DATE DUE			

Liberty's Chosen Home

Other books by Alan Lupo

(WITH FRANK COLCORD AND EDMUND P. FOWLER):

*Rites of Way: The Politics of Transportation
in Boston and the U.S. City*

Liberty's Chosen Home

The Politics of Violence in Boston

Alan Lupo

Little, Brown and Company   BOSTON TORONTO

FIRST EDITION

T 02/77

Library of Congress Cataloging in Publication Data

Lupo, Alan.
   Liberty's Chosen Home.

   Includes index.
   1. School integration — Massachusetts — Boston.
I. Title.
LC214.23.B67L86   370.19'342   76–29639
ISBN 0–316–53672–5

Designed by D. Christine Benders

*Published simultaneously in Canada
by Little, Brown & Company (Canada) Limited*

PRINTED IN THE UNITED STATES OF AMERICA

To Caryl, a wife who supported and a journalist who understood. To Steven and Alyssa for their unquestioned loyalty and unassailable confidence. To Esther, Max, Helen, and Hugh, for caring. To all the white, black, Hispanic, and Oriental people in the neighborhoods, who tried to keep the peace and make the Yankee legacy livable.

And to Dick McDonough, an editor who loves this city and who made this book readable.

Author's Note

The opinions expressed by those quoted in this book are not necessarily the author's opinions also. This is especially true of the opinions expressed by some public figures about other public figures who do not play a large role in this book, even though they were certainly important actors during the busing crisis. It was the author's decision not to write a book solely on busing in Boston. It was my decision to concentrate in the last third of the book on how the government of the city dealt with the crisis. To me, both the mayor's administration and the crisis are symbols of the city and its history.

Fall, 1975   Alan Lupo

Acknowledgments

Much of this book would not have been possible were it not for the people of Boston — those with whom I grew up, those whom I have covered as a reporter, and those whom I have met and talked with socially in the last decade. Another large chunk of this book exists because I asked for and was given access to Mayor Kevin White's strategy sessions.

"Put away that damn pencil," he would often say, when noticing me trying to blend into a wall. Sometimes, I would put it away, knowing that if the subject were important enough, I could run out into the hall and into a men's room and write the notes from memory. Usually, I didn't put it away, and usually he didn't mean it either. I thank him and his scores of loyal aides and workers for their help. They are too numerous to mention by name.

Finally, I must thank certain institutions in Boston, for without their resources, another important segment of this book would have been much more difficult, perhaps impossible, to write. They include Boston University's School of Public Communications morgue;

Mugar Library at Boston University; Gutman Library at Harvard; the College Three library at the University of Massachusetts–Boston; the Boston Athenaeum; Boston Public Library, and the Boston City Council and Law Department reference rooms.

And a special thanks to Glea Humez of Little, Brown.

The historic and background material was drawn from many sources, including old newspapers and clippings, City Council minutes, official city documents and reports, Finance Commission reports, the *Boston Municipal Register,* the *1880 Federal Census,* and 102 books and magazines dating back to the mid-nineteenth century.

For someone who has spent so much of his working life writing stories for the day or the night or the following day, to have been able to spend months with old files, reports, news clips, and magazine articles was a rare luxury. It was also as necessary as being on the street when the buses rolled and being with the mayor as the city creaked and groaned about him. Neither historic research alone nor reporting alone could have told the story of Boston. I hope a combination of those techniques has served me well in telling that story.

Preface

BOSTON IS A much misunderstood city, perceived by the rest of the nation with cliches worn thin and ragged by time.

By 1974, when many of the events of this book took place, the "proper Bostonians" were as dead as Honey Fitz and Jim Curley and their colorful followers. There were a few here and there, along with one horse of precisely that name, Proper Bostonian, who had gained some measure of prestige by beating a nag called Shecky Green. So much for that legacy.

As for baked beans and brown bread, nobody I know eats them together. Hardly anybody I know eats baked beans, unless forced to by their income. And everybody I know who eats brown bread makes sure it's Jewish dark rye. Very little is "banned in Boston" anymore, and most of those who would do the banning — "bluenoses" they were called — live in the suburbs, as do most Brahmins. The suburbs, however, have managed to ban just about everything and everybody they don't want.

Perhaps the biggest cliche this city had to bear is that it is a liberal city. Indeed, its working stiffs voted for McGovern, and its transient students and issue-oriented residents of Beacon Hill and the Back Bay will rally on the Common and collect money for grape pickers, Indochinese peasants, and Chilean revolutionaries much as Yankees did generations ago for John Brown and his guerrillas and the patriots of Hungary. But the same Boston was for Al Smith, when most were rallying to Franklin Delano Roosevelt. The same Boston gave Father Coughlin and Joe McCarthy their most avid support. And the same Boston has come down very hard on a doctor for having performed clean, sanitary abortions.

And that is the story of this city. It is, and always has been, a city torn apart by the extremes, a city both liberal and conservative, both enlightened and parochial and stifling. At times in history, it has been very hard to be an Irishman in Boston, or an Italian, or a Jew, or a black, or, lately, a Yankee. It has *always* been difficult to be a moderate.

In 1974, Boston began integrating its schools under a federal court order. It did so with a measure of violence, and the violence did not easily diminish. Those who always had believed in the cliche of an enlightened Boston were shocked. Those who knew better were also shocked — that the violence wasn't worse, for they knew their beloved Boston for what it was: quaint, historic, livable, colorful, and potentially deadly. The violence among whites and blacks in 1974 and 1975 was, to them, a reminder of earlier battles, waged on the grounds of religion, country of origin, or neighborhood turf. The violence of busing was the inevitable result of the city's history, in which one group dumped on another, and in which each group left the next with less to fight over, less to claim.

If the research and writing of these events is lacking, I must shoulder that criticism. But if the content disturbs the reader, then we had all better take that rap, for the insanity and hypocrisy of a society that sets poor against workingman, black against white, city against suburb, a society that deludes itself that it has even set up the machinery capable of dealing with redressing its most onerous social grievances.

It is not enough to outline forces of history, as if some vaguely defined issues — racism, corruption, poverty, whatever — dictated the events of our times. It is necessary also to describe the specifics of those events, because it is often a specific incident, action, or decision that helps determine their outcome. The trouble with too many histories is that they deal only with sweeping and cosmic issues and rarely portray the actors as humans, as human as the writers and readers of these histories. The persons charged with implementing busing in Boston are not supermen. Nor are our presidents, our ambassadors, our quarterbacks, our special heroes or villains. This book is, in part, a story of how those persons dealt with an historic event that none of them had wrought.

This is also the story of a particular actor in Boston's drama, its mayor, Kevin Hagan White. It does not purport to be a complete story of Kevin White and what he has done and failed to do as a mayor. This is not a biography. He is important in this book not only because he was the mayor at the time, but because he represented, in his inheritance, his emotions, his instincts, and his politics, so much of what Boston has been and is. It seemed to me that the city and mayor were as one, and to have written about one without the other would have been an act of inaccuracy.

This is not the story of James Michael Curley or the Pilgrims, of Sacco and Vanzetti or the Boston Police Strike, or Harvard-Yale games or the Kennedy family. Curley and some of the Kennedy family and some unnamed Pilgrims appear in the book, but as background to the story that I wanted to tell, the story of the past and present of a city that has often raised issues for the rest of this republic, issues that the nation would rather not have faced, issues that had to be faced if the nation were — and is — to survive.

For this story is also the story of the American city, forced to shoulder the nation's social debt, and to do so with precious little help from Washington and even less from its affluent neighbors, the suburbs.

Boston has been called often, and accurately, a manageable city, a livable city. If such a place is allowed to flirt so closely with disaster, then what can the message be for the great urban centers of this republic?

With a couple of small exceptions, the conversations, quotes, epithets, screams, shouts, orders, moans, and wisecracks set down as part of the city's recent history are based on my notes of events and conversations as I witnessed them and not secondhand reports. These included scores of closed-door meetings and private conversations, which I witnessed because Kevin White agreed to open doors to me that would normally have been closed.

Contents

CONTENTS

Liberty's Chosen Home

ONE

Athens, It Ain't

In what is called the living room in the office of the mayor of Boston, Kevin Hagan White sits with his press secretary, Frank Tivnan, and stares at the human horseshoe of reporters.

There are thirty or more of them, packed into the room, sitting on sofas, on chairs, on the edge of a table, on the floor, standing with their backs to the wall. They have come not only from within the city but from out of Massachusetts to cover a national story, to see the Abolitionist City, the city of William Lloyd Garrison and Wendell Phillips, the city that financed John Brown's raid on Harper's Ferry, the city that welcomed runaway slaves, the city that voted against Vietnam and for George McGovern and sent righteous soldiers to Selma and dollar bills to Cesar Chavez.

They want to see how Boston integrates its schools, and when they see that Boston can do so only with white and black violence, they want to know why.

Kevin White knows why. The grandson of an Irish immigrant workingman on one side, and a reform city councilman on the other, the son of a man who had been both president of the City Council and chairman of the school committee, the son-in-law of a Charlestown ward heeler who had also become president of the City Council, Kevin White, by virtue of genes alone, knows his city.

Inevitably the question is asked. It comes from a young local reporter sitting with his back to the wall. "Mister Mayor, speaking just personally, did you expect Boston to reach this point?" The question hangs in the air for a few seconds. The mayor presses the reporter. Just what does he mean by "this point"? The reporter says, "I ask the question in light of the reputation of Boston as a liberal city, an enlightened city."

Kevin White, who knows an opportunity when he sees one, shoots back, "Are you a local reporter?" The young man says, "Yes." The mayor twists his lips in sarcasm and turns to his right, a piece of showmanship that says, "Then you should know better." Everyone laughs. The people who know the city laugh, and the people who do not want to appear not to know the city laugh.

A few minutes later, almost as an anticlimax, Kevin White says, "If you're familiar with the local scene, you'll know that a liberal constituency has never been part of it."

About that time, downstairs in the war room that has been set up to process information and kill rumors, the police radio crackles that students are pouring out of English High School and are headed for Huntington Avenue. The Tactical Patrol Force is dispatched to the scene. They have fought whites, they would fight blacks. In this most "liberal" of cities, the Police Department would liberally take on all comers, all colors.

The morning of September 12, 1974, is humid. The air is hazy with smog. It will not rain. The streets will remain dry and full of people. Some of the people will not remain dry. It will be a good day for drinking. It will be a bad day for almost everything else.

At 5 A.M., Larry Quealy, a tall, husky, and handsome man who has served three of Boston's mayors, picks up the phone in his West Roxbury home and calls his boss, Mayor Kevin H. White, at the latter's Beacon Hill townhouse. Quealy says he is worried and that he expects trouble. Now, the mayor is nervous too. He trusts Quealy's judgment on such matters. Quealy has good lines into the white Catholic community of Boston, and Quealy has been on the phone most of the night.

"There are reports of blockades at the schools," he says, "and a possible assault on Bill Reid, the headmaster at South Boston. There's one guy driving around with a loudspeaker trying to incite people."

At about 6 A.M., Rich Kelliher, a mayoral aide, opens the door to the old Civil Defense room in the basement of Boston's modern City Hall. It has a new name now. Everybody is calling it "the bunker." With its multicolored phones, its maps, its lists of emergency phone numbers, its police radios and clacking teletypes, it looks like a war room; a new room for a very old war, a war between the races, between classes.

In South Boston, the morning breaks a bit cooler than elsewhere in the city. Southie is a peninsula, cooled by the waters of Boston Harbor. It is a very tight peninsula. It is, in fact, a white ghetto. In case anyone wasn't sure, the citizens painted "White Power" signs on fences, on pedestrian overpasses and on the walls of schools and homes. In case the point was still not made, there is the kid with the white T-shirt with the words "Black Sucks."

Across the traffic-clogged Central Artery, slicing through the city for the benefit of those who had fled Boston for its suburban South Shore, another ghetto awakens. The blacks of Roxbury, like the mayor and Southie, are also nervous. The two worlds will come together today, and the shape of each will forever be altered.

"I don't usually eat breakfast," Kevin White is saying, "but I got the nerves this morning." He is walking out of the back of City Hall, across Congress Street, past the statue of Sam Adams, who stands stubbornly with arms folded, past Faneuil Hall, where more than a century ago, men fought for and against the cause of Abolition.

A man yells at him, "Good luck, Mister Mayor. You're all right!" Mister Mayor nods and smiles. He walks into the front entrance of the ancient Quincy Market, where the Jewish and Italian butchers have been up and working even before Larry Quealy called the mayor on the phone.

In Marion's Restaurant, he orders two glasses of orange juice, one piece of hot cornbread, and a couple of poached eggs. He makes small talk with some reporters and his aides, but it is forced. In the middle of it, he shakes his head and mutters, "Sometimes I think I gotta get outta this. I feel like saying screw it. It must be nice being in Washington and eating breakfast in the Senate dining room at 11 in the morning."

As the mayor and his retinue walk back to City Hall, the Boston Police Department confirms that a crowd of two hundred to three hundred whites are gathered near South Boston High School and booing and jeering the buses as they roll up with black students. Between the buses and the crowd is a line of husky cops from the Tactical Patrol Force.

In the bunker, John Coakley, an associate superintendent of schools, looks up and says, "We're ten minutes past the opening of high school now. There are four buses in South Boston with sixty black kids. They're *in* school."

In the "parlor" of his office, Kevin White sits on a couch, sits in his shirtsleeves with Quealy, his deputy mayor, Bob Kiley, and his speechwriter and advisor on national issues, Ira Jackson.

They are beginning to relax. Southie is a problem, as expected. Roxbury seems quiet. The rest of the city is tense, but there are few reports of violence. Buses are arriving at some black schools half-filled with whites.

Bob Kiley puts on his suit jacket and tells the mayor, "I'm goin' out on the street." For much of the next three weeks, Kiley will be out on the street, in a car with a phone, calling his observations back to Kevin White and back to the bunker. For three weeks, young Mark Weddleton, a former basketball star at English High School and now an aide to Kiley, will drive Kiley up and down streets that cabdrivers don't even know about.

As their car approaches Southie, Kiley is worrying out loud. "It's hot and muggy. Our people think they'll get some refreshment and come back this afternoon." In Southie, you don't have to get into a car to get to a bar. There is no lack of refreshment.

On this first day of busing, South Boston is already beginning to look like an occupied zone. The police are all over, on motorcycles, in "paddy" wagons, standing at traffic crossings, gathered on foot and in cruisers at special checkpoints. The people seem sullen, but not beaten. At one of the projects, one of the four red brick masses of apartments that house one-fifth of Southie's population, three kids, one with a megaphone, get ready. On the wall of the high school annex, the old L Street bathhouse, it says clearly, "South Boston Ku Klux Klan."

The car takes a left at L Street and moves up the hill, past the lines of police. This is the bus route in. On the right is the water. On the left are projects and three-decker houses and side streets, a battlefield ready-made for urban warfare.

Out on the street in front of the high school, the school where a lot of cops graduated, the kids of Southie and their mothers and fathers and younger sisters and brothers stare at the cops, who do not dream now that the community that once canonized them would come to hate them. The kids stand face-to-muzzle with the horses of the mounted police.

A paddy wagon pulls in as close to the school as possible. Some police rush to the door in its rear. The door opens, and out comes a cop with a young black woman. You hear the sound before you see the woman. The sound here travels faster than the light of its cause.

At first, the sound is incomprehensible. It is just a din, a roar, a rumble. But then the noises filter out, and the words ring clearly on the top of the hill. "Niggah! Niggah!"

She walks through the schoolyard toward the steps. She walks with swinging hips, and shoots back a grin at them. Uppity. Who the hell do these people think they are anyway? The crowd goes crazy with noise, with frustration. Why isn't she scared? "Niggah!" they yell. "Niggah! . . . Have a nice day, niggah!" Someone throws a soft-drink can. It clanks safely behind her onto the pavement.

"Niggah!"

She walks into the school, the old school with its peeling paint, its cracked plaster, its dirty basement, the school, which for a lot of Southie men and women, is the high point of their lives. "Here we go, Southie, here we go!" Clap. Clap. They will chant and clap against the busing, as they do for their team. But there is no team so far this year, because the white kids, encouraged by their parents, are staying home from school, the school the black woman is now entering.

Over the urinal in the boy's room, someone has scrawled "Niggers Suck." In a few days, over the next urinal, someone will scrawl, "Happy St. Patrick's Day, you Irish Bastards."

On a muggy, uncomfortable day in the late summer of its three hundred forty-fifth year, the Cradle of Liberty, the Athens of America, the Hub of the Universe is integrating its schools.

TWO

The Holy Commonwealth

THE LAND, such as it was, groaned under its burden of ice. The ice built upon itself, one glassy sheet over another, until the very top layer covered the highest hills. The ice was a vise stronger than any other natural force. When the handle of a vise is tightened too fast, it will crack the wood within it, and so this glacial ice crunched and smashed the earth within its 200-foot-thick grip, ground away the surface of the country, reshaped the land as it crept 50 miles into the ocean.

The ice of the last glacial period gave shape and substance to what lay beneath it. Rocky, often cold, sometimes barren, the landed legacy of the Ice Ages was ready for the character of those who would come from across the sea to inhabit it.

As the ice wall moved from the shoreline, it left the land depressed below the ocean, as deep as 300 feet in some places. The land did not remain still. It struggled slowly to recover its position, but the ocean gave battle, and earth and water locked in combat for turf, for ownership, for the rights of property.

The ice had left behind its mounds of waste, hills of rubbish, a mix of pebbles and dirt, clay and boulders, and the sea now assaulted the shore, washing over the waste, rearranging its contours. Land pushed up through water, and water drained away silt and flooded land in a contest that would never end.

The creation of these forces was a peninsula connected to the mainland by a narrow isthmus that was flooded regularly by high tides. The tides burrowed into the land and made three coves, and beyond the coves rose three hills: one, Fort Hill, would become an early home for the Irish immigrants and would soon thereafter be obliterated; one, Copp's Hill, would become a graveyard for the Yankee founders, in the shadows of Italian tenements; and the third, Beacon Hill, would become the last symbol of political power for those Yankees who remained alive and fighting and a home for an Irish mayor who was to inherit their city.

In time, the Indians would come to the peninsula, which they would call Shawmut. In the waters, there were cod and lobster. In the forests beyond the peninsula, there were moose, caribou, and deer. Across the great waters, farther than the Massachusetts dared to imagine, there was trouble in an older world that boasted at once of civilization and progress and yet could brook no deviations from what its leaders insisted were the mores of their time.

An aging Queen Elizabeth and her Anglican bishops, beleaguered by constant rebellion in Ireland and fighting with Spain, were faced by a growing challenge from within, a most dangerous challenge for the times because it questioned the Church, and when one questioned the Church, one threatened the State.

The Puritans called for a simpler form of worship than that practiced in the Anglican Church. Some were holding secret religious meetings, in which they preached that a church should be governed by its members, not by the State or by an order of bishops. If their democracy were not suspect enough, their self-righteousness seemed to leave their enemies no room for compromise.

Censored and persecuted, their meetings banned, some of their numbers killed or banished, they left the kingdom of Elizabeth and later of James I, her successor. Later, those who had taken refuge in Holland joined their brethren from England in a journey westward to that rocky and barren coast. They took with them their righteousness and, unbending through the years, it would linger forever in Boston, this frigid Puritan sense of purpose, as cold and hard as the glacial ice that had imprisoned the land that had become their home.

It lingered long after the passing of the Puritans' Holy Commonwealth. Those who followed them to the Shawmut Peninsula, to Boston, were not Puritans. There were thugs and adventurers, indentured servants and intellectuals, preachers and farmers and merchants.

To the south of Boston, in Plymouth, Governor Bradford wrote in 1642, "It may be demanded how came it to pass that so many wicked persons and profane people should so quickly come over into this land, and mixe themselves amongst them, seeing it was religious men that began ye work, and they came for religion's sake."

Some were arriving as laborers, a commodity so badly needed in the Holy Commonwealth that nobody was checking their pedigrees. Private transportation companies were ferrying over anyone who could pay the tab. Families were taking up collections to send their misfit cousins and brothers to the New World.

"There were knotts of rioteous Young Men in the Town," the Reverend Cotton Mather complained to his diary in 1713. "On purpose to insult Piety, they will come under my Window in the Middle of the Night, and sing profane and filthy Songs. The last Night they did so, and fell upon People with Clubs, taken off my Wood-pile."

History would obscure distinctions between the Cotton Mathers and the knots of rioteous young men. They would all become "Yankees." Their descendants and newer English immigrants would riot in the streets at Sam Adams's call. Time made patriots of wharf rats and brawlers. And their descendants would rail at the European immigrant.

The Puritans brought the chimera of religious freedom and denied it to Roger Williams and Ann Hutchinson. They found witches among them and purged them. They executed three Quakers and banned the rest. The Yankees who followed began a revolution, and denied its promise to others. They smuggled in rum, and later preached Prohibition. They traded in slaves, and later preached Abolition. They founded public schools for all, and not so subtly fed Protestantism to the children of Irish Catholic immigrants. They held out the hand of friendship to the black man in Dixie but patronized the black man in Boston.

In his poem on how the Quakers had been banished from the town, John Greenleaf Whittier wrote in 1880:

> *I see the vision of days to come,*
> *When your beautiful City of the Bay*
> *Shall be Christian liberty's chosen home,*
> *And none shall his neighbor's rights gainsay. . . .*

But Whittier's poem was filled more with hope than with historic accuracy. Protestant mobs had burned down the Ursuline Convent.

They had run wild through the streets of the Irish settlements. While some Yankees preached that this was not what the Holy Commonwealth had intended, others of equal prestige would organize politically to restrict the immigrants and dilute the power of those they could not restrict.

For the rest of the nation, two distinct messages were continually sent out from Boston. One was of compassion for the less fortunate, education for everyone, toleration for differences, freedom for the enslaved. The other was of self-righteous bigotry, a denial of opportunity to others, a limit to toleration, a patronizing of the workingman, the black man, the Catholic, the Jew.

Not always did the messages come from two different sets of Yankees. Some of the most strident Abolitionists fanned the flames of those who loathed the Irish. Some of the most educated of Yankees rejected the possibility that other cultures could contribute to their schools.

Too often, however, the messenger was confused. Harvard was confused with Boston, long after the Brahmins so closely associated with that institution had left the city for the suburbs. When the city would face its own dichotomy, it was too late. For the preachers of racial justice, the latter-day Abolitionists, lived in areas that would barely be affected by the coming conflagration. When the expected erupted, outsiders reacted as if events were really unexpected, as if Boston were really different.

"Well, heavens to Betsy! My eyes and ears must be deceiving me! Is it really true that Boston, the cradle of American liberty, freedom and democracy, is experiencing integration difficulties? Were Boston's citizens really seen throwing rocks and yelling at other American citizens? Is this the same Boston that is the home of that leading liberal institution known as Harvard? . . ." — A Virginia woman, writing to the Boston *Globe* in the fall of 1974

THREE

"... A Sad Day for Boston"

EVERYTHING IN MASSACHUSETTS that doesn't move is named after somebody. There is patronage for the living and for the dead. The former are given non–civil service jobs or "provisional" appointments; the latter are given highways, buildings, streets, street corners, municipal bathhouses, playgrounds, and safety islands. If it's nailed or cemented down and shows no sign of disappearing in a half-year or so, it's knighted.

On this night late in August, 1974, white people who don't want kids bused are filing into the auditorium of the Robert Gould Shaw School in West Roxbury. It is possible that they don't sense the irony.

Shaw, a promising young man of one of the oldest of Bay State families, was colonel of the Massachusetts 54th Regiment, black volunteers. He was killed in the assault on Fort Alexander in South Carolina, but the city would never be without his presence. A settlement house in the black neighborhood bears his name, as does this school, and when busing protestors would mass on the Common to march, the spirit of Shaw would again hover near them.

Tonight, the antibusing leaders are in West Roxbury to whip up

sentiment for their cause, to warn the residents of this almost suburban neighborhood that it's only a matter of time before their children are bused back to the old neighborhoods, the neighborhoods
from which their parents had fled.

For the upwardly mobile and the city's middle class, West Roxbury
is one of the last outposts in Boston. It is a big sprawling ward at the
southern tip of the city. Once, it was farmland. It was where Nathaniel
Hawthorne and his friends organized the Brook Farm commune.
There are probably some Yankees left in West Roxbury, and certainly
some Protestants. There is an increasing number of Jews forced out of
the neighborhoods to the north. But today, West Roxbury is a largely
Catholic community, whose members number politicians, well-paid
appointed officials, civil servants, police, firemen, realtors, small business proprietors, doctors, and those blue-collar guys who will mortgage
their grandmothers to live there.

The main street, Centre Street, is Little American Suburb — stores
newer than the variety stores in the old neighborhoods, more plate
glass, fewer iron gratings, more concern with vandalism than with
muggings. There's Weinstein, the tax man, and Christos, the hot oven
grinder man. A Chinese restaurant. An Irish bar. Italian names.
Armenian names. Their own post office. Their own library. Their own
bowling alley.

Bingo night at Holy Name Church will lose some of its regulars
tonight. They will drive or walk past the church and continue down
Centre Street, past stores and public facilities, and a police substation
and the Theodore Parker Unitarian Church. Staring down grimly at
them from his pedestal is the Reverend Mr. Parker, who preached
Abolition in the days of Garrison, Phillips, William Ellery Channing,
and Lyman Beecher.

Parker digested Old and New Testaments for breakfast, rather than
food. Sometimes, he would get through as many as five books of the
Bible on a morning when he was hot. He brought his intellect and his
religious fervor to the cause of Abolition and preached to large antislavery audiences every Sunday in the Melodeon and the Music Hall.
Before anybody ever conjured up radical chic, the Reverend Mr.
Parker was helping fugitive slaves to escape and even hiding them in
his house.

But in true Yankee form, Parker's heat for the issue was cooled
somewhat for the individual involved. "He is the least acquisitive of
all men," said Parker of the black man he insisted on helping. "He is
an equatorial grasshopper." To Parker, "The Negro is a slow, a loose-
jointed sort of animal, a great child."

Nor did his charity extend as far as the Irish, of whom he said, "Dirt and rum, with pestilence and blows, follow their steps; their voices have already debauched the politics of this city. . . ."

Parker died five years before the slaves were freed and about three decades before the Irish began taking over his city. Parker's sculptor chose to show his subject scowling. Tonight, the old Abolitionist will have much to scowl about.

The Shaw School is a large red brick structure at the foot of a tree-lined hill of modestly middle-class wooden homes. It was born in 1937 as "Federal Emergency Administration Project No. 4217." It smells of fresh paint and cleaning liquid. Over one hallway door is a sign, "Keep to the right. File promptly and quietly to all classes." If you follow those orders, you can make it through the Boston school system.

Jim Smith, treasurer of his class at nearby Roslindale High School, is a young handsome man who has no trouble talking to crowds. There is a crowd here tonight, for almost all six hundred seats are filled with the angry, the confused, the curious, the observers from other camps. With some people who don't like blacks. With some people who are indifferent to race, but don't want their kids bused out of the neighborhood. With some people who might be willing to try it, but fear the not-so-subtle pressures of their neighbors. With people who are just trying to find out what's going on.

"We have watched the bumbling in the mayor's office long enough," he says, though no one makes it clear just how the mayor's office has bumbled. There is great applause. He says he has never seen such lousy planning. He is seventeen years old. Busing, he predicts, will be "the death knell of the city." Who are the villains in this piece? everyone keeps wondering.

"Perhaps the real culprits are the politicians, the so-called servants of the people," Jim Smith yells. And the applause is heavy and long, and they are shouting, "Yay! Yay!"

It was getting to be an especially bad year for politicians. If Watergate had never happened, it would still be a bad year here for the pols. The people of Massachusetts love and hate their politicians at the same time. As long as the Yankees ran the corporations, the financial institutions, as long as the Yankees kept their headlock on the real source of power, the others in Massachusetts would have to make do with lesser sources of power — with sports and crime, with unions and politics.

So for a century now, politics has been a sport and a vocation, a source of employment for the many and a degree of limited power for the few. In parts of Cambridge and the wealthier suburbs of highly educated people, politics is connected to issues for the Jewish and Catholic liberals. For the Yankees in those communities, politics is something you are expected to engage in, for it is really public service. Public service is something that is *expected* of you.

But in the wards of Boston, politics is a little bit different. It is a means of daily survival.

It is getting your boy into a community college or out of jail. It is alerting your cousin to a civil service exam for firefighters. It is getting close to the man, who, if elected, will not pledge to end the world's poverty, but might do something about ending yours. It is often patronage, but semantics tends to cloud it. When a Harvard type gets a job with a politician or an administration, he is "given an appointment." When his neighbor in East or North Cambridge gets a job with a politician, he is, simply, "getting a job."

To these getting leaned on in life, such rhetoric was just more hypocrisy. The good-government reformers had never provided jobs anyway, only sermons. You don't heat your flat with sermons. You can't eat morality. So, for the local politicians who made no bones about using the system to employ himself, a relative or two, some close friends, and his constituents, there was some measure of respect. But not of love.

Lately, a new element had crept into the on-again, off-again love affair between the white man on the street and his elected representative. The former was learning, finally, that the latter was growing more impotent every year.

"We never got any real power," said a Boston city councilman, Jerry O'Leary. "They [the Yankees] still control the banks." That was a given. Everyone knew that. When the suburban bankers, who commuted to the city's financial district every day, refuse to float low-interest mortgages, when the suburban realtors blockbust and insurance men redline neighborhoods, parts of the city become doomed. And the city councilman, the state representative, the state senator, and even the mayor are left to moan or cajole. Impotence.

It was one thing to call the man in office and get a personal favor. Even when civil service replaced patronage, even when that reform became a monster of a bureaucracy devouring any real effort to promote good government, even then, the local pol could do favors. But the options become more limited every year. For a decade, the people's pols had promised there would be no busing of their children, even when they must have known it was inevitable. And now, it was happening, and when young Jimmy Smith from Roslindale High School says, "Perhaps the real culprits are the politicians . . . ," the people in the auditorium of the Robert Gould Shaw Elementary School go wild with applause and shouts.

School Committeeman John Kerrigan has been waiting at the back of the hall. Kerrigan has a pockmarked face and a street-corner frame, but it's sagging just a bit now at the belly. Kerrigan is the ultimate wise guy. He has come to symbolize Boston Irish politics, to the disgust of his liberal critics. Kerrigan is a clever man. Once, at an annual State House hearing on a bill to repeal the state's Racial Imbalance Act, he quietly joked to a *Globe* reporter, "Hey, they better not repeal this thing. My political career will be through."

Kerrigan's political career has been built, sculptured, molded around the foundation of racial fear. It is not an unfounded fear, for the black street violence of today is as vicious as was the Irish brand a century ago. But to play on the fear is to exaggerate it.

Now, with both the primary election and the first day of busing only two weeks away, John Kerrigan is listening to the people cheer the kid, when he says you can't trust pols. He listens to the kid and the crowd as the kid does a routine that the Kerrigans have capitalized on for years. Not race, but class.

"Where does Governor Sargent live?" Jimmy Smith asks, and answers his own question. "In Dover." And Judge Garrity (the federal judge who handed down the busing order)? In Wellesley. And the mayor's kids go to private schools. Who are the villains? Not just the politicians. It is the well-off who will not do what they tell others to do. And just as there is some truth to justify the fear of racial violence, a fear that exists as strongly in the black community as the white, there is also truth to this plot theory. But somehow, liberals, suburbanites, Communists, the NAACP, street hoodlums, and Harvard academicians have all been lumped together. It is tragic. As the world they once knew begins to disintegrate around them, the whites of Boston look for a scapegoat.

Now, pushed to the wall, even "one of our own" is no longer sacrosanct. Kerrigan tries to joke with them, when it's his turn. "I didn't like the way everyone applauded when the young fellow said what he did about politicians." Some chuckles. A few laughs. Some rumbling. "It's true!" yells one in the audience. "We don't care what you like," yells another, and there is some applause for that, too. Kerrigan moves on to another subject. He attacks Ted Kennedy; he says the federal judge, Arthur Garrity, worked for the Kennedys to get where he is. Earlier, he had said quietly to somebody in the audience, "Was it you I told I'd hang Garrity around Kennedy's neck?" Now, he proceeds to do it.

But a man in the audience starts arguing with him. A woman, angry at the man, yells, "Throw him out!" Now there are rumbling, mumbling, insults, yelling. Kerrigan is trying to regain control of the audience. "One thing the news media would like to bring back is that you're rowdy and disorderly," he says. "And we're unhappy," a woman yells out. Kerrigan urges them to join a march September ninth and a school boycott. Marching and boycotting in large numbers, he promises them, can work.

There are signs here. Is no one reading the signs, the forecasts? There must be someone savvy enough, some high priest of politics, who having caught the bird can split it open and read its guts. The Ides of September. The Kerrigans have been promising there would be no busing, yet busing is coming. They still promise. The promises ignore the social forces that are pulling and tugging at this old city, that are ripping apart what is good along with what is bad. But the promises no longer work, and the people are angry at their own impotence. Like a lover who cannot one night bring himself to love, they strike out in anger.

All night, there will be minor disruptions in the crowd. Some will stand up to suggest only some facts, and they will be shouted down. Others will suggest moderately that they ride as monitors to protect their *own* children, and there will be shouts and a waving of fists. And this is not the toughest community in Boston. This is not black Roxbury or Irish-Polish Southie or Italian East Boston. Something has been let loose that cannot be controlled. It is bigger than Kerrigan.

It is bigger than city councilman Albert Dapper O'Neil, heavyset, jowly, an Irish bachelor who dresses well, sings well, speaks well, tells jokes well, Dapper who tells them he didn't fight Hitler to come back to this, Dapper who says to applause, "I know of other groups in this city who have demonstrated and demanded and got everything they wanted. We will march September ninth and anytime we want to."

It is bigger, even, than Louise Day Hicks, who shaped a national reputation as the school committeewoman who vowed — Never! For her, there is applause as she enters the room with her little blond granddaughter. For her, there is the chairman of the meeting introducing the symbol of resistance with these words, "In the beginning, there was just one person yelling, 'Stop the buses,' and no one listened." For her, there is a standing ovation.

She is a big woman, tall, broad-shouldered, thick in the ankles. She can be an emotional person, given to tears. But, now, as usual, what comes out is the almost syrupy sweet voice of a child, so surprising to everyone who hears it for the first time.

"This is a sad day for Boston. . . . Can anyone guarantee that if a child is placed on a bus, that child will be safe? I cannot get anyone to guarantee that. You make your choice. If you feel your child will be subjected to any harm, until someone proves to you that he will be safe, I believe you should keep that child off that bus. We believe in freedom of choice. There will be parents who for reasons best known to themselves will place their children on the bus, and we'll guarantee we'll never harm those children. We are concerned about their educational welfare as well as their moral welfare. . . . We must unite now, if ever in the history of this city. This whole plan's purpose is to divide and conquer us. I can still see Khrushchev pounding his shoe on the table at the UN and saying he does not need troops to conquer the United States, that we will destroy ourselves from within. We are not going to divide or politicize this city.

"Senators Kennedy and Brooke have abandoned Boston. These are sad days for Boston. They'll have neighbor against neighbor. I tell you the whole city will be involved by February. So don't sit sure and smug; unite, and help each other. We believe in quality education. . . . The only weapon we have is the people. The voices of the people will be heard. . . . If we can only hold together, all will not be lost, the children will be saved. And that's what we all are looking for. To save our children."

What lay ahead was bigger than Louise, so big that for a time, she and others would lose control of a situation they had helped create. But only helped. For the situation had begun long before their time, and what would happen in and to Boston was only the inevitable result of its own history, for there had always been sad days for Boston.

FOUR

A Riot

Kevin Hagan White sits at one end of a long table in a small playroom-bar of a Dorchester basement, crowded with his fellow white Catholics. He is drinking coffee and chainsmoking Marlboros, drinking coffee in every neighborhood, and trying to keep the city from committing suicide.

"There'll be a black mayor someday," he tells them, "and the city won't fall apart."

"It won't be our city anymore," says a young woman.

"That's what the Yankees said about the Irish," he tells her.

The group erupts in protest. "It's not the same," one says. "It's not the same," another says. And a third yells, "The Irish weren't dangerous."

They had come because they were hungry. The potato had rotted away to an inedible mass. A half-million had died in three years. They had come because there was nothing to look forward to but the tenant-slavery of their fathers. The prophesies of the Shan Van Vocht, the poor old woman, had come to naught.

Oh, the French are on the sea,
  Says the Shan Van Vocht....
Will Ireland then be free?
  Says the Shan Van Vocht.
Yes! Ireland shall be free,
From the centre to the sea.
Then Hurrah for Liberty!
  Says the Shan Van Vocht.

Their starvation coincided with the needs of Yankee shipowners, whose vessels arrived in English ports laden with the bulky raw produce of America and were destined to return lighter with the condensed manufactured products of England. Immigrants made good ballast. More important, their fees made the return trip more worthwhile for the merchantmen.

With what little they owned on their shoulders, with their children trailing in the dust behind them, they traveled to the docks in Liverpool, stood humbly before the doctor who checked them for contagious diseases, and prayed all their tickets would be properly stamped.

"There was not a wet eye on board," wrote an English journalist who watched a batch leave one day in 1850. "There had been no fond leave-takings; no farewells to England; no pangs at parting. Possibly there was no necessity for any. To ninety-nine out of hundred of these emigrants, the Old Country had been in all probability an unkind mother, a country of sorrow and distress, associated only with remembrances of poverty and suffering."

If hope lay in the future, there was precious little sign of it on the ships. Thousands died and would never see the New World. And many who made it would long remember the crowds in the hold, the pitch and roll of the wooden cargo ships, the loss of all privacy and sense of family that had held strong on the farm even in the famine, and the stench of vomit that lingered in their quarters.

They came spilling off the filthy boats, their captains glad to be rid of them, rough men dressed in strange hats and frocks and boots, with pipes stuck in their belts, their emaciated and frightened children and women trailing behind them, all speaking in a high-pitched babble that barely could be understood.

Back home, a home which generations of them would come to drink to, cry over, eulogize, and which most would never see again, thousands of their brethren starved to death, while English landlords sold native Irish corn to Britain. They were used to death. Death was what they so often talked about, wrote about, sang about, fought about.

Two centuries before, Cromwell the Puritan warrior had massacred them at Drogheda and Wexford. A half-century after Cromwell, a new generation of fighters was slaughtered at the Boyne by William of Orange.

Too often, they had seen hope rise on the horizon like the awaited French fleet, and always it had died. Now, Lord Edward Fitzgerald was dead of Protestant wounds. Wolfe Tone was dead of suicide, they said, in prison. Daniel O'Connell had fought his way into a Protestant English Parliament and was now shouting into the winds for peaceful accommodations, but the excesses of the past would come to breed only murder in the future. And now, the potato crop, on which 90 percent of the peasantry subsisted, was gone. And the peasants were going. To America.

America had a use for their brawn. America would not ask if they had bought with them centuries of culture, song, poetry, writing, philosophy. America couldn't care less. The Massachusetts Puritans had as much use for the Irish Catholic as had the Puritans of Cromwell or the Protestants of Parliament. Cotton Mather had made that clear in 1700. Efforts to bring Irish to the colony were nothing more than "formidable attempts of Satan and his Sons to Unsettle us." But that was before America was building dikes, canals, railroads, before American men needed others to dig ditches, before American women needed others to mend clothes and clean kitchens.

For dikes, canals, railroads, and ditches, Satan & Sons, it was learned, would work hard for low pay, ask few questions, and get no overtime. Given good mercantile motivation, the grandsons of the Puritans could bend the rules a little. If the employer needed cheap labor, he could send a messenger down to the labor exchange run by the Society for the Prevention of Pauperism in Boston. In the same year the English journalist left Liverpool "with remembrances of poverty and suffering," the labor exchange found work for 3,137 Irish immigrants. Unlike those in New York City, this labor exchange did not provide breakfast, supper, and a place to sleep. And whoever did get a job was paid only half of what the unskilled worker in New York City was getting. As for the mending of clothes and the cleaning of kitchens, the laborer's wife was lucky to get $1.75 a week for eighty hours' work. If the domestic was single and lived in with the family, Yankee business ethics often required the woman to fork back 75 cents of her weekly pay for board.

At what point did the Yankees begin to question the price they were paying for cheap labor? From the countinghouses of granite block that jutted out into the harbor, the merchants could look out on their own fleets and down on the increasingly Irish dockworkers who man-handled their wares and who, themselves, stopped a moment to watch the arrival of another ship cluttered with more of their brethren.

But to the Yankee eye, these were men given too much to the flow of liquor and the teachings of priests. Paddies. Good-natured, jolly, yes, often hardworking. But reckless men not to be entrusted with the heritage of the Mayflower Compact.

Down on the wooden docks, rank with the stench of fish, splattered with the droppings of molasses and oils and blobs of produce rotting in the sun, the Irish workers looked up and saw that the granite facade of the Yankee was as harsh as the granite walls of his counting rooms. Did these people never laugh? Why, their weddings were less joyful than an Irishman's funeral!

As they moved into new neighborhoods or into villages and towns that had never seen them before, they were stared at, followed by children and adults, ridiculed by bright and compassionate people who, when not discussing the Irish, could be downright liberal. Whiskey, Hawthorne concluded, was "doubtless the first necessity of life — daily bread being only second" for the Irish. So they were, at first, objects of curiosity, but it is a very short step from provoking curiosity to presenting a threat, from quaint brogues and drinking habits to raucous threats and street brawls, from an Irish Stepin Fetchit to an Irish Stokely.

In 1850, Mayor John Prescott Bigelow warned at his inaugural, "Foreign paupers are rapidly accumulating on our hands. . . . Numbers of helpless beings, including imbeciles in both body and mind, — the aged, the blind, the paralytic, and the lunatic, have been landed from immigrant vessels, to become instantly, and permanently a charge upon our public charities."

Was it then that Yankee leaders began questioning the price in dollars and cents? By Gawd, *they* were paying for Europe's paupers! Bigelow's remarks were more hysterical than accurate, but he did say that the new jail might prove to be the most expensive building ever constructed by the city. And there was all over the Bay State a welfare problem, with 320 local Boards of Overseers of the Poor drawing on state funds to support the unemployed paupers, drawing enough to warrant the state sending out inspection teams to make sure the recipients were worthy and that the middlemen were honest.

Was it by then that the guardians of Yankee ethics and morality began wondering what price they were paying beyond dollars and cents? If the real or imagined challenge to those ethics was blatant, the response was anything but subtle, and it would serve succeeding generations of officials.

"At the rate with which violence and crime have recently increased," Mayor Bigelow warned, "our jails, like our almshouses, however capacious, will be scarcely adequate to the imperious requirements of society. [The] causes are in substance, — the increase of the intemperate use of intoxicating liquors; the unwillingness of juries to convict culprits, although guilt be ever so apparent; the leniency of judicial sentences; the facility of procuring pardons; and that morbid philanthropy, which practically prefers the escape of the offender to the security of the innocent."

By 1857, more than half the paupers and criminals in the Deer Island House of Industry were Irish. By 1864, almost three-quarters of all persons arrested by the Boston police were Irish. By the 1860's, some policemen, spotting suspicious characters in crowds, were given to yelling, "Pickpockets! Look out for your wallets!" — a cry that would be taken up more than a century later by Irish subway authorities as they eyed black youngsters working their way through rush-hour crowds. Increasingly, for the Yankee, the Irish came to be associated with street crime, and unless business or a night out on the town warranted otherwise, the average Yankee steered clear of his old neighborhoods that he no longer recognized as his.

As the Irish residents of Deer Island had increased by 1857, so too had their more law-abiding or luckier brethren outside the prison walls. In the decade that began with the famine of 1847, Boston's Irish population grew from 5,000 to 50,000, from one-fiftieth of the total population to one-sixth. "Suffolk County is only a New England 'County Cork,' the Reverend Theodore Parker wrote in 1860. "Boston is but the 'Dublin of America.' " But perhaps most frightening for the Yankees, the Irish were beginning to vote in large numbers.

The appointment of an Irishman to the police force in 1851 caused as much curiosity as it did controversy. People followed the poor man around town until they were convinced he would not suddenly whip out a bottle of brew, slug it all down in one gulp, do a strange jig on the cobblestones, and turn into something awesome and green.

But the next year, when the Boston Catholic diocesan newspaper, the *Pilot*, attacked Protestant ministers, public education, and cooperation between Catholics and Protestants, there was less curiosity provoked than controversy. The observations were met in kind by the "nativists," the immigrant-baiters who warned that illiterate "brutes" were being shoved into the voting stations and that only a papal takeover could result.

How, then, to deal with the Irish before the Irish dealt a death-blow to whatever it was the Yankees held sacred? The solutions ranged from the well-meaning but patronizing suggestions of Edward Everett Hale to discriminatory proposals of Know-Nothings and nativists, who wanted the Irish kept in Ireland and their local brothers kept in the ghettos.

Hale counseled that America must welcome the Irish, spread them out numerically to prevent any heavy concentration in the cities, "absorb them into our own society and make of them what we can."

In 1854, the Know-Nothing Party swept up the state election, carrying both the governor's office and a majority of the legislature. As the Know-Nothings later faded, the anti-Irish sentiment would be inherited by Abolitionists, and later by Republicans.

The nativist sentiment was part of the Yankee dichotomy. It grew in spite of the progressive spirit among the writers and philosophers of New England and perhaps because of what the Yankee wanted to preserve and conserve — a hazy mix of convenient democratic government and profitable commercial enterprise.

Even if there had been no elderly survivors of the Revolution to remind the populace of their peculiar inheritance, others were up to the task. At his inaugural as second mayor of Boston on May 1, 1823, the popular Josiah Quincy orated:

"Let there exist, elsewhere, a greater population, a richer commerce, wider streets, more splendid avenues, statelier palaces. Be it the endeavor of this metropolis to educate better men, happier citizens, more enlightened statesmen; to elevate a people, thoroughly instructed in their social rights, deeply imbued with a sense of their moral duties; mild, flexible to every breadth of legitimate authority; unyielding as fate to unconstitutional impositions."

Quincy would be proven somewhat of an oracle. Boston would fall behind other cities in the statistics of population and profits. Its streets 150 years later would be as narrow, as winding, as confusing as they had been when they were Indian paths. And down those streets would march generations of men and women "unyielding as fate to unconstitutional impositions." Except that such impositions depended on who was defining and who was marching.

"Impositions" were contrary to the New England character, be they a stamp tax, the War of 1812, or the Fugitive Slave Act. New Englanders could and had reacted violently against what they perceived to be threats to their freedom or their commerce. Now, there was to be a threat of their life-style — subtle at first in the days of Quincy, more blatant later as the Civil War approached.

To the teachers, the thinkers, the philosophers, the writers, the more statesmanlike politicians and merchants, the Yankee carried with him for the rest of his days an awesome, God-given responsibility founded in a base of Unitarianism, Transcendentalism, patriotism, mercantilism. It was their lot to serve the less fortunate, the less educated. It was an ethic both charitable and patronizing, and in the coming years it too would be strained by those men fresh from the bogs who had known precious little charity, less-educated men who questioned how it was that the Yankee was so sure of so much.

"The atmosphere of education in which he lived," Henry Adams wrote of his youth in Boston, "was colonial, revolutionary, almost Cromwellian. . . . Resistance to something was the law of New England nature . . . for numberless generations his predecessors had viewed the world chiefly as a thing to be reformed, filled with evil forces to be abolished, and they saw no reason to suppose that they had wholly succeeded in the abolition; the duty was unchanged.

"That duty implied not only resistance to evil, but hatred of it. Boys naturally look on all force as an enemy, and generally find it so, but the New Englander, whether boy or man, in his long struggle with a stingy or hostile universe, had learned also to love the pleasure of hating; his joys were few."

From this common base sprung the diverse philosophers and statesmen in whose company Quincy had exulted.

For Henry David Thoreau, sitting alone near his pond in Concord, the lesson to be preached was one of resistance. In 1847, the year of the Great Famine in Ireland, Thoreau argued against the United States war with Mexico, "It is not desirable to cultivate a respect for law, so much as for the right. . . . Law never made men a whit more just; and, by means of their respect for it, even the well-disposed are daily made the agents of injustice. . . ."

For Horace Mann, the Yankee inheritance was nothing if it was not secured in education for everyone. In his twelfth and last report as Secretary to the Massachusetts Board of Education, he was clearly worried. "With every generation, fortunes increase, on the one hand, and some new privation is added to poverty, on the other. We are verging towards those extremes of opulence and penury, each of which unhumanizes the human mind. . . . Now, surely, nothing but Universal Education can counterwork this tendency to the domination of capital and the servility of labor." Education, he insisted always, was "the great equalizer . . . the balance-wheel of the social machinery." Sadly for him, in the last years of his life, Yankee and Irish Catholic would clash bitterly over his beloved public education.

For William Lloyd Garrison, working on his newspaper in a filthy office, its small windows splattered with printer's ink, his press in one corner of the room, his bed in another, the Yankee inheritance was the cause of Abolition, a cause in which he and his loyal supporters would be as unbending as their Puritan forebears. "I will be as harsh as truth," he promised in his first issue of *The Liberator,* "and as uncompromising as justice. On this subject, I do not wish to think, or speak, or write with moderation." For Garrison, there could be pleasure in hating injustice.

Garrison's histrionics were too much for the establishment Yankees, both the moderates, who favored eventual emancipation of the black man, and the commercially minded, who saw no harm in free labor producing the raw materials for their mills. They might swallow Emerson with his idealistic notions of reform and his criticism of the mercantile environment as one "not of giving but of taking advantage," but Garrison and the Reverend Mr. Parker and their ilk were a threat to the Union and financial stability.

On a fall day in 1850, Parker sermonized that were he a juror at the trial of a man accused of helping a fugitive slave escape, he would find the man not guilty. "Then men will call me forsworn and a liar, but I think human nature will justify the verdict. . . . The man who attacks me to reduce me to slavery, in that moment of attack, alienates his right to life, and if I were the fugitive and could escape in no other way, I would kill him with as little compunction as I would drive a mosquito from my face."

A few days later, a notice for a "constitutional meeting" was distributed. The issue was law and order. The notice appeared in newspapers and, significantly, was posted on the wall in the Merchants' Reading Room and signed by 5,000 citizens. And on the appointed day, the men of property assembled in Faneuil Hall and cheered their president, the elderly Dr. John C. Warren, a venerable man and a venerable name, a professor of anatomy at Harvard and founder of the Massachusetts General Hospital, son of a man who helped found Harvard Medical School and nephew of a hero of the Revolution. To these men, a way of life was being attacked by people who should have known better, by Wendell Phillips, the son of the city's first mayor, himself a cautious and conservative man, by women who spoke out regardless of their husbands' sentiments, by people named Sewall, Whipple, and Phelps, by Yankees, by God!

Now, Dr. Warren was brought forth to balance the prestige of the radical roster of Abolitionists. And as the market men on the street below began closing their shops, as the dark shadows of late afternoon fell across the rows of seats in this historic meeting hall, the old man spoke of what it was many Yankees were fighting to preserve.

"Under the Constitution a new order of things has arisen. Commerce and agriculture have revived. Manufactures have everywhere grown up. Education, literature, and science have been diffused in all our cities and towns. The highest prosperity has pervaded the nation, and presented to the wondering eyes of Europe the spectacle of a federal republic, free without licentiousness, and rich without luxury. I stand, then, at all hazards, for the Constitution and the Union, one and indissoluble, now and forever."

There was great applause. Here it was, finally, in case anyone had missed the point. Somehow, the pursuit of successful commerce and democracy were one, were somehow guaranteed by the Constitution. The laws were made to be obeyed, and if that included the Fugitive Slave Law, then so be it. Those who encouraged disobedience to such laws should be severely punished, those assembled resolved.

As for the nitpicking issue of slavery, one B. R. Curtis raised the following arguments in this meeting that would foreshadow by more than a century the antibusing rhetoric of even larger meetings.

"Do we want in any way to encourage the immigration of the colored people?" Curtis asked. "What would be the effect on the white population of this State of the influx of half a million of negroes, possessing all the political rights of the white man? It could not be otherwise than disastrous, perhaps fatal, to one or the other race; for experience teaches that the two races cannot exist together on terms of equality — equality of numbers and of rights. Strife, if not bloodshed, would inevitably follow such a condition of our population, until the superior race obtained the mastery.

"The day-laborer, the farmer, the mechanic, all men who labor — the merchant, the capitalist, all who pay taxes are interested in excluding the colored population, that labor may not be degraded and capital burdened by contact with an ignorant, improvident, inferior race, with whom it is politically and physically impossible for the white man to amalgamate."

Whether he knew it or not, Curtis's words would have struck a responsive chord with men who were not at that meeting, men who worked downstairs in the market stalls and who lived a few blocks away near the docks and wharves, men from the bogs, men from whom many of Curtis's allies *and* Parker's allies had much to fear.

Abolition was the obvious issue of the day. It had cracked the social infrastructure of the small town that was the city of Boston, the town where Warrens and Choates and Cabots and Lodges and Adamses lived in comfortable homes with gardens and chestnut trees and elms, all in a walking distance from their shops and law offices, the town where family name, intermarriage, and Harvard cemented social solidarity. Now, there were rifts in the families. Once socially acceptable people had become outcasts and radicals.

The streets were filled with the vulgarity that must accompany any such crisis. Men had almost killed Garrison one fall day in 1835. And now, Yankee youths once given to illegally sleigh racing down the ice-packed "neck" connecting Boston with Roxbury, once given to snowball fights on the Common, now such men gathered in the street to cheer, to riot, to help colored freemen wrest fugitive slaves from federal authorities and deliver them unto freedom.

And while the inheritors of that God-given responsibility called Massachusetts watched the action in the very fronts of their homes and shops and offices, they would sporadically turn their heads to the back, for there lay the other threat to all that Massachusetts and Boston had come to mean.

The Irish were being expropriated for their brawn and for their minds. The Yankees told the Irish how lucky they were to be working. As low as the pay was, as harsh as life was, it was better than no life at all, was it not? The black citizens of Boston were among the first to feel the brunt of the Irish immigration. For the Irish and the blacks were competing for jobs, and the Irish, by dint of numbers, were winning. The Irishmen had economic reason to fear the sudden arrival of freed blacks, and both the Catholic press and Yankee merchants played to that fear.

To the Irishmen, the Abolitionist Yankees were dangerous men bent on replacing them at their work with "niggers" and destroying their Catholic faith with their Protestant preachings and their public school prayers and propaganda. For the Irishman, Abolition was a luxury of liberalism that only middle- and upper-class Yankees could afford. Abolition and all do-goodism associated with it opened a wound in the city that would never really heal and would fester again a century later.

To Abolitionists like Parker, the Irish were slovenly and hostile, opposed to Abolition, opposed to the Free Soil Party and its Republican heirs, opposed to the advancement of the human condition.

To the likes of those who assembled in Faneuil Hall that afternoon, the Irish, while a potential ally against the radical antislavery leaders and their black friends, were a health menace, a crime menace, and a voting menace.

The reaction to the Irish spilled from sedate parlor conversation and Congregationalist tirades against popery to mob action in the streets. On August 11, 1834, a mob of truckmen — tough teamsters who hauled freight and were trotted out in white frocks and black hats on their big horses for city processions — marched into neighboring Charlestown, where they were joined by their Protestant brothers in labor from the brickyards, and proceeded to sack and burn the Ursuline Convent.

Rumors spread that 20,000 Irishmen would retaliate. The Yankee thugs made ready, and Harvard students armed themselves to protect their school. Mayor Theodore Lyman prepared to call out the militia.

On August 12, the city and its suburbs waited in fear for the expected retaliation. There were rumors that Irish laborers were coming in by train from Worcester, from Lowell, from Providence to stand by their Boston brothers. Mayor Lyman called a meeting of Yankee leaders at 1 P.M. at Faneuil Hall. There, former Mayors Quincy and Harrison Gray Otis denounced the mob action, and the meeting adopted resolutions attacking the "base and cowardly act."

Lyman had good intelligence too. He knew that the Charlestown mob planned to march through Boston with a brass band to show off the trophies stolen from the convent. This would assure an Irish counterattack. Lyman sent for the leader of the band. "You are to play at the *head* of the procession," he told him. "The militia are under arms. They will fire. You are a stout man, and will be surely shot!" The bandmaster hurried back to his friends and announced his temporary retirement from the music business. But a small number of men still insisted on marching and began moving across the Charlestown bridge. Lyman had stationed a man on horseback at the Boston end of the bridge. As the crowd drew near, he turned and galloped off, provoking a cry, "He is going for the military!" The mob returned to Charlestown.

That evening, the Catholic Bishop Fenwick spoke to several hundred Catholics in a church downtown and preached nonviolence. "Turn not a finger in your own defense, and there are those around you who will see that justice is done you." But the trial of what few mob leaders were caught was a farce, and no one served time for the deed in Charlestown.

Whatever justice awaited the Irishman, be he patient or violent, it was overwhelmed by hostility. Tension increased in the city. The attack by Yankee mobs on Garrison took place the very next year, and on a Sunday in June, 1837, a Yankee volunteer fire company collided with an Irish funeral procession on Broad Street. At first, it was a donnybrook that saw the Irish outnumber the Yankees for a change, but more of the rowdy volunteer fire companies arrived on the scene, and the fighting took on the proportions of an anti-Irish pogrom that only the cavalry could stop.

While Lyman was busy protecting the Irish, he was clearly worried about his Yankee city. In his 1835 inaugural address, he had raised the specter of Great Britain's sending more of its paupers to Boston and warned, "If these persons should actually come in great numbers, they will of course cluster in the cities, forming separate communities or colonies, detached and alienated from the general habits and associations of the people . . . we shall have among us a race that will never be infused into our own, but on the contrary will always remain distinct and hostile. Their children will be brought up in ignorance and idleness; disregarding themselves every comfort and neglecting every decency of life, they will be found living in filth and wretchedness, crowded, of either age or sex, into foul and confined apartments. This course of life is the fatal and teeming source of epidemic or malignant diseases."

In a time to come, in the Boston of 1974, Irish politicians would warn of black and Puerto Rican hordes traveling north to Boston to live off the city's charity and infest neighborhoods and bring down property values and commit crimes. Kevin White would try to counter the fear by quoting Mayor Lyman's speech that the Irish would always remain hostile. And a lady would shout at him one afternoon, "No matter how poor we were, Kevin, we always had clean lace curtains on our windows. We took care of our property. Have you seen what *they've* done, Kevin? Have you been down there? It's a shame, just a shame!"

"*The influence of unacclimated foreign immigrants and the great number of families crowded into the houses in Broad Street, Ann Street and other densely populated parts of the city, render the air very impure and expose the lives of infants, who are compelled to breathe it, to disease and death.*" — From an 1845 census conducted by Lemuel Shattuck

Shattuck was a pioneer in public health policy. He made it his business to visit the slums forsaken by his Yankee neighbors, and what he saw made him fear for the future of the city as much as Mayor Lyman had. To Shattuck, dirt and disease led to social and moral deprivation. He warned his fellow Bostonians, "Pauperism, crime, disease and death stare us in the face."

In June, 1846, a public assembly at the Warren Street Chapel named a seven-man committee to study "the expedience of providing better tenements for the poor". Later that year, the committee reported back that Boston was more densely populated than Liverpool or the "old city of London within the walls." There were 11 persons per house in Boston, they concluded, the same as in Dublin, but in

Dublin, the houses were larger. On Broad Street, the average was up to 37 persons per house, and the committee estimated that each individual enjoyed only seven square yards of room. "Here," it concluded, "is a density of population surpassed, probably, in few places in the civilized world!"

Things promised to get worse. Irish were still coming in, settling on top of one another. From Broad and Ann Streets, they had moved into the once respectable Fort Hill neighborhood and were taking over the North End and working their way up Copp's Hill, leaving one hill, Beacon, to the Yankees, who would hold on to it tenaciously. The year the committee made its study, there were almost 2,500 baptisms in Greater Boston, five times the number in 1830. The birth rate in the Broad Street section alone was double that of the city, and both that and immigration offset the infant mortality rate among Catholics. In Boston, 47 of every 100 persons died before the age of five. For the Catholics, the rate was almost 62 in every 100. About 15 percent of the average Bostonians made it past the age of fifty. For the Catholics, only 6 percent lived that long. Boston's Catholics were dying off at a younger age than the average of the lowest class of laborers in England's filthy industrial towns.

The committee pondered the possibility of building houses for laborers out in the country, but agents for the railroads were cool to the idea — they feared that settlement of Boston's poor along their roads would depress land values. They worried about what their patrons would think if they saw laborers gathered daily at the depot to commute. And as the Lymans and the Shattucks worried, as committees pondered, the Irish kept coming.

If there was a contagious disease to be had, the Irish got it wholesale. Of 700 cholera fatalities in 1849, 500 were among the Irish. In the humid summer of 1854, the cholera struck again.

Edward H. Savage, then a police officer responsible for the North End, would later recount how he visited one tenement after another, one dead body after another.

"I assisted with my own hands in removing more than fifty bodies of the dead and dying, where necessity for the safety of others required it. In some instances, where life had departed by a few hours, the corpse would be so swollen, that the largest coffin could not contain it; in others the flesh would actually fall to pieces, a putrefied mass, before it could be properly laid out, the stench arising therefrom being almost suffocating."

In the narrow streets of the North End, the Irish had found refuge. By 1850, half the neighborhood's 23,000 residents were Irish. They were close to the wharves and the industries associated with Boston's maritime and railroad economy. For the Yankees, it must have been especially painful to see the Irish tread on the turf of Cotton Mather and Paul Revere, to see them loitering in the hallways in the shadow of the very church from whose steeple were hung the lanterns that signaled Revere's ride. But there was no going back.

It was a raucous neighborhood from early in the morning, when fishmongers and produce dealers began peddling their wares, to early the next morning, when sailors poured out of local brothels and dram shops to scurry back to the ships that carried the China trade, the trade that made smart Yankees rich, the trade that produced front-end investment for textile mills, banks, and railroads.

The women who stared out the windows and looked down on the sailors, the men who lounged in the doorways of the shanties, the urchins who stared up from the gutter dirt or the sewage of the backyards knew nothing of the merchants in Canton. They did not go with the wealthy of Boston, the men in long waistcoats, the women in off-the-shoulder gowns, to dance under the ornate chandeliers of the new Union Hall at Washington and Essex Streets. They were not given to the radical chic, who were sporting "Kossuth hats" and quoting that Hungarian patriot. No, the populace of the North End would make their own amusements.

In the nearby National Theatre, a police captain reported to the City Council, "On any evening when the theatre is open, in the upper part of the house, may be found from fifty to one hundred boys from eight years old and upwards, generally poorly clad, and worse fed. When the theatre closes (as it does at very late hours) many of these boys find lodgings in sheds, hay-barns, or at station houses.

"Very few of them attend school; some of them (such as will work) are found peddling matches, papers, etc., by day, earning barely enough to keep soul and body together, (their parents, if they have any, not caring for them); but at all events they must raise the necessary twelve cents to go and 'see the play'. In very many cases, the perpetrators of petty larcenies, which occur so often at this season of the year, are found at this place."

For the entertainment of the men of the North End, there was a renowned rat pit in the cellar of a tough barroom. The saloon itself ran narrow and deep. It featured bad gin and cabbage-leaf cigars, and catered to a clientele of pickpockets, petty thieves, street brawlers, and those who came to stare at the barmaids with their "vermilion cheeks" and low-necked dresses.

In the rear of the barroom, a trapdoor led to the cellar and the rat pit, an octagon-shaped wooden crib about eight feet in diameter and almost four feet high. On three sides of the crib were rows of boards for the sportsmen. On the fourth side stood the owner, Barney, his assistant, and a flour barrel half full of live rats. The room was eerie, lighted with oil lamps and with candles resting in candlesticks made of potatoes or turnips or empty bottles.

At showtime, Barney would lift the wire mesh from the top of the barrel and with a pair of long curling tongs fish out the rats and place them inside the pit. Meanwhile, his assistant would keep a tight grip on Flora, a dog with a neighborhood reputation as one of the great ratters of her time.

"A dollar," shouted a gambler. "A dollar she kills twenty rats in twelve seconds!"

"I take that!" yelled another.

"Half a dollar on the rats," a third yelled. There was always a longshot guy in the crowd. "Don't put in them small rats."

Flora was dropped into the pit and in a matter of seconds wiped out twenty rats. Score: Flora, 20, Rats, 0. Everybody back upstairs for drinks, and later, downstairs again for more contests with different dogs, until the barrel's rat population was depleted.

For a local black man named Jum, Barney's rat emporium was good business. Jum every night would walk to the stables with a burlap bag, a lantern, and his own set of curling tongs and spend a few hours bagging rats. Barney would pay Jum a shilling each. A bag of thirty meant a finif for Jum, happily hoisting his bag down Salem Street every night. But Barney one night got wiped out in a drunken brawl in a North Street barroom; one of his young protégés, a two-legged rat, stabbed Barney through the heart. And Jum was out of work.

The alliance of economic convenience between the Barneys and the Jums was not pervasive enough to bring the Irish and the black of Massachusetts together. The poorest of them lived in the same tenements and shared more than either group did with the Yankee establishment. When war finally came, the Irish and other immigrants were eagerly recruited by both sides, but the blacks would have to fight just for the chance to fight. There lay the irony. The Irish, willing to fight for pay, status, glory, and the Union, were taking part in a crusade that would free the black man to compete with the Irish. The blacks, wanting to fight for the freedom of their brothers, were not allowed to take up arms. When the Abolitionist governor, John Albion Andrew, urged that blacks be armed, Catholic spokesmen warned that such a policy would lead to slave insurrections.

To Andrew and the Massachusetts hawks, the Civil War was a crusade that had begun three decades before in the small parlors of some Beacon Hill townhouses, in the ratty offices of Garrison's newspaper, in the pulpits of Parker and William Ellery Channing.

The struggle, said the Boston *Journal,* "is one between the Puritan ideas of morality, religion and self-government, as represented by the schoolhouse, the church and the town meeting; and the aristocratic ideas brought to this country by the free and easy cavaliers of Charles the First, and which find their natural expression in the institution of slavery, in the love of ease and political power, and in the impotence of moral and religious restraints, so characteristic of the South."

Flagg's Boston Brass Band played songs of war and country, and both Irish and Yankee, and later black, marched down State Street to board the ships that would take them southward. They marched to the cheers of people who broke through three lines of guards to wish them well. They marched with the reassurance of John Andrew's words — "The sympathy of the old Bay State accompanies you to the field; the progress of good men whom you leave behind shall attend you in every conflict; and the blessings of God himself will be with you and our holy cause forever more."

The regiments going south might carry with them the glory of Massachusetts, but they would not suffice. By the end of 1862, both the President and the Congress knew this War of Secession would eat up more men than anyone had imagined. So Congress passed the Conscription Act, and early in June, 1863, Lincoln issued a proclamation calling for 300,000 men.

It was one thing to volunteer to go gloriously to battle to save the Union, to sound the battle cry of freedom and all that. It was quite something else to be ordered to go, especially when the letters reaching home indicated this war was not as glorious an affair as the orators back home had promised. And it was even more grating, when wealthier draft-age men could avoid conscription by forking over a commutation fee of $300.

But the federal government plodded on with it and appointed provost marshals for each congressional district to supervise the draft. For Massachusetts, the quota was more than 18,000, of which Boston was to provide 3,300. Some political leaders insisted that the draft was unjust. Some men proclaimed that if drafted, they would refuse to either go, pay a fee, or find a substitute. Somebody had been boning up on his Thoreau.

For the most part, the men of Massachusetts swallowed their reluctance and submitted to the law. On Sunday, July 12, the Boston *Herald* commented: "The draft is received in this State without the faintest show of opposition, so far as we have learned. . . . Nobody can complain but that the draft is impartial. It hits here and there indiscriminately, and the only thing that varies one's chances from another is the possession of some physical disability or of three hundred dollars. The best humor prevails about the draft. . . ."

In New Bedford, the draft just missed a whaler, who had shipped out. In Salem, it grabbed up four lawyers and six ministers. And in Taunton, the conscripts were singing:

> *I'm a raw recruit with a bran' new suit,*
> *And three hundred dollars bounty.*
> *I'm goin' down to Springfield town*
> *To fight for Bristol County.*

Beyond Springfield town and the peaceful Connecticut Valley, beyond that vast spread of Massachusetts still relatively untouched by Celt or black or tenement, in the city of New York, the Irish rose up against the conscription on July 13. To the newsroom of the Boston *Herald,* the telegraph clacked out the gory details, and on the morning of the fourteenth, Boston's readers stared at the long bank of headlines. "The Conscript Riot in New York . . . Scenes of Flame and Blood . . . 50 Persons Killed . . . The Mob Led by Women and Children . . ."

Deputy Police Chief Savage was not overjoyed to read the papers. Every hour, there was a new edition, each with new and more bloodcurdling details. He would recall later, "There began to appear certain indications that the same dreadful contagion lay hidden beneath the surface in our own city."

A half year later, Savage's boss, Police Chief John Kurtz, would report that on July 12, his central office had received information of a large organization forming to resist the draft. Several kinds of evidence supported the rumor, he said, and the police were sent out into the streets to pick up more information. By the fourteenth, they had reason to believe the "organization" numbered "many thousand men" both in the city and in nearby communities.

That day, Kurtz reported his intelligence to Mayor Frederick W. Lincoln, Jr. Lincoln already had one taste of rioting in an earlier term, when a mob ran through the streets protesting the activities of the Abolitionists. Now, he, along with the rest of the city establishment, was scared by the events in New York.

According to Kurtz, Mayor Lincoln issued orders that every precaution be made for an uprising, which was expected in 48 hours. While the chief and the mayor conferred, Provost Marshal William G. Howe arrived to report that one of his men was assaulted and nearly killed, that several police had been injured, and that a mob of 5,000 were running loose.

The day had been muggy, unpleasant enough for most of Boston's toilers and citizens, particularly so for those stuffed into the North End tenements. It was that dangerous kind of weather that brought memories of the cholera. Even the nearness of the harbor's waters could not bring relief to the tenement district. Two of those toiling in the heat were Wesley Hill and David Howe, both assigned as assistants to Provost Marshal William Howe for the Northern District. The Northern District included the North End, where at about 1 P.M., the two men were distributing draft notices. At 146 Prince Street, a house not far from the gas works, Howe handed a draft notice to a woman to deliver to her husband, and the two began arguing.

A crowd gathered. Some said later that it was mostly women and children. Others reported that employees of the gas works, hanging around outside on their lunch hour, joined in.

The crowd, some of them yelling threats, moved in on Hill and Howe. Hill was able to escape, but Howe was beaten up, and a by-stander who tried to help him was also attacked and forced to flee. The noise drew the attention of two or three policemen, returning to their station from lunch, and they rushed to the scene. As one of them, Officer Trask, tried to arrest one of the mob leaders, a man stepped behind him and slashed his face with a knife. Trask, a strong man, pushed his way out of the crowd and ran to the station house.

Meanwhile, another officer, Romanzo H. Wilkins, arrived and wrestled Howe away from the crowd. He rushed him to a store on the corner of Prince and Commercial Streets and washed the blood from Howe's face. Wilkins looked outside and figured it was safe to get Howe out of there, but when they hit the street, the crowd, grown larger, attacked them again.

Somehow, Howe made it to a house. By then, he was suffering from five or six head wounds, which were bleeding heavily. His right eye hurt, and he was badly bruised. Outside, the police were taking a shellacking not only from close combat, but also from an artillery barrage of rocks and other missiles. Three officers were badly injured, before the police retreated.

"When the rioters had lost sight of the officers," Savage said, "they ran howling through the streets like so many demons, in quest of some object on which to vent their fury, and meeting with nothing seemingly worthy of their notice, a large number headed for the Hanover

Street Station House, and in a few moments a mass of many hundreds were crowded together in that locality; but as no one was in custody, and nothing appearing there to furnish fuel for the flame, they offered no violence."

Savage, in charge of the central office, headed for his old beat, the North End. When he arrived at the station house, he found a crowd of about 2,000 persons "perfectly quiet, strikingly so." Inside the station were a dozen or more police, but no one had ventured out to make any arrests. Savage, who figured most of the crowd knew him, stood on the station house steps and reassured them that no one was in custody, that .there was no cause for alarm. He begged them to go home or return to work, but he was met with silence, and some of the faces in the crowd looked anything but friendly.

Savage began working the crowd, talking with people he knew, and in a few minutes, they confirmed his worst fears, that there were men in the crowd who were armed. Savage consulted with Captain Nathaniel G. Davis, of Station One, and they agreed that Savage should get reinforcements and that the police should try to clear the streets. So, Savage started off for Station Two "and at least fifteen hundred of every age and sex (there was little diversity of color) formed a most uncouth escort up Hanover Street, without, however, offering any abuse save a continued round of shouts, half complimentary and half defiant."

Savage's action dispersed the mob, but knots of people were all over the North End. Storekeepers began shutting down early. Meanwhile, Provost Marshal Howe was delivering his report to Mayor Lincoln and Police Chief Kurtz. Kurtz ordered all men armed and ready — no one was to go home that night — and Lincoln began dictating the orders for calling up state militia companies and regular army units. The rioting in New York had fully panicked Boston's leaders. Kurtz ordered his men to reconnoiter any suspected rendezvous places, and put into operation a rumor control center.

A short time later, the commander of the First Battalion of Light Dragoons and his company commanders were given their orders. The Dragoons were like most volunteer units. Its members were "men of substance, but not wealthy."

Captain Lucius Slade, commanding Company A, took the official message and began reading, "Whereas it has been made to appear to me, Frederick W. Lincoln, Jr., Mayor of the said City of Boston, that there is threatened a tumult, riot and mob of a body of men acting together by force and violence, with intent by force and violence to break and resist the laws of the Commonwealth . . . and that military force is necessary to aid the civil authority in suppressing the same."

Slade was being ordered to call in his entire company, arm them, and form them up at the Sudbury Street Armory for his orders. "Hereof fail not at your peril; and have you there this warrant with your doings returned therein. . . ." Captain Slade was not the only officer getting this message. A similar order was being read by Captain Edward J. Jones, of the 11th Battery, Massachusetts Militia, a unit of light artillery. This group of men, dressed in their worn, surplus U.S. Government issue uniforms, would, in a few hours, be called upon to fire upon their fellow citizens of Boston. Jones and his men proceeded to the armory on Cooper Street in the North End.

Out in the waters of Boston Harbor, far from the tumult and squalor of the North End, Major Stephen Cabot had finished lunch and was dozing off in his bunk at Fort Warren. The day had been foggy and muggy, and Cabot was tired from his duty as officer of the day. Hardly had he fallen asleep when he was awakened by the whistle of a steamer. Cabot walked outside and saw the city boat *Henry Morrison*, docked at the fort wharf. A Colonel Brown, representing Governor Andrew, hurried off the boat and asked to see the fort commander, Colonel Dimick.

Andrew was requesting troops to suppress a riot, Brown said. He told the officers that the mob was beating up the police, that there were signs of serious trouble and Andrew wanted all the soldiers Dimick could spare. Dimick ordered Cabot to order up three companies and issued 20 rounds of ammunition to each of the 166 men. Dressed in battle fatigues, the men boarded the boat for Boston, most of them never having dreamed that their role in America's Civil War would be on a battlefield in the North End.

The fog was thick enough to delay their arrival until 6:15 P.M. When they disembarked, they loaded their weapons with ball cartridges, and Cabot marched his command to the State House. Meanwhile, regular troops from Fort Independence, another harbor fortification, had arrived in the city and had reported to state officials. Governor Andrew told Cabot he was under Mayor Lincoln's command. Cabot was to leave one detachment of men guarding the armory of the Fusiliers and take the rest to the Cooper Street. armory.

As the militia units were posting men all over the city, as police scouts wandered through the streets and alleys of the North End and Fort Hill and South Boston, as regular army units arrived at the docks, as the cobblestones began to echo to the clop-clop-clopping of the Dragoons, the crowds of curious men and women and children began reassembling after dinner. As evening approached, it was rumored that young men in groups of six to a dozen, some of them carrying sticks and clubs, were moving toward the North End from other parts of the city.

By 7 P.M., a large crowd had gathered on Cooper and North Margin Streets near the armory. They mumbled, muttered, and milled around and could not have been arrested for more than loitering until Major Cabot marched his men down Cooper Street. The crowd began hooting at and jeering the soldiers, and a few stones sailed into the ranks. Cabot marched his men into the armory and ordered the doors and shutters closed. He hoped that if the soldiers were out of sight, the crowd would disperse.

Captain Jones, of the militia, strode up to Cabot, saluted and reported for his orders. Cabot told Jones to place a six-pounder cannon on the floor facing the Cooper Street door and a second one facing the North Margin Street door and to load both of them with double canister shot. Jones hesitated. He urged Cabot to use blank cartridges. He said he could not be responsible for firing canister at a group of Boston civilians.

"I told him that I did not intend to fire at all if it could be avoided," Cabot later said, "but that if I were forced to fire, I intended to do all the damage I could, and that I alone was responsible and that he could obey my orders or I would place my own officers and men in charge of the guns. At this, he had the guns loaded, and did his duty like a man."

Cabot made sure men were posted at the Cooper Street gun and at each upstairs window to make sure no one climbed onto the roofs of any nearby buildings. Outside, the crowd was getting wild. They had pelted the armory with bricks and stones, and now women and children were tearing up the sidewalks and carrying the ammunition to their men and boys in the front lines. "We boys," a nineteenth-century wag said of the Irish, "is sociable wit' pavin' stones."

The armory was now under siege. Rocks smashed through windows and thudded against the walls. Sporadic reports of gunfire were heard. "Various persons in the streets who had been attracted by the tumult were knocked down and beaten," Savage wrote later, "the rioters seeming to be determined that none but their own gang should remain in the neighborhood."

At 7:30 P.M., a detective rushed into the Margin Street entrance and said that the mob was beating up a soldier. Cabot ordered a lieutenant to take twenty men, drive the crowd back with fixed bayonets, and rescue the man. When they did, they found a Lieutenant

Sawin of the militia, who had been severely beaten and trampled underfoot and was covered with blood. As the mob began closing in on the rescue party and stoning them, Cabot sent another detachment out to rescue the rescue party. At some point, a few soldiers fired over the heads of the mob, an action that Cabot said later he did not order, an action that only aggravated the mob. Some soldiers were badly hurt by stones, and a captain was knocked down.

"Quite a good many gun and pistol shots were fired by the mob," Cabot reported. "This firing over the heads of the mob encouraged them to suppose we were using blank cartridges and rendered them more bold and aggressive. As soon as the doors were closed, the attack began in earnest."

Some men were now smashing at the armory door with axes and sledgehammers, and the door was beginning to buckle. Fifteen feet behind the door stood the six-pounder. The men outside had smashed open the upper part of the door, and rocks were flying in. Cabot ordered the gun primed and then ordered it fired. Boston was not going to let the Irish get to the weapons.

Canister sprays like buckshot, but is more deadly. Those young veterans wounded south of the Potomac could attest to its power. When the brass cannon opened up into the face of the mob, one man fell dead immediately, and another looked at his right hand and saw a shattered mass of bones and flesh, the fingers practically severed. Drogheda again. Wexford. The Boyne in miniature. The riotous Celts pushed back before the Athens of America.

The firing continued, not from the cannon, but from the infantry-men, and Cooper Street began to clear. Inside the armory, seventy-one-year-old William Currier, of 23 Cooper Street, lay dead of gunshot wounds. Currier, the father of a policeman assigned to Station One, had been killed by a shot fired from outside the armory, authorities concluded. But in the confusion, who really knew? No one even knew how many outside had been injured or killed, for the Irish were drag-ging away their own. Who but the residents of those slums, people rarely interviewed by journalists, people whose opinions were seldom sought out, who but they would know and take quietly to their graves the stories:

Of Mary Beadman, twelve, shot near the heart, who lingered for two days at her home before dying.

Of Francis McGrath, seventeen, of Church Street, who probably died immediately but was such a mess that he could not be identified for at least two days, "shot in eleven places," a reporter wrote. "The body presented a frightful appearance. One arm was nearly shot away. His head and body were perforated in every direction."

Of John Dolan, forty-two, of 144 North Street, shot in the arm and dead four days later.

Of John J. Norton, eleven, of 166 Endicott Street, who died of wounds before morning.

Of Michael Gaffey, fifteen, of 30 Cross Street, who had been standing on the opposite side of Cooper Street, when the grapeshot caught him in the abdomen and sent him to his eternal rest sometime between midnight and one o'clock in the morning of July 15.

Of Patrick Reynolds, twelve, of Bolton Place, who died on Friday from a severe wound in the hip.

Of Dennis Hogan, twenty-two, of 101 Cross Street, who was hit in the shoulder and lungs and from whose back the doctors removed a minié ball bullet, and who died Thursday and whose body was taken home. For the wake, you know. Such quaint people.

So Cooper Street was cleared, and as doctors walked about treating the wounded on both sides, as the clouds of gunsmoke lifted while the stench of powder hung in the thick air of a humid Boston night, the survivors and whatever friends they could pick up made for downtown Boston, for Dock Square near Faneuil Hall.

As alarm bells rang, some of the mob tore down the shutters covering the windows at a hardware store, crawled inside and distributed some guns, knives, and cutlasses to their friends. The Irish were now mucking about in the Cradle of Liberty.

Dock Square was laid out like an imperfect spiderweb. It spun out from its gut assorted radial streets and alleyways. If the mob could arm well and get organized, it could hold off half an army.

But the Yankees never gave them a chance. The police, bolstered by infantry, cavalry, and artillery units, overwhelmed the mob and dispersed them. By 10 P.M., the Dragoons were patrolling Cooper Street, and Dock Square was still but for an occasional shouted order, the clank of steel, and the snorting of horses.

As the sun rose from the mists of Boston Harbor on the morning of July 15, the morning found a city with most of its physical structure intact. At Dock Square, there were broken glass and ripped-up shutters. In the North End, some stores and homes had been damaged, some sidewalks and a street ripped up, and the armory had become an instant slum in concert with the neighborhood. Its windows were broken; the front door had been smashed by stones from the front and by grapeshot from the rear.

For their morning papers, Bostonians could continue to read of the bloody mayhem in New York, but now they had their own riot news to entice them: "The Draft Excitement in Boston! . . . Riotous Demonstrations Last Evening . . . Sacking of Gunsmith's Stores . . . The Military Called Out . . . Attack on the Armory on Cooper Street . . . The Mob Fired On . . ."

And elsewhere in the papers, Mayor Lincoln's proclamation to his fellow citizens: "The peace and good order of this city have been violated by an assembly of rioters and evil disposed persons, and still further violence is threatened." There would be no more "tumultuous assemblages," he warned, no further assaults on property or people.

On the night of the fifteenth, the Constitutional Democratic Club of the Commonwealth met and called the provisions of the Draft Act unconstitutional, producing "exasperation and tumult," and demanded that it be tested in the courts.

As the Democrats debated the Republican draft, some Harvard alumni dining at the Parker House decided to adjourn to the State House and offer their services as volunteers. Once there, the First Corps of Cadets, in charge of protecting the State House, elected the Harvard grads as members and drilled them in how to handle the new Spencer repeating rifle.

Over in South Boston, some of the "good citizens" feared an outbreak in their neighborhood and received muskets and ammo to form a Ward Guard. They remained under arms all through the night of the fifteenth.

But it was over, this little Irish rebellion against authority. "It was pretty clearly understood throughout the city early last evening," the *Herald* noted on July 16, "that there would be no dilly-dallying with riotously disposed individuals and that blank cartridges would be entirely ignored."

On the morning of the sixteenth, court proceedings continued on five Irishmen charged with the murder of old Mr. Currier, not because any of them had shot him, but because of what Deputy Savage described as "the well established principle of law that where persons acting in concert commit a crime, each is responsible for the act committed by either of the others."

That day, a packet boat from New York arrived with twenty-five "negroes, mostly women, who seemed to think Boston a much safer place for them at the present time than New York." The previous day, there had been rumors that the Irish were going to get the blacks, and the military units assigned to Beacon Hill and the State House, not far from the city's small black neighborhood, were alerted. That confrontation would come another day in another time, when both Irish and blacks would regard Boston as no longer safe. While there were some who felt that the bloodshed could have been avoided, Mayor Lincoln came closer to the opinion of the majority. Shortly after the riot, he reported to the City Council: "The fair name of our city is too precious to be stained by lawless mobs — peace and good order must be preserved at all hazards."

For a time, there would be some measure of peace, or at least good order. But it was the chimera of it, rather than the reality. For the classes were at war now, and there would be no peace.

That year, a legislative committee, smelling of nativist sentiment, called for metropolitan government to replace city government, for a metropolitan government was one the Yankees could control. "Moreover, large classes having the right of citizens but not the welfare of government at heart, always run into large cities as the common sewers of the state, and are ready to make use of just such machinery as the present system affords to them to make the material, moral and legal interests of society and the state subservient to their passion and their will."

In years to come, before the century's end, a Yankee legislature would wrench away some of Boston's powers for political reasons painted in moral hues. But, for now, Boston remained municipally intact. The middle-class Irish exhorted their poorer brothers to work for "the good parish — remarkable for its orderly, well-dressed people, who take a pride in appearing decent, and of being proper in their homes and conversation, and no brawls or tumults are ever heard within its walls." And the Yankees and middle-class Irish would soon begin to make accommodations that were mutually beneficial.

So, when Charles Francis Adams returned home from duty as a Union officer, he wrote, "Notwithstanding many local and individual changes, streets which were fashionable in 1837 are fashionable now; the same families not seldom live in the same houses; the wealthy names then are wealthy names still, and the men of note then are men of note now. . . . In literature, also, the Athens of America still sounds the old harp-strings. In the year 1837 R. W. Emerson delivered a Phi Beta Kappa oration, as he did in 1867; Caleb Cushing declined to address the societies of Dartmouth College, and Mrs. George S. Hillard took his place. Dr. O. W. Holmes brought out a little volume of poems. . . ."

But the Yankee blood was thinning, Western stock was growing more sturdy and adventurous, and Boston and Massachusetts and New England would wilt industrially and culturally in years to come.

And the Irish blood, spilled on the broken sidewalks of Cooper Street, simply fertilized seeds planted long ago by the Shan Van Vocht. Some men, of both Yankee and Irish vintage, had to know by the time

Adams returned from the war, that the Irish would be free, if not in Ireland, than certainly in Boston.

> *From the centre to the sea.*
> *Then hurrah for Liberty!*
> *Says the Shan Van Vocht.*

FIVE

The Very Old Boston: A Parade

They march often, now, the white people of Boston.

They gather in South Boston or East Boston or West Roxbury or with their former neighbors now living in the suburbs south of the city, and they get in their cars and wave American flags, Irish flags, Italian flags, and homemade banners of dissent, of resistance to what the Fourteenth Amendment has come to mean to them. They drive slowly in their cars, the drivers honking their horns, men joining their wives and children on a Sunday, a day off, to protest something they feel powerless to fight. The cars snake through suburb and city on their way to a judge's house, a governor's house, past a mayor's house, to a park or a stadium. Inevitably, the same speakers rise to stride to the podiums to address them, to say the same things, to cheer them on, to beat their own breasts.

They parade on foot and they chant, "2-4-6-8-, we don't wanna integrate" or "Here we go, Southie, here we go," clap, clap. Adolescent high-school girls lead their mothers in song, "Over there, over there, oh the kids aren't going, the kids aren't going, the kids aren't going over there."

Over there is the black man. Over there is everything they had fought to keep away. Over there is yet another change piled on top of all the changes that have been forced on them. This is, unlike the high rises, the highways, the urban renewal, the airport runways, the fast food franchises, the cost of living, a more moral change. Yet they are unprepared to bear the brunt of it, and others, more prepared, are unwilling. So, they march and chant into the winds that blow off the whitecaps in the harbor, they march and chant into the winds of change, the most biting and chilling winds of all, trying to snuggle close to them what little power they have accumulated in all those years.

Mayor Frederick Octavius Prince looked over his lectern at those assembled in Boston's Old South Meeting House, looked at the people who, applauding and attentive, were shifting in their wooden seats and waiting for him to begin speaking again. It was sad that there weren't more people. There were still vacant seats in the Old South, but he knew that whatever the audience lacked in numbers, it made up in prestige.

On a large platform were not only the city aldermen and common councilmen, but U.S. Secretary of State William Evarts and a whole pack of federal and state politicians, judges, ex-mayors, and even mayors from other cities.

A moment ago, they and the citizenry down in front had enthusiastically applauded after Prince finished reading a four-stanza poem:

> *So shall all nations come*
> *To make our land their home.*
> *No more o'er earth to roam.*
> *God save the state.*

Fred Prince liked this part of his job the best. His political friends and enemies could debate his Democratic Party politics, his administrative ability, his tendency to hire the Irish. When Prince was elected to his first term as mayor in 1877, he had promised to continue the previous mayor's policy of holding the line on city expenses. The financial panic of 1873 had been particularly harsh on the real estate speculators in those areas newly annexed to the growing city. They had demanded and got a reduction in assessments and in city expenses to boot. Prince proceeded in his first term to knock another half million dollars off the city tax rate, but he soon learned, as would all Yankee Democrats and Republicans, two basic lessons. One was moral, and one was political.

The moral lesson was that decreasing the city budget made life even more difficult for the thousands of poor who, by now, lived not only in the North End, but had sprawled into the West End and parts of the South End, South Boston, the Roxbury flats, and East Boston. The political lesson was that a Yankee victory depended on Irish support, and Irish support demanded, in return, some patronage and some contracts.

Prince knew something about patronage. His own grandfather supported Thomas Jefferson and was handed federal appointments for his loyalty. The new Boston *Globe*, fighting for Irish rights and Irish readership, jokingly referred to its friend, the mayor, as "Mayor F. O'Prince."

But now, on this pleasant, cloudless September seventeenth, Fred Prince, once a Harvard class president, was all Yankee, as was most of the audience, as was the occasion. On the wall to his right had been ornamented the date, "1630." On the wall to the left, the inscription read, "The Day We Celebrate — 1880." Boston was today celebrating the two hundred and fiftieth year of its very being, and Mayor Prince, a lover of theatre and the classics, a sparkling dinnertime host, a raconteur, a great public speaker, dapper in his sixty-second year with a manicured bush moustache, was the man for the occasion. On this issue, there was no debate among his friends and foes.

As the applause for the poem subsided, Prince launched into a long historical oration. He reminded his listeners that they were sitting where John Winthrop, their founder and first governor, had lived and died. On these grounds, he intoned, Otis, Adams, Quincy, Warren, and Hancock "prepared the people for revolution and independence."

"Scarcely a feature of the landscape remains to tell us how nature looked before she was subdued by civilization. The sea has been converted into land; the hills have been levelled — the valleys filled up, the sites of the Indian wigwams are now those of the palaces of our merchant princes, and where 'the wild fox dug his hole unscared', art has reared her beautiful temples for the worship of God and the dissemination of learning. . . . Today the population of our municipality with that of its suburbs . . . is nearly half a million."

Beneath the physical changes, the new housing, the new landfill, were more wrenching changes, less conducive to the sunshine rhetoric of celebrators.

The city of Boston and the nation were at odds with themselves over values — the value of a protective tariff against the value of a not-so-protective tariff, the value of gold against the value of silver, the value of civil service reform against the value of patronage, the value of the woman at home against the value of the woman at the polls, the value of capital against the value of labor. These divisions were not as traumatic or bloody as the war of fifteen years before. Great armies would not clash at Vicksburg or Malvern Hill over the tariff issue or civil service. But these questions were beginning to penetrate deep into the American hide, to lay back layer after layer of protective skin and expose the reality of America. Their very existence indicated that America was no longer what its orators and poets imagined it once had been, what it may indeed have been before the merchant prince replaced the Yankee craftsman, before the draftee replaced the Minuteman, before anyone dared recognize the need to address the inevitable issue of class warfare.

New England was losing its grip on itself and its monopoly on the finance and culture of America. The nation had grown too large to be dominated by any one section, and the great figures were growing old and dying. Thoreau, Emerson, Longfellow, Garrison, and Mann were dead. An elderly John Greenleaf Whittier was well enough to write a poem for the *Memorial History of Boston*. James Russell Lowell was entering the last decade of his life. Wendell Phillips was still a fiery orator who, in January, had brought Bostonians to rousing cheers as he introduced the Irish patriot Parnell, but he was seventy years old and tortured with reservations about the republican form of government. As New England's population fell behind the rest of the nation, so too did her political power weaken, and New England Yankees had begun to get defensive about just what it was they were contributing to the nation.

"Who cares," declared a minister one July Fourth, "for the growth of New England? Who cares, so long as she can continue to give principles and institutions and men to the Nation?" Indeed, people may have cared, but there seemed to be precious little they could do about it. It seemed to many that the sons and grandsons of the Yankee traders and thinkers didn't have the stomach for adventure or the brains for original thought that their ancestors had claimed as their Pilgrim heritage. Those who did were moving elsewhere, or, at least, investing elsewhere.

The action was elsewhere, and the action was different. It was in Colorado, where the population had increased 387 percent from 1870 to 1880, and where jobs were up 476 percent. It was in the Dakota territories, where the population had risen 853 percent; in Kansas, 173 percent; in Nebraska, 268 percent; in Washington, 214 percent. New England investors looked to Pennsylvania and Virginia for coal; to Missouri and Kansas for lead and zinc ore; to Michigan and Arizona, to California and Montana, to Ohio and Tennessee for copper ingots;

to Bradford, Pennsylvania, where 3,086 oil wells had been drilled and more than $1.2 million in rigs installed. Massachusetts investors made handsome profits in western railroads, but somehow lost that ingenuity or desire to obtain a locally owned line that could barrel through the Middle West to Chicago.

For some men, there was more money to be made outside New England than at home. They created fortunes for new generations of men and women who would learn the art of clipping coupons. The day was coming when the Yankees would talk a good game about investing in the future of Massachusetts, of Boston, but the money was flowing west. The day would come when too many important people would hold little or no confidence in their city and state. Some would blame it on the Irish, but the seeds of that were being planted now, even as Fred Prince proceeded to praise the city's progress.

The port was dying. Massachusetts could still boast of shoe factories and textile industries, but her fishing industry was disappearing even then. Boston no longer built the ships that Maine did. Months before Mayor Prince rose to this occasion of oratory, the nearby community of Medford ceased building ships. Across the harbor in East Boston, where Donald McKay had bred his mighty clippers, the last wooden square-riggers to be built in those yards were underway. In three years, Newburyport would push out into the Atlantic waters the last full-rigged ship to be built in Massachusetts. It was steel and coal that America demanded, and New England provided precious little of either. The profit motive, which some equated with economic progress, was an unscrupulous lover. It caressed a chunk of America as long as that section had something it needed. When it had taken the countryside for all it was worth, the lover left for more promising companions, and two and one-half centuries of tradition, companionship, heritage, and education meant nothing.

The sons and daughters of Massachusetts farmers walked sadly away from the 40,000 farms, and the farms continued to shrink in size to an average of 87 acres, smaller than they had been in 1870, in 1860, in 1850.

It was to the mill towns and the cities that the farmers' sons and daughters came, to join the Irish, the French Canadians, and the Protestants from the Canadian provinces. For a number of them, the destination was Boston, for if Massachusetts, despite reality, was still the center of the universe for the New Englander, for others of poetic nature in the republic, then Boston was the Hub.

It had grown from a two-square-mile peninsula of hills and oozy saltmarshes to a city of 37 square miles, from a handful of Pilgrims seeking good water to 363,000 people seeking security, comfort, money, a piece of action, learning, skills, something. There were still a score of Indians in Boston, but they were outnumbered six to one by the Chinese. More than a third of the population had journeyed from overseas, and half of those were from Ireland. Some 3,500 men and women had traveled down from Vermont. Almost 10,000 had come from New Hampshire. More than 20,000 had once lived in Maine. From New Brunswick had come almost 6,000, seeking their fortunes. From Nova Scotia, almost 10,000 "Novies" had come to make their way in the Hub. Two-thirds of the people were immigrants and their American-born offspring.

The very face and depth of the city had changed. Fort Hill, with its Irish shanties, had been demolished. Downtown, once the home of Yankees, had been destroyed by fire in 1872 and rebuilt from the pavement into a major commercial center. The city was extending south to gobble up Roxbury and Dorchester and the farmlands and pastures of West Roxbury. To the east, it was blocked by water. It turned to the west and absorbed Brighton and to the north it had annexed the proud town of Charlestown. There were 3,700 industries worth $47 million, paying 60,000 men, women, and children almost $25 million in wages a year. There were universities and teaching hospitals, lecture halls and museums, all symbols of Yankee beneficence and pride.

But the orations of the times belied the confidence expressed in the present, for the orators, indeed the very establishment of the city, were prone to talk increasingly of the past.

On July 5, 1880, they dedicated a statue of Sam Adams in Dock Square, near Faneuil Hall, and the orator, Robert Dickson Smith, reminded everyone, "The descendants of these Puritans . . . have peopled a great belt of the continent with men of ruling minds. Whenever a mind rises to eminence in the northern range of States, it is found that the bones of his ancestors are resting in the old grave-yards of the Commonwealth, which should be the Mecca of the now imperial West."

If there was a touch of jealousy in that, it was overcome by the complacency that marked Smith's view of Massachusetts in 1880. "I venture to say that never in the whole history of the world, from the building of Babel to the present time, have there been seen a million and a half people living together in such material prosperity, — so well fed, so well clothed, so well housed. May we not add, so surrounded by the means of education for themselves and their children . . . "

Dickson Smith could speak complacently of a million and a half

Massachusetts citizens sharing material prosperity, but the facts, for the few who cared to seek them out, portrayed a different picture, a picture that clearly illustrated good intentions unsupported by reality. To the more cynical, the picture suggested hypocrisy.

There was, for example, the state law limiting child labor in the factories. But when the state surveyed 160 factories in 1879, it found only three or four strictly complying with the law. A truant officer who visited about 30 factories in greater Boston found children working illegally in all of them. It turned out that some 25,000 Massachusetts children between the ages of five and fifteen had never gone to school. The factory owners could say righteously that they certainly were not pulling the youngsters out of their homes and classrooms. They could say accurately that it was the parents who came to them, begging the owners to employ their sons and daughters. The children became to their families an important source of funds. For many families, a job for a twelve-year-old boy or a fourteen-year-old girl made the difference between survival and disaster.

Too many Yankees were living in the real or imagined past, in a time when single-minded, independent farmers tilled a rocky soil for subsistence, shared some of their produce with their neighbors, and bartered the rest off for whatever else their families needed. But now the farm boys were in the mills with the Irish and French kids, working long hours so that young men and women named Lowell and Appleton could dabble in the arts. Because too many Yankees lived in the past, they did not understand the industrial present, they feared the future, and they preached frugality.

Late one May afternoon in 1876, when their nation was but one hundred years old, some of Boston's most prestigious and well-educated politicians and businessmen gathered in a room at the Bureau of Charity on Chardon Street. These were important men, men of affairs, men with a premium on their time. There were F. W. Lincoln and Theodore Lyman, Martin Brimmer and Thomas Amory, Samuel Eliot and Francis Minot, Dr. James J. Putnam and J. E. Lowell. They had gathered to talk about how to register Boston's poor. There were many "disconnected charitable agencies," Brimmer complained, and a lack of cooperation was resulting in "evils." The chief of those evils, according to Dr. Putnam's minutes, "is that the same person is often helped unnecessarily by different societies, so that the active mendicant has a better chance [of relief] than the more modest."

It was clear what must be done. The poor must be registered, listed, cross-filed, accounted for, checked, and double-checked. J. E. Lowell suggested a double list, one of names and one of streets, "so that if it were found that a suspicious number of persons in one house received help, the attention of the Committee would be drawn to that fact." The Committee? Of course, a committee. You must have a committee. This would be the Registration of Charities Committee, and it would insist to existing charities, some of whom chose not to believe it, "We believe that greater familiarity with each other's work would tend to diminish imposture and street begging, which all are desirous to prevent; and would greatly benefit the deserving poor."

No, insisted the committee, they have no desire to brand anyone as "unworthy," but simply to improve communications, and they set about the arduous task of figuring out how to set up card files.

"Josephine M. Dillon, 2nd St., South Boston, married to John H. Dillon, moved from Charlestown. Seamstress. Irish. Two children sick with scarlet fever."

"Each society," a committee memo suggested, "will report its cases on these cards and they will be sorted and filed in drawers or boxes. The difficulty of this plan is that each case may be represented by 20 or more cards. The advantage is that it saves writing. . . ."

"James and Mary Kelleher and six children. Nov., 1876, Oldest child cripple and half-witted. J consumptive, no work. Feb., 1887, J got a little work, baby better. July, 1877, Oldest boy died."

So the committee went on registering and filing. The Female Benevolent Society managed in 1879 to find work for fifty women, who got 50 cents a week. A Beacon Hill minister aided those of his own church, personally giving them a ton of coal but discouraging them from seeking aid elsewhere. If they did, he dropped them, cut them off. In the North End, the small colony of Portuguese tried to help themselves. Their priest, Fr. John Hughes, would work for the poor box of St. John the Baptist Church, but "the amount is small. Sometimes not more than 70 cents a month."

In the same year those prestigious gentlemen gathered to complain of undeserving poor, hyperactive mendicants, and competing charities, state health officials were getting a bit closer to reality. The Board of Health's 1876 report warned, "The high death rate that has characterized Boston for some years past is largely due . . . to the excessive mortality among infants and children under five years of age, the mean death rate under one far surpassing that of London, and almost equalling that of Liverpool, the most unhealthy of English cities."

A Charlestown doctor, commenting on the alarming incidence of diphtheria, reported, "Nearly every case that I have seen has occurred in houses with defective drainage, which in this district, is fearfully bad in all houses which have been built from twenty to forty years, or more. They were laid on planks, which have become decayed and broken away, allowing the drain to become clogged and the cellars to become filled with the fluids from sinks and waterclosets."

The Commission on Sewerage complained of sewers extending through annexed territory without any semblance of a system. At low tide, sewer gases were released into the newly built houses, and 20 million gallons of sewage were being discharged daily at different points, "polluting the atmosphere."

Yankee businessmen, the ones who had complained about high assessments and city expenses, and some Irish businessmen-politicians were making fortunes in real estate and paying precious little attention to the side effects of their handiwork. The South Boston flats stank. At low tide, raw sewage lay uncovered in the stagnant Roxbury Canal.

It was one matter to preach stringency of values and mores to the poor and quite something else to apply that to one's business practices. If there was immorality on the street, as poor white toughs mugged innocent citizens on their way to the railroad station, there was a good dose of it in the establishment too. The enforcement of either law or morality among those who were supposed to know better was lax, and the results were inevitable.

John Donovan, while delivering goods on the fourth floor of 298 Devonshire Street, fell to his death through the elevator opening to the first floor. The elevator shaft had not been provided with any trapdoors or railings.

Joseph Brannan, while reaching for a shifting-rope of an elevator on the second story of 54 Chauncy Street, fell to the basement through the elevator opening and died. No railings for protection.

John Donohue, while climbing a ladder secured to an elevator shaft in a Charlestown building, fell to the basement and died. No trapdoors or railings.

There were 500 of these hoist-ways and elevators in Boston by 1880, and for more than three years the Inspector of Buildings had been fighting for railings and trapdoors, which could be closed during non-business hours. Such a request, he said, would be "neither onerous nor burdensome." But he wasn't having much luck. "From a fire standpoint," he said of the elevators, "they constitute at the present time one of the most dangerous features in building construction the department has to contend with."

John E. Fitzgerald, chairman of the Board of Fire Commissioners, complained, "Property owners barely comply with the building laws and try to evade them all they can."

There were precious few men of private influence who could watch out for the interests of those living in sewage flats or fire-prone tenements or for those delivering packages in unsafe elevators. Only 66 of the 1,200 attorneys in 1880 were not of English stock. Only five local architects were not "American." Only 30 to 40 of the city's 1,000 doctors were foreigners or of immigrant parents. To the Yankee theoretician, all this made no difference. It shouldn't have. Almost a century later, when people fought to integrate unions and businesses, they were told that a good doctor, lawyer, shop steward, whatever, would watch out for any man's interests. It shouldn't make any difference. But it would, and it did in 1880.

By then, the Irish had realized that. They had not invented patronage. They saw it all around them. In the post–Civil War years, as their numbers increased in the city, their influence increased accordingly. They might not run banks, nor were there many of them practicing law, financing Western railroads, treating the ill or setting municipal, state, or national policy. But they did one thing, if they did nothing else. They voted, and a small, but growing, number of successful Irish businessmen were willing to act as power brokers for those voters.

Smart politicians like Fred Prince could orate as much as they desired about Pilgrim heritage and Yankee destiny, but when they left the speaker's podium, took off the ceremonial clothes, and donned their business suits, they were prepared to meet with men named Collins, O'Brien, McEttrick, and Doherty.

It was not just Fred Prince, or any mayor alone, who could provide contracts and jobs. The mayor's power was nothing compared to what the City Council might offer. The council included a 12-man board of aldermen, elected at large every year, and a 72-member common council, comprised of three men from each of the city's 24 wards. The City Council appointed most major officials, and joint committees of councilmen and aldermen controlled the appointments of all municipal workers. Those who peddled influence and sought spoils went to these committees, and both the seekers and the givers were predominantly Yankees. In years to come, journals and reformers and assorted statesmen would express great shock over the state of American cities and would promptly blame Irish and other immigrants for their sad state, but the Irish had simply improved upon the lessons they had learned so well from their Yankee masters.

Together, the aldermen and councilmen each year picked 33 first assistant assessors, who got $7 a day for street duty and $3.50 a day for office duty, and another 33 second assistant assessors, who made $5 a day. The bridges over streams and railroads were under control of the aldermen, who annually appointed bridge superintendents. As with the assessors, most bridge superintendents in 1880 were not Irish. Nor was the superintendent of police, Samuel G. Adams, nor were any of his top assistants; nor were the police captain and two lieutenants assigned to the North End, nor were the truant officers.

By 1880, some of the seekers and givers were not Yankees.

A contractor named Timothy McCarthy got $413.10 that year for some heavy work on Boston Common. Patrick Meehan made out even better — he grossed $1,057.85, and that included an $897.60 gravel and filling job.

It was true that one-third of the House of Correction inmates had been born in Ireland. But 100 of the 697 cops who helped put them there also had been born in Ireland.

The chairman of the board of aldermen was Hugh O'Brien, an old Fort Hill boy who had dropped out of school and who rose from apprentice printer to successful businessman. One of his 11 colleagues was a James Joseph Flynn. To be elected, they had to run citywide. Over in the other chamber, in the common council, the men from the North and West Ends, from parts of Roxbury and from East Boston were Irish.

All three members of one ward were Irish, and two of them were named Daniel J. Sweeney. From the West End came John B. Fitzpatrick, who would engage in what would become typical internecine Irish wars for the control of wards. Someday, he would lose to a man named Martin Lomasney, a man who became the master of ward and voter control and one of the nation's experts on the brokerage of power. But in 1880, Martin Lomasney was just a twenty-one-year-old lamplighter, one of 130 men hired by the city to light and clean the 10,139 gas lamps at 1.5 cents a lamp per night. In the mornings, they would reappear and douse the lights in the copper lanterns. The rest of the day and night was theirs. Lomasney and others spent part of it running political errands in the precincts.

The city, no longer a small, cohesive unit, was divided into 24 wards, many of them run like little kingdoms by coalitions of elected officials and local bosses. Within the wards were the precincts, and they too had their leaders, the counts and dukes of the duchies, who answered to the kings of the ward. The precincts elected their own vote wardens and clerks — a strong ward organization could insure that the right people were elected to protect their interests. And throughout the city, an increasing number of these wardens and clerks were Irish. While the casual citizen of Boston, whose political interests were limited to the annual act of voting, might notice only Yankee names in the most prestigious places, the Irish were building strength down in the precincts.

A whole new generation of American-born Irish was in its youth, and in time, it would not only push the Yankees out of City Hall, but also the generation of older, middle-class Irish bosses, who, in 1880, listened politely to the Yankee speeches, made what deals they could, and reprimanded brash young men who would move more quickly and upset the delicate Yankee-Irish political balance they had engineered.

Up in the North End, John F. Fitzgerald, at age seventeen, was going to school and spending the rest of his time organizing social and athletic events and helping the local parish priests with their picnics. His friends nicknamed him Johnny Fitz. In later years, he would be known as Honey. And much later, as the maternal grandfather of the nation's first Catholic president. In 1880, he was building power.

Across the waters in East Boston, Patrick J. Kennedy, then twenty-two, was in the saloon business. He was a somewhat reserved, but pleasant, young man who befriended many and increasingly was called upon by his neighbors for advice and favors. Pat Kennedy was on his way to controlling all of East Boston. He was the paternal grandfather of that president-to-be. In 1880, he was serving drinks and building power, and were one of his customers to lean over the bar and predict that the Irish precincts would produce anything bigger than a mayor, it would have given Pat Kennedy a good chuckle.

For any Irish precinct captain looking around his neighborhood, the last thing on his mind was the presidency. It was not that relevant to him whether Garfield the Republican or Hancock the Democrat won the White House. Life had not changed perceptibly for the majority of the Irish since the days when Police Officer Savage carried the cholera victims out of the North End slums.

Samuel Adams Drake, the author, walking through Boston and taking notes for a guidebook, was moved to note in the North End, "The rain had been falling as we continued our walk through the filthy street along the water. The air was filled with the stench arising under the warm sun from the mud and garbage of the gutter, and from every door and window of the overcrowded tenements peered forth a swarm of dirty humanity. Someone has called the Irish the finest peasantry in the world, but perhaps he had not seen them herded together in our cities."

Indeed, one could find a Hugh O'Brien. Now in his fifty-third year and president of the board of aldermen, O'Brien, a school dropout who became a business success, was one of those Irish the Yankees pointed to when they were insisting that the system really did work, that if a man has energy and brains and will and vision, he could make it in America. By 1880, O'Brien had served four years on the board of aldermen, where he fought for the regulation of payment to workingmen by those who secured contracts with the city, where he urged the abolition of the poll tax as a prerequisite for voting, where he pushed for public parks and improved sewerage and water systems.

For all of his advocacy for the workingman, O'Brien was enough of a businessman to know a buck when he saw one. He would become treasurer and general manager of the Brush Electric Light Company and president of the Union Institution for Savings. O'Brien was middle class, but he was not typical. There were at least 577 O'Briens trying to make a living in Boston by 1880, and probably a few more not even listed in the city records. They were teamsters and plasterers, grocers and peddlers, clerks and blacksmiths, coppersmiths and coachmen, a marble polisher, a cop, and a bootmaker. More than a third of them were laborers, or helpers or porters, working at the jobs they or their fathers did twenty years before and living in the same neighborhoods.

Hugh O'Brien, the businessman, and Patrick Collins, the statesman, and John Boyle O'Reilly, the poet and patriot, would be the first invited to dinner and to power, but it was among those other O'Briens that the Pat Kennedys and Pat Maguires, the Honey Fitzgeralds and the Martin Lomasneys were raised to prominence. Their propensity for large families would solidify that power, and that was important, for while the Irish immigrants still landed and settled in Boston's wards, they were not coming over in the same numbers.

Now, there would be others.

The others had been patient. They had waited and suffered, not in silence, and often with resistance, but they had waited as long as the human animal can, and now that time in history had come when they could wait no longer. The respectable, middle-class audience sitting in Old South and listening to Freddie Prince knew nothing of them. The saloon-keepers and lamplighters and liquor dealers and smalltime real estate operators building power in the precincts knew almost nothing of them, but perhaps the more aware among these power brokers had seen the first signs of these others.

Living a few blocks up from John O'Brien, a Hanover Street laborer, was one Abraham Levy, a man who made suspenders, and not far from him, an Abraham Levy who said he was a salesman and who boarded out at 170 Hanover. Down from John O'Brien, the porter who lived on Salem Street, resided one Morris Levi, a shoemaker, and around a corner in the rear of 34 North Bennett Street lived a laborer named John Leverone. They were the beginnings.

In Ireland, the potato had been marked for death by heavy rains and a lingering cold spell. In the south of Italy, where rain would have been welcomed, there was, as usual, little of it, and every year, the lands, bereft of large rivers or irrigation, would be plagued by the drought. Both peasants and landowners had chopped away at the forests on the slopes of the mountains, chopped away to till more land to either survive or make profit, and now the slopes were barren, so when it did rain, there would be landslides to destroy the farms and fortify the marshes. The people would go hungry, but the mosquitos, bearing their malaria, would eat.

In the guts of Sicily and in the provinces around Naples and in the bottom of the Po Valley, thousands of men wandered from farm to farm, looking for work, thanking their particular saint if they could manage between 100 and 200 working days a year. The *braccianti*, landless men, were given to malaria and the *pellagra*, the last elements of which were the loss of mind and the loss of life. Some said those who contracted pellagra were living on nothing but an inferior quality of Indian corn. In Italy, they came to call the disease *la malattia propria della più squallida miseria* — the disease of the worst poverty and wretchedness.

Of that commodity, there was a surplus in the Italy of the 1880's.

In the province of Vicenza, more than four-fifths of the people never ate meat; a third of them never drank wine. The peasants lived in houses open to the wind and the elements, but too small for the families. Often, the men would sleep in the outhouses and the cattle sheds. In the winter days, the women also would go to the cattle sheds. They were warmer there.

In the province of Mantua, the houses were not houses. They were huts of mud, thatched with canes. They reminded a visitor of the dwellings of Australian aborigines. In 1880, about 109,000 Italians left their home. By 1881, the average was up to 154,000; by 1886, it was 222,000. At first, only a quarter of them journeyed across the Atlantic. By the mid-1880's, more than half were going to the Americas, many of them enticed by North American industrialists and shipping concerns, who found it profitable to bring over cheap labor for the American industrial machine.

For years, the Italian "birds of passage" crossed and recrossed the Atlantic, a new generation of Italian explorers, looking not for great lands to settle or even great wealth, but for sustenance. Depending on whose records one believed, the Italian laborers were sending home anywhere from $4 million to $30 million a year. Only a fifth of the more than 300,000 Italians migrating to America in the 1880's would be women. But, each year after that, the number of women and whole families would increase. The Italians would come to stay.

In the growing Italian communities of Boston and New York, they would tell the story of Gian-Battista Foppiano, brought to America at fourteen months of age by his parents and taken back with them a few years later to their native Ciceagna. Gian-Battista, it was said, pleaded with his parents to return to America, but to no avail. Gian-Battista, it was said, wrote letters to his young friends in America and asked for money so he could return. Gian-Battista, it was said, was taken with the melancholy and at the age of eighteen now wandered about in the insane asylum of Genoa, his heart broken for want of America.

In the already large Irish communities of Boston and New York and elsewhere, the insecure Irish were telling other stories. They told of how Italians were replacing Irish on labor gangs, especially if the Irish showed signs of dissatisfaction with wages or working conditions.

P. J. Maguire, a Boston Irish boss, ran a newspaper called *The Boston Republic,* in which he attacked Republican attempts to redistrict Democratic wards, counterattacked Yankee irritants like the race-baiting Henry Ward Beecher, and commented on other real or imagined threats to the still very wobbly Irish-American power base.

One such threat apparently were the Italians, whom he described in 1890, as "the very scourings of the slums of Italy. . . . They are a dangerous as well as undesirable element. . . ." That was a harbinger of things to come from a whole class of parochial and insecure Irish Catholic leaders who would reject any liberal Yankee Catholic versions of what the Church could be in America and opt instead for what it was in the parishes back home. The Irish, still being castigated and discriminated against by Yankees, had become a defensive lot. They had enough troubles with the Yankees. They figured they needed Italians like another potato famine.

But the Italian population in the North End was destined to grow from 1,000 in 1880 to 7,700 in 1895, almost 1,000 more Italians in the North End that year than the Irish.

"Nowhere in Boston has Father Time wrought such ruthless changes, as in this once highly respectable quarter, now swarming with Italians in every dirty nook and corner. In truth, it is hard to believe the evidence of our own senses, though the fumes of garlic are sufficiently convincing. Past and Present confront each other here with a stare of blank amazement, in the humble Revere homestead, on one side, and the pretentious Hotel Italy on the other; nor do those among

us, who recall something of its vanished prestige, feel at all at home in a place where our own mother-tongue no longer serves us." — Samuel Adams Drake

Young Johnny Fitz was less disturbed than Mr. Drake. He would learn that one could preserve one's political base by providing services to the Italians, as one did to the Irish. A few streets away in the teeming West End, Martin Lomasney learned the same lesson. There would be decades of bad blood between Irishman and Italian. In the end, they would be brought together only by intermarriage, when it was allowed, and by a mutual fear of the black man. For the emerging Irish kings and king-makers in the Boston wards, accommodation would prove more valuable than confrontation. And what worked with the Italians could work also with others. Yet others.

Inorozhdi, they were called in Russian. The "otherwise born." There were between five and six million of them, most of them confined by law to only one small portion of so vast a country, and some of them had lived in Mother Russia for centuries, but all of them together were considered outsiders. The Jews of Russia, of Poland, of Lithuania, of Rumania had endured migrations, revolutions, annexations, wholesale emigrations and murder, and discrimination of all degrees, but now, there were signs that further endurance might not be worth the price.

If you were a native Russian, the army would not take your only son for the service. If there were more than one draft-age son, the army would take only those earning no wages. If you had a son already in the army, your other boys were exempt. If you were a Russian Jew, you could not depend on any of those exemptions. For you, they did not apply, and if the recruitment officer felt your eighteen-year-old boy was really twenty-one or older, the boy was drafted.

If you were a Jew in Russia, you did not live wherever you pleased. You lived in a specific area called the Pale of Settlement. In the cities of the Pale, you were among a majority, but your representatives were limited to one-third of the municipal councils, and no matter how educated or active you were in the community, you could never serve as burgomaster. Outside the Pale, certain categories of Jews were allowed to live and work, and some even had the ear of the Tsar's court, but in the 1880's that would be of little use.

For centuries, in Russia, in Rumania, in Poland, in Lithuania, the Jews lived where they lived and how they lived purely by the dispensation of those who ruled. A Jew lived from day to day and expected little. He was rarely disappointed.

"One needs luck even in bad luck," they said in Yiddish. They had developed a sense of resignation to reality, their reality. That they had developed it with humor did not lessen the reality. "Jewish wealth," they said fatalistically, "is like snow in March."

So, in the villages of mud and thatched huts, in the small towns of wooden houses and dirt streets, in the cities, the Jews watched the sun set every day, knocked with their knuckles on their bare wooden tables and, if they were religious, thanked the God of Abraham, Isaac, Jacob, and of everybody else in the neighborhood for his blessings. Religious or not, they learned early to mutter upon every rare occasion of good luck, "kayn aynhoreh" — no evil eye!

Less than two months after the murder of Tsar Alexander II in 1881, the "Christians" of the city of Yelisavetgrad began a pogrom against the Jews, destroying their homes and stores, attacking Jews wherever they were found. It would be the first of more than two hundred pogroms in the next year or so, and while they would vary in the amount of property destroyed, the number of women raped, the number of Jews killed, they would all bear frightening similarities — Jews who defended themselves were often arrested; the authorities rarely could control the mobs; and officials either encouraged the pogroms, silently condoned them, or acted too late to stop them.

In December, 1881, the Jew-baiters went to work in Poland, and a pogrom in Warsaw destroyed 1,500 Jewish homes, synagogues, and places of business. In Rumania, the news had never been good. All through the 1870's, there had been riots and assaults on Jews in Vaslui, Ploeşti, and Darabani. The Jews in Rumania had been confined to the provinces of Moldavia and Wallachia. In 1878, the Congress of Berlin had urged Rumania, Serbia, and Bulgaria to afford civil rights to their Jews. In 1881, King Carol I of Rumania responded with laws that banned Jews from rural districts and barred them from certain trades.

In eastern Europe, the message the Jews were getting was as clear as the hunger pangs in the guts of the peasant farmers in Italy. There was one escape valve with some chance of a future: emigration. And the Russians, pressing more and more discriminatory laws on the Jews as the decade wore on, were as happy politically about that escape valve as the Italian government was economically. So, they went. The Jews crowded into the Russian border towns, often without passports and with little or no money, and sat in the streets and waited for their more politically potent and affluent brethren in western Europe to get them out of there.

Through the 1870's, an average of 7,550 Jews a year left Russia. In the 1880's, that grew to 20,000 a year, and in the 1890's to 40,000. In the 1880's, they were still trickling into Boston; by the 1890's, they were pouring in, and the flood would burst again when new pogroms took place early in the next century. Sometimes, as with the Italians, the men came first and sent later for their wives and children. The latter arrived with the clothes they wore and some more in a bag, and, if they had just a bit of money and luck, with two candlesticks, a samovar, and some feathered pillows. In America, there were no pogroms, but America was no bargain either.

"Their inborn love of money-making leads them to crowd into the smallest quarters," an observer wrote of the immigrants. "Families having very respectable bank accounts have been known to occupy cellar rooms where damp and cold streaked the walls. . . . There are actually streets in the West End where, while Jews are moving in, negro housewives are gathering up their skirts and seeking a more spotless environment."

"James J. O'Brien, a resident of the North End, is at the Massachusetts General Hospital with a knife wound three inches long on the left side of his neck and a similar wound on his left cheek. His alleged assailant, a Hebrew, Lewis Cohen, is in a cell at Station 1." — Boston *Globe,* June 13, 1893

Into the North End they moved with the Italians, crowding the equally poor Irish. Into the West End they moved in such numbers that Martin Lomasney would not, could not, ignore them. Into East Boston, into the South End and Roxbury. Into the neighboring city of Chelsea.

With their Italian and Irish neighbors, they did what they had to do to make a living. Sometimes, it was clean, and sometimes, it was dirty. From the North End, 10,000 Jews over the years would take the three-cent Winnisimet Ferry ride to Chelsea, turning then from an aristocratic suburb where the rich summered to a densely populated tenement city, where the poor bought, sold, and stored rags and junk.

In 1908, after a fire destroyed 492 acres of Chelsea and left more than 17,000 homeless, 300 injured, and 18 dead, a Yankee resident penned his version of a Tsarist directive: "The residents of Chelsea are determined to drive out the Hebrew junk dealers, and the insurance companies are helping by cancelling all policies on rag shops. The people of Chelsea have tolerated these undesirable citizens as long as they propose to; fire after fire of incendiary origin has taken place until there is no alternative — they have got to go."

So, apparently in America you also had to knock on wood, throw salt over your shoulder, beware the evil eye. In Russia, the evil eye was easily definable. It belonged to the state. But here, in America, the evil eye could be in a dozen sockets or more. It could be an Irish monopoly on jobs that kept out Italians and Jews. It could be Italian and Jewish peddlers pushing out Irishmen. It could be Irish workingmen fighting newly imported Protestants from the Canadian provinces for construction jobs. Or it could be that most deceptive of eyes, that Yankee cornea, which perceived shades of good and evil according to preconceived images of the morality and worth of other cultures.

". . . Immigration to this country is increasing," wrote Henry Cabot Lodge, congressman of Massachusetts, in 1891, "and . . . it is making its greatest relative increase from races most alien to the body of the American people and from the lowest and most illiterate classes among those races. In other words, it is apparent that, while our immigration is increasing, it is showing at the same time a marked tendency to deteriorate in character."

He was a culmination of Cabots and Lodges. He was a Brahmin, living on the wealthy, restricted North Shore and looking down on his city with great foreboding. Henry Cabot Lodge was obsessed with foreigners — not all foreigners, he insisted, but those ignorant and dirty people from southern and eastern Europe who did nothing but turn cities to slums and lower the wages of the American workingman. Henry Cabot Lodge would become one of the most insistent and famous spokesmen for restricting immigrants, a movement that got its impetus in Massachusetts and was as much Massachusetts as Abolition had been for an earlier generation.

Somehow, the once searching and progressive spirit of the learned Yankee had become prostituted. It was never pure, myths to the contrary. The Rev. Theodore Parker had proven that with his disdain of the Irish, as had the Know-Nothings with their mixture of social reform and anti-Irish discrimination.

But the Irish, defensive and parochial, had rejected the good Yankee along with the bad. The Yankees were pulling inward into their souls and geographically away from their cities. Now, these new people, these others, were arriving, and some saw only one way to save civilization as they perceived it. So, in 1894, three Harvard graduates — Prescott Farnsworth Hall, Charles Warren, and Robert DeCourcy Ward — celebrated their fifth year as alumni by organizing the Immigration Restriction League of Boston. It would lay the foundation for the restrictive measures the nation would adopt years later.

When the story of Gian-Battista Foppiano, the Italian boy driven mad by his longing for America, was published in the *North American Review*, Prescott Farnsworth Hall, as secretary of the Immigration Restriction League, wrote to the magazine, "Personally, I do not believe that boys who have to be shut up in Italian lunatic asylums for insanity produced by longing for the United States, would have been desirable immigrants."

Meanwhile, the League's big gun, Henry Cabot Lodge, was writing articles in every national publication he could with newly discovered conclusions drawn from immigration figures, census tracts, and other sources.

". . . While persons of foreign birth and parentage furnish a little more than one-third of the total white population of the country, they furnish more than half of the criminals . . . persons of foreign birth or parentage are a little more than one-third of our population, and yet they furnish nearly two-thirds of our juvenile delinquents, the inmates of reformatories. . . . The foreign-born constitute only 17 percent of our total white population . . . and yet they furnish *over half of all the paupers in almshouses throughout the country.*"

As busy as he was expounding his restriction theories nationally, Lodge was hard at work back in his home state using the same techniques politically. The problem in Massachusetts, apparently, was not just that immigrants tended to be poorer than people who lived on Lodge's North Shore turf, but that they showed this foolish inclination to vote Democrat. A coalition of city Irish and Mugwumps — those kamikaze-like defectors from the national Republican party — had elected William E. Russell governor of Massachusetts, and Russell was a Democrat. In continually unsuccessful attempts to defeat Russell, Lodge reached into his ever-present bag of statistics and showed that the crime rate was worse in the Boston wards that voted Democratic. It was a technique that Irish Democrats would use more than 80 years later to convince their neighbors that their children should not be bused into the city's black wards.

"These are the localities that give Democratic majorities," Lodge told his listeners. "Go where they are and look, and then say whether you think a party that gets its votes in such quarters . . . is likely to give Massachusetts good government."

Russell gave Massachusetts as good a government as anyone, but there was truth to the statistics. The truth was poverty, and it was as rife in the city then as it had been in those humid dog days of 1863.

In 1899, some consultants for the city reported on tenements in the North End and West End, where they had found "dirty and battered walls and ceilings, dark cellars with water standing in them, alleys littered with garbage and filth, broken and leaking drain pipes . . . dark and filthy water-closets, closets long frozen or otherwise out of order . . . and houses so dilapidated and so much settled that they are dangerous."

All this had come about under Yankee rule, some of it benevolent and some of it regressive and ignorant. It had come about partly because of that ignorance, partly because the economic system would not readjust to new realities and partly because of forces in St. Petersburg and Calabria and Dublin, forces far beyond the control of even the most well-intentioned Yankees.

In that same year, the year of that report, a young politician from Roxbury, James Michael Curley, was elected to municipal office. An increasing number of Irish names appeared on the roles of the City Council. From then on, the Irish, and specifically Curley, would be blamed for the ills of the city.

But all this was not even a vision, a dream, a nightmare, a fleeting thought for those who sat assembled properly and quietly that nice fall day in 1880.

On this day, despite the signs of change, despite the transformations that already had occurred, Bostonians felt they were still living in the Boston they had always known. Fred Prince was soothing them, reassuring them that "most of the important events of our history will be found, when effects are traced to their causes, to have had their origin in the Puritan principles which first germinated here."

Now, the mayor was winding up his long oration, for there was much yet to do this historic day. "We have reason to be proud," he said, "not only of our political history, but of our material growth and prosperity.

"All this," Prince concluded, "is the product of industry, frugality and intelligence, and of those moral and religious principles implanted here by the early Puritans. It is our duty to transmit these blessings with the good government and free institutions we have inherited, unimpaired, to the generations that are to succeed us. This trust is a solemn one and can only be executed by monitoring the virtues of our ancestors, for the same agencies which enabled them to acquire will be needed to enable us to preserve."

As Prince was speaking, the Ancient and Honorable Artillery Company was forming in line on Washington Street. After the mayor finished, he walked outside and took their salute. Everyone then proceeded to the Common, about a block or two away, to eat lunch at the city's expense. Before most of the guests reached dessert, a cannon sounded, signaling the line of march. Horse-drawn carriages rolled up and were filled with guests.

A thirty-one-piece band led off the march, followed by the Ancient and Honorable Artillery, acting as escort to the sixty carriages, as they pulled onto Boylston Street for the march downtown past the department stores and offices bedecked with flags and bunting. In the first carriage, with the mayor, sat Robert Charles Winthrop, in his twenty-fifth year as president of the Massachusetts Historical Society. Here was Winthrop, now seventy-one, the symbol of all that had been. He was a direct descendant of John Winthrop. His mother, Elizabeth Bowdoin, was the granddaughter of a Massachusetts governor; his father, Thomas, had been a lieutenant governor of Massachusetts for seven years. From Latin School, he had gone to Harvard at age fifteen. He had studied law three years in the office of Daniel Webster. His own political career had taken him to Speaker of the U.S. House of Representatives and then to the U.S. Senate. Robert Winthrop had left politics in 1852 to devote his life to arts and letters and history. Now, Winthrop, his white hair just balding in front, his face framed with thick, wavy sideburns and an old-style high collar, sat in the first carriage and looked to the front and rear on the seemingly endless parade. This would be symbolic, for this parade was the last Yankee gasp, the last really big show of an era that was ending. Even the historian that he was, Winthrop could not know the speed and depth of the change that was coming.

In front of the carriages marched Superintendent of Police Samuel G. Adams and his men; then the Second Corps of Cadets, whose predecessors had guarded the State House during the Irish insurrection of 1863; Chief Marshal Augustus P. Martin and his aides; the Military Order of Loyal Legion; the Massachusetts Volunteer Militia.

Far behind the carriages were the Scots Charitable Society, the Charitable Irish Society, the French Canadian Society, the Portuguese Benevolent Society of Massachusetts, and behind them, the Italian Mutual Relief Society, and behind them, more Irish societies from Boston and other communities — the Boston Shamrock Society, the American Society of Hibernians, the Ancient Order of Hibernians of Suffolk County, the Montgomery Guard Fenians.

The past was marching in front of Robert Winthrop and Fred Prince. The future was marching behind them.

The newspapers that editorially gushed over "New England enterprise and ingenuity" that they found apparent in the parade also carried ads that read, "Wanted by an American woman, a situation as a housekeeper . . ." and "Wanted in Walpole, Mass., a competent girl for general housework in a small family. Protestant preferred. Wages, $3."

The signs were there for every sense, for those who could smell the frying of garlic next to Paul Revere's house in the North End, for those who could read newspapers of the events in southern and eastern Europe, for those who could discern brogues and read voting results, the signs were there.

Two carriages behind Prince and Winthrop rode Alderman O'Brien. In five years, he would be the city's first Irish mayor. In five years, Prince's political career would come to an end as he failed in a bid for governor, and he would, as had Winthrop, become more engrossed with literature and the past than with precinct counts and the present. In five years, the Yankee legislature would take from the city control of its own police department and licensing authority.

That day, as the Yankees paraded in their last great garish display of pride and patriotism, an Irishman playing left field for the "Bostons" baseball club, got to first on an error, to second on a wild throw, to third on a passed ball, and came home on a wild pitch. In his second time up in the same inning, he sent the ball into left field for a triple, and 1,100 persons watching Boston play Providence in a field in the South End applauded and yelled.

In the back of the parade and in the backyards of the city, the Irish were flexing muscle.

SIX

The Old Boston: Political Genes of a Man and the City

"I was thinking this morning — how many guys, how many mayors run a city and need a whole law enforcement force to keep down a minor civil insurrection? I don't mean a riot. I mean planned civil insurrection, where you've mobilized for months against your own people, or an element of them. It's getting to be an annual event with me. There's something awful about that. Awful." — The grandson, contemplating his political inheritance, fall, 1975

Part One: A Grandfather

When Thomas White left Ballinasloe in the county of Galway, he did so for good. He was a young man on his way to becoming an American, so American that in years to come, you would not know on meeting this dapper man in a straw skimmer and suits from Kennedy's department store that this was an Irishman. There would be no cloth caps for Thomas White, sir, and no trace of a brogue, but for a bit of trouble he'd have every so often with the word "Massachusetts." He'd accent the "chu" as if he were sneezing.

The White family was very businesslike about this immigration business. Thomas and his older brothers found an apartment in the Jamaica Plain neighborhood, its outskirts still rural and Yankee, its insides opening up to the workingman, and they sent for the rest of their family.

Thomas was the father's name too, and Thomas the father got placed in employment at the Forest Hills Cemetery, while Thomas the son got himself the proper license to get himself out of the merchant marine and into the breweries as an engineer. In 1895, he married Bridget Theresa Dolan, the oldest of five Dolan sisters and brothers from Ballinasloe, of all places, and for the rest of her life their confidante and advisor.

So he left his family in Jamaica Plain, and, with his wife, found an apartment in Roxbury. The young man named James Michael Curley was beginning to move around in one ward there and would soon make quite a reputation as a hard political worker, a fine speaker, and an accomplished doer of favors. But Thomas White showed little interest in the corner gangs, or the boys who would gather in the barbershops to talk ward politics endlessly, or in the scores of societies and clubs springing up by the blockload. He and Bridget stayed in Roxbury long enough to have two children, Mary and Joe, and then — business being as it was in the breweries and opportunities being as they were — they moved uptown to Forest Hills, at the tip of Jamaica Plain.

In Forest Hills, seven more children would be born to Bridget White, and the boys would sleep two and three to a bed, but outside there was more space than anyone in Roxbury had thought possible. The kids would grow up playing relievo in the Forest Hills Cemetery, rolling down the grassy hills of the Arnold Arboretum, playing baseball in open fields in sight of farms and herds of cows.

Into Forest Hills would come the Boston Elevated, taking the Irish to work and bringing them back out to the kind of home they had saved for — a small duplex wooden house, or one of the spacious apartments in a wooden three-decker.

In 1905, the year Thomas's son Bill was born, the brewery workers went on strike for nine months. Some places closed down and would never reopen. It was long, and it was hard, but when it was over, the workers would never strike again, and Thomas White was a union man, 1000 percent. A union man who would march every year in the Labor Day parade.

He cared little or nothing for the politics of Irish nationalism at home or the politics of ward bosses in Boston. But a union man he was, and he made sure that every piece of clothing bought downtown for his children carried the union label, and if Joe or Bill or any of the kids had to pass the neighborhood bakery to go farther for union-label bread, then they would go farther.

Tom White was a tall, husky man of few words, respected in the neighborhood, a good father to his nine children, and, soon, the chief engineer of the Commercial Brewery in Charlestown. During Prohibition, when some breweries made beer to be watered down for the legal 3.2 brew, when some breweries closed, and others cut down their work shifts, the union took good care of Tom White, and made sure he stayed employed.

Tom White figured he had a respectable job, running a power plant, taking care of the boilers and such. It was something you needed a license for, and it was a job that paid good money. You wouldn't get wealthy, but you wouldn't know poverty either. And White figured if you could work like that and live the way he was and be a union man and an American, and all that, you should dress well. So he wore no beard on his face, and he walked about in a suit and a good straw hat. And when his wife's cousins came over for work and stayed with the Whites, he wouldn't let them wear their cloth caps, their suspenders, their britches. "If you're going to be an American, you'll have to dress like one," he told them and down they went to the downtown stores, looking for the union label.

Back in Roxbury, life for Jim Curley was much more exciting than Thomas White was finding it. Further back, in the older wards, life for Martin Lomasney and Pat Kennedy and John F. Fitzgerald was certainly more exciting. And that was just fine with Thomas White. He wanted none of it. He had what he wanted, a large healthy Catholic family, financially secure and living in a nice neighborhood.

It was not an exciting life. It was a good life.

Part Two: The City

One discernible difference between Thomas White and other young men of his time was that he cared little for politics, and they cared a lot. And that led to another marked difference. While he went to work in private industry, the others sought employment or contracts in the biggest growth industry in Boston — the public service.

In the last years of the nineteenth century, the third and last Josiah Quincy to govern Boston expanded public employment, because he believed government was meant to serve people, and in the bargain, such expansion provided opportunities to hire men recommended by the increasingly influential Irish ward bosses. For a politician to trifle with that trend, as a Republican mayor tried in 1900 by cutting the payroll, there was no lack of resistance.

"Men are being discharged indiscriminately," the young city councilman James Michael Curley roared, "for their political belief and nothing else. . . . I live in a district . . . composed largely of working people, who have large families of six or eight; and I have seen those same families in actual want or suffering during the last month or two, due to no other reason than the men were Democrats."

To immigrants, Yankee reform came to mean cutting down the supply of jobs. Reform was something for the rich. Reform was preached by people who lived somewhere else. So, the seeds of distrust of the very word "reform" were planted early, nurtured for a half century with a parochial Catholic distrust of anything Protestant or liberal or Jewish, seeds fortified by those who destroyed neighborhoods in the name of municipal reform and progress and later sown onto the streets by reformers who preached racial integration.

The newer immigrants turned, then, not to the Yankees, but to the Irish, not out of love, but of necessity. Irish and Italian workingmen fought viciously in the streets of the North End over jobs. A West End Jew would recall years later, "My father was a big guy, and he worked hard. The only time I saw him cry was in the Depression. The men would line up in the morning, and they'd pass out shovels, and you'd get so much a day. He'd wait in line, but he hardly ever got a shovel. The Irish would get them, always the Irish."

The trouble with patronage and the power to give contracts was that not all the recipients of such goodness were worthy of the jobs thrust upon them. This problem seemed to escalate during the mayoral regimes of John F. "Honey Fitz" Fitzgerald and Jim Curley.

The Citizens Municipal League, the Good Government Association, and other self-appointed guardians of the city politic cried "shame," and Curley answered that good government people were just a "bunch of goo-goos." So they would be known for decades. The goo-goos, for all their pomposity, arrogance, and insularity, did turn up issues worthy of reform.

A goo-goo watchdog organization, the Boston Finance Commission, churned out reams of reports, finding graft and incompetency to be the hallmarks of Honey Fitz's administration.

"Did you know anything about coal?" the commission asked Fitz's appointee to head the city's Supply Department.

"No."

"Did you know how to test it?"

"No."

"Did you know whether a test could be made?"

"No."

"What difference would it make whether you bought Georges Creek coal, New River coal, or other coal?"

"I don't know."

"Did you ever see a bill of lading?"

"Never."

One could only admire the man's forthright answers, just as one could only admire the resourcefulness of Fitzgerald's constable, the one in charge of killing unlicensed dogs. In 20 months, he allegedly bumped off 6,532 doggies at a buck a dog. When the commission went to investigate, it found no books or financial records worthy of the name. He had kept such a book, he explained, but way back in the winter of 1906, someone broke into his place, wouldn't you know, and hooked the book. The commission tried a body count, but to no avail.

So outraged were reformers at what they were discovering, that one of them imported Lincoln Steffens, the muckraking journalist, to expose graft and corruption in Boston as he had done in other cities. Steffens, instead, ended up pals with Martin Lomasney, who clearly knew more about the city and its immigrants than the reformers. Steffens left town, concluding that Boston and New England were "dying of hypocrisy" and pinning the blame for graft not on the Irish but on the Puritans. They, he charged, believed in Christian ideals but founded an economic system rewarding "thrift, cunning and possessions." They had successfully separated religion and culture from politics and business, and they had become hypocrites. So, the working stiff's perceptions of the reformer, the outsider, the preacher of goodness were again fortified.

The old masters of the city were distraught. They had been pushed out of their neighborhoods by Irish, Italian, and Jew. They had been pushed out of City Hall by the Irish. Now, the more learned and worldly among them could not even preach, because the flock was changing.

The Catholic Church was as fine an inheritor to Puritan rigidity as could be found. Had the Mather family gone on a talent hunt for a parochial, hidebound successor, they could not have done better than William Cardinal O'Connell, who took what had been a fairly flexible church somewhat out of touch with its own people and turned it into a strict disciplinary organization. The Church in Massachusetts was being reworked in the image of the monk Jansen, of the rigid moral code.

It was something of what the old nativists had feared. It was Romanism, with its disciplined hierarchy, its laity kept subservient to the priests, its stifling of initiative and intellectual curiosity. From here, it was only a few short steps to patience for those who would decry all that was Yankee and patience for those who would distrust the Jew. Not until the 1950's, when Richard Cardinal Cushing, his raspy talk bubbling with one-liners and good humor, his arms around Protestant and Jew alike, began peeling off the layers of hate and parochialism that had grown around the cocoon of the Church, not until then did the Catholic power in Massachusetts begin assuming a sense of progressive leadership, to inherit not the mantle of Puritan bigotry, but that of Yankee enlightment. Then, it would be too late.

For the Yankees in Boston, the growing immigrant vote, the changing neighborhoods, the street gangs, the blatant political immorality, the influence of the Church were all they had feared. They escaped by the hundreds to the suburbs, where they consolidated their political power and kept control of the State House as long as they could. To completely escape, they would have to relinquish their economic power also, and this they could not and would not do. So, they traveled to State Street and Commerce Street, to Milk Street and Water Street and Congress Street and carefully watched their money. And that's pretty much all they did with it. They watched it, carefully put aside in protective trusts, and because they didn't have the guts and imagination of their ship-captain ancestors, they saw no reason to invest anymore in a city that wasn't even theirs. Even if they had wanted to, they were discouraged by the antics of the Fitzgeralds and the Curleys. If only, they and their mouthpieces in the newspaper editorial rooms reasoned, if only some good men would run for office!

Part Three: The Other Grandfather

"He speaks of being a businessman," Jerry Watson was chiding one day in May, 1921, on the City Council floor. "Why, anybody would think the gentleman opposite, Councilman Hagan, calling him by name with your permission, Mr. President, was a big businessman! Why, he runs a two-by-four shoe store on Washington Street and sublets an alleyway in the rear to a little stand where they sell peanut shells and indulge in other kinds of shell games, perhaps. . . . He came here with fourteen or fifteen pencils, all sharpened, and never used the point of one."

On and on Watson went. On and on and on. "Oh, Henry! Henry! May your Maker take from you some of the ego or conceit. May He add a trifle to your manhood, if you have sufficient wisdom to drink it in; and believe me, you can take wisdom to advantage, even if it comes from the lips of an enemy, or even from 'Jerry' Watson, so called by you and those who believe in your methods. . . ."

Jerry Watson had mastered such banter that he could lie without losing a beat. But he was absolutely at his best when he simply exaggerated the truth, and the truth was that the handsome, distinguished looking, well-dressed, white-haired Hagan was a touch conceited. He wore a square derby and a black cloth coat with a mink lining. He was a meticulous man, in his dress, in his speech, in the way he laid his clothes out in the dresser drawers. In the style of the times, his gregarious wife, Mary Elizabeth Shields, while sewing layettes for unwed mothers with her friends in the Thimble Club, would refer to her husband as "Mr. Hagan." Mr. Hagan was a small businessman and proud of it, at a time when Chambers of Commerce and service clubs were growing, and an increasing number of men, emulating the wealthy and powerful mill owners and railroad barons, were preaching that good government was the same as good business, what was good for business was good for government, and that what was good for government was a businessman who would deign to serve in public office.

Very few businessmen were volunteering themselves, however. A few did so, because, they said, it was their civic duty, a phrase which made the Watsons and Curleys of the world want to throw up. Henry Hagan talked often of a businessman and his civic duties. One day, responding to a Watson charge that he, Hagan, was being favored by the Edison Company with low utility rates in exchange for favorable votes, Hagan intoned, "I am here to try to do my duty, believing that every public man in any sphere of action should contribute at least 20 percent of his time to public work." Yankee ethics, word for word, and from a lace-curtain Irishman.

A few years after the American Civil War ended, Henry Hagan's parents joined the trek from Nova Scotia to Boston. They were Irish, and Hagan later married a woman whose people had also come from Ireland, but in mannerisms and speech and attitude, Hagan was more American than Thomas White, the engineer, was trying to be. Shortly before the turn of the century, Hagan had some bad luck in business — an event that would give Jerry Watson great material to exaggerate and build upon for his councilmanic routines — but by the second decade of the new century, Henry Hagan was a man of respect in his adopted city. He ran a shoe store in a ritzy downtown location, and his brother Fred managed another one for him in the South End.

Hagan's business activities led him into that strange alliance of businessmen, immigrant baiters, educators, and sincere reformers, the goo-goos, the cost-conscious exponents of municipal reform who looked at government and fantasized balanced budgets as the weapons to be used to restore public service as a public trust.

In January, 1914, James Michael Curley won his first election as mayor, and Henry Hagan lost his first try at the City Council by 366 votes. He was forty-eight years old and a leading light in the Boston City Club and the Citizens Municipal League. The goo-goos were not giving up, by Gawd. They had not pushed reform for nothing, not so the Fitzgeralds and Curleys and Watsons could take over. The Good Government Association kept fielding candidates, and one of them was Hagan.

Hagan was elected in 1915, and the GGA even enjoyed a majority on the City Council for a short time. Just how grateful Boston was is not a matter of historic record. If there was anyone building up gratitude, it was Curley. He was busy building on a citywide basis what he had done for years in his own ward. He was building a mystique. He was becoming and would remain even after death a folk hero, a symbol of the Irish wise guy telling off the Yankee, a symbol of the poor boy who makes good and doesn't forget his friends and his old neighborhoods.

There were times when Curley made money from his position, and there were more times when other men made money from Curley being where and what he was. He was familiar with the insides of courtrooms and prisons. But he would also forever remain the source of money and jobs to those who most needed them. If that meant spending every municipal penny in the till and borrowing more to do it, then that's what would be done, other people's priorities to the contrary notwithstanding.

Jim Curley's machine consisted of one basic moving part, and that was Jim Curley. When the people lined up at City Hall or in front of the beautiful Jamaica Plain home with the green shamrocks on the window shutters, they were not there to see some precinct captain or lieutenant. They were there to see Curley. It was Curley, the individual, and while men might imitate his voice and mannerisms and style, no one could imitate the man. For Hagan, and this was the difference, there were no lines of petitioners. For Hagan, there were no imitators.

In 1915, to people like Hagan, Curley was the corrupt representative of a corrupt system. For almost a decade, Hagan would do battle in the council chambers against that system, a determined and sincere fighter who, unlike his adversary mayors, would never be remembered in popular history. To his critics, he was a humorless and strange man.

"He comes in here with his order, written by himself, like all of his orders," Watson said of him. "He never trusts the members of this body to assist him in drawing his orders. He never consults with any of the officials of this body. . . . In his little office he draws his orders crudely but conveying his thoughts, and doesn't dare to let them see the light of day until they are introduced here, for fear that he may lose a little glory for himself. . . ."

Hagan saw himself differently. One day, railing at his critics over a vote he had taken — "I had the courage of my conviction when that amendment was presented, believing that it is harmful to the men in the Police and Fire Departments — I had the courage of my convictions even to get in the odium of members of the Police and Fire departments by voting 'No,' and I stood alone in that vote. . . . I voted against that with courage, for it takes courage in this or any other matter to be alone, a minority of one, on a popular proposition."

Undeterred by Watson and others, Hagan became a gadfly. He was given to visiting street repair sites and bringing back firsthand reports to his fellow councilmen about shoddy wood blocks and cracked pavement, wasted money and poor supervision. His reports were usually followed by a burst of Watson sarcasm. "Why, he is a lawyer and everything else! We ought to congratualate ourselves on having him with us. We cannot go wrong!"

To the Watsons of politics, the goo-goos were unfair fighters. When a Watson wanted something done, he sat down quietly with another politician, and they talked. They compromised. When the goo-goos wanted something, they too talked among themselves, to others influential in the community, quietly, and then, when it served their interests, loudly to the press. Among the more sincere goo-goos, and there is evidence Hagan was among them, there was a tendency to go down in flames, sticking to the issue you believed in, whatever the cost. There would never be any real understanding between the two groups — the pols regarding the idealists as flaky, preachy, and given to suicidal tendencies; the idealists seeing the pols as parochial, narrow-minded men given to backroom deals and penny ante patronage.

"I know that when people come to me for help," Watson lectured Hagan one day, "when they want a job or a favor, and a letter is suggested, they want me to do something personally. Letters don't mean anything; orders don't mean anything. You wouldn't sell any shoes, Henry, by writing letters. You have got to get people into your store and get the personal element into play. Of course, they don't always get the best of it, when they get in there, but, at the same time, the personal element enters into it."

Watson pierced close to the real Hagan during a playground debate, when he turned to the chair and said, "I want simply to say that there are members of this body, like this gentleman I have just referred to, who hobnob with certain men and who think that they are just a little above the ordinary man. They attend Chamber of Commerce banquets, City Club conferences, where four or five meet and form themselves into a Good Government. . . . I am satisfied that my thrusts are reaching the mark where I can disturb a gentleman with the coldest personality I have ever seen in a human being."

Hagan was, if not cold, certainly reserved. He was not garrulous and full of exuberance like his wife, Mary Elizabeth. For the era in which he lived, he was the prototype father, not a pal to his kids, but the authority. Hagan had business associates, social acquaintances, political allies and supporters — Lomasney, for one — and admirers, but he was a loner, an introvert, given neither to slapping backs nor pumping hands.

He would leave the house at midday and return late at night. Mary Elizabeth would lay out a glass of brandy and a siphon of soda water for his one evening drink, and on Sundays, he would take some beer with the family dinner, which no one was allowed to miss for anything so foolish as a date with a boy or a previous engagement.

As the children dozed off upstairs at night, Hagan would stoke the coal furnace and then return to the kitchen or the living room, and long after Mary Elizabeth Hagan went to bed, he would remain up, reading Shakespeare, Balzac, reading often all through the night, and in the morning, one of his daughters would find him sleeping with a book in his hand, or reading still.

Occasionally, he would joke about Jerry Watson's jibes and antics, but he rarely talked politics at home. You did not talk politics with women, and Mrs. Hagan, while she would vote for school committee members, because who knew better than a mother about the qualifications of such who deigned to set policy for one's children, Mrs. Hagan was anti-suffragette.

Unlike Watson or Curley, Hagan found nothing enjoyable in campaigning. He rarely campaigned. He'd rather play poker and was doing so the night before one election, to the amazement of the newspapermen with whom he was playing. In Boston, election eve was, for most others, a rowdy night filled with last-minute rhetoric, torchlight parades, rallies, and fistfights. Not for Hagan.

In the summer, in the mountains of Maine, Hagan, nattily dressed in leather knickers, would wait until the golf course was clear of all players. Then, he would golf. Alone. At night, in the main house of the hotel where they vacationed every year, there would be social gatherings and dances, and Mary Elizabeth and her brood would be laughing and dancing, and one of them would look out onto the porch and see the small flickering red light that they knew was the tip of their father's cigar. Henry Hagan, sitting alone at the end of a dark porch in the mountains of Maine, would wait for his girls to come kiss him goodnight, and then would sit quietly again with his own private thoughts.

He was a deeper man than Watson gave him credit for being, and while he remained aloof, middle-class in philosophy and bearing, he was, in reality, not even the businessman that his connections and political support would have indicated. Between his penchant for public service and his love of books, Hagan let his business slide. When finally defeated for reelection, he left the Council in 1923 with the good wishes even of Watson, to whom the whole business of politics was not business at all, but fun. If the political defeat hurt him, he did not let on to anyone, and his family heard nothing more about it. It was his style not to show anger, but to hold that inside of him. One result was bleeding ulcers. A few years later, Henry Hagan lost his shoe stores and went to work as an agent for a large shoe concern. It was a grievous blow to his pride, to his image of himself as an American businessman.

His daughter Patricia had married a robust and gregarious young man she had met a few years earlier at an afternoon dance. She was a pretty girl, but somewhat reserved like her father. The man she met was not anything like her father. Joe White, an athlete and an organizer of dances and sports clubs, had worked his way through Boston College. He was one of nine youngsters of Thomas White, the engineer. Joe White was a shaker of hands and a memorizer of names and faces. He was a natural for Boston's biggest industry — politics.

"It's the fastest-moving game in the world," he would tell his wife. It replaced sports for him. Hagan was not overly enthusiastic over his new son-in-law — it was the snob in him that Watson had seen so clearly — and he remained somewhat aloof, though cordial.

One day in 1933, Hagan left his downtown office, walked across the street to a restaurant and collapsed from a ruptured ulcer. He lay in bed one week and died.

Once, when his son-in-law had first run for office and lost, Hagan had told him, "Remember, you will never find a friend in politics."

Part Four: "Mother"

By the 1930's, the neighborhoods had been carved out and assigned labels. The North End was Italian. The West End was everything. East Boston was mostly Italian, with some Irish and Jews left. South Boston was Irish, with some Poles and Lithuanians and Albanians, but mostly Irish. The South End and lower Roxbury were a mix, and most of the city's blacks lived there. Roxbury and the northern tier of Dorchester were Jewish; the southern tier, Irish, as were Roslindale and Hyde Park. Irish lived in Allston, and Jews were moving to Brighton, where there was an Italian colony. Within each ward, there were pieces of turf, laid out by religion, by country of origin, by county of origin, by village of origin. There was no city of Boston. There was simply this collection of neighborhoods, parishes, transplanted villages, duchies, principalities.

Each neighborhood was insular and stuck to itself and told its children to stick with their own kind. The most insular neighborhood of all was Charlestown.

Once, it had been a large sprawling town of its own, proud of having repulsed the British at the Battle of Bunker Hill and proud of its Federal-period brick townhouses that formed a square around the monument to that battle. In the old days, Charlestown was home for rich Yankees who'd raise $30,000 for the annual Bunker Hill Day parade simply by passing the hat door-to-door around Monument Square. By 1874, Charlestown was annexed to Boston, and by the early twentieth century, its merchants and leaders were already expressing regret. Almost as soon as the elevated train structure was built, part of Charlestown began to deteriorate and was forever consigned to gloom even on the sunniest of days. In 1910, the population reached 41,000 and promptly began decreasing, and by 1965, Charlestown counted only 16,381 persons.

The ward was cut off from the rest of the city by a stretch of blue and gray pollution that emptied into the slimy waters of Boston's inner harbor, waters fed with the grime and oil of the tankers and freighters and navy vessels that docked at Charlestown's piers. Across an old bridge, Charlestown sent its women, laden with scrub brushes and pails, to clean Boston's office buildings. To the docks went her men to haul freight and join the Longshoremen's Union, or wait long hours for work that didn't come, wait in the dingy bars under the elevated and drink boilermakers. Charlestown gave Boston priests and plug-uglies. And all of them, to a man and a woman, were townies and proud of it. In its isolation, Charlestown was a very tight community, and could be a very rough one, too. That it was tight was its strength. But the roughest guys on the docks could not give Charlestown the strength it needed to deal with unwelcome change and forced progress. For a while, at least, the politicians could do the dealing.

William Galvin was a Charlestown boy, one of nine kids spawned by a couple from County Cork. His father had died a relatively young man, and Billy worked so everyone else could go to school. He worked two or three jobs at a time, and one of them was running a bar, and another was real estate. He got pretty well known around the ward, which depended on visiting ships and longshoremen for its revenues. When his patrons got so drunk they passed out, Billy Galvin lifted them up and deposited them on their front steps. For that and other services, they began calling him "Mother Galvin." And when Mother Galvin got into politics, he kept on the second floor of his brick townhouse a waiting room, where the people of Charlestown would sit in straight-backed chairs against the walls and wait to talk with their Mother.

Billy Galvin knew and understood Charlestown. He had run once for office and was licked, but in 1937, he knew it was his year. It was a time when those sensitive to the precincts could discern that changes were about to take place. The newspapers kept calling it reform, but the press, which has a short attention span and little sense of the past, has always confused "change" and "youth" with "reform."

A Curley protégé and school committeeman, Maurice Tobin, was tired of waiting for his mentor to move aside and let younger men take a shot at mayor. Tobin, nowhere near Curley in political stature, was a handsome man who spoke nicely. To younger pols on their way up, men like Mother Galvin, Tobin represented an opening to a political future. To the Yankees, Tobin wasn't much, but he was better than Curley.

One such Yankee was Henry Shattuck, the bachelor Brahmin from the Back Bay. He was a tall and trim man, given to boating and hiking. The blond hair of his youth had receded, but his blue eyes were the clear and perceptive agents of a brain that worked overtime as lawyer, computer, accountant, and goo-goo. By 1937, Shattuck had been a member of the city's most prestigious clubs, financial institutions, and law firms and had served as a state representative.

When critics called him cold, cruel, "deaf, dumb and blind to the masses," when they said he was nothing more than a "State Street informer," his supporters recalled how he had fought high coal prices and Prohibition and the powerful utility companies. Henry Shattuck was not a jovial backslapper. But he was a man of respect and man of his word. Like other Yankees who fled Boston for the State Department or New York finance houses or western mining interests and railroad ventures, he could have skipped town. But Shattuck stayed, knowing he would never be mayor — "an angel from Heaven couldn't get elected as mayor of Boston if he were a Republican." So, in 1933, he had run for City Council to become one of the last of the Brahmins on that once totally Yankee body.

Shattuck was very busy in the spring of 1937, seeking the right man to beat Curley. He did this quietly in the style of his people, in the style of people used to power. The man he and his friends turned to, without the press knowing it, was John McCormack, then making this way up the ladder in the U.S. House of Representatives, but McCormack wasn't interested.

Shattuck and his Yankee allies then went all out for Tobin, giving the Curley protégé two things he needed — money and prestige. And some say it was then, in 1937, that Shattuck helped organize "The Vault," a coalition of financiers that would meet quietly and support either their kind of candidate or at least somebody who didn't remind them of Curley, the man who had threatened to flood their vaults and start a run on their banks.

In a vicious campaign that saw Curley subjected to dirtier tricks than he had played himself, Tobin won. That night, outside the hotel that had served as Curley's headquarters, the victory banners were drenched in rain. Two bands hired to lead a march through the city packed up their instruments. Jim Curley choked up and could hardly speak. His daughter Mary cried. "Goodbye, Jim," the faithful yelled, as he walked unsteadily out. The press dispatched Curley to a home for ex-pols, speculating that he was finished. Curley would fool them all. He would outlive Tobin and he would be back in office long after Mother Galvin was involuntarily retired from the City Council.

As for Galvin, his election to City Council in the Tobin sweep solidified his clout in Charlestown. When journalist Samuel Lubell and the *Saturday Evening Post* came to Boston to learn why the poorer sections of the city went 9 to 1 for Roosevelt in 1940, they talked to Mother Galvin and took pictures of his constituents waiting to see him. Galvin rattled off the statistics of how the New Deal was helping the unemployed, the sick, the hungry, the aged, and the *Post* noted, "Of nine Galvin breadwinners, five rely on public employment."

Mother Galvin remained mother to his ward. He was not a Henry

Hagan goo-goo. But like Hagan, he was not much of a backslapper either. He liked his ward and he liked his home. He got up at 5 o'clock in the morning to begin working and he was in bed by 7:30 at night. Like most who have run saloons, he never found liquor particularly useful, and he was not a party-goer. William and Ella Galvin produced seven girls and a boy, and they sent every one of them through college. For most of the girls, it was St. Mary's parochial school and Catholic colleges — Newton College of the Sacred Heart or Georgetown Visitation. Ella made their dresses and dressed them identically, which pleased the photographers for the newspapers. The girls knew there was a waiting room in the house, but they were told not to hang around there.

Mother Galvin left the mothering of his daughters to Ella, who made a career of it. She took the girls to Brookline for elocution lessons. There were ballet lessons, ice skating lessons. They were living an existence that more resembled the suburban life of a 1950's family than that of a pre-World War II Charlestown family. The Galvin girls, until they reached junior high school, were told to be back in the house by 3:15 P.M. and into bed at 6 P.M. They didn't like it, but that's the way it was going to be. Billy Galvin knew his ward, and his son, Billy Galvin, Jr., would know it, but the Galvin girls would be protected and would be given the best Catholic or Ivy education.

It didn't take long for the not-so-Ivy world to take a poke at Billy Galvin. Just two days before the end of 1938, councilman Clem Norton, whom Galvin considered a windbag, urged the Finance Commission to investigate charges that four councilmen, including Galvin, discussed rumors of a $10,000 bribe fund with officials of the Independent Taxi Owners' Association (ITOA). At the time, the ITOA was asking the council to approve open taxi stands in front of hotels, and the powerful Checker Cab Company was fighting it. The rumor was that ITOA, to counteract Checker's political influence, had collected a slush fund to buy votes.

Three of the five Boston Finance Commission members concluded that the councilmen's "primary interest" in visiting the taxi office "was to find out if money could be obtained for votes favorable to the Independent Taxi Operators cause. . . ." Two other commissioners disagreed — the four had acted unwisely, but not improperly.

This was the kind of political mud-throwing contest that Henry Hagan had detested. Mother Galvin understood it, and he knew how to play it. Now, Norton, no mean debater himself, was Galvin's enemy, and Galvin occasionally went after Norton in a manner that would make Jerry Watson proud.

"At the present time," he said one day, "this gentleman holds a public office. He lives at the ninth hole of the George Wright Golf Course. In order to reach him, you have to take a car to a distant section of Hyde Park and then walk a mile and a half to reach his place, where you may find him at home after eleven o'clock at night, but you will be greeted by two ferocious police dogs before you are able to get into his home."

A couple of years later, as the British were bombing Cologne, Mother Galvin went on his own bombing mission. He walked into a school committee meeting, being chaired by Norton. According to one account, Galvin called Norton "Boston's number one political faker," and Norton, rarely at a loss for words, replied that his accuser was "Boston's number one political gangster," thus prompting Galvin to fling a seven-inch plaster ashtray at Norton's head. The ashtray narrowly missed a white-haired lady secretary. Both men were restrained, and as Galvin was escorted out, Norton banged for order and intoned, "Galvin has started his campaign for Congress."

But Billy Galvin was not about to enter Congress. By then, in fact, he was already through with elective office. He had been beaten after his second term, even though he had been council president, and he took it like a man and went about the business of making money so he could send all those kids to college. His old friend Tobin appointed him superintendent of markets and made sure the job got civil service protection, so Galvin would be set, and when Maurice Tobin became governor, some people said it didn't hurt to see Mother Galvin if you wanted the governor's ear.

Galvin would tell his family and friends that what beat him were his own good intentions to do something for his people. Galvin's political mistake, by his account, was to fight so hard for public housing in Charlestown.

By 1935, one-third of Charlestown's buildings were at least eighty years old, and almost 80 percent of its housing stock was wooden. One quarter of the homes needed major repairs or were unfit for occupancy; 121 of them had no toilets. Charlestown was, in miniature, what all the old cities were becoming: what, in fact, many neighborhoods always had been from the time the fast-buck Yankees and their Irish students began putting up ready-made slums for the workers.

In a scene that would be played out repeatedly in Charlestown and in Boston's other old neighborhoods, the people felt more threatened than consoled by the "help" they were getting. On the night of June 8, 1939, more than 400 residents of the slum area to be demolished for public housing shouted their disapproval at a public meeting and threatened to barricade their homes unless they were offered apartments elsewhere at the same rents. Only 20 persons rose in favor of Galvin's project.

"I pay $17 rent," one woman told the councilmen, "and after the government takes our house for the new project, I go to look for a new house. The best I can get is a four-room, back-alley place and then they ask me to pay $18 rent."

A newspaper reporter noted, "There are no worse conditions in Boston, perhaps none elsewhere equally bad," but he couldn't convince the people in the neighborhood. Because it was a neighborhood, and that had come to mean something very special to the immigrants and their offspring who had precious little else.

By August, 1939, the wrecking crews were at work, tearing up the 1,039 apartments, obliterating them from history, whacking down both the vacant, boarded-up rat holes, and places that used to be home for 781 families. Two months before, the court had ordered everyone out, but the court order bore no relationship to either reality or realty.

An old woman, sitting in a doorstoop, watched the wrecking crews and told a visitor, "I was born in this house and I wanted to die here. I had planned to die here. It's too bad they can't wait just a little while. I won't live much longer."

Across the street, a mongrel picked away at the trash, and a boy said, "That's Teddy. He used to be Eddie's dog, but Eddie moved away, and now the dog just comes there every day and guards the house." The air was fetid with the dust of what had once been life. The earth movers groaned and squalled, as they tore apart what the courts had said was theirs for the eating. A dumb dog stood in front of what he thought was his home and barked at the workmen, barked at court orders, barked at a whole wrenching of history that would come to leave gaping holes elsewhere in the city, leave mongrel dogs rooting in the trash of generations of families.

SEVEN

The "New Boston"

LONG AGO, the economic dry rot had set in, and for years, the Yankees watched, while the city limped and choked and rattled on its way to the grave. To die because it was no longer the first port of call for those who did their business by sea, because the state's mill barons were packing up and moving to Dixie, because it was no longer the center of imaginative, shrewd Yankees who were willing to take chances in their own town, perhaps because it was no longer their own town.

By 1950, the city's population was up to 790,000, but that was an increase of only 40,000 over 1920, and it included the beginnings of the postwar baby boom. Some 110,000 persons had left the city since 1920. In the next fifteen years, the population would drop off another 170,000, helped along by the insanity of the times, which suggested that to make the city economically viable and more livable, people's homes should be taken and smashed for highways, high-rise luxury apartments, tunnel approaches, and airport property.

With many of those who voluntarily crossed the borders into the suburbs went not only tax money, but leadership. These voluntary refugees would provide a middle-class base for political, cultural, and economic leadership in the suburbs.

They left behind a city with the most serious economic disease one can have in a society that taxes its real estate to pay for its public services — a shrinking tax base.

As the Church had expanded its holdings, as government became a major industry needing new buildings, as one university after another burst out of its confines and bought property in Beacon Hill and Back Bay, in Allston and Brighton, the tax base shrank even further. As the Massachusetts Turnpike Authority extended its interstate marvel right through the city, as engineers laid out the Central Artery, built at a cost of more than $3 million a mile across the length of the city, as men planned ill-conceived highways that would never be built, the tax base shrank. By the time Kevin Hagan White would fight for his third term as mayor in 1975, 54 percent of the property in Boston was tax-exempt.

Financial confidence in the city was nil. Land prices were high. Assessments were spotty, inaccurate, high where they should be low, low where they should be high. Downtown was beginning to feel the pinch of the suburban shopping plazas. Department stores were closing. Newspapers were closing. Buildings were razed and replaced by parking lots, pizza dispensaries, discount outlets, and joke shops. From two years before the Great Depression until thirteen years after World War II, not one new office building was constructed in downtown Boston.

Even the most progressive administration with support from business, ward heelers, labor, and intellectuals could not have governed Boston. Boston was part of a mishmash of government that Massachusetts had developed over the years. Boston could not raise new taxes without legislative approval or appoint its own police commissioner. Boston had to foot the bill for the Finance Commission, whose members were appointed by the governor. Boston had to pay the costs of running Suffolk County's courthouses and jail, while the three other municipalities in the county contributed nothing. Boston could not collect taxes from the properties at the airport, because they were ruled tax-exempt, even though they were profit-making. Boston's clout in the legislature was limited, even when it changed from Republican to Democrat, because as it did, so did the suburban influence on Beacon Hill grow. Rural and suburban citizens, raking in money with zoning and real estate and highway deals, pointed to Boston with accusing fingers, said "Boston politics," as if that brand were dirtier than theirs, and did as little as possible for the city.

The tax rot from within, the declining quality of services, the pull from the suburbs, the planned federally-funded destruction of homes and neighborhoods and life-styles, all of this was tearing away at the fragile ethnic and economic alliances that had held the city together for the previous two or three decades.

Back in 1944, the goo-goos had run "The Boston Contest," soliciting groups for plans for a better Boston. The groups were top-heavy with academicians and businessmen. The experienced pols, and, more importantly, the residents of the neighborhoods seemed not to count. Prizes were given out. The winner of the third prize actually had suggested that the North and West Ends be completely transformed into "first-class residential sections."

Perhaps it was well meant. So were other reforms. Perhaps the authors believed so deeply in enticing the middle and upper economic classes back to the city that they were willing to sacrifice two decent, safe, and historic workingman's neighborhoods. In print, the proposal seemed vicious, unthinkable. It was filed away, as were most proposals on most issues. Yet, forces were at work to destroy the guts of Boston, to disembowel the city in the name of economic progress and enlightenment.

Across the harbor in East Boston, the community's large waterfront park was handed over to Logan International Airport. The picnic tables and ballfields disappeared. They became a runway.

In Charlestown, 80 families were pushed out for the approaches to a bridge that would make life easier for those who had left the city to commute back in every day and take their earnings back out to the suburbs.

Down in the South End, 22 acres were cleared near the new expressway for industrial development, and 700 more families were displaced.

"On the street where I grew up, there were Polish, Italian, Chinese, Cape Verdeans, Greeks, Albanians, Lithuanians. I went to the Abraham Lincoln School, and they called it the Little League of Nations. There were 33 ethnic groups in the area. One day, the Armenians up the street had a wedding. They blocked off the street, cleaned it up and invited everybody. Across the street, we used to help the Italians bring in the grapes for homemade wine. I was weaned on more kinds of food than anyone I know. It was normal to talk about someone's ethnic background. I knew about the Jewish holidays. I knew the Albanians went after school to Albanian school. I knew the big hero for the Italian kids wasn't Ted Williams but Tony Cuccinello and Joe DiMaggio. I knew about the Civil War in Spain, because all of a sudden, some refugees showed up, and their kids showed up in the Lincoln School.

"When I went to college down in South Carolina, that's when I first learned I lived in a slum. The Traveler was doing a series on skid row, and my family sent me the stories, and they were talking about where I lived. That's not to say we didn't know we were not living in luxury. But they were exaggerating. As it turned out, the new Herald-Traveler *wanted to move in that area and rip off that land, which is what they ultimately did."* — State Representative Melvin King, a black legislator who grew up and lives in Boston's South End, 1975

All over the city, the red brick of public housing replaced dilapidated wooden tenements, forcing the poor, but longtime, residents out and creating with one sweep a new community, filled with poor from everywhere, having little in common with one another except their poverty. By the 1960's, 8 percent of the city's residents no longer lived in neighborhoods, but in public housing, ranging from Galvin's Bunker Hill legacy to Columbia Point — the latter, a conglomeration of diarrhea-colored high rises, constructed next to a rat-infested dump, and equipped with lots of parking spaces but no bus service. Columbia Point, sitting out on a spit of land jutting into the harbor, one mile from Dorchester and Southie, became a textbook example of how not to build public housing.

But there was another textbook case being written in Boston, one that would begin to fulfill the expectations of that insensitive Boston Contest proposal. It was called the West End Project, and it arrived on the scene as a companion to political reform. What was about to happen to Martin Lomasney's old ward, to what was once the most powerful political base in an American city, was devastating — devastating not only in the way the steel wrecking ball smashed against people's homes, not only in what it did to people's lives or to the lifestyle and history of the city, but devastating politically. For the refugees of the West End spread throughout the city and beyond. Instead of packs on their backs or oxcarts laden with belongings, they carried emotional scars and a willingness to explain how they came about.

Wherever they went, those West Enders who did not benefit from the project, those who had wanted to live and die where they grew up, planted more seeds of distrust in ground already fertile with the distrust of outsiders. Neighborhoods that needed renewal projects would turn their backs on any proposals now. And outsiders, always watched warily by the neighborhood leaders, now labored under the added burden of the West End, regardless of the programs or issues they were supporting.

The 48 acres of tenements that had been a neighborhood were swept clean of rubble. The modern, low-cost housing West Enders had been told would be theirs for the asking was not built. Instead, luxury towers arose to obliterate anything but the memories of what had been. For the 2,600 families moved out of the way, for hundreds of others who had left before them, knowing there was no longer a future for them in the old neighborhood, the high rises, with their architecture-school textbook lawns and sidewalk patterns, their swimming pools, their high walls and security force, were a reminder of how little power the ward leaders and their constituents really had when faced with big money and real power.

By the 1950's, the developers and consultants and architects of America had replaced the paving contractor as the wheelers and dealers. They spoke not with brogues or Yiddishisms or Italian accents. They were and are very clean-cut men — usually men — and while they certainly were not all Yankees, they seemed cut from similar molds. They were well-dressed, well-educated, well-financed. They made important alliances, not only with elected officials, but with technicians in government, and they contributed to political campaigns. They wanted to "fit" with the ruling political powers, though they would never, ever, ever use such a word.

They worked with a new nine-member City Council, elected not by wards but citywide and made possible by another charter reform pushed through by goo-goos.

Henry Shattuck had argued that an at-large council would see city problems from a citywide perspective. But there were other fringe "benefits" to a nine-man council, elected at-large. While there might be less logrolling, fewer tradeoffs on voting, there would also be less pressure on the councilmen from the neighborhoods. Places like the West End, Charlestown, East Boston, and Roxbury — older and poorer neighborhoods — would lose whatever little power they had. The more populous, higher-numbered wards to the south of the city would become crucial in determining at-large elections. But it was not the southern half of the city that developers were eyeing for profit. If a councilman voted for a plan to destroy the West End, he would not be punished in Dorchester, Hyde Park, or West Roxbury. And with a strong-mayor form of government, in which the council had limited powers anyway, all kinds of wondrous things were possible. The charter passed in November, 1949, symbolically, the last year that Jim Curley served as mayor of Boston.

The night before Jim Curley lost his last reelection, the Curley crowds took every seat at his rally and lined up three deep against the walls. A kid sang, "For it was Curley, Cuuuuurrrrrlllleeeeee, long before the fashion changed. . . ." Knocko McCormack, the big and beefy brother of Congressman John, assured everyone that "the folks were loyal to Jim." But Knocko was out of touch, and the fashions had indeed changed. John Hynes, a low-key city clerk with bland features and less-than-stirring oratorical abilities, beat Curley by more than 11,000 votes.

Curley had ridiculed Hynes as "a little city clerk" and had called his Democratic opponent "the Republican candidate from the State Street wrecking crew." Newer and younger Bostonians shrugged off the tirades as old, tired Curleyisms.

From the Back Bay, Henry Shattuck directed his forces for Hynes, forces that included a few hundred college men and women. They worked under the direction of a brilliant twenty-one-year-old Harvard Law student from New York, Jerome Lyle Rappaport, who would become the darling of the press, the goo-goos, and the businessmen.

Curley and his cronies, having spent all their lives in overcoming the disillusions and handcrafting the subtleties of their trade, looked at Rappaport and his upstart college friends and poked fun at them. But Rappaport and his friends won, and Curley and his diminishing admirers lost.

By 1950, Curley's first wife and five of his nine children were dead. Before that year ended, he outlived two more of them. Mary and her brother Leo died of cerebral hemorrhages on the same day, about an hour apart. He loved all of them, but perhaps he had been closest to Mary, and now she too was gone, along with his old haunts, his old friends and enemies and the old habits. Torchlight parades were still held, but more in respect to tradition than to necessity. Men who spoke in the old style were regarded as interesting relics, walking and breathing memorabilia. There was still a glut of chicanery, but it was less violent and more subtle than it used to be.

In the depressing years to come, when, on occasions, men could sincerely point to outside influences, to alleged reformers as the creators of havoc, the accusations sounded too much like Curley, and Boston had convinced itself — the so-called leadership had, if not the people — that it could no longer afford such language. Yet dispersed throughout the city were thousands who deeply believed that the only thing that ever barred the door to social and financial destruction for them was Jim Curley. As long as he survived, they would vote for him. And as long as he lived, Curley would keep running for office. He had no other options. It was all he ever knew. It was all that was left for him. He died in the winter of 1958 at the age of eighty-two. He left behind an estate of $3,768 and thousands of men and women standing in the cold of Beacon Hill, outside the State House, where they were

waking him, standing the way they used to stand and wait in front of
the house in Jamaica Plain, except now they were crying. They cried
and mourned the man and the city that had once belonged to them
and now belonged to no one. Now, it was up for grabs.

Johnny Hynes was hardly upper-crust Harvard. He was a Dorchester
boy, and he would die in Dorchester. His mother had died when he
was seven, and his father spent forty-five years inspecting railroad cars
for the Boston and Albany. He started out as an office boy and ended
up as mayor for ten years. Between him and John F. Collins, the tough
Jamaica Plain pol who succeeded Hynes for eight years, the face and
soul of Boston were reshaped, and once again, Yankee contours
marked the face of the city. The Yankees now had to share power with
Irish, Italian, and Jewish businessmen, even with Protestants from,
God save them, the Middle West, but liberal accommodations were
made in the name of money and what they called progress.

Once again, the civic committees returned, both the ones that operated openly and "The Vault," which met quietly and agreed to support John Collins. When elected, Collins continued to meet with "The
Vault," not in City Hall, but in the confines of the city's boardrooms,
and shape public policy. Old names like Coolidge, Cutler, Lowell, and
Shattuck were returning to the headlines. New names like Rappaport
figured in the daily conversations of those who worshipped at the idol
of progress.

Rappaport had organized the New Boston Committee, hailed by
most of the press as an energetic, youth-oriented, public-spirited group
who fought for good government, reform, and a healthy city. The
committee, which included a fair number of Hynes's friends and supporters, enjoyed a couple of years of political success and came close to
becoming the first citywide machine Boston ever had, but internal
dissension tore it apart, and Rappaport wandered off to become, first,
a successful lawyer representing people who had business in City Hall,
and, then, the representative for the developer intent on obliterating
the West End.

Reform and good government and progress and making a buck were
intertwined now. When some screamed that the whole West End deal
was a "land steal," the press preferred to listen to Rappaport denying
such a thing, insisting the conditions of land taking and construction
were "as onerous as any imposed on any developer in the country" and
reminding the press that Charles River Park, Inc., had committed
itself to 2,400 units of housing "in a city which has built only 270
apartment house units since 1941."

In the 1950's and 1960's, the crusaders were no longer sounding calls to arms against incumbent pols. They didn't have to. The mayors were with them, and it didn't make much difference if the city councilmen were or not. The crusaders were playing a new game. It was played quietly, behind closed doors at City Hall or in State Street offices. Its name was redevelopment. Its proponents, including the leading newspaper publishers, said it was Boston's salvation. Unlike the old crusaders, these reformers made less passionate pronouncements about democracy. In fact, most of them had little desire to be quoted. These men were very big on business and efficiency, two elements that often clash with the openness, compromise, and bloody combat inherent in a democracy. The newspaper publishers saw no conflict of interest in participating in creating the New Boston, while their employees purported to cover it. Such an issue would have been academic anyway, for the coverage of the emerging New Boston was anything but objective or fair. It was a paean of praise for the new heroes, the real estate developers, who also sat on the same civic committees that were creating a policy of redevelopment — a policy that could insure a good rate of return to those committee members. Every tax concession, every groundbreaking, airport runway extension, or new highway plan was hailed in the press as yet another rung in the city's ladder of progress.

All right, so the West End was quaint. Boston had no more time to be quaint, said the molders of public opinion. Boston must move now. Move quickly, before the rest of the nation passes Boston by. Move quickly or else. There was always an "or else," whenever anyone dared raise a question or objection. Move now, or else the federal government will give Boston's urban renewal money to Seattle or Bangor. Move now, or the 90 percent federal highway funds will disappear. Move now, or the Federal Aviation Administration will withdraw approval of that new runway.

"We have furnished this nation with patriots, with statesmen, with poets, with authors, with educators, with scientists and with leaders," an editorial reminded everyone. "We will now furnish the nation with a blueprint of a modern city."

Buy. Sell. Pave over. Dig up. The suburban growth mentality, slowly blighting the countryside, destroying watersheds and flood plains, straining the economy with shopping plaza overkill, draining the city of jobs and businesses and people, the growth syndrome had come to Boston. As its ancestors had practiced their Puritanism, their Abolitionism, their Know-Nothingism, their Irish retribution and Catholicism to an extreme, so the New Bostonians attacked the old city, with a vengeance.

"The city was a dime away from bankruptcy," a former urban renewal crusader later remembered. "Something quick and visible had to happen. There wasn't much attention paid to jobs for Bostonians. The development was seen as producing construction jobs, and it was sold on bringing in tax money. And the hope was that if you could satisfy the bankers, maybe you could get them to do some investing and get some tertiary ripples in the economy."

Under Collins and his master builder, Ed Logue, the urban renewal chief, Boston became the cutting edge in America's renewal programs. If it did something well, other cities got similar grants. If Boston made mistakes, they became object lessons for the feds. One problem was that the feds were not funding cities for much of anything except redevelopment. "Boston," the planner remembered, "was in the forefront of change, but you didn't go beyond what was fundable."

Some asked why not? Why couldn't the city say no, this plan will hurt people. Let there be no clearance, no redevelopment, until the human factors are settled. But mayoral administrations were measured by what they built in a four year term. If John Collins could not produce on John Hynes's promises and his own, the bankers, the businessmen might go elsewhere with their money, to the suburbs.

But Logue's massive program went beyond traditional redevelopment and into the older neighborhoods, where, he hoped, a combination of slum clearance and rehabilitation would stabilize them.

Logue, in appearance as cold and removed as Collins, displayed a knowledge and sensitivity about the neighborhoods. As he moved into them with his blueprints, he found the traditional distrust and resentment, now refueled by the West End disaster, the Central Artery boondoggle, the slum clearance in the South End, the tax concessions for the Prudential Center. Logue instituted what he called, "Planning With People," but it often meant that the people were Logue's people — those neighborhood residents selected for their tendency to cooperate with him. Perhaps there was no other way to do it. Perhaps the crisis of the neighborhoods demanded action as abrupt and quick as had the crisis of downtown. But most neighborhoods resisted.

Back at City Hall, Collins had made it clear that the priority was downtown. That had to be saved first. The priority, he insisted, was cutting taxes, which he managed to do year after year. That the quality of service was bound to decline as tax funds declined and as the need for public services escalated in the city was something the boosters did not discuss much.

The pungent aroma of progress was everywhere. It was a smell of asphalt and cement and blueprint ink and fresh wood and fresh money. But to a lot of people, it was beginning to stink.

It smelled in the very plans drawn up by highway engineers from Massachusetts and Washington and their highly paid consultants, drawn up with no real input from the citizens whose lives the roads would disrupt. If the highway builders were to be allowed to build that which they wished, they would be removing from $89 to $221 million worth of taxable property from Boston over a twenty-year period, 4,600 jobs in a high unemployment area, and 1,155 acres of land in already densely populated communities.

The stink of progress was clearly perceptible in the neighborhoods affected by the expansion of Logan Airport, with its commodities of jet noise and fuel discharge. The Massachusetts Port Authority, given free rein to run the airport, given tax-free properties, given limited powers of eminent domain, had transformed the goo-goo theory of civic boards independent of politics into a travesty. Yet flights were disrupting the peace of South Boston's beaches and what little peace there was at the Columbia Point Projects. The whine of warmups and the roar of reverse thrusts continued throughout the night, to drive East Boston residents out of their homes. Heavy trucks, illegally overloaded with fill for the expanding airport, roared through East Boston's streets, while a hungry port authority took waterfront parkland and turned it into a runway extension.

In the heart of black Roxbury, urban renewal machines smashed apart wooden slums, cleared the land for the construction of brick duplex homes. But the project forced slum families to crowd into Dorchester, and as the neighborhood turned black, the area suddenly became known as North Dorchester to distinguish black Dorchester from white Dorchester. The black refugees were even worse off than the West Enders, for, as a group, they had even less money and, because of color, fewer options as to where they could move. Young Jews moved away, leaving the parents and the old behind to cope with dirt-poor black families born and bred in the repressive South and swept north to dreams that rarely materialized. The Jews moved south from what had been their turf for two generations, south with their landsmen in Mattapan, only to move again a few years later when Protestant bankers, stricken with civic conscience, handed blacks low-interest mortgages to buy homes — in Mattapan *only*. The blockbusters of both colors went to work. The Jews sold low and left for good. The blacks bought high and drowned in debt.

All over the city, there was movement, there was change. There were also anger and fear, and in the summer of 1967, while the press speculated over John Collins's intentions, while others made ready to run for mayor of Boston, the people spoke to their fears and frustrations.

All over the city, people asked why streetlights were busted or not working, why streets were not repaired, why sewer lines blocked up, why cops were no longer visible, why they couldn't get mortgage money and insurance and police protection, why there was no bus service, why slumlords couldn't be identified or prosecuted, why the projects could not be maintained, why some playgrounds were locked up on weekends and others were consistently vandalized. For all the millions of dollars of renewal and development, for all the national publicity, for all the newfound confidence and reputation of Boston, the city was dying. Its people knew it and they feared it.

John Collins, Ed Logue, "The Vault," and federal money had saved corporate Boston from self-destruction. But they could not cope with social Boston, and they were getting the messages of discontent.

In 1966, Collins ran in the Democratic primary for his party's nomination to the U.S. Senate. A former governor, Endicott (Chub) Peabody, beat him badly in Collins's own city. Collins's campaign manager told a reporter he doubted Collins would run for a third term. "He really hasn't been enjoying the job in recent years. There are too many problems in the city. I'll be surprised if he runs for reelection."

By 1967, even John Collins couldn't hope to hold the tax rate down again for the coming year. In June, Boston's ghetto erupted in violence, and a few days later, John Collins said thanks, but no thanks. He had had enough. He tried to pass the mantle to Ed Logue, but Logue, the symbol of the New Boston, would be rejected by the people of old Boston.

"Logue had spent a lot of time crawling through alleys," a Logue admirer recalled, "trying to figure out how to help poor people live. But there were no weapons he could use, and with his left hand, he ended up building Government Center. . . . He became known by what he did."

What he and John Collins did, what Hynes and Shattuck had begun to do, was to build what they and the national press called "The New Boston." Their legacy was a city with two personalities. One was that newer Boston, brimming with confidence, attracting money and the middle class, sporting its new and often ugly high rises like an immigrant kid who just made it into the white-collar crowd and shows off his two new suits. It was a chic Boston, of specialty shops and bars and steak houses with hokey names and walls plastered with pictures of sports heroes. It had little or nothing to do with the other city, but it symbolized growth and money and good bond ratings, and it was oh so much fun for the thousands who came to dabble at the universities in and around the city.

The other personality was the old Boston, increasingly angry at the threats to its life-style and existence, convinced that somebody else was getting everything, while it was getting nothing more than the shaft, angry at what it perceived to be an insensitive government that could no longer provide the basic services needed for survival in the neighborhoods and distrustful now of all outsiders, preachers, planners, reformers, and do-gooders.

EIGHT

The Inheritance

WHEN HE WAS YOUNG, Joe White wandered. He tried teaching in Puerto Rico and playing football. He promoted semi-pro baseball for a while, and he dabbled in the oil business in Boston. By profession, Joe White was a teacher. By instinct, he was a politician, and about the time the stock market crashed, Joe White's political fortunes began looking good. He served four years in the state House of Representatives and four more in the state Senate.

Henry Hagan's warning that politics was a lonely business that left you no friends was clearly meant for others than his son-in-law. Henry Hagan's daughter, Patricia, well-schooled and -read, found herself in a household that bore little resemblance to the sedate one in which she had grown up. It was noisy and full of political friends and campaign workers. Patricia White became a short-order cook, feeding election workers who would spend the night sleeping on the floors at her house. She became a chauffeur, driving Joe to christenings, weddings, and wakes, where he would deliver the proper congratulations or condolences and drink with the best in the crowd.

Like all proper middle-class Catholic women, like her mother and Tom White's wife, Patricia White stayed home to raise three sons and a daughter, stayed home, knowing Joe White might or might not be home for dinner, knowing he would never call one way or the other and that if he did, something was wrong. Life with Joe could be hilarious. And it could be lonely, because with all the tumult, with all the action that swirled around her, Patricia White did not have anyone to talk to. Joe would talk about local politics. His wife listened, and she spoke when she felt she should, but her interests were more cosmic. Her companions became her books. She read late into the night, as Henry Hagan used to, not going to sleep until she was sure her three boys and her daughter were back home from wherever they had been.

Meanwhile, Joe White hustled. He got into the oil business, which he put in the name of his sister, Mary Scanlon. Mary's husband, Jim, was a politician from the nearby workingmen's city of Somerville. He and Joe ended up in the Senate together, and it was said that nothing passed through that body that Jimmy Scanlon and Joe White didn't approve first.

White hitched his fortunes to one Joseph Ely, a Yankee Democrat who became governor, much to the disgust of Jim Curley. There was no love between Ely and Curley, so, as far as Curley was concerned, Joe White was as useful as Curley's old nemesis, Henry Hagan, had been.

In 1932, Ely and the state's middle-class Irish U.S. Senator, David I. Walsh, were sticking with Al Smith. Curley went to work for Roosevelt in a state that had given Al Smith more votes than his own New York. Curley's slate to the national convention was smeared, and 25,000 persons cheered Walsh, Ely, Joe White, and the others who headed off for Chicago. Quietly, Jim Curley traveled to Chicago too, used his influence to replace the chairman of the Puerto Rican delegation, and when the roll was called, "Jaime Miguel Curleo" cast six votes for Roosevelt.

Ely, being a good Democrat, swung over to Roosevelt when he got back to Massachusetts. Being a good Democrat, he did other things too, such as reward those who supported him. For Joe White, the award was appointment as director of the telephone and telegraph division of the state Department of Public Utilities. White's friends made sure Joe could take a noncompetitive civil service exam, much to the disgust of a department official who insisted Joe White didn't know anything about phones or telegraphs.

White was dispensing neither law, nor real estate, nor insurance, the three favorite occupations of men who seek political office. While the offices they seek pay little or nothing, their law, realty, and insurance businesses miraculously increase in volume once they're in office. But the state job and the oil business, which was not averse to getting a few state contracts from the Ely administration, gave White some financial security while he continued in politics.

That would haunt him occasionally, as when he ran unsuccessfully for lieutenant governor in 1938 and his opponents ran a sound truck up and down Boston's busy streets with a parody of "Snow White and the Seven Dwarfs." It was called "Joe White and His Seven Jobs." They ran the truck past Filene's department store one day, as Patricia White was shopping with her oldest boy, Kevin, then nine years old. She had to explain that that's the way it was in politics, and he should not worry about it.

Joe White certainly wasn't worried about it. On balance, his public image was that of a reasoned Democrat, not given to ethnic tirades but to responsible government. It's the image he was not averse to promoting, and it's the one the press chose to buy.

Where Mother Galvin was an organization Democrat, a clubhouse man meticulous about recording the needs of constituents and recording also his responses, Joe White was a freer spirit, an independent, who worked outside organizations. He was gregarious, but as he grew older, he became more of a loner, and whatever power he had, he had created himself. And he had much.

It would take Joe White an hour to walk the two blocks from City Hall to the State House, because he was besieged by those in need of favors. Years later, Mother Galvin would say to Joe White's boy Kevin, "There wasn't an election in this city between 1937 and 1952 that someone didn't fear your father. There was no one who would contend with Joe White."

By 1945, Joe White was seen as the most prominent pol in Boston, the only man who could lick Jim Curley in a two-man race. So, Joe White took out nomination papers, and his boys ran from door to door to get signatures on them. But Governor Maurice Tobin had other ideas, and he came to Joe White's house one night to talk of those ideas. Tobin wanted his old friend, the fire commissioner, William Arthur Reilly, in the race. Tobin was adamant. Would White consider dropping out? Tobin left the house, and left Joe White to ponder that question.

He knew he was strong. He had friends all over the city. The press, he knew, would be favorable to him. Just the previous year, one editorial said that as a school committeeman, he had "rendered valiant service in the cause of public education in the city."

But he was convinced he couldn't beat Curley if another strong candidate were in the field, sapping strength that would otherwise go to him. Reilly had the clout of Tobin and Galvin and Hynes and others behind him.

Kevin Hagan White — all Joe and Patricia's kids shared that middle name — was sixteen years old. He had collected the nominating signatures for his father. He had waited quietly upstairs while the Governor of the Commonwealth sat downstairs talking to his father.

The deadline for filing papers was a Tuesday. Kevin White was returning to his house in the dusk of Monday, when he saw his father, leaning against his car, talking to his mother. His father carried his nomination papers in his hand.

"What are you doing?" Kevin White asked. "Putting in your papers?"

"No," said Joe. "I'm not running for mayor." And he got into his car and drove away.

"Why doesn't he run?" he asked his mother.

"He doesn't think he can win in a large field. Your father knows best."

For a few moments in the dusk of a Monday afternoon, he had bared the face and soul of disappointment to his boy. He had not done that before, and he wouldn't do it again. And his boy, becoming a man and a pol, would try not to show his disappointments to his kids.

Tobin's man, Reilly, lost to Curley, and in 1949, another of Tobin's men, John Hynes, came to call on Joe White. White had sat out the 1945 election, and Hynes wanted to make sure he didn't sit out this one; he needed Joe White. Even then, there were those who felt White should have run himself. But there, shortly after dinner one night, was Hynes standing at the door, saying hello to Patricia Hagan White, coming into the parlor, where Joe and his girl, Maureen, were listening to the radio. Hynes took only five minutes of Joe White's time. When he left, he had White's support.

So Johnny Hynes, not Joe White, was the man to usher in the New Boston. White went on to serve as president of the City Council, where he would always have respect, but the years would whittle away at his power and influence.

A decade after Johnny Hynes went to him for support, Johnny Powers, the powerful Senate president from South Boston, went hat-in-hand to Joe White to back him in his race against John Collins. Joe White's support in 1959 was not as vital as it had been in 1949. Ten years had made the difference between real power and courtesy. Johnny Powers was being courteous. Joe White was being evasive. He wouldn't commit himself. In the summer of 1959, Yankee goo-goos were subtly and quietly building the campaign that would destroy Johnny Powers, the most powerful local pol in Massachusetts. He could deliver things, like jobs. He could be very helpful to a third and fourth generation of Irishmen on their way up, something Kevin White kept reminding his father. Kevin was nearing thirty, in his third year as an assistant district attorney for Suffolk County, a nesting place for future politicians. Support Powers, he and one of his brothers, Terry, urged Joe. "No," Joe said, "when you've got experience in these things, you wait."

But Joe White was getting older. He was less sure of his own instincts. He let his boys convince him to go with Johnny Powers. At the time, no bookie would touch a Powers race. He was considered that safe until a "dirty tricks" campaign that linked Powers with bookies— then, the bookies were more likely to give odds. Kevin White knew his precincts very well then. On election night, Kevin White was in Johnny Powers's headquarters on Berkeley Street, right across from police headquarters, and he began counting returns. After only three precincts, he knew Powers was gone, and he called Joe White, who had hesitated, and said, "He's gone. He's through." Kevin White learned a little bit about instincts.

Kevin White would come to be proud of his instincts. When all the plans were set before him, when all his aides were finished arguing, Kevin White would bury his mouth in his knuckles and come up with a decision. On the occasions when he could not do this, he would torture himself with the possibility that somehow, perhaps, he was losing that political gift of reading into your own guts. But then he would find himself making another decision the same way, and the blatant pride would return. He did not learn his trade in school.

At Tabor Academy, a private school, Kevin had managed to finish eighty-third in a senior class of 85. When he told his headmaster he wanted to go to Williams, the man appeared stunned. "Kevin," he said, "you can't even punctuate a sentence." But Kevin White made out the application anyway as he sat at the kitchen table in his West Roxbury home, while his mother — "She was the only one of them that ever read anything," Clem Norton would say — looked over his shoulder and saw her boy put down "political science." She was surprised. A lot more people were surprised when Williams accepted Joe White's oldest boy, because a scholar he wasn't. The headmaster told Williams he'd be personally responsible.

The picture in the 1952 Williams College yearbook is of a very young Irish face, a handsome face with a full head of hair. The eyes look slightly upward, and the lips form a half-smile. The face is pleas-antly cocky. Cocky is what some people used to call the Irish before they called Jews cocky, which was before they called black folks cocky. Sure, they were cocky, now. The grandfather worked in a brewery, and his boy Joe went to Boston College, which so much as told the Ivy League it knew where it could stick it, and now, here was Joe's boy going to Tabor Academy and then to Williams College and in a fraternity, too.

In those days, those faraway Cold War and crewcut days when col-lege fraternities did not have to advertise for members, there was on the American college campus the institution of "best." Best dressed, best looking, best personality, best left lung, best car, best car keys, best this, best that, and of course, "most likely to." He was not voted most likely to succeed or best athlete. Nor was he in the running for best build or most original or best dressed. He got no votes for being the hardest worker, nor did he receive any for being the laziest. Of ten men getting voted handsomest, he finished seventh. He was neither a socialite, nor a highway menace nor the funniest man in his class. But he placed third for class politician. He tied for fourth place for "Shov-els It Fastest."

Twenty years later, he could still shovel it with the best of them. At least that's what his critics said. "He's the sizzle without the steak," an opponent, Joe Timilty, liked to say. "He missed his calling. He should have been a performer." Mother Galvin's daughter Kathryn saw him a different way. She remembered him, a long time ago, walking toward her, down a long corridor in a building at Newton College of the Sacred Heart. "All I can remember was his smile, a beaming smile that seemed to say he was so glad to see you. He has that genuine warmth." She liked it so much, she married him. They had five kids. Billy Galvin became Grandfather Mother.

At forty-five, he had not lost that striking face. The eyes commanded attention. The grin was wide, like a living smile button. But the hair had turned gray, and it required careful combing to cover a small, round bald patch. Early in his years as mayor, the hairline had begun to recede. He had only a third of his stomach left, because an ulcer and a surgeon's knife had claimed the rest in 1970, the year he ran for governor, the year he won battles like primaries and debates, and lost wars, like conventions and the election. At forty-five, he was still trim, because a buddy would come by his Beacon Hill townhouse, pick him up at 6:30 in the morning and take a run or play some handball. But the trimness, by early 1975, had seemed something quite different, when the cameras caught him at a distance. He sometimes seemed emaciated. For all his energy, this man in his mid-forties looked at times as if he were a decade older.

The face is chameleon-like, a reflection of mood and strain and time of day. It can be pale white or radish red. It tightens. It collapses. It breaks into a landscape of crevices. It is a contagious face. Its smile makes you smile, and its grimace makes you worry. The face, like the owner, is open and disarming. It hides very little.

Kevin White became both performer and politician. There is much of the former within the latter. It comes with the ambition. It comes with the trade. The politician is in every ambitious human. But most humans play at it, use it only part time. Even most of those who run for office play at it. Kevin White *is* a politician. That's what he does for a living. He is afraid of ever having to do something else, because he thinks it will bore him, and boredom will destroy his mind.

To keep her mind alive, Henry Hagan's daughter Patricia read books, newspapers, everything she could find. She argued, debated, discussed, queried. To keep his mind alive, Kevin White ran for office, raced from crisis to crisis, failing at times to deal with the little way stations of detail that make government perceptibly more efficient. He began reading, more as an adult than as a kid. He talked to people he barely knew about whatever was on his mind. The visitor found it disarming and warm; his staffers groaned and grimaced as their boss spilled out to unlikely receptacles the latest innermost secrets of mayoral Boston. More often than not, the staff needn't have worried. The mind worked faster than the tongue. His speech often failed to keep up with the mind. It was hard to follow him, but he shamed you into it with his punctuated phrases — "You understand . . . You know what I mean?"

He is petulant, abrasive, curt with those who are close to him, quick to anger, quick to soothe. His ego and his pride are abundant, as with any public figure, and they are out on the line for everyone to see and react to and balm and attack. As was Hagan, he is often a man unto himself.

"Where is the mayor?" an aide asks.

"Out," a secretary says.

"Out?"

"Out." She shrugs in resignation.

Out, maybe taking a drive, or walking alone through the busy downtown streets or wandering about the docks with a plainclothesman or slurping an ice cream somewhere. Out. And when he is good and ready, he will come back in. Out, without an audience, handing a buck to a bum.

He came to insist that he was tough, as if he had to convince people. He could be tough and play the game of pressure and use the tools afforded by power, tools of incumbency, of patronage and assessment adjustments and zoning decisions and contracts. He came to believe that one could parlay political power into good government, and that it did not hurt if the results strengthened the man in office. Unlike the professional goo-goos, he did not believe that ambition and power were the handmaidens of hell.

He began grabbing power in 1960 with the capture of a Democratic ward committee; a dozen years later, he would almost become the party's nominee for vice president. Almost.

The same year White took control of the ward committee, he decided to move out of his job as an assistant district attorney and run for Secretary of State, a low-profile office that can be either a safe sinecure for a safe Democrat or whatever one wants to make it. For a young Democrat with ambition, the Secretary of State office was a good beginning. Its record-keeping functions could give the holder a ready-made excuse to drive all over Massachusetts and visit all 351 cities and towns, to meet the town clerks, and to palaver with local pols.

Two weeks before the Democratic state convention, White announced for Secretary of State. "Uh-huh," mumbled that part of the public which bothered to read such news. "I was the darkest horse the Democratic party had ever seen," White would recall. A week before the convention, White was asked to drop out of the running to make life easier for another candidate. White refused, and was then forced to resign as assistant D.A. His replacement was another young member of a Boston political family who was looking around for some paying work to flesh out a somewhat thin résumé — Edward Moore Kennedy.

White and his young friends — Dick Dray, who had known Kathryn Galvin White since she summered as a teenager on the South Shore, and Larry Cameron, his buddy and law partner, and Herbert Gleason, a tall, young Yankee lawyer and reformer from Beacon Hill — began campaigning in earnest. White used a relative's office to make phone calls to anybody who knew of any kind of gathering of two or more Democrats and wangle an invitation. When the convention opened, the White forces used wives, girlfriends, old college buddies to pack the hall as workers, all wearing White buttons, and all moving around a lot. Meanwhile, Mother Galvin talked to those who had worked with him and Maurice Tobin, and Joe White did something he had rarely done for himself — he called in all those favors he figured people owed him. "Listen, you sonofabitch, you owe me one." The balloting began shortly after midnight. By 3 A.M., some delegates had gone home —

who the hell really cared who the Secretary of State was going to be? But White's enthusiastic young friends were still there, and so were the old-timers who had pledged themselves to Joe White and Galvin, so when a distant relative of the Whites convinced the gubernatorial candidate, Joe Ward, to throw his support to Joe White's boy, the votes were there. White went on to take a tough party primary in September and, in November, beat another young man on the political make — a black Republican named Ed Brooke — in the final election. Now, Kevin White had the bug. Whatever he might have learned about politics at Williams was of questionable use. Now, he was a full-fledged student, thirty years old, and he wanted to go to the best schools, and on his way, he learned something else about power: that it was not timeless and without end.

"We wanted to go to the Kennedy convention in Los Angeles, and we asked my father to become a delegate so we could go out with him. He didn't really want to, but he went and asked John McCormack. My father felt funny asking for himself and his sons. It's a trait of the Irish — you don't ask for your own. For somebody else, yes. But not for your own. So there was my father, having asked for something, having had John McCormack put his arm around his shoulder and told him he'd take care of it."

There was a time when, if Joe White wanted to go to a National Democratic Convention, he didn't have to ask anybody. And Kevin White knew that, and he knew that now his father had done something he would not have done, had his boys not asked it.

That summer, as the grandson of Honey Fitz and P. J. Kennedy was being nominated for President of the United States, Henry Hagan's son-in-law, Joe White, was badly injured in an auto accident in Los Angeles. In the hospital, he suffered a stroke. Later, they flew him back to a Boston hospital, where he slowly regained some strength. They took his phone away from him because he was on it all day campaigning for his boy Kevin for Secretary of State. Joe White looked at them, waited until everyone left the room, and went down the hall to use the pay phone. But he would never be quite the same. By the spring of 1961, he had resigned from the City Council. A newspaper called his 33 years in office "a model of public service." In July, 1967, as his boy campaigned for mayor, Joe White died. Fourteen priests, including one of Joe's brothers, concelebrated the mass. The church was packed with pols and friends, a lot of people for a guy who had never been mayor. He had not lived to see his son take the office that had tempted him, the office he probably could have won had he but tried.

For a long time, Kevin White was "Joe White's boy." The boy

didn't like what that implied. He didn't figure he had inherited power from Joe. He said Joe never really wanted him to run, but once he was in it, Joe supported him. What father won't do for his son, right? Some fathers gave their kids a slot at Harvard. Joe White gave his boy delegates. By the time Joe White died, his boy Kevin had run four times for Secretary of State and had racked up record pluralities. The very first paragraph in Joe's obituary identified him not only as a politician but also as father of "Secretary of State Kevin White." The roles had been reversed for a new generation of readers, viewers, voters, and consumers. Kevin White was pretty much his own man.

Secretary of State had not been a bad job. One made contacts, and one could enjoy himself and fantasize about the bright future. One day, Secretary White's helicopter landed for some ceremony at one town and found the entire high school standing at attention while the band played "Hail to the Chief." It was only 1962, his friend Dick Dray remembered, "when everyone thought Kevin White was Rinso White's brother." Dray couldn't stop laughing, and White walked behind him, poking him in the ribs.

Those were the days Kevin White flew, boated, or drove all over Massachusetts, to town clerks' offices, political receptions, picnics, and clambakes. One cold morning, he sat alone in his car in the rain, alone in a nondescript middle Massachusetts city, waiting for a parade to begin so he could join it. And all through his career, the politicians and the political writers would speculate over which parade Kevin would join next.

He used the office for some reform, for pushing through a campaign fund disclosure law that was honored by those who thought it harmless to do so. But those who watched him watched substantive issues less than the personality of the man in the office. John Kennedy had reintroduced style after fifteen years of Truman and Eisenhower, and now the newspapers and the voters and, most of all, the television cameras sought out style, of which Kevin with the blue eyes and warm grin had much.

By 1966, he was thirty-six years old and clearly had to move off the dime, or else he would die in office and be recorded in local history as the longest running Secretary of State in Massachusetts. In 1966, his friends threw him a "time," which brought in around $50,000, and Kevin quietly told some of those friends to do a little research on Boston to document just how crummy life was. The speculation increased that he would go for mayor in 1967 and, once there, would be strong for governor in 1970. The speculation was accurate.

In the winter of 1967, White formally announced his intentions to marry the city. He did so with a statement that set a style and a purpose that his people insisted eight years later was still their goal. There had been, he said, too much emphasis on buildings and not enough on people. It has since become a cliché, but there was much truth to the cliché. "There is an alienated voter in Boston, a citizen who has been locked out, who feels no common bond with those who he believes play with the mechanics of government. . . . If we cannot encourage people to stay in the city — and we have not — if we fail to foster and sustain our human resources, then any other achievements will mock our efforts for the future."

The West End was gone, politically and physically. The heart of Roxbury was physically transformed by urban renewal, but the initial displacement had helped force Jews out of Dorchester and helped lock blacks in. Charlestown was fatigued and wary from persistent warring with the Boston Redevelopment Authority. Allston, sliced in half by an extension of the Massachusetts Turnpike, watched commercial properties creep up to its homes. Next door, Brighton saw apartment buildings turn from residences of families and the elderly to student pads. The South End was in turmoil, as competing ethnic and economic forces vied for control of that one square mile of ancient turf. East Boston felt it was just a place somewhere across the harbor, belonging to no one, fighting all alone against Logan Airport expansion, against a Port Authority that no newspaper or government body dared challenge. Dorchester was falling apart in the north and frightened to death in the south. Mattapan was ready to pack up and go suburban. Hyde Park was schizophrenic. The North End and Southie were still proud, but increasingly angry. The Fenway was full of elderly people afraid to walk out of their apartment houses for fear of being heisted in broad daylight.

The wise guys in the State House were saying Kevin Hagan White was a lightweight. "Kevin from Heaven," they snickered; "if ya threw him outta a window, he'd float up."

White took out full-page newspaper ads, announcing his candidacy and soliciting volunteers. Every volunteer who answered was asked to bring in friends to meet with White over coffee. Between March and June, White held 75 coffee klatches, and would come to use the technique again. At each one, he listened to complaints about the city, so he was building a campaign organization and formulating a platform at the same time. He needed the organization. When he was Secretary of State, he had treated Boston much the same as any other city or town. His statewide contacts were good, for he had thought often of being governor, but his city strength was not such to make one jealous.

Joe White was a sick man and could do little. Galvin still had some Charlestown friends and a few others here and there, but that wasn't enough.

White drew on a politician's only constant source of support — one's old friends and associates. His brother Terry, who ran a street line-painting business, was the campaign manager. When Kevin was an assistant D.A., he worked part-time painting lines for Terry; now, Terry worked for Kevin's campaign. There was Ted Anzalone, a street-wise guy from East Boston, whom Kevin had inherited from the previous Secretary of State. There were Larry Cameron, who had led the old Democratic ward committee takeover in 1960, and Herb Gleason, the establishment lawyer who riled the city with his exhortations for an integrated school system. Cameron's wife, Barbara, was treasurer.

By the early summer of 1967, the campaign that had begun fairly smoothly was thrown off stride. A black welfare mothers' revolt in Roxbury presented complications as new to the candidate as they were to John Collins and his businesslike administration.

Boston had kept relatively calm for more than two years, while other cities exploded in racial warfare. But in June, 1967, angry welfare mothers locked city workers in a Roxbury welfare office. Police responded forcefully; black youths went on a rampage. Stores were looted. Fire engines with all-white crews screamed through the streets of Roxbury and North Dorchester to extinguish the flames of arson in old Jewish-owned stores that would never reopen. Police wagons full of police sharpshooters roamed the streets in search of snipers. Blacks gathered on street corners and repeated the latest rumors of real and imagined police brutality. Collins called the actions of the welfare mothers "the worst manifestation of disrespect for the rights of others that this city ever has seen." Not quite, but then, it had been years since others had taken to the streets.

As with all disorders, the rioting burned itself out. It had not matched the violence of Watts in 1965, nor would it come close to the looting and shooting of other incidents in other cities that year. But the rubble on Blue Hill Avenue would remain; the plywood would work its way south through Dorchester and into Mattapan as the last vestiges of a Jewish community disappeared from the map. The plywood remained for years, a testimonial to the germs incubating in the New Boston.

For close to two weeks, White and his friends debated — do they avoid the issue, deal with it head-on, condemn somebody? They steered clear of it; it was John Collins's immediate problem. Next year, and for every year after that, it would be theirs. As the shouting died down in Roxbury, as the White campaign began getting off the ground again, Joe White died, and for another week, his son's campaign faltered a bit. By mid-August, Kevin and his friends were ready once more, only to find themselves spending valuable time playing a game thrust upon them by someone else, a game that would help them hone more finely their own political instincts, a game that, if lost, could put an end to White's career.

Two of the primary candidates that year were national figures — Logue and Louise Day Hicks. In came the national press to document their foregone conclusions that Logue was progressive and Hicks was a dangerous racist. One John Sears was interesting, being a Yankee Beacon Hill Republican and all that, running on a progressive brand of goo-gooism that spoke to the ills of the neighborhoods. As for young Kevin White, one national journal labeled him "bland." The local pols and writers still mumbled that he was "light."

"First I was a 'nice young kid.' Then, when I started moving on reforms, I was 'a new breed Democrat.' Then, when we went with Frank Bellotti against Chub Peabody (for governor), I was a 'vicious young kid.' When I ran for mayor, I was 'bland.' When I got elected mayor, I was called 'a progressive liberal.' Then, when I ran for governor, I was 'ambitious for state office.' Now, I'm back at City Hall, minding my own business, and they say I'm 'too concerned with national affairs.'" — The mayor, remembering what others say, on a winter day in 1973

In the neighborhoods, in 1967, the people began calling him Kevin. He waded into crowds of elderly at housing project receptions, of kids at schools, of guys on the corner, with a style, a disarming technique that would help save the city during the rebellions of minorities and the student confrontations with police in the 1960's and in the harsh and endless days of confronation in the 1970's. An admirer who could be critical of the mayor said of him once, "There is probably nobody better in the country with a coat over the shoulder. He's a master at street style, better than Lindsay."

Kevin White was doing well at the polls, and something had to be done to stop that, and the weapon chosen by a White opponent was to challenge his nomination papers. A few minutes before the city elections department closed on the last day that challenges were allowed, a young technician from Jamaica Plain walked in with a formal challenge of Kevin White's nomination papers. His name was Richard Iantosca. Nobody in politics seemed to know who he was, and they weren't about to find out either, because Richard Iantosca promptly disappeared from his house and his job. His challenge, however, did not disappear, and canny people got the sinking feeling that Kevin from Heaven was suddenly going to Purgatory. Iantosca — whoever he was — had discovered some shoddy work among the signatures on White's papers, and if wholesale graft was not the conclusion, embarrassment was, for here was the reformer Secretary of State who had been responsible for eight years for election procedures, and he was about to be ruled off the ballot.

Nobody in Kevin White's camp believed that Richard Iantosca was acting on his own. Someone was behind him. But who? Here was a political nobody from a moderate-income Jamaica Plain neighborhood being represented in his challenge by an attorney from a prestigious Boston law firm. As they looked into it, White's friends turned up one strange coincidence after another, and one of them was that the case had been referred to that firm by another big firm, one that represented the Boston Redevelopment Authority, whose director was Ed Logue.

No, said some. Not Logue! He wasn't a Boston pol. He was Logue, the technician, the progressive rebuilder of cities and their images. Hicks maybe. Or Chris Iannella, a tough city councilman who knew the ways of city politics and wanted to be Boston's first Italian mayor. Or one of the lesser candidates maybe, but not Logue. But others in the White camp were not so sure. They knew that the two candidates who most threatened Logue and his padrone, John Collins, and the whole New Boston crowd of bankers, publishers, developers, et al., were White and Sears, and White was clearly up in front of Logue and Sears.

White's lawyer nosed around and came back and said, "You got troubles. Collins is tight with the ballot law commission. I have no way of knowing who's behind this."

Meanwhile, Anzalone, who had contacts everywhere, was getting phone calls from friends and friends of friends. Each caller suggested that the perpetrator was a different candidate. One woman said, "Ed Logue." How did she know, he asked. Well, she said, she knew Iantosca, and he was telling her how Logue lived on Beacon Hill in a fancy townhouse and all, but how he had a frayed couch, a hole in his couch. Anzalone related all his information back to Kevin, who turned to his friends and announced with a snap of the fingers, "It's Logue."

Of course, Kevin figured. It had to be. "A kid from Jamaica Plain goes to Logue's house on *Beacon Hill*. What would he remember about it? That's what he would remember." But it was one thing to know who was challenging you; it was quite something else to prove it.

Anzalone and Dick Dray received a tip that the missing Iantosca was being kept in the Parker House, a hotel down the corner from old City Hall, that he was up in an eighth-floor room facing the rear alley. Anzalone went up to the eighth floor to nose around.

In a few minutes, Anzalone came down and reported he was certain the mystery challenger was in a certain eighth-floor room. They rushed to Kevin's house and began plotting, while a tired and somewhat disbelieving candidate stood looking at them, wondering what had become of their sanity. "We'll call the room in the Parker House and see who answers," Dray said. White walked upstairs, slumped down in a chair, and picked up the extension phone as the boys downstairs made their call. Suddenly, Anzalone came crashing up the stairs. "He's there, Kevin. Somebody's there! We hear him breathing!" White looked at his friend — "That's me, you stupid bastards!"

While his friends and relatives worked the barrooms, old political haunts, hotels, and the phones, the candidate called in the press and charged that Logue was behind the Iantosca challenge and prodded him — come out and fight in the open. Logue denied it, but slowly, the bits and pieces of the story were falling into the public's lap. The politician's grapevine, more dependable and quicker than anything the press or the FBI has developed, was producing clues. One night, a Cambridge pol called Kevin and said, "I've been talking to a guy in a bar who says he knows the connection between Logue and Iantosca. . . ." At midnight, the tipster knocked on Kevin's door and talked about an attorney who had put Logue and Iantosca together.

Soon afterward, Iantosca's attorneys announced the challenge would be dropped.

For Kevin White, the Logue-Iantosca affair brought a sympathetic press and no loss of votes, possibly even a gain. For Edward Logue, there was a backlash. He might have been on his way to a defeat anyway, but the mystery challenge insured that. When the preliminary election was over, Ed Logue placed fourth. White finished second and in the money, but he was more than 13,000 votes behind Louise.

Quietly, Ted Kennedy began raising money for White, who was $50,000 in debt after the primary. Dick Goodwin, the Kennedy speechwriter, offered his services. Samuel Huntington, a Harvard political scientist and a Beacon Hill neighbor, helped write position papers. The *Globe* broke its rule of not endorsing candidates and asked White whether endorsement of him would help or hurt his cause. The money, the academics, the establishment, and the liberals were coming over, but most of them didn't vote in Boston.

Hicks was banking on the alienation of white neighborhoods, an alienation triggered by race and crime. White saw it in a larger con-

text. The *Globe* that summer had run weekly articles on each neighborhood, and it was clear — to some candidates, at least, White, Sears,
and Tom Atkins, a black running for City Council — that the New
Boston image had left Boston's wards far behind. The alienation was
there all right, but it was more complex than race and crime. It spoke
to all the unlit parks and ripped-up streets and deteriorating housing
and teenage vandalism, all the issues that were never alleviated by
downtown redevelopment, issues that were made worse by a tight
budget policy.

For every man who stood in his front doorway, as one Jamaica Plain
man did, and said, "I'd like to see the next mayor take a gun and
shoot every goddamn nigger in the city," there were a half dozen who
complained, as did an East Boston man, "The sewers are wicked. The
odor will hit you from fifty feet away."

For Louise, the campaign was simple. She was against busing and
for law and order. She had nothing to lose in the black community,
whose voting record was spotty anyway. "You know where I stand,"
she said occasionally, though the press would play it as if she said that
upon waking, eating, and going to bed each day.

For White, the campaign was more difficult. He knew that if all the
liberals and blacks in Boston got together and voted for him en masse,
he would finish out of the running. He needed the votes of those people
who had put Joe White and Mother Galvin into office, the votes of the
Catholic kids with whom he had grown up in West Roxbury, the votes
of every Irishman, Italian, and Jew who, while not ecstatic over black
power, worried about the deluge that might follow Hicks into office. A
white cop predicted bivouacs in Franklin Park; a black militant fore-
cast Molotov cocktails. Businessmen looked at Louise and wondered
what the hell a woman was doing, running for mayor. Jews looked at
Louise and heard echoes of old gang fights with Irishers. Blacks looked
at Louise and panicked. The Irish true to form, looked at their
friends. But a lot of people who fit all those descriptions, but black,
looked at Louise and listened to her and heard their own fears and
frustrations coming back at them.

White was playing not only on what he thought were his strengths,
but also on what he perceived to be Louise's weakness. Hicks was a one-
issue candidate, if racial fears and law and order are truly mingled
into one. She was short on substance. She could turn a clever phrase,
for she was a politically clever woman, but if pressed hard enough on
just about anything besides racial imbalance or law and order, she did
verbal waltzes. Emotionally, she seemed unprepared for the pressures.
White lunged. "The thing most voters don't consider, but which is

vitally important, is emotional stability. You've got to remember that's power you're giving a man."

Kevin had refrained at first from attacking Louise — it was hard to attack a woman — and chose to come across as a reasonable man who could control uprisings, crises, and the nagging problems of just administering Boston day after day. Privately, Kevin's new allies found a man who equally enjoyed pols and professors. They opened up his eyes. He liked to be challenged, and he challenged them. It became clear to those who clustered to him that Kevin White was not bland and was not light. Petulant, moody, given to fits of anger and visible depression, yes, but not light. He had his own virtues, and he borrowed a few from others — the Jack Kennedy self-effacement routine, in which the politician opens up to reporters more than their own publishers ever would and becomes, in their eyes, accessible. In his years as Secretary of State, White had grown, in substance, from a fairly lousy public speaker to a smooth, almost glib, off-the-cuff speaker and, in style, from a man with eyeglasses to a man with contact lenses. He could take a briefing better than most and retain what aides told him. In style and substance, it was all there, waiting to be cultivated by contact with others and by every new experience.

On election day, White pulled heavily in his areas of strength. The Italians were not rushing to Mrs. Hicks. The blacks were voting heavier than they had in years, and they were voting for him. The pockets of Jewish votes left in the city were his. The elderly, some out of loyalty to Mother Galvin and the late Joe White, many out of fear that Hicks represented traumatic change, were voting for White. Hicks was not pulling as much strength as expected in the Irish and Italian precincts. When it was over, she had won half the wards and 90,000 votes, and she had lost the election. She lost by only 12,000 or so votes, but she lost.

White had not been mayor ten months, when some of his political allies began putting together the nucleus of a campaign organization for governor. By the spring of 1969, young men who had been beating the bushes for an opening into Boston's political system, men like Jackie Walsh and Bo Holland, who had grown up in the Dochesters and Hyde Parks and West Roxburys and had played football at Boston Latin, the kind of men who previously were fleeing the city for the suburbs, were now searching for delegates who would support Kevin White for governor in the 1970 state Democratic convention. White lost the convention to a clique from the Legislature and promptly entered the party primary, which he won. In the final election against a progressive Republican Yankee, Francis Sargent, the mayor was whipped. He was whipped by the very people he had governed — the precincts in his own city. He lost the final election a few weeks after he lost part of his stomach, and the loss would remain in what was left of his gut, to nag him and tear at him. He was not used to losing, and he was hurt, because the people who helped him lose were the ones in the neighborhoods, the neighborhoods he had promised to help.

The next year, 1971, White had to prove something special to himself. He had to win reelection as mayor in the same neighborhoods that beat his head in when he ran for governor, and he wanted to win big. In the closing days of his campaign that year, he would say to a visitor, "This last year was a great test for me, to bounce back. If I lose this time, I'll get out. I don't want to be a hack."

Once again, the final election would be the Kevin and Louise show, with some differences. Louise was less strident, and Kevin looked a lot older. And now, he was the incumbent, not the fresh young, unknown glamour boy, which meant that with all the strength of incumbency, there was also the weakness — former supporters who had soured on him, job seekers who had gone jobless, neighborhood leaders who felt he hadn't produced what he had promised, allies of pols he had beaten, old enemies. Unlike 1967, White now had his very own block of negative votes. He had solidified his own base of support, and it had stopped expanding. Now, he needed new blood, new people.

Jackie Walsh, Bo Holland, and others went to work. They called on the bright young men they had seen perform in other campaigns of other politicians who had run with, against, and apart from Kevin White. They plucked these people out on a talent search. The people said yes. The prospect of working for "a winnah" was enticing. The new men recruited were to become Little City Hall managers and election commissioners and such in White's second term.

In 1971, White was the strongest candidate. The goal was not to win the election, but to win big, to reconstruct Kevin White as the most viable, progressive, liberal mayor around. He would need a mandate enabling him to do what he'd want to do in the city — create community schools apart from the influence of the school committee, expand the Little City Halls, shove reform down the throat of the Police Department. That same mandate would force other important people — the chairmen of legislative committees, the speaker of the House, and the Senate president — to pay attention to him as a powerful party figure who would be around for a long time, a man whose phone calls had to be returned immediately. And a mandate would not hurt his national image either, as a young and viable liberal candidate in case anyone were looking around.

The 1967 campaign had been run by a handful of persons. It was a family affair, very quaint and folksy, but the 1971 campaign was computerized, automated, sophisticated gimmickry and public relations. John Marttila, a bright young political consultant with headquarters in Boston, took a potential victory and turned it into a runaway, into the mandate White had wanted.

In November, White trounced Hicks 113,137 to 70,331, one of the worst routs in Boston's political history. He had beaten her not only in his areas of strength, in the Italian, black, Jewish, and liberal precincts, not only in Charlestown, where he always had strength, not only in neighborhoods inundated with transients, outsiders, and students, but he beat her in West Roxbury, in Hyde Park, even in two white Catholic wards of Dorchester.

Kevin White would pay more attention to his city now, not with the same eye for detail that a small city mayor or a Richard Daley might, but with more time and energy than most Boston mayors had devoted. Yet, still, there were those sirens that kept luring him away, sometimes to disaster. He got it in his head that he could put together a coalition of Massachusetts mayors to fight for statewide tax reform, and it went nowhere. His young political men, like Jackie Walsh, the men he was so proud to be "bringing along," worked hard at capturing the control of about half the city's ward committees, but not much more was done to build an ongoing organization. The Democratic party in Boston, in Massachusetts, remained a collection of tribes, each with a leader commanding a personal following or loyalty. And now, nationally, there were sirens calling the mayor of Boston, for men were running for President, and the 1971 reelection of Kevin White indeed showed him to be a man of political strength and savvy.

George McGovern called and asked for a car to go to New Hampshire. Vance Hartke called and heard a City Hall operator break into his conversation with White to announce, perhaps as a clarion of Hartke's political fate, "Mistah Mayah, there's a Hartke Vance on the line." Ed Muskie called. The operator knew who he was, and he already had a car. What he wanted were delegates, and he got the top Democrats of Massachusetts, including the mayor. The mayor went to New York City to meet with other big-shot Democrats in a hotel room and talk about Ed Muskie. The mayor, until then, had not exactly rushed to the spotlight, when traveling with the U.S. Conference of Mayors, but when he came back from New York, he started laughing and telling people, "There we are, the biggest Democrats in the country. I figure, okay, now I'm gonna hear the pros. Fah Chrissakes, it was like a meeting in Precinct One, Ward One."

Kevin White began learning what Martin Lomasney had learned seventy-five years before, that the pols on a national scale were not much different from the pols locally, that, in fact, the pols in the U.S. House and Senate were farther removed from reality in relatively safe sinecures. Now, White was not going to be so hesitant to speak up in national forums.

When the McGovernites assembled in Miami later that year — without the Kevin Whites of the nation, who had found themselves on Muskie tickets in McGovern states — White almost got something from his party that he never expected. For a few hours one summer day, White was the leading candidate for McGovern's vice president. But McGovern changed his mind, or had it changed for him, possibly by a lack of enthusiasm on the part of either the staunch, inflexible "liberals" in the Massachusetts delegation or Ted Kennedy. Just who did Kevin White in that day in Miami would forever be a subject of speculation, but the slight taste of the morsel dangled by McGovern left White ready and willing to grab any similar opportunities.

White remained the essence of a good party Democrat. One of his aides, Ann Lewis, honchoed the city precincts for McGovern in 1972 to help keep Massachusetts in the party column, while the rest of the Union went elsewhere. When the debacle was finally over and Bob Strauss came out of Texas to attempt reuniting and rebuilding the national party, White was one of the first leaders he called on, and White spent part of the next two years touring the nation.

In the Bronx, with his friend Bronx County boss Pat Cunningham looking on, White said, "So let us be able to say in 1976 that the birthplace of Democratic victory began in the Bronx." White was preaching that Democratic victory in 1976 was possible, but it would depend on new faces. When asked to name the new faces, he listed every Democrat in the Western Hemisphere except Humphrey, Muskie, McGovern, Jackson, and, of course, himself. Himself was left for the inferences of the press. Some people around White had the temerity to suggest that Kennedy was another old face.

On Beacon Street, just past the State House, White and his wife and friends had renovated the old Parkman townhouse, and the mayor would use it as a retreat, a place to think and sleep and work on a speech. Now, he said, it was an urban institute, a think tank, where mayors, legislative aides, union men, academics, corporation executives, and journalists would be invited to dine and drink brandy and discuss cosmic issues. That such meetings were destined to make White a more familiar figure in a variety of circles in the U.S. was a fact not lost on his critics.

He knew now that his instincts were as good as, if not better than, the instincts of those who had busied themselves for years in running for national office or in helping others to do so. When Nixon was on his way out, White argued in a closed-door meeting of Democrats for a special midterm national election. Go for it, he warned, or Gerald Ford would only gain strength in office and be a real presidential contender in 1976. They practically laughed him out of the room. By the time the Washington *Post* and *The New York Times* and the rest of the press picked up the idea, it was too late.

Now, in his mid-forties, Kevin White knew much about power. He understood it better than most men do. He knew it the way a lover knows the creases and folds and furrows of a partner, and he caressed it daily, and he knew it wasn't everything it was cracked up to be. Power, he found, was not elusive. It was real enough. It brought interviewers from *Time* and *Newsweek* and *The New York Times*. It brought words of praise from the Washington *Post* and the Atlanta *Constitution*.

Power meant he could halt a skyscraper to pressure its developers to support yet another development, a pet project of his, which he believed they were sabotaging. And power enabled the mayor to detail plans dramatically for more foot patrolmen on the city's streets about the time he was running for reelection. And power enabled him to give a little shove to some young pols running for City Council and state rep and state Senate, help in the form of staff people who had leverage and organization in the neighborhoods in which those young pols were running.

White had brought a new tone to Boston's government, or, perhaps, an old tune with fresh lyrics. It was markedly different from the Collins regime, when Logue went about the city, seeking community people who seemed amenable to what he had in mind, and then went about doing what he had in mind. Now, White was indicating he would bend a bit to community pressures.

The neighborhoods did not always win, but what often was happening now was a compromise between what the neighborhood wanted and what a developer wanted. Before, the neighborhood factor had generally lost out. Often, it had not even been considered. Where once "culture" was something the Brahmins indulged in at a museum or the Symphony, now it was something brought into every neighborhood by a "Summerthing" program.

He created a network of Little City Halls all over the city, operating usually out of trailers and staffed with city employees who would be his eyes and ears and who would respond to the grievances of their turf. Even in their most imperfect form, the halls worked far better than any parochial ward and precinct organization commanded by the contemporaries of Henry Hagan. The system took a lot of forms. It meant something as simple as getting a Social Security form or filing a complaint without taking a subway downtown and without dealing with some faceless civil servant on the phone. It meant that agitation to stop airport expansion, to stop highways, to hold down rents, to light up secondary shopping centers at night all got translated into official city policy.

Seven years later, after repeated changes in the management of that system, it had yet to force through the most basic change of all — to force city agencies into any kind of neighborhood-oriented planning or cooperation with one another. Seven years later, Little City Hall managers and their bosses and planners would gather together in a monthly meeting and wonder how to make the system work.

By 1975, White had yet to straighten out the assessing department, as he had promised he would, but he did begin remaking Boston's police force into a younger and more sensitive outfit. He hadn't cracked down hard on the building inspectors, but he made sure that some blacks and Puerto Ricans did their own rehabilitation in their own neighborhoods. By the eve of his third shot at the office of mayor, he had yet to use his Little City Halls as leverage to reorder the priorities of the traditional city agencies, but he had made sure that Little City Hall veterans were involved in the city's budgetary process.

Those in the neighborhoods who had thought Kevin White's arrival would mean more community control were disappointed. White wanted neighborhood needs to set the priorities, but he refused to share his authority. He was too much the professional politician for that. He was the mayor, he said, and he was in charge.

To the critics of White, this would come to mean that if you weren't in the mayor's camp, forget it. To a degree, that's what it did mean.

If you applied to the city "personnel office" on the sixth floor of City Hall for a summer job or a "provisional" appointment, you didn't have to pledge your life to Kevin White, but expressing loyalty and a willingness to work for his reelection did not hurt. If you got the job, the people in the personnel office might never approach you again, but your department head probably would, less for a donation to the campaign than for one of your free nights to put up signs, lick envelopes, or make phone calls. The department heads, in turn, were occasionally reminded by the mayor that they had political obligations as well as administrative ones.

For all the years of the White administration, the commodities of

power and control were tugged back and forth between neighborhoods and City Hall, as White decentralized power with one hand and
pulled the strings of it tight with the other. His philosophy had
emerged fairly early as mayor — the best mayor was the one who governed with all the powers available to him. Let the mayor use
judgment and discretion, but let him never forget he has the power,
and let no one else forget it either. He consciously tried to walk a line
between the charisma and goo-gooism of a Lindsay and the dictatorship of a Daley.

Kevin White sincerely wanted to change Boston. Not to change it
into some East Coast version of a Dallas or a Phoenix, but to change
its government so that it would sustain the very strength of the city, its
neighborhoods. That was one reason why he picked a classy staff that
included old friends and associates like Anzalone and Ed Sullivan and
professionals — "outsiders," some of them — like Bob Weinberg, from
the U.S. Budget Bureau, and Hale Champion, former aide to Governor Pat Brown of California, and Barney Frank, a disheveled, over-
weight New Jersey liberal who was faster on his feet than any man half
his size and owned a machine gun for a mouth. The mayor wanted to
lean on this staff, to let them run the day-to-day city, while he ran the
big-picture city. And Frank filled that bill until filling it day after day
and night after night wore him out, as so many of White's aides would
be worn out.

Two terms after his election, on a platform of turning government
to the needs of the neighborhoods, Boston's neighborhoods were still
in dire need. But as Curley used to like to say, where there were once
filthy vacant lots, there were new parks; where there was once a slum,
there was now a rehabilitated home. White could point to parks, playgrounds, housing, fire stations that did not exist in 1968.

He was the essence of Boston, not only because he was its mayor, but
because he was so much of what Boston was. He was the culmination
of the hard pols and the goo-goos, of the Hagans, the Joe Whites, and
the Mother Galvins. They were in his blood and his genes. And the
city, like its mayor, was also on public trial. Was Boston something of
substance, as Josiah Quincy and Wendell Phillips and Governor John
Andrew had believed, or was it all style, all a shiny veneer of an image
that would crumble apart in a crisis?

Because it was old and because it was Boston, the city had led the
nation for so many years. For many years after that, it had lain close to
dead, suffocating in its own parochialism, which, ironically, also kept
it alive and colorful, if not healthy. Now, this allegedly new Boston
was emerging, not only with brash new high rises but with small yet

distinct signs that the various hearts that were its neighborhoods were beating again and could be massaged into a new, full life. But soon, sooner than it wished and perhaps later than it should have been, the lingering issue of race would again thrust Boston into the national limelights. Again, the nation would look to this old city of the sea. Some would look for the key to resistance; others, for the grand new battle hymns of Abolition. America would look to Boston, and, in doing so, would look to see what Henry Hagan's grandson had learned about power and politics.

The virus infecting the city was stubborn, the virus of race and class. It had within it the elements of destruction. No matter how many apartment rents were controlled, no matter how many fast-food franchises were kept out of a neighborhood, no matter how many three-deckers might be rehabilitated, the sporadic violence bred by that virus could wipe out everything and destroy both the city and its mayor.

In that summer of 1967 when Kevin White first ran for mayor, there were some very hot days, very humid days. In the North End, the Irish had long gone, the Jews had wandered through and left, and the Italians now gathered in the streets in front of their old but immaculate tenement homes and waited for the darkness and relief from the sun. It was a day not unlike that very hot day more than a century ago in the same North End, when tempers flared and the germ bared itself to a frightened city.

On this particular day in 1967, the two city pools, separating the North End from the fetid harbor, were closed to the people. On the stoops were the women of the North End, women in light print housecoats, one with a broom with which she had swept her steps and sidewalk. In the North End, there were men who used muscle to keep the peace, to keep out the "beatniks" and anybody else they didn't like, to keep out junkies and muggers, to keep the streets nice and quiet so the cops wouldn't be all over the place and start leaning on the bookies. In the North End, the women used their eyes and ears to maintain the early warning system, to check and make sure the life they had made for themselves remained sacrosanct. Given the hot tenements, given the low wages, it was not a bad life. There were neighbors. There were stores and churches nearby. There were relatives and friends to watch the kids. You could walk down the streets in the middle of the night and no one would bother you. You could grow vegetables on the rooftops. You could live and die in peace.

On this day, a mechanical problem closed the pools, but somehow, the city failed to communicate that to the people, and the women were complaining, for it was indeed hot.

"*What did the Italians ever get?*" *one woman says.* "*Two stinkin'
pools, and one's polluted.*"

"*It's the colored,*" *says another.* "*They let them swim in the pool
and it got polluted.*" *The others are embarrassed. No, they say. That
didn't happen. And then the first one speaks up again and says:*
"*They're comin' to our schools now.*" *And the second one looks up in
shock and says only this.*

"*Oh, my God!*"

NINE

School Days

In Ireland, the day is holy and calm.

In Ireland, families pray to the missionary who brought them Christianity.

Not far from the River Boyne, he had lit the Paschal Fire. At Ballintupper was his church and the well where he baptized those he had converted. At Tara, it is said, he plucked the leaves from a shamrock to explain the Trinity.

St. Patrick, they called him.

He was a missionary.

Before that, he had been a slave.

The piece of brick is ragged and comes to a point. A long time ago, Marty Gopen shined it up and made his own inscription on the brick: "Souvenir of South Boston. March 17, 1964," it says on one side. On the other, he wrote, "Erin Go Bah! A Stone's Throw from Ole Ireland." Now, in 1975, he laughs about it. When the brick came crashing through the truck window and broke his eyeglasses, he did *not laugh. With or without the souvenir, Marty Gopen remembers that St. Patrick's Day parade.*

The black and white communities were divided within themselves. White sentiment ranged from a clearly expressed distaste of associating with the blacks to white radicals who supported every demand of the black militants. Some blacks were demanding an immediate end to segregated schools. Others wanted black schools for black kids and black teachers. A third group was willing to go with black schools and progressive, sensitive white administrators.

The politicians wished the issue had never been raised. It would only exacerbate existing hostility, especially among the poorer whites. To the majority of the school committee, there were good colored and bad colored, and those agitating for integrated schools were in the second group.

Year after year, in petitions to the school committee, in newspaper articles, in suits before the courts, in pleas to the Legislature, in public speeches, the black militants and their white allies were making the same point: separate schools were not equal schools — they were bad for both black and white. Separate schools made black kids feel inferior and convinced white kids of black inferiority.

Besides, they argued, such schools were illegal. And worst of all, their white attorney argued one day in court, they spawned and furthered ignorance and prejudice. "Prejudice . . . is sure to prevail where people do not know each other."

The issue in Boston was segregation, pure and simple. The battleground was in the school system that was supposed to be open to all and classless. The fight had been waged for eleven years. The year was 1855, and the issue was about to be resolved. Before the year was out, black kids would be going to white schools in Boston.

Compared to the Irish, the black presence in Boston was minimal. There were, perhaps, 1,950 of them, most living on the north slope of Beacon Hill and the West End. An increasing number had made their way out of slavery, and a few were wanted by the authorities in the South as fugitive slaves. Blacks had been in Boston as long as anyone could remember, and some could trace their local lineage back as far as many Yankees.

The early Yankee attitude toward slavery was, typically enough, a confused conflict of religious and mercantile motives, with the result that black slaves, paid servants, and freedmen coexisted in Massachusetts until the state finally wiped out the first category in 1789. Long after slavery and long before the Abolition movement, Massachusetts got the reputation among blacks as a liberal state. In 1808, a member of the African Society in Boston wrote, "Massachusetts is greatly to be valued for the peculiar advantage which we enjoy, as it respects our freedom. . . ." The blacks had done their bit for the Revolution. One of them, Crispus Attucks, had been killed in the Boston Massacre. Another, Peter Salem, picked off a Redcoat major during the Battle of Bunker Hill.

By the nineteenth century, the blacks in Boston, few as they were, already had a sense of local history, a sense of belonging. When they wanted to set up their own school on Beacon Hill, the city was only too glad to cooperate. The Yankee power structure didn't particularly care how high a black got, but it could get nervous when one got too close. Such a state of affairs might linger for generations in most cities, but not in Boston, not as the Garrisonian Abolitionists and outspoken blacks insisted on attacking local segregation even as they poured out their broadsides against the South. One after another, the racist institutions gave way — segregated church pews and public facilities, a ban on intermarriage, separate train compartments for black and white. The blacks could count among their own dockworkers and laggards, tailors and musicians, saloon workers and brawlers, and a growing number of businessmen, artisans, and intellectuals. Not only had they worked together with Garrison and Wendell Phillips and other white Abolitionists, but some of them had begun taking their white allies to task for patronizing them. Slavery had caused the alliance; the Fugitive Slave Law had solidified it. With every instance of federal officials grabbing black men off the streets of Boston to be bound and returned south, the sympathy increased for the other causes of local blacks. There was no shortage of such incidents. As the nation moved towards self-destruction, Bostonians found they had a list of black heroes and martyrs: Frederick Douglass, the former slave who became an international symbol of resistance; Eliza Small and Polly Ann Bates, two black women rescued from a courthouse by a mob of black and white men and women and spirited away by horse and carriage to safety; Anthony Burns, almost saved from slavery but for the intervention of federal artillery detachments; Lewis Hayden, born one of a family of twenty-five slaves and later a successful Boston businessman, whose home and store were key stations for the Underground Railroad; Thomas Simms, a fugitive slave from Georgia arrested by Boston cops on a hoked-up theft charge and escorted past angry Bostonians by hundreds of police and militia to a ship that returned him to bondage.

Such incidents, giving heart to Yankee Abolitionists and grief to law-and-order merchants, kept Boston in a constant state of turmoil before the Civil War, and they were forever the backdrop to any local issue that blacks felt moved to raise. Those pushing such issues often found a ready vehicle in Garrison's strident newspaper, *The Liberator*. The name that appeared under articles urging the desegregation of Boston's schools was William C. Nell.

In 1829, he had gone to class in the basement of a colored school. The school examiner, Samuel T. Armstrong, showed up one day with Mayor Harrison Gray Otis in tow. Three children, including Nell, had done well enough to win the honors of the city. Normally, when a youngster won such honors, he received the Franklin Medal. Instead of medals, the three black youths were each promised a copy of a book on Franklin's life. Meanwhile, the white medal winners were invited to the annual Faneuil Hall dinner. Nell persuaded one of his friends, a waiter at the affair, to let him pose as a waiter. Mr. Armstrong recognized Nell and whispered to him, "*You* ought to be here with the other boys." Years later, Nell told his friends, "The impression made on my mind by this day's experience deepened into a solemn vow that, God helping me, I would do my best to hasten the day when the color of the skin would be no barrier to equal school rights."

Nell became a business agent of sorts, a combination of accountant and preparer of legal documents. He lived on Beacon Hill, where every day, he could look at the Smith School, where every black child in Boston was supposed to attend classes, regardless of where he or she lived. By early in the 1840's, the blacks were making noises about segregated education, and in 1844, they began petitioning the politicians to end it.

In a pattern that would become familiar to a later generation of blacks, the school committee turned down the petition. This triggered a series of protest meetings. The activists reasserted that the "support of separate schools, at the public charge, for any one class of the inhabitants in exclusion of any other class, is contrary to the laws of this Commonwealth." They urged black parents to take their kids out of the Smith School. It was the beginning of what was to become a fairly successful boycott.

Each year, a majority of the school committee would try to discredit the petitioners. They called the agitators "unworthy successors" of the black leaders who had set up the schools in the first place.

When the blacks insisted that separate schools depressed the black children, the school committee majority asked rhetorically, "Did our Pilgrim fathers become depressed, and degenerate, by keeping distinct from the aboriginal Naragansetts and Pequods . . . ?" It was fortunate that they asked rhetorically.

As far as most committeemen were concerned, "the less the colored and white people become intermingled, the better it will be for both races. . . . Amalgamation is degradation. . . . Let them cultivate a respect for themselves, for their own race, their own blood, age, and for their own *color*."

As for the white kids, ". . . If these separate schools were abolished and the colored children were mingled promiscuously in the other schools, the white children would not associate cordially with them. The whites would vex and insult the colored children, who would retort by blows, and thus continual quarrels would arise. It is also certain, that many scholars would be driven from our schools, by such a change . . . many parents would not allow their children to associate with colored children; and these, too, from among the class who most need instruction: for the prejudices against color are strongest among the most ignorant."

On that count, the school committeemen were right, even though they were about 130 years off, but their predictions of white scholarly flight would be made accurate not by the arrival of some black children, but by the increasing enrollment of white immigrant kids.

When the blacks argued that the separate school system "secures to the child of the Foreigner a privilege that is denied to the native Bostonian," the Yankees replied, "This word 'Foreigner' applied to another class . . . is a 'noun-multitude.' It extends to nearly a third of the people of this peninsula; and to a race ever multiplying, and now shoaling upon us, at the rate of a thousand fresh recruits weekly . . . a huge and constantly swelling mass of heterogeneous materials thrown in upon us from abroad." As the foreigners come, the committee said, "they are provided for in the best way practicable; the children being absorbed into our established public schools, and obliged to enter the race of competition with our home-born offspring, at great and manifest disadvantages. And what is the consequence? They seldom rise above the humblest forms in our schools. They crowd the lower rooms and classes; and there, in the inferior departments, the instinct of association, or some other combining cause, has produced a practical exclusiveness; — the report of our annual Examining Committee for the present year showing, that in a school room containing some 60 children, only one of them was an American; all the others being Irish. And there is no question that an entire separation of that part of our population in schools by themselves, would, if permissible, be chosen by them generally. Already they have demanded it as a rightful concession in New York; and signs there are, now indicating a threatened movement in the same direction, amongst ourselves."

The inverted logic of the Yankees was that the blacks who wished to mingle with the Yankees should be kept separate, even though they were only a handful and even though it made them feel inferior in this classless American society; the Irish who would just as soon have stayed away from the Protestant Yankees must be kept in school at all costs, even if it made them feel inferior.

The school committee minority dissented. "Our Common Schools," they argued, "are common to all; and each and all are legally entitled . . . to the equal benefit of all the advantages they may confer — as common to each and all, as the public highways, the courts of law, or the light of air. It is the peculiar advantage of our republican system that it confers civil equality and legal rights upon every citizen — that it knows no privileged class and no degraded class — that it confers no distinction and creates no difference between rich and poor, learned and ignorant, white and black; but places all upon the same level, and considers them alike entitled to its protection and its benefits."

Their arguments against separate schools, the arguments that the Abolitionist lawyer Charles Sumner and the black lawyer Robert Morris would bring unsuccessfully to the courts, were the basis of a Supreme Court decision that would come crashing down on the heads of Americans in 1954. Long before scholars and jurists and pols would debate the merits of a Coleman Report or *Brown vs. the Board of Education*, the school committee minority and the Abolitionists of Boston outlined the devastating harm that separate schools were doing to black and white.

If the blacks were to be "shut out and separated, they are sure to be neglected and to experience all the evils of an isolated and despised class."

Every year, the arguments were made, and every year, an increasing number of school committeemen and others influential in the community raised their voices in support. Meanwhile, Nell's boycott continued. Parents pulled their children out of the Smith School and did not return them even when the white administrator was replaced with a black man. Some blacks were willing to go along with this appointment, but Nell and his friends were militant to the point of intimidating other black youngsters from using the school when it opened for the fall, 1849, semester. When the state Supreme Court ruled in 1850 that each local school system could decide whether to segregate or not, the militant blacks began a taxpayer's boycott — black taxpayers simply moved out of the city, taking their investments and their children with them.

By 1854, a lot of influential politicians were arguing that separate schools were doing more harm to the proud Boston school system than anything else. That year and the following year, Nell, with help from blacks and whites in other communities, submitted petitions to the Legislature. It was the Know-Nothing Legislature, filled with Yankee artisans and farmers suspicious of or hostile to the Irish and hostile to the Fugitive Slave Law. The Know-Nothings saw less of a threat among a handful of black Protestants than they did among the masses of Irish Catholics. In 1855, the Massachusetts Legislature outlawed desegregation in the public schools. True to the style of Massachusetts, an historic piece of liberal and progressive legislation was enacted into law by men who could hardly be called liberal, men who were elected to office partly because they detested a minority called Irish.

More than a century later, Boston would integrate its schools again. By then, the Irish and their white Catholic supporters were the power structure on the defensive, and the blacks were the "swelling mass," growing in numbers and threatening the power and life-style of those who had succeeded the Yankees.

The route they would choose was through the schools, that much-trampled road, its banks littered with the bodies of old reforms, old corruptions, old traditions gone sour, old antagonisms. The schools were, at once, the pride and bane of Massachusetts.

Massachusetts invented the public school system for the rest of America, a fact that Massachusetts would never let anyone else ever forget, even when the system showed signs of falling apart. What education industry Babbitts and politicians too often have forgotten is that for all its precedent and progress, inferior schools did not arrive with Irish school committees or black students.

By early in the nineteenth century, the reformers and defenders of public schools were hot at it, and some of the criticisms of the Boston system made in 1846 read as if they were written in 1946 and 1956 and 1966.

". . . Such scholars as are bright force themselves to the top; but the dull, the mass, not being favorites, not having the particular assistance and encouragement they need *and ought to have*, never rise. It has always been so in the Boston schools, and always will be so under the present inefficient mode of instruction and supervision. . . .

"The error has been that the teachers, not looking beyond the textbook, have become short-sighted, and their pupils are in danger of becoming stone-blind. . . . In geography, the children know the catalogue of names, but they cannot give an answer to any rational question naturally flowing from the text; they cannot sketch an outline of the most familiar country in the world. In English grammar, they can parse by rule sentences that they do not understand; they can repeat rules for writing and speaking the language correctly, but they can neither write nor speak according to them. In reading, they can pronounce correctly, mind the pauses, and sometimes hit the inflections; but they do not understand what they read. . . ."

Poor teaching and learning were only part of a larger problem, the critics insisted, and that was a political problem, in which teachers allegedly pledged their loyalty to those selecting them for jobs.

The Yankees held to the ideology of Horace Mann, propagated it as one would the Scriptures, that the very foundation of a democracy is its educational process, that the state is duty-bound to provide that education and to do so to a social and economic mix, one in which the less fortunate are dragged into a world of Yankee American–classical values.

One problem with this lust for quality education was that Yankee standards, Yankee teachers, and Yankee schools proved inflexible to a growing, stubborn minority. When the Yankees of Massachusetts gathered in Boston in the spring and summer of 1853 to propose changes in the state constitution, the members found themselves in the middle of one of those keep-our-public-money-out-of-religious-school debates.

While Yankee legislators went to great pains to note that the schools were nonsectarian because the law said so, a Fitchburg lawyer named Nathaniel Wood brought them back to reality.

"We have, growing up, between three and four hundred Irish children. About one in twenty of these go to our common schools. Many of the intelligent Irish do not and and will not send their children to our schools." Wood said he asked an Irishman why he would not send his children to the public schools.

"His answer was, 'I will not send my children to a sectarian school.'

" 'A sectarian school?' said I. 'Heavens! I did not know that our schools were sectarian.'

" 'Well,' said he, 'that is just the way with you here in America, and with religionists all over the world. Our sect is not sect; everybody else is sectarian. Now, what constitutes a sectarian school? It is where you will have all the Protestant forms of worship introduced. You will insist on having prayers according to the Protestant forms. You introduce your Protestant Bibles and other Protestant books, and you will have none other. Now, I put it to you, would you be willing to send your children to be instructed by Roman Catholic priests; to be compelled to read their Bible, and have comments upon it?'

"I said, 'No.' . . .

"It is all important that our Irish children should be educated,"

Wood continued. "It is as important to us as it is to the Irish themselves. We do not want them to grow up amongst us, ignorant and vicious, first to rob our hen-roosts, and afterwards to commit more serious offenses. . . . If we cannot educate them in such schools as we have, let us give them such schools as they can accept. And I would appropriate money for the purpose."

Others stood up and spoke as if Wood had never related that conversation held one day in the town of Fitchburg. No, they insisted, Protestants and Catholics were taught alike and treated alike, because that's how the system was set up and, therefore, that's how it must be working. So, on a Friday in July, 1853, on the seventieth day of the convention, a motion to reconsider a resolve prohibiting money to "sectarian" schools failed by almost 100 votes. Inside the school system, the virus of racial and religious and class warfare incubated, while Yankee officialdom spoke glowingly of a germ-free system.

As the immigrants began filling up the wards of Boston and the mill towns, the old Yankee schools creaked and groaned under a burden for which they had never been prepared. In Boston, there were almost 2,800 primary school kids unable to attend because of a lack of space.

Beyond the sheer numbers, there were in the classrooms, in living size, shapes, and color, Irish, Italians, Russian and eastern European Jews, Greeks, Poles, French Canadians, and Portuguese. Some youngsters, less than inspired by their Yankee instructors, were moved to attack same in the schoolrooms. The situation prompted one Boston school committeeman to complain in 1889, "We have in one of our schools 280 boys from Russia and Italy. The teachers in some of these schools who are trying to rescue and save these boys from ruin are engaged in a mission almost as holy as the ministers of religion."

Upper-income Yankees began pulling their kids out of the public school system and sending them to private schools, a remarkable break with generations of Yankee tradition and fealty to the gospel of Puritans and the beliefs of Horace Mann. At the other end of the economic and religious spectrum, the Catholics were beginning to build and populate parochial schools.

By 1873, about 7,500 Massachusetts youths were in parochial schools; by the turn of the century, their number had grown to 61,500. By 1915, Boston's parochial school population grew to 18 percent. It would come to be in Boston that the public schools were increasingly left to Catholic families who could not afford parochial schools. Where, in the suburbs, middle- and upper-income families would lobby hard for innovative education and the best facilities their tax money would buy, no such force would exist in Boston. The vacuum would be filled instead by Cardinal O'Connell, who railed against the forces of progressive education and warned that they not be allowed to infiltrate the public schools. Those forces generally took the warning, and along with their ideas and their money, they went to the suburbs, awaiting them with open arms. Parochial Boston would turn into itself, and the Irish would produce an inbred, highly political school system that rewarded loyalty and discipline more than intellectual curiosity.

But the Irish were not to come by such power easily. Despite the increasing Irish population in Boston, the last years of the nineteenth century witnessed Protestants defeating Catholics year after year for seats on the then 24-member school committee. They did so with the support of fairly recent British immigrants, who happily joined the American Protective Association and, more importantly, with the support of a variety of temperance leaders and suffragettes, who organized ward committees and got out the anti-Catholic vote. Feeding fuel to their efforts were a claque of brimstone-school preachers who made much of a successful Catholic effort to heave from the schools a textbook with a slight Protestant bias. The preachers were joined by influential Yankee businessmen and some scholars, one of whom urged that "Protestant men and women who have Catholic servants in their employ should say to them on the eve of election day that if they intended to vote at the dictation of the priests they must look for work elsewhere."

Let the school board never become "a way station for ward politicians," warned the suffragist Edwin Mead. But it would become precisely that. Let it be a responsible and dignified body of those who know the most about education, he urged. But it had long ago stopped being that. Yet even moderates like Mead seemed unable to understand the very nature of the democratic school system they worked so hard to defend.

". . . The proportion today of our better educated men who are Catholics is but small," he said. "Leaving out the question of sectarianism therefore, which always should be left out, I should expect that the large majority of the Boston School Board today would not be Catholics. Such a condition would only be proper."

The Irish politicians understood that what counted in a democracy, for better or for worse, was not one's education, but numbers. Despite the Catholic clergy's campaign against Catholic women registering to vote, the overwhelming numbers of Irish in certain Boston wards meant that they could recoup whatever setbacks were dealt to them in the late 1800's. In waves of goo-goo-inspired reform, the school committee, elected by wards, was reduced to 5, all to be elected at large. Half the school population was Catholic, the Boston *Pilot* protested, and an at-large election would render Catholic voters helpless and produce, at best, one Catholic school committeeman. The Yankees had pressed ahead, convinced that they must not turn over their pet educational system to Irish control. The Irish assumed control over the decades, of course, as their numbers spread throughout all the wards, and by the early 1960's, they became the staunchest defenders of the at-large system, a system that had come to assure one Irish school committee after another, to the exclusion of "reform" Yankees, Jews, Italians, and even Irish of the older and smaller and lower-income wards, and, of course, blacks.

The blacks were among the least noticed of Boston's minorities. By 1880, the year Boston celebrated its 250th anniversary, only 5,873 blacks could be counted in the city, a mere 1.6 percent of the population. The city registrar was satisfied that the small numbers justified "the averment that the colored race finds its congenial home in southern latitudes, and that the struggle to make it take root in northern regions will prove, as it always proved, a difficult one."

Black Republicans were given a share of patronage by the Yankees, and blacks were elected to both the state House of Representatives and the City Council. Their ability to send a man on a short walk up the street to represent them at the State House came to an end, however, when, in 1895, the Democratic pols gerrymandered the West End. This effectively tore apart the Republican majority that the blacks had built up over the years. By splitting the black neighborhood in two and attaching each half to a Democratic ward, the Democratic pols made it nearly impossible for the blacks to send a state Representative to the Legislature.

Less than a decade later, the goo-goos engineered their "reforms," directed at Honey Fitz and his cronies, and the ward council was replaced by the at-large body. Blacks had served on the council since the time of Abolition, but the at-large elections effectively removed access to that pocket of power and patronage.

Boston's black power and influence, such as it had been, was diluted not only in local politics, but nationally also. By the twentieth century, the black Abolitionists were dead, and the younger men who had taken them as heroes were now old men. As the white Abolitionist spirit also faltered, as the South regained its political clout, concerned blacks and whites began realizing that the civil rights struggle was in danger and would require constant vigilance. Nationally, the blacks would split between those who followed the more cautious Southerner

Booker T. Washington and those college-educated, younger, and more militant Northerners, headquartered in Boston. The emerging leader of the militants was William Munroe Trotter, born to a black veteran of the Civil War and raised an upper-class Negro in Boston's Hyde Park neighborhood. Trotter's newspaper, the *Guardian,* became the strident successor to Garrison's *Liberator.* There was never a loss for material, for not only was the South ruthlessly discriminating against blacks, but the North too was having second thoughts. Some hotels. and restaurants in Boston were beginning to refuse blacks; gerry-mandering and "reform" were diluting local political gains, and prestigious Yankees like Charles Francis Adams, Jr., businessman, re-former, and veteran of the Union Army, were suggesting that the black man lacked the "essential qualities of alertness, individuality, reliability and self-reliance."

As Trotter aged in the years after World War I, the face and makeup, the style and composition of black Bostonians changed. While their numbers accounted for only 3 percent of the city's popula-tion, their rate of growth was faster than that of the whites. The new mix of old Boston black families, rural southern migrants and West Indians did not fall in line behind Trotter or any other learned phi-losopher-king, nor did the groups get along with one another.

By the Depression, Boston's new "colored district" was solid and growing in the South End–Lower Roxbury neighborhoods, and once again, the politicians — this time, the Republicans — sliced up the black neighborhood, parceling out its pieces like a great power dis-tributing chunks of Africa to colonial allies. Now, the new leaders were the black ward pols, and the most powerful of them, Dr. Silas F. (Shag) Taylor, medical school graduate, pharmacist, and alleged boot-legger, switched loyalties to the Democrats and lost some friends and customers in the shuffle. For Shag Taylor and his brother Balcolm, the switch was made on pure political grounds. For thousands of other blacks who were switching, the reasons were idealistic and economic and all tied up in a bundle named Franklin D. Roosevelt. For all these reasons, the Massachusetts Colored League became something to be recognized by the Irish Democrats in control of local politics. The Massachusetts Colored League was Shag Taylor's Ward 9 organization. There was more political wisdom dispensed over Shag Taylor's counter than prescriptions.

Bal Taylor, in later years, once told a black reporter, "This area needed a voice, and we've tried to supply it, by George; it's worth our while to see that the people are taken care of." So, on a smaller scale than Lomasney and old Pat Kennedy, the Taylors wheeled and dealed, and if it was smaller potatoes, that was not due to any lack of abilities on the part of the Taylor family, but instead to the small numbers of blacks and even smaller number of black voters. In the 1930's, the forties, and fifties, the local black pols — the Taylors never ran for public office; others occasionally ran and often lost — were the focus of what little power existed in the black community. They and the clergy were the leaders. Shag and Bal Taylor worked closely with Curley; they served in the high councils of local and state Democratic politics. They were the house niggers, but they traded in on that for jobs, housing, or anything they could get. And as the post–World War II migration from the South increased, the demands on the Taylors, on the clergy, on the small neighborhood associations, on the old black Boston elite were more than anyone could handle.

The white pols said the Negroes didn't vote anyway. It was a somewhat inaccurate charge. Blacks voted, and they voted in both parties. The politically active black, allied with the Jewish pols of nearby Roxbury and Dorchester wards and with the Irish pols up top, could live a very interesting life. But most transplanted Southerners living in the worst parts of Boston, getting the worst housing, the worst jobs — if they got any jobs at all — most of them saw no reason to vote. Unlike the Irish and their Jewish neighbors, they did not translate votes into political power and power into clout. Even with clout, the social ills of urban America were beyond the abilities of most ward politicians. Once again, as in the days of the Underground Railroad, it would take issues to force new leadership into the open. In the black community, patronage and public housing would not be enough.

In the 1950's, it was still possible to find white and black children playing together in the streets of Roxbury, but this was changing, and beneath the picture of an integrated community was a simmering white fear and distrust of "niggers" by the Irish in Roxbury, of "shvartzehs" by the Jews of Roxbury. By the 1950's, as Jews and Irish continued to square off in the Dorchester playing fields just south of Roxbury, those Jews living in a changing neighborhood talked more of blacks than of Irish.

As long as the situation remained stable, as long as the black population remained small, white Boston could afford patronage, friendship, hatred, whatever it chose. The threat was far removed from most of the neighborhoods. Boston had experienced gang wars between Jews and Irish, between Italians and Irish, between integrated gangs of whites and blacks, between groups of blacks and groups of whites, but, unlike Detroit or New York or Chicago, there had been no race riots. The Legislature busied itself in the postwar era by passing bills further banning discrimination in public accommodations, supporting fair employment, attacking discrimination in the sale and rental of private housing. The black community was not making any threats. The state was solidly in the Roosevelt-Truman column. Old Republicans felt loyalty to old Republican ideals; liberals felt loyalty toward civil rights; the pols regarded the whole thing as relatively harmless. In the black community, the old families pursued grace, glory, and money; the clergy preached weekly; the pols lined up behind Johnny Powers. As a transplanted Washingtonian named Ed Brooke began his climb up the prestigious ladder of law–politics–public service to the U.S. Senate, the upper-class colored folks of Boston could once again point with pride. To the transplanted dirt farmers and welfare mothers and Boston-bred teenage dudes learning the tricks on old Irish and Jewish corners, there was also pride, but the whole business seemed so distant as to be rendered academic. Ed Brooke was one role model. The hundreds of unemployed men, welfare mothers, and school dropouts were also role models, closer to the reality of what was.

By 1960, the black population of Boston, long hovering at 3 percent, had grown to 10 percent of the city's total residents. Something like 20 percent of the blacks were already in public housing projects, a number made even more awesome by the fact that a number of projects made sure no blacks moved in. Between 1950 and 1960, when Boston was losing about 100,000 whites to the suburbs, almost 25,000 blacks were born or moved into the city. By the end of the long Eisenhower "sleep" and the beginning of a decade that would see a black revolution in city streets, Boston discovered that it had a predominantly black neighborhood. Where once the "colored" had been somewhat dispersed, now the blacks were concentrated in Roxbury, the northern fringe of Dorchester, the South End, and part of the Back Bay. By 1960, 21 percent of Boston's housing was classified as deteriorating or dilapidated — for the blacks and their immediate white neighbors, the rate was 49 percent. The banks were no longer granting mortgages in the older neighborhoods; insurance companies were pulling out coverage whenever possible. Two black contractors who wanted to rehabilitate two apartment buildings were refused loans by every bank they visited. Blacks who could afford homes in Roxbury and Dorchester were paying inflated prices, and the city's checkerboard assessment policies, when translated, showed that assessments were higher in Roxbury than in most neighborhoods. Unlike the downtown businessmen with money and access to abatement lawyers, Roxbury blacks felt they got the short end of the stick on abatements, because they had no political clout. Many of those who didn't own homes — and by 1960 only 4,000 of the city's 63,000 blacks did — complained that absentee landlords were gouging them on rents and that they were paying through the nose for necessary, but dangerous, space heaters to keep their apartments warm against the northeast winds that roared over the harbor waters and slipped through the cracks and gaping holes of the wooden Roxbury tenements.

Once again, Boston's health care officials trooped out over the city and found what their predecessors had found years before in the once-fetid North End. The death rate from tuberculosis in 1959 for blacks was 27.6, compared to 11.1 for whites. The infant death rate for 1955 to 1959 in the neighborhood with the most blacks was 36.9; in the whitest neighborhood, it was 12.5 percent. When a social service agency ran comparisons of 64 Boston neighborhoods on social and health characteristics, none of the predominantly black neighborhoods was among the top ten "healthy" areas.

"The seeds of discontent among Negro unemployed, unemployable and underemployed are being nurtured by the black nationalist groups operating in the most mobile section of Roxbury–North Dorchester," some concerned blacks wrote in 1961. "There is growing evidence that unless constructive and practical leadership is forcefully exercised by both whites and Negroes, the uneventful slumber of Boston's rapidly increasing Negro community may be drawing to a close."

In time, the militant blacks cited by that report would come to the forefront in Roxbury, the South End, and North Dorchester. Some would capture the attention of the press and the loyalties of young men and women and then disappear from the scene. Others would settle into one niche or another, establish their base of support and lay the foundation of political power for blacks in Boston. But the group that first publicly shattered the chimera of interracial harmony in Boston was the NAACP's Boston branch, which, like its counterparts most everywhere, was a middle-class outfit in which middle-class blacks were steadily taking over leadership from middle-class whites. When the NAACP spat hard enough to hit the mark, the issue it chose was a middle-class issue — schools. Not patronage or contracts or pissing contests over some precinct captain's loyalties or a fight for more public services, but schools, for the NAACP had looked around its growing community and it had found de facto segregation. In 1961, it began complaining about that state of affairs, and pretty soon, it was 1844 all over again, except that this time around, the resistance did not bend.

Irish numbers had overwhelmed Yankee-sponsored structural changes. By World War II, two-thirds of those who had served on the five-member school committee were Irish. But now that the Irish had control, what was it exactly that they controlled?

The journalist Louis Lyons wrote that a narrow-minded Catholic establishment had rejected federal aid to education and had opposed "every advance in public education." He found bigotry evident "in the almost hysterical anxiety to control the public school system and to subvert its teaching to the mediocrity of the product of the local teachers' college. This trend was accelerated after 1939 when a local residence rule gave a monopoly of teaching positions to the local system."

In 1944, a school survey commissioned by the Finance Commission found a school system run by politicians, a system that was failing to spark the imagination or the curiosity of its pupils, a dull bureaucracy that was doing no more to help the children who needed help the most than did the system criticized back in 1846.

"Members of the staff of the school system reported again and again to the survey staff," the surveyors wrote, "that 'politics' has dealt a paralyzing blow to progress in Boston schools. 'Politics' is given as the cause of relatively incompetent persons holding responsible positions, of decisions being made that are contrary to the best judgment of those most concerned with the result, of staff members failing to deal with problems courageously and frankly, and of a pervading fear which survey members found existent among school personnel. . . . The result is deadly to honest thinking, professional initiative, courageous leadership, and progress in all portions of the school system."

A 1970 report on the schools found basically the same problems of dirty politics and classroom insensitivity that the 1944 report had found.

A school committee, the 1970 report insisted, "cannot play favorites. Nor can members expect staff members to purchase tickets to annual testimonial dinners or parties for members, a practice which substitutes loyalty for performance, gratitude for results."

The old Yankee reform of 1905 had fallen in on top of itself. By creating at-large elections, it had banned from the school committee representatives of minorities and of the older city wards. It had forced candidates to run citywide. An upper income goo-goo could do that easily, but a hungry Irish pol had to raise the money somewhere and a lot of it, for it cost a lot to run a citywide campiagn. The very situation that the reformers hoped to prevent had occurred — an inbred and insensitive bureaucracy, sacrificing curiosity for discipline and order and catering to special-interest groups of masters, teachers, custodians, and other school employees.

"Dear Friend:
Friends of Boston School Committeeman John J. Kerrigan are planning to honor him with a reception and Cocktail Party at the New

*England Aquarium on Thursday evening, October 19, 1972, from 5:30
to 7:30 p.m. The purpose of this party is twofold. The first to honor
John, an outstanding dedicated public official, who is an unpaid member of the Boston School Committee. The second is to honor John on
the occasion of his fourteenth Wedding Anniversary. . . . Enclosed for
your convenience you will find both a reservation card and a postage-
paid return envelope. . . .*

> *"Gentlemen: Please reserve____tables at $250.00 each.*
> *"Please reserve____tables at $500.00 each."*
> — Typical invitation to a testimonial for a Boston
>   school committeeman

*"It came to my house in the mail. I had heard of it a couple of days
before from department heads. They had said they had gotten invita-
tions, and they were discussing it, saying how awful it was. They
felt — why should we give him money for something he sought and
knew was unpaid? And that Fourteenth Wedding Anniversary thing is
silly. Twenty-five dollars for two hours and a drink! . . . It annoys me.
You know you're on a list, and somewhere, someone is checking your
name. . . . People think it's important, especially if you're looking for a
rating. If two teachers come up with the same score, and one buys
tickets and one doesn't, they will take the one who buys the tickets."*

> — A teacher reacting to the invitation

For years, while Boston's pupils struggled with their ABC's, a number of school committee members majored in PPP's — politics, pressure, and patronage. The school committee was just another part of
the political system. While many of Boston's high school graduates
found themselves unemployable, school committee graduates could be
found in prestigious political positions all over town, or at least *trying*.
Joe Lee and William Arthur Reilly had tried to become mayor and
failed — Lee ended up back on the committee, and Reilly ended up in
the Hynes administration. Joe White became president of the Boston
City Council. Maurice Tobin became mayor, governor, and U.S. Secretary of Labor. Louise Day Hicks launched a national reputation from
the chairmanship of the school committee. Jimmy Hennigan became
register of probate, and a school committeeman named Paul Ellison
worked as his clerk. John Kerrigan ran twice for district attorney and
lost. Thomas Eisenstadt became sheriff of Suffolk County.

The testimonials, or "times," as the Bay State pols call them, could
be useful in paying off old campaign debts or bankrolling upcoming
campaigns or, as some allege, just having some money around because

it's nice to have money around — even if you are, as many committee members have been, a practicing attorney. So, the school committee for decades spent most of its meeting time on contracts and personnel matters and very little on the business of education. The Finance Commission members held hearings.

They heard the secretary to the school committee testify that he had bought testimonial tickets because "it seemed wise." Wise? "In case the question ever came up perhaps of pay raises, I didn't want to be forgotten."

An instructor said that evening school teachers normally receive their checks at home, but that the previous winter, one paycheck didn't arrive in the mail. It arrived by way of a principal, who interrupted the teacher in a machine shop and asked him if he'd bought tickets to school committeeman Paul Tierney's time. The teacher didn't even know how the principal got the paychecks in the first place.

David Rosengard, an assistant superintendent, resented the implied pressures on those who didn't fork out dough and became a vocal critic of the testimonials. In 1972, he was not reappointed.

Another administrator, John Coakley, associate director of the system's Education Planning Center, was number one on the rating list of those qualified for promotion to day school principal. Coakley refused to buy testimonial tickets or to sell them either. He was not promoted.

School employees were not the only persons solicited. Contractors who did business with the school system were sent tickets by an employee active in awarding no-bid contracts, which had totaled more than $2 million in 1972. For almost two years, the FinCom investigated Boston's legacy to Horace Mann's dreams and concluded in 1975 that the whole school committee should be abolished.

The system could work both ways. When the school custodians threw a banquet in 1973, the whole school committee attended, as did city councilmen, state reps, and senators, other state and local politicians, and priests. Custodians were each getting more than a lot of teachers — about $6 million in salaries and overtime. Truant officers were making as much as police lieutenants, and a school nurse could make about $5,500 more than a nurse in the City Hospital.

For these services, the average Boston high school student who stuck it out had less than a 50 percent chance of ending up in a college or prep school or trade school. In predominantly white neighborhoods like East and South Boston, only 30 percent of the high school graduates went on to higher education. In racially mixed Dorchester, it dropped to 28 percent. The system's own figures showed that by 1973, the dropout rate for white South Boston High School was 12.3 percent, for predominantly black Dorchester High, 12.5 percent. While the dropout rate in the showcase Latin schools averaged one tenth of one percent, the rate for Boston Trade was 14.2 percent, for Boston High, 32.5 percent, for Trade High for Girls, 20.4 percent. And critics insisted that the school department figures were conservative.

One East Boston mother active in school reform became fond of saying, "When a woman finds out she's pregnant in Boston today, she prays for two things: one, that the child is healthy; two, that he gets accepted to Latin School."

When the inevitable demonstrations, protests, and revolts broke out against such a system, an angry young teacher took the floor at a public meeting and asserted that the system's curriculum was outmoded and failed to encourage independent thought, that Boston's kids were being trapped into low-paying jobs, the draft, and early pregnancy.

The school system, state officials charged, was violating the state bilingual educational law by allowing high pupil-teacher ratios, failing to serve hundreds of children, and passing off courses as "bilingual" that really were not.

A special Task Force on Children Out of School contended that at least 4,000 school-age children were not attending school in Boston. "The majority of these children remain out of school because the School Department provides no educational programs for them. Children of Puerto Rican, Italian, Chinese and other ethnic groups comprise the larger proportion of excluded youngsters. Other children — those who are crippled and girls who are pregnant, for example — are excluded from school in large numbers too."

After Massachusetts passed a law and provided funds to protect the educational and civil rights of handicapped children, the Boston school system was still failing in its charge. Half the special-needs children in Boston remained totally unidentified and unserved. As usual, the system used money to hire unqualified personnel to work in the special programs — patronage à la school committee. The training programs ranged from "meagre to non-existent," and at least a fourth of the special education classes were being held in basements, storage rooms, old offices, and isolated buildings.

Meanwhile, the system's consumers were responding in kind. In 1973, officials reported 664 incidents of vandalism costing thousands of dollars in equipment and the destruction of two school facilities; 139 teachers said they had been assaulted or robbed, along with a dozen custodians.

A new associate superintendent looked out over the system in which he had served for thirty-seven years, declared that the biggest problem facing the schools was providing protection for teachers and property, and acknowledged that at least 15 percent of the high school graduates were not reading at grade level.

Occasionally, in any municipality, people get angry enough to throw out the rascals, even in Boston where people condone as "politics" what others might label corruption. But by the mid-1960's, the Boston voters were returning their school committee members to office with regularity, for the committee had come to symbolize something far more important than corruption to those white people who, like the two women in the North End, feared the growing power and population of Boston's black community. The committee symbolized resistance.

Black parents were complaining by the mid-1950's that predominantly black schools were getting the short end of the financial and political stick. The tight, often inflexible, school system could not bend to the new culture swarming into its classrooms, just as the Yankee schools had been shaken by the influx of Irish. Blacks complained that the vocational training and counseling ran from lousy to nonexistent. They called for remedial reading and cultural programs. They said the schools refused to recognize or deal with the special needs of many children. They were angry at the number of inexperienced and substitute teachers at the black schools. The black parents and the white Catholic school committee were having trouble understanding each other. The school committee seemed hard of hearing, especially when blacks complained of segregation. The school committee denied segregation the way Yankees had denied the existence of secular teaching to Catholic critics. Segregation was not allowed; therefore, there was no segregation. Yet by 1960, 14 Boston schools were 50 to 85 percent black, and another 15 schools were 90 percent or more black. The names engraved on the school granite were Irish and Yankee; the consumers inside were black. The city's residential patterns were creating segregated schools, and the Boston school committee, when it finally did recognize segregation, refused to do anything about it. After all, the members argued, weren't the schools in Southie predominantly Irish? The ones in Mattapan's northern tier predominantly Jewish? The ones in the North End and East Boston predominantly Italian?

The answer was yes, and that very fact was the symbol of Boston's split personality, a personality both beautiful and ugly. Boston was not a cosmopolitan city. Its late Yankee literary giants were exceptions to a narrow-minded, parochial, self-servant merchant society. And now, the ethnics were in charge of the same parochial town — each claiming pride in a neighborhood or in a section of a neighborhood. In power they were, but with less power than their predecessors and, therefore, even more protective of what little they had. The tightly knit, parochial neighborhoods were at once the boast and the bane of Boston. They gave the city a quality that most other cities had lost, yet to keep that quality, they forced their sons and daughters to look inward, to keep to their own kind.

There were Jews who had gone to school with Catholics, and both who had gone to school with blacks, but between the ethnic neighborhoods and the parochial school system in the city and with most of the Protestants and an increasing number of middle-income Catholics and Jews in the suburbs, Boston had not exactly turned out a healthy mix of graduates. Each group submitted itself to a school system which, like most in America, tore away all vestiges of that group's culture, to make them "better Americans," of course. So they became Italo-Americans, Irish Americans and Jewish Americans, knowing little or nothing of Italy, Ireland, or eastern Europe, knowing little of one another and, too often, expecting little. The same process was put to work on the black Americans, but with two different factors. One — the blacks figured that as bad as the white schools were, they were better taken care of than the black ones. Two, black parents and leaders did what the whites had failed to do — they raised a stink. They said what Thomas Nell and Robert Morris had said a century before, that separate schools were harmful and illegal.

"As I got into the fourth grade and above, then I got some sense of how teachers felt about folks where I lived. In the seventh grade, there was Mrs. McNamara. She used to walk around the room with a wooden mallet and go around bopping people on the head. It hurt, too. I told her she better never hit me with that thing. Other kids would grab it from her if she tried to hit them. She would call you 'guttersnipe' or say, 'You act like you're from the gutter.' I sensed it, the attitude, but I couldn't articulate it. That kind of hostility ended up in the school yard, where the youngsters took it out on each other. If the teacher ridiculed you, then you figured it was okay to ridicule other kids.

"The teachers were either Irish or Yankee. There were some Jewish teachers and a few Italians. I didn't see my first black teacher until I was in the seventh grade, Mrs. Woods. When you go to a school and see a black teacher, it kind of jumps out at you. I thought Mrs. Woods was the greatest person ever, and I had a seventh grade crush on her. I never had a black male teacher while I was in school in the city."

— State Representative Mel King, a black South Ender who had run unsuccessfully for school committee

By the early 1960's, Boston history began repeating itself, as blacks and their white allies accused the school committee of perpetuating segregated schools, as they petitioned for redress, as the school committee majority cut off debate, rejected the allegations and began running for office with the pledge that there would never be any massive desegregation of Boston's schools as long as they were in office.

But integration was, by 1962, an issue and would remain so, and no gaveling down of protests or rhetorical end runs could obviate that. The forced integration of Boston's schools became the greatest social and political issue to confront the city since the Irish reach for power. More than black community control, black business power, black patronage, black employment, integration was the one issue that could finally fuse Boston's diverse and relatively quiet black community into a political force. The means and scale of its being carried out would determine once and for all — beyond the threat of urban renewal, airport and highway expansion, deteriorating building stock, changing life-styles, beyond all those other assaults on them — whether the city's distinct Irish and Italian neighborhoods would survive, or whether Boston would become, like most cities, a place where white people worked during the day and which they abandoned every evening.

In 1963, half the city's 5,000 black high school and junior high pupils formally boycotted the public schools one day to protest segregation. The next year, church and civil leaders, supported by some school officials in the suburbs, sponsored a boycott that drew 14,000 black youngsters out of Boston's schools and put them into Freedom Schools, where they were joined by 1,000 white kids from liberal suburban families. The school committee fumed and went on and on about irresponsible acts. A black man, possibly not realizing that he was echoing the anti-Yankee Curleyisms of the past, looked at the committee and concluded, "Theirs is the old way of life — and that's changing, whether or not they accept it. Time and right are with us."

It would take time, and it would test the liberal posturizing of the suburban politicians in Massachusetts. In 1963, Royal Bolling, a black state representative, filed a fourteen-word bill to ban state aid to communities with racially imbalanced schools. The bill contained no definitions, no procedures for withholding the money, no details, but it was the concept that two years later would be embodied in a complex piece of legislation supported by pols from all over the political and ideological lot.

On the night of March 16, 1964, the black and white members of the

Boston chapter, NAACP, completed a float. It wasn't very fancy, and it wasn't very militant. One panel carried a picture of the recently assassinated John F. Kennedy, who had managed to be a hero to both Irish and blacks. To the right of his picture were these words: "From the Fight For Irish Freedom to the fight for U.S. Equality. NAACP." Three shamrocks decorated the sign, and yet another one had been painted on a map of Ireland outlined on the door near the driver's seat.

When the volunteers finished banging and nailing and painting, they had to pick two people to sit in the truck, one black and one white. A young black man, Bob Howells, worn down by his civil rights activity in his native South and recently arrived in Boston, volunteered. When it came turn for someone to drive, people were saying, "No, not me. . . . I ain't gonna drive it." Marty Gopen looked up and said, "I'll drive it."

The NAACP was going to put that float into the St. Patrick's Day parade in South Boston. It had gone through the proper channels; a nervous parade marshal had given permission after warning that discretion might be the better part of valor. The NAACP had been talking a lot the last couple of years about Boston being a racist town, and a lot of white people, including the racists, did not take kindly to that.

Marty Gopen had grown up Jewish in Roxbury. He knew South Boston by reputation. His father would take him along to the L Street bathhouse in Southie, but they'd never stop on the way.

Early in the nineteenth century, the Irish laborers began leaving Fort Hill and crossing into what Boston then called the Neck in search of jobs at iron foundries and glassworks and shipyards. They settled where they could walk to work, so tenements and three-deckers and industrial plants all grew up together. Southie's lower end turned into something dirty and tough. Its upper end came to represent upward mobility from soot and dirty brick to lace curtains, fringed lamps, and little white doilies, but it too was tough. The neighborhood, the Church, and politics were the three institutions that held Southie together, as together as it could be as the twentieth century progressed, as some industries polluted their backyards, as others closed down, as the Italians, Poles, and Lithuanians, led by the Irish, saw young families move out for lack of housing and saw another one-fifth of their population become residents of public housing. In Southie, men played ball longer than most men did in most other neighborhoods, and men continued to wear warm-up jackets long after they stopped playing ball. South Boston High School was producing some of the city's best football and baseball players and some of the city's worst scholars. But for years, for a husky kid who played a little ball and didn't care much for the books, for those kids the priests got to before the rackets did, for those kids, there were always jobs in politics.

By World War II, Southie had sent John McCormack to Congress and had produced four City Council presidents. Suffolk County District Attorney William J. Foley lived in Southie, and his son would become a city councilman. Judge William Day lived in the upper end with his daughter Louise. Southie had produced one City Hospital superintendent, a public health commissioner, the city messenger, the city censor, the chairman of the transit commission, a few judges, a coterie of court clerks, and hundreds of cops, firefighters, civil servants, and patronage beneficiaries. Through the years, Johnny Powers and "Billso" Hickey the traffic commissioner and John McCormack's brother Knocko were, along with the boxers at Connolly's Gym, the priests, and the dock workers, the symbols of Southie's success. Even when the city returned to at-large elections, Southie could count on one or more favorite sons on the council.

But Southie's politics were ward politics. Ward politics were good enough to produce a job, lower bail, get a kid into a community college, fight a zoning exception, and combat urban renewal proposals. But ward politics couldn't stop poverty and increasing unemployment. Ward politics couldn't change basic attitudes in Southie about outsiders. By the time Marty Gopen got behind the wheel of his truck and slammed the door behind him, South Boston had long grown into itself. It was wary of outsiders, of pols who didn't come from Southie, of scholars and civil libertarians and reformers and preachers of change and kids who didn't seem in a hurry to marry and settle down. It was especially wary, its street kids said, of niggers.

The blacks of Roxbury were as foreign to the Irish of Southie as the Irish had been to the Yankee. In fact, the Yankee had been a lot closer to the black. In 1840, when the St. Patrick's Day orator in South Boston said, "Sixty thousand Irish in Boston and yet not a one in the Watch, the police or on jury duty," there were Yankees and blacks who could come together and speak in peace.

Now, the police and juries were filled with Irish, and so were the streets of Southie for the March 17, 1964, parade. Marty Gopen and Bob Howells were worried, because the damn truck seemed to have 3,700 forward-moving gears and a spring clutch. They were worried about panicking and jolting forward and hitting somebody. Gopen turned the ignition key in the truck, paneled with messages linking Irish and Negro civil rights. But the Irish in Southie, most of them, knew little of the struggle for Irish freedom. To them, Parnell was a guy named Mel who used to pitch for the Red Sox. As the parade moved out, Gopen saw four youths in front of his truck with a banner decorated with three shamrocks and a quaint message, "Go home nigger. Long live the spirit of independence in segregated Boston."

Gopen stopped dead so he wouldn't hit the demonstrators. That's when the first barrage hit the truck — bricks, cherry bombs, garbage. Somebody made like Parnell, Mel, and pitched a rock that shattered the bottom of the truck's rearview mirror. The tone was set for the rest of the parade. Within minutes, the windows on both sides of the cab were broken. Miraculously, the windshield remained intact. Early in the parade, at least two youths managed to jump on the running boards. Howells had removed a tire iron from a toolbox under his seat, and he and Gopen began a morbid conversation on how they would defend themselves.

By then, the police went into action. Two unmarked cars, each carrying plainclothesmen, were escorting Gopen's truck. Two cops were seen on a rooftop over the parade route on Broadway. Senator Ted Kennedy, marching in front of the NAACP truck, looked back, saw what was happening, and ordered his police escort to help.

The police presence kept the tough guys from charging the truck anymore, but it could not stop the garbage or the invective. Gopen saw an opened gallon of white paint come flying down on a motorcycle cop, knocking him to the street. An ice cream with fudge sauce hit the "Q" in "Equality." The jocks were getting early into spring training with ice creams, eggs, beer cans, tomatoes, and a crabmeat sandwich. Gopen was driving a mobile buffet.

He had expected the violence, but he was shocked to look out the cab and see women, holding babies with one arm and shaking the other at the truck and spewing out some less-than-kind utterances in the style of the local longshoremen.

"Go home, niggers."

Gopen kept driving, jerking to a halt, grinding up the gears and driving again.

"Niggah lovah!"

And he was Jewish too, to boot. That also would not go over very big today.

"Fuck you! Fuck you! Fuck you! Fuck you!"

It was getting boring, Gopen thought. Two hours of "fuck yous."

A local newspaper reporter had started out with Gopen and Howells. After 25 yards of abuse, he jumped off the truck. Now, two hours later, Gopen and Howells and the cops figured enough was enough.

Why press your luck? They had passed the reviewing stand, and the crowd seemed to be getting more vicious. One of the last bricks had come through the already broken window and had smashed Gopen's glasses. The police extricated the NAACP float — what was left of it — and escorted it across the bridge. Gopen's truck limped into the South End. Later that day, the NAACP board was briefed. Nobody seemed surprised but Howells. He said it was worse than the South. He moved back there.

Tom Atkins, then the executive secretary of the NAACP, likened the incidents to "the viciousness of the type you might expect to see in New Orleans or in the back woods of Mississippi. But it happened in Boston, and this is where it must be dealt with. There have to be a lot of changes here — and right away."

The NAACP leaders called a press conference. They said the "silence of the white majority" had created an atmosphere of bigotry in Boston. Their pronouncement went out over the wires. The incidents in Southie made national news. It didn't look good for the New Boston. The NAACP guys might be pushy, but nobody ever accused them of being dumb. Atkins counterattacked the ice cream, the eggs, the crabmeat sandwich. "If there are sections of this city," he said, "that are off limits to Negroes, they'd better take the signs down, because we're coming."

In 1965, the Irish Maginot Line was blitzkrieged. The NAACP filed a federal court suit, alleging that black kids were being denied equal rights under the Constitution. The feds began investigating discrimination in Boston schools. A State Advisory Committee on Racial Imbalance and Education, one of the greatest collections of goo-goos ever assembled in Massachusetts, released a 131-page report on segregation in Boston's schools.

In Boston's City Hall, a lonely voice called out and suggested that the only way to erace racial imbalance was to bus black kids into suburban schools. For his efforts, Ed Logue was told to mind his own business, and the state education commissioner said such a move would place a great burden on many communities, because they'd have to build new schools. So the burden, as ordained by the wisdom of the day, would be the city's alone.

As blacks maintained a vigil outside school committee headquarters for 114 days, liberal Democrats and Republican Governor John Volpe worked the racial imbalance concept into a law, the first in the nation. It was full of carrots and sticks, money for new schools that promised to be racially balanced, no money for those communities that refused to end segregation. To end it, one could redraw school districts, build new schools near changing neighborhoods, play all kinds of games, and do all kinds of tricks. To end it in Boston, it would be necessary to do some busing — not a massive amount, but some, and that was the word that nobody wanted to touch. Busing was poison ivy, poison ivy with germs. Louise Day Hicks and other school committee members used it. The matadors shook it up and down in front of their bulls. With every shake, another vote was assured. But others in the drama preferred not to use it, for they knew it was a killer. From the very beginning, they knew that, and in the end, they were right. Volpe, who pushed for a hard-line version of the bill, refused to comment on busing youngsters from one district to another, preferring to mouth the inanity "We are not going to dictate to local school committees on how to carry this out." A liberal legislator said, apparently with a straight face, "There is adequate protection in the bill now [for those who feared busing] since any parent who does not want her child bused has only to object to the school authorities."

The Boston representatives fought a losing battle. At best, it was a series of small holding actions, attempts to delay the inevitable. Members of the Massachusetts Federation for Fair Housing and Equal Rights were lobbying their hometown legislators. The white people whose money and kids had gone south in Abolition's latest crusade were now working the lobbies of the State House, right in front of the mural showing the Union troops getting mugged in Baltimore. This was liberalism's shining moment — a Jesuit named Robert Drinan headed up a team of six civil rights lawyers, working with a Jewish Democratic legislator from Brookline named Beryl Cohen and Henry Shattuck's nephew, Lieutenant Governor Elliot Richardson, while black ministers stood outside school committee headquarters down the street and prayed and stood silently in the grand variety of climate with which Boston is blessed at any given hour.

On August 18, Volpe signed the bill into law. "Massachusetts is once again leading the nation in educational reform," an editorial cawed. Volpe said basically the same thing and handed out 38 pens. The Reverend Virgil Carter ended his vigil down the street, concluding in the fashion of Pilgrims, "At the ending of this vigil, I want only to say, Thanks be to God." By the winter of that year, the state said Boston now had 46 racially imbalanced schools — those with a majority of nonwhites. And before the year was out, Mrs. Hicks and friends filed their first bill to kill the Racial Imbalance Law.

By the mid-1960's, white Boston looked at black Roxbury and Dorchester the way Yankee Boston had watched the North End and Fort Hill a century before, as neighborhoods that you did not visit unless your job required it and then only during the day. The most obvious and the most publicized crimes in America are not the white-collar crimes, but the street crimes, and every rumor or story about a handbag-snatching, a fire, a gang assault further confirmed white fears and resistance. Every assault on a black, every word of resistance by a white further strengthened the posture of the militant blacks, be they Muslims preaching a separate, powerful, and proud society, or budding black pols on the make saying the things that brought applause, or that new generation of community leaders challenging the older and more middle-class "colored" institutions.

By fighting the imbalance act, by stirring up the existing fears and spreading them throughout the city, Hicks and the rest of the school committee helped assure the inevitable disaster that would befall Boston, a disaster that they would be unable to control, a disaster so violent in nature that it would make Hicks look like a moderate.

Their unalterable opposition couldn't get her elected mayor, but it served to thwart the intent of the Legislature. Seven years after the Racial Imbalance Act had become law, the number of racially imbalanced schools had increased from 46 to 67, and the percentage of nonwhites attending them grew from 68 percent to almost 79 percent.

The Boston school committee would brook no political compromise with a community that was growing more and more impatient with the thought of any compromise at all. The committee misread the stubbornness of the blacks, the political climate of the era, the forces that were at work. So ridiculous were the committee's efforts to circumvent the law, to avoid the issue, that they even classified 671 Chinese kids as white, much to the surprise and anger of the Chinese community. There will be no busing, the fearful white constituency was told, because that's what it wanted to hear. Why, they would go to jail, committeemen pledged, if anyone tried to bus Boston's children.

The busing that would come to Boston was embodied in a plan that was poorly drawn up, a plan destined to wreak havoc and violence. It was drawn up by state education officials, "outsiders," that breed of human so distasteful to Boston's white neighborhood residents. It was based on a theory that the mixing of black and white students was fruitful, even if you were mixing only poor black kids with poor white kids. The liberals avoided the whole issue of class as they sounded their clarion calls for Boston to desegregate. The school committee avoided anything that approached public responsibility, as it made promises that could not be kept, and raised false hopes and made a bad situation truly tragic.

Early in what became a Ping-Pong game over the Racial Imbalance

Act, the Boston school committee proposed the construction of new schools as the way to fulfill the law. The state looked at the proposal and found that of the twenty-two construction projects, five would increase racial imbalance, or, at best, fail to reduce it; another half-dozen might not even affect racial imbalance, and eleven of them had nothing to do with eliminating racial imbalance.

The state rejected the committee's plan. Thwock. Back to the committee went a state plan. Educationally indefensible, said a school administrator. Thwock, back to the state went the committee with another plan. Thwock, the state rejected the second plan.

As the school committee successfully avoided dealing with the issue, the imbalance increased every year. Committee members threw up their hands in frustration and asked, what could one do, the neighborhoods were changing so fast, it was difficult to even figure out where to build fringe area schools because the fringe kept changing. That was the nature of de facto segregation, they reminded everyone — housing patterns. But by the latter half of the 1960's, some integrationists were contending there was more de jure than de facto to Boston's segregated schools.

For a group that saw nothing but chaos and deficits in busing, the school authorities seemed to have no reservations about busing black pupils past white schools with empty seats to other predominantly black schools. By its system of pupil assignments, district lines, and the manner in which students were "fed" from district schools to citywide high schools, the Boston school committee was perpetrating a segregated school system.

The school committee was not going to do anything to promote white flight — not so much because the committee was racist, but because it was highly political. Like the turn-of-the-century Yankees, who continued to try to control the committee long after they were a minority, the Irish committeemen of the 1960's watched the black school population break over one-third of the total public school students. With blacks spreading throughout the system, whites would flee, and the black student population would increase proportionately. Black families continued to live in Boston; when they moved, it was to another neighborhood, not another city or town. The major shifts of white population *within* the city had ended; when the whites moved, the chances were pretty good they were off to suburbia. The Irish had pushed the Yankees out of the city; the Irish, Italians, and Jews had pushed one another around *inside* the city. As long as the latter held true, white politicians could seek out and find a base of support. Now, the blacks were pushing the whites out of the city, and the whites moving into Boston were young white-collar professionals, single or recently married or married with one or two kids, Catholics who didn't make mass quite as often, Jews who didn't go to *shul*, "outsiders," people from Minne–goddamn–sota who talked funny and pronounced their *r*'s. They were the legacy of the New Boston, come to haunt the ward heelers of the old city. Between them, the blacks, the Chinese coming in from Hong Kong and Taiwan, the Puerto Ricans and Colombians and Cubans, between all those folks and white flight, it didn't take a political genius to see what could happen.

Whatever the motivations of the school committeemen, political or racist, there were, from the early days of the resistance movement, some elements of truth to which the modern Abolitionists paid little heed. A theory that segregated schooling was harmful, a theory supported by the Supreme Court, had become a vehicle of what Hicks called "social engineering." Children would be transferred about the city like so many digits in a computer. It was a soulless numbers game, in which adult human beings tried to measure integration and education with quotas and percentiles. Somehow, the din and smoke of the battle clouded the real issue, which was less the separation of the races than the separation of the classes. For one class lived in Boston and some older communities nearby, and quite another class lived in most of the suburbs. The responsible leadership in more than thirty of these suburban communities would participate in a program that brought some black youngsters out to their schools, but the key tactic in most suburbs was to resist, to let the city fight its own battle.

"It will be no more than five years," Ed Logue predicted in 1967, "before Boston's schools are more than 50 percent in Negro enrollment. We need the help of our friends in the suburbs. They have nothing to be frightened about." Logue was statistically off by eight years, but his plea made great good sense. It was the good-government thing to do. After all, most of the goo-goos lived in the suburbs. But the suburbs would have none of it. The city, whose economy, whose culture, whose very geographic setting had made the suburbs possible, was told to go it alone. A century of social and racial neglect was to be redressed not by opening the job market to minorities, not by building low-income housing in a metropolitan area, not by making quality education available to lower-income blacks and whites, but by forcing an institution least able to cope with change — the Boston school system — to arbitrarily shuffle around its children from one lousy school to another, by telling oppressed whites and oppressed blacks that they must mingle for some greater social good.

For the whites in the city, for most of them, the answer was no. They resisted, and the resistance sprang, in part, from the blatant bigotry of the heirs to Father Coughlin and Joe McCarthy. The youngsters who had been babies held by their shrieking mothers at that St. Patrick's Day parade in 1964 would be old enough in 1974 to shout "nigger" on their own. They spat at the blacks, the Puerto Ricans, the Yankees in the suburbs, the "experts," the suburban Irish judge who would send down the inevitable order to integrate, the Jews who had moved from Dorchester and thereby had removed the wall between Irish and black. This resistance came from the ugly profile of Boston's parochialism. The more beautiful and poetic profile of that same insularity also produced resistance. It was milder, less violent, less racist. It pleaded to society to preserve what little the neighborhoods had managed to save over the years through the endless assaults on their life-style. Its proponents included those who could welcome blacks, but could not dispatch their children to Roxbury, and those who could and would put their kids on a bus, but who wondered why only they were doing this and not their white relatives and neighbors a few feet over the city's boundaries.

For the blacks in the city, for most of them, the answer was yes. They would put their kids on a bus. Most would do so with great resignation and fear, but they would do it, because they believed nothing could be worse than what they had. Bringing white kids to black schools, their leaders figured, would force the white school committee and its patronage army to pay attention to those schools. For the blacks reasoned that the school system would respond to its white constituency. To a degree, it would, but only to a degree, for the system had done little for its white consumers. To the degree that it wouldn't, the blacks would have to take power. They had not found it with Garrison or Trotter or the Taylor brothers. Now, their numbers were greater, their consciousness was being raised by every televised racial incident, and their vehicle to power would be neither the pen nor the sword, but the bus.

TEN

Boston: 1974

"*I'm gonna play Saint Ant'ony.*"
"*Saint Anthony?*"
"*Yeah, a lotta guys I know play him. A big book in the No't End, he plays him. 613.*"
"*Why do you play saints? Hah?*"
"*I might get lucky. Who says there's no God, hah? You see that priest who won the lottery? Two hundred t'ousand dollahs!*"
"*Yeah — but he's a priest.*" — A conversation, 1974

"*So life goes on, although on a much simpler scale. Bostonians have never been drawn to Bar Harbor, preferring the simplicity of North Haven, Dark Harbor, and Islesboro. At North Haven, Boston Cabots have a resort-within-a-resort and call it Cabotville. They live in Spartan-like cottages and never dress for dinner.*" — Boston *Globe,* July, 1974

Somewhere in that hazy land, where the real earth ends in the illusions of those who view horizons, Boston groped through the summer of 1974, as if much of the city were not aware of the impending war.

Forces born more than a century before had clashed repeatedly, and now they were giving shape and substance to the ultimate battles of class warfare.

By 1974, a decade of irresponsible debate over school integration had hardened the lines of battle. The trenches had been dug long ago. All that remained was the filling of them with cannon fodder.

State education officials and state courts had finally come around to taking the hardest of hard lines with the Boston school committee, after that body had cleverly shifted field, delayed, and backtracked over racial imbalance since 1965. In March, the state Supreme Court ordered the committee to comply with the state's timetable for implementing a state plan to balance the schools. It was not the best possible plan for Boston. Ten months earlier, Harvard Law School professor Louis L. Jaffe, conducting hearings on the state plan, urged that South Boston be exempted from it, that to include it would do more harm than good. "The people there are intensely hostile to blacks. Almost no blacks have elected to go into available space in South Boston, either under their district assignments, which give them a preference, or under controlled transfer."

To mix Southie and Roxbury, to bus students from each into the other, was not to ask for war, for the war was inevitable, but it was to insure that the war would be bloody. The accepted wisdom, however, was that hostility should not exempt a neighborhood. Was not the South hostile? Southie remained in the plan.

And the plan remained. Whatever the school committee did, whatever Louise Day Hicks and her minions of busing opponents did, the plan remained. It was like a scab that had grown out of the virus. One might scrape at it, hack at it, medicate it, but it remained, impervious to all attack. By June of 1974, the protestors of busing and that state plan had finally realized something of what they had been trying to do for almost a decade. The state of Massachusetts — the predominantly Catholic Legislature and the liberalish Yankee Republican Governor Francis Sargent — took the clout out of the Racial Imbalance Act of 1965 by removing the state Board of Education's power to redistrict and order busing. Instead, there would be magnet school programs to draw whites and blacks together, and there would be incentives — the blacks angrily called them "bounties" — for schools accepting black kids.

Running against Sargent was another liberal, a Democratic lawyer named Michael Dukakis, from the liberal suburb of Brookline, and he too was calling for some options to busing.

Both Sargent and Dukakis were talking about suburban involvement. Both contended that without the suburbs, busing in Boston was doomed. One of Sargent's liberal aides reportedly said at one staff meeting, "Busing is an idea whose time has come and gone." From the busing crusaders came a shower of invectives. No deviation was to be allowed. Everyone was to be locked in place.

Quietly, stories were circulating that some blacks who had fought the long battle to integrate Boston's schools now had second thoughts about busing, wondering whether sending black children to Boston's lousy white schools was perhaps less worthy than fighting for community control of their own schools.

There were no easy answers, yet when political candidates or the mayor offered alternatives, which reflected the very complexity of the issue, the immediate response from some busing strongholds was that the pols were taking a dive, that they were simply protecting their political flanks. Perhaps. And then, perhaps, the pols were closer to reality than their critics too. "Cowards," yelled voices from the rear of the battle area, at Harvard.

Yet who were the cowards?

Were they those who preached integration to Boston from the whitest of suburbs? Were they those who told Boston how integration was supposedly working somewhere in California but who never told Boston the fate of those black and white kids who *had* been attending classes together in the city? Were the black, Puerto Rican, and white parents who wanted their children in neighborhood schools cowards? Or were they just ignorant of what was really good for them, as some experts seemed to imply?

Maybe the real cowards were the speech-making pols who didn't fully inform their constituents where and how integration had worked in the system, who played on fear, the most vile kind of politics, and who promised that the war they helped start would never come. Maybe they were those black and liberal leaders who no longer believed integrating schools was the priority it once was.

What would happen in September in no way would resemble what the progressives in this society wanted, those who dreamed of a truly integrated society — housing in the suburbs and jobs at all levels, not just a bunch of tired, ill-equipped schools in the central city trying reluctantly to suddenly, on their own, redeem two centuries of inglorious racial history.

So the Sargents and the Dukakises and the Whites sought political compromise. They sought it to protect their political flanks, and they sought it to avert disaster. For this, they were vilified. It was too late to turn back. Indeed, racial justice demanded no turning back, but who was to say racial justice would not have been served by turning ever so slightly a few degrees away from the path that led to Sarajevo?

Cowards?

One year later, James Coleman, author of the 1966 school study that integrationists used to justify busing, said, "My position has changed. I don't think I foresaw the kinds of consequences about disorders in schools of large cities and the white flight."

About the same time, a Superior Court judge in California suspended his five-year-old busing order in Inglewood, because there were no longer enough whites with whom the minorities could integrate. There were in the suburbs of Inglewood, just as there were in the suburbs of Boston, but the Supreme Court was still protecting America's suburbs.

Realists, perhaps.

Moderate critics and worried politicians and the diehard opponents of busing, that motley group that ran the gamut from those who had worked with blacks for common causes and loved their neighborhood schools and identities to those who ranted and raved about niggers and crime, had come as close as they would to a victory when Frank Sargent signed the bill tearing the club and enforcement powers away from the Racial Imbalance Act.

But Sargent's signature was not the prelude to the inevitable. That most important event took place not at the State House, but about one mile away, where a third branch of government would do what neither the executive nor the legislative had done. A tall, thin, balding, and unimposing suburbanite named Wendell Arthur Garrity, Jr., a judge of the United States District Court, had drawn a case back in March, 1972, *Tallulah Morgan et al., Plaintiffs,* v. *James W. Hennigan et al., Defendants.* The case was a class action suit filed by the NAACP against the school committee and the state Board of Education. It alleged that Boston's separate schools violated the plaintiffs' rights under the Fourteenth Amendment. On June 21, 1974, the last day of the school year, Garrity finally issued his findings.

To Garrity, the evidence was clear, and the evidence, he said, established that school officials had knowingly carried out a systematic program of segregation and had intentionally maintained a dual school system, a system that was unconstitutionally segregated. In almost every facet of the school system, in building new schools, in changing district lines, in setting up feeder patterns for high schools, in the much vaunted open enrollment and controlled transfer programs, in the transfer policy for teachers, the school committee and its underlings kept Boston's schools segregated.

Garrity found de jure segregation and ridiculed the committee's arguments that it had no control over changing neighborhoods. He contended that the committee's highly praised policy of maintaining neighborhood schools was no policy at all. Even if segregated neighborhoods and the purity of neighborhood schools were cogent defenses for the school committee, Garrity said, they were partial defenses at best — "neither argument has any relevance to the defendants' practices with respect to faculty and staff, open enrollment and controlled transfer or feeder patterns."

The school committee knew long ago what neighborhoods were changing and how they were changing and could have planned a desegregated school system based on such knowledge. Instead, the committee pandered to the fears of whites.

The specific findings were damning:

"Teachers are also segregated. Seventy-five percent of Boston's black teachers are in schools more than 50 percent black. Eighty-one schools have never had a black teacher. . . .

". . . The defendants deliberately dragged their feet in formulating plans to lessen overcrowding as well as racial imbalance generally. They constantly delayed the presentation of plans requested by the state board until the last possible moment. . . .

". . . The defendants have made districting changes for the purpose of perpetuating racial segregation.

"In September, 1965, a private group of black parents raised funds for private transportation of black pupils transferring under open enrollment to predominantly white schools. Called Operation Exodus and led by a black parent, Ellen Jackson, who testified at the trial, it bused approximately 250 black students in 1965–66 and grew steadily to approximately 1,100 students in 1969–70. At some of the transferee schools, the students encountered locked doors, physical segregation in separate classrooms, auditoriums, and corridors, and placement in the rear of classrooms. Anticipating the arrival of black students, administrators of some transferee schools had desks unbolted from the floor and removed from classrooms."

The suburbanite judge made the only findings he could make. The realists in Boston knew that Garrity's conclusions were inevitable. Garrity had spent little time physically looking at Boston schools. He may not have really understood the sense of neighborhood most whites felt, nor the extent of their fear of black crime. Perhaps he would be surprised in the days to come to read and hear of black and Puerto Rican parents protesting busing, complaining that their children would be removed from community schools that they, the adults, had worked so hard to improve. Whatever the faults of the opinion or the man who made it, the realists knew the conclusions would stand. They knew long before June, and some people in the city had moved to deal as early as possible with what they foresaw as impending disaster.

Bob Schwartz was among them. Schwartz had grown up in the nearby suburb of Newton, once a Yankee-Republican enclave that had since become liberal, Democratic, and heavily Jewish. He had organized and had been principal of an experimental, racially integrated high school on the West Coast. He had moved to Boston and settled on Beacon Hill, and walked to work every day. Work, specifically, was as the mayor's aide on education.

The problem for Schwartz was the problem that had been facing White from the days he campaigned for office — how to deal with the lousy school system without being caught up in the racial imbalance controversy.

The prospect of busing had made campaigning uncomfortable for the moderates in politics. When asked about busing, White had talked about building new junior and senior high schools that would attract students from all over the city. "No person, white or Negro, has a natural desire to bus, at the elementary school level. Most mothers, though, won't care what type of transportation is necessary to get their children to English or Latin or Boston College High School if the educational facilities they need are provided."

Hicks had campaigned to eradicate the Racial Imbalance Law; White had proposed amending it to eliminate the first four grades from its coverage. He stuck to the letter of the law, by insisting it did not require busing, but she argued, pragmatically, that the law made busing unavoidable. At one point, White promised, "There will be no busing in this city as long as I am mayor."

Early in his term, long before Schwartz arrived, White had said that "Boston's white students, as well as its black, have been cheated. The physical plants available to predominantly white student bodies are, in too many cases, old and dilapidated. Let us not delude ourselves into believing that we are confronted solely by a racial issue when in fact we face the betrayal of all children by a system not equipped to provide them . . . with the very best of educational experiences."

White began visiting the schools, where he'd meet and talk with student assemblies, with both teachers and headmasters barred from the room. He moved fast to insure that his Public Facilities Department built new schools, either from the ground up, or renovated new ones out of an old car dealer's showroom and a former bowling alley. There were not a hell of lot of things a mayor could do with schools, which are run by the school committee, but White showed signs of taking as much control as he could. He began a community school program, where the new schools that he built were open after hours to community groups and were run by local councils whose loyalty was to the mayor rather than the school committee. But the issue of ultimate control was put off — delayed by the race for governor and the reelection campaign. When Schwartz arrived during the mayor's second term, the problem handed him was: how does the mayor take control of and reform Boston's schools without being destroyed by busing?

Behind all the deliberations was the one nagging moral issue that bugged both Schwartz and his boss, the conviction that the wrong problem was being addressed, that the real issue was not the separation of races inside the city, but the separation of classes in and outside the city. When the mayor would go to court to force suburban involvement, Garrity would throw the problem back to the city. So, the issue was not faced, and other tactics had to be drawn up.

Schwartz hoped that the mayor's office could develop a position on schools credible enough to attract people on both sides of the busing issue, that these people would build a coalition to take on the school committee. That would be difficult, he knew, because there were whites who were deeply suspicious of the mayor's entry into school affairs and blacks who felt Kevin White was not firm enough on school integration. It would be difficult also because Kevin White was still of two minds over school reform — his earlier instincts had told him that messing with schools was a no-win issue; but the uprisings of high school students in both black and white schools had not been contained within the buildings, and the problems became *his* problems. In 1972, White told Schwartz he'd go for school reform if it wouldn't kill him politically; he said, "We started 50,000 things, and not very many of them came to much. Now, I realize I've gotta pick my shots. You take as much time as you need." He left Schwartz convinced— "If he comes in on it, he'll do it with both feet."

White kept his promise to give Schwartz time to develop positions for him. Early in 1973, as the pressure built on the mayor to take a stand on busing, he was in the midst of a budget meeting with Ed Sullivan, his deputy mayor and old companion from the Secretary of State days, and Sullivan was worried.

"If you've got to do something on racial balance, do it before March first. I was talking with Alice Christopher over in East Boston, and she says they're hitting you in East Boston on it."

White shook his head, no, he said, let Schwartz have the time he needs to develop something.

"Last Wednesday," Sullivan went on, "they had a meeting in Orient Heights, and the place was crowded . . ." White cut him off. "Hey, don't worry about that."

But Sullivan was worried. He shook his head, as the mayor plunged ahead with the budget discussion and said quietly, "It's a big issue in East Boston." Indeed, it was. The year before, Msgr. Mimie Pitaro, a priest who had stopped racial combat at the Maverick Projects in 1964 and who had since become a community leader and a state representative, was defeated in his reelection bid. Pitaro had voted his conscience on racial imbalance, and Eastie tore him apart for doing so. Among the leaders in the successful anti-Pitaro campaign were twin sisters, Elvira (Pixie) Palladino and Rosamond (Trixie) Tutela, who, earlier, had stopped dead a White administration attempt to construct two low-cost houses on vacant lots. Pixie and Trixie had vowed then there would be no "infill" housing in Eastie, that Pitaro would go along with other progressive priests, and that busing would never come to Eastie. Pitaro had been one of the best state reps in the history of the Legislature, but out he went. And the constructive leadership in East Boston, fighting against Logan Airport, fighting for elderly housing and recreation, was now battling to survive against a new community force with one major goal — to fight busing. The East Boston scenario was being played out across the city, and it would escalate in the next two years and drive the moderate white leadership against the wall.

From the beginning, the integration question had made life difficult for the few liberal white politicians in Boston. Not unlike former Senator William Fulbright, the liberal Dixie Democrat who survived by being all Southern on civil rights issues, men like congressman Joe Moakley, of South Boston, an early hawk in the fight to force Nixon out of office and a man deeply committed to low-income housing and other liberal programs, were forced to re-pledge their antibusing vows.

White's liberal critics, most of whom lived outside the city in predominantly white communities, could not understand why he did not run to the front of the bus and lead the charge. "What's he playing to Louise's constituency for? He won't get those votes anyway." But it was more than Louise's constituency. The issue had spread; the virus had spread. The Pixies and the Trixies of Boston might just peak at some point, and the same names and faces would reappear at ROAR rallies, but the prevailing sentiment among Boston voters was against busing. So, for White, there had to be a middle ground, some knob of a hill, some dry spot of land in the middle of the river, where his feet would get wet, and his pants might get drenched, but where he would be safe from drowning.

On March 1, 1973, Schwartz appeared before a legislative committee holding its annual hearing on the Racial Imbalance Act and read the mayor's position, which, he, Schwartz, had drawn up — "I have now come to the conclusion that the Racial Imbalance Law is fundamentally unworkable, and that rather than being amended, the bill must ultimately be replaced." But, he quickly added, replace it only if and when equal opportunities and resources were guaranteed in *all* city schools, when financial inequality between city and suburb was eliminated, when voluntary busing programs were strengthened. No forced busing, the mayor insisted.

The strengthening of voluntary busing programs made more sense than forced busing, but they alone might never meet the court test. Massachusetts was not about to equalize opportunities or provide the fiscal tools for Boston to do so, nor was it about to take from the suburbs to give to the city.

Back inside the mayor's office, the debate continued. One group of aides — Sullivan, Barbara Cameron, Quealy — would urge a hard line against busing. They feared what they heard in the neighborhoods. Others, Schwartz, Paul Parks, a black civil rights leader, and Bob Kiley, would urge the mayor not to lose his progressive image, not to dive, but to stay on the board and keep his bearings. Sometimes one side would prevail, and sometimes the other, and pretty soon it was difficult for observers to figure out exactly where Kevin White was, but *he* knew where he was most of the time — where Schwartz had put him in a position paper made public on April 10, 1973.

"The issue isn't busing; it is whether the busing is mandatory or voluntary, and whether the destination is feared or desired." He argued that whereas the state courts had forbidden massive busing, a federal suit would result in just that, and he attacked the school committee for its failure to cooperate with the state in what he said would be a less disastrous plan. He reviewed his attitude toward the schools and how he had become more involved — "the problems and failures of the school system affect every other aspect of city life; and the lack of authority to solve these problems does not and should not absolve a mayor of responsibility."

He was ready to try to shift the public discussion away from busing to the more "fundamental" question of improving the city schools for everyone. He talked about discrimination among classes of people, how white and black in the city were locked together into a deadly school system and how many busing opponents were really angry "that there is something inherently unfair in a system that gives people with money choices about schooling that others are denied."

White talked about equalizing state aid to schools, increasing money
for voluntary busing programs, building new high schools in West
Roxbury and Hyde Park to attract and hold middle income whites,
attracting suburbanites into the city school system with experimental
programs in the arts, to end the parochialism and isolation of Boston's
schools from the greater Boston community of Yankee-endowed arts,
sciences, and culture. He urged that the school committee be abolished
and replaced with an education commissioner responsible to the
mayor. Whatever the pros and cons of busing, whatever one's feeling
that the issue be class or race, Kevin White wanted to make one thing
perfectly clear — the goddamn thing wasn't *his* fault.

"The school committee is now doing everything in its power to find
a scapegoat for its present problems, but the committee members must
bear the responsibility for the mess they have created. Had the school
committee committed itself in the early '60's to seeking equal educational opportunity for all children, there would have been no need for
a Racial Imbalance Law. Once the law was passed, had the committee
moved firmly and swiftly to implement the law, integration might
have been achieved with a minimum of community disruption. Instead, the school committee adopted a posture of defiance and resistance to the law, and with each passing year they have made the
possibility of peaceful desegregation more difficult and have increased
the likelihood that a federal court will impose a desegregation order
on Boston that will go further than anything required under the
Racial Imbalance Law."

In June, 1974, that's precisely what happened. Schwartz had known
it. White had known it. Everyone close to the situation had seen it
coming. By January of that year, six months before Garrity's decision,
Schwartz was wondering, "How does Kevin prevent the city from
blowing up and being fucked up to a fare-thee-well, and at the same
time not be seen as the guy who desegregated the schools?"

On January 2, six months before Garrity's decision, Schwartz had
sent White a memo under the subject, "preparing for busing." He
said, "The city has nine months to prepare to implement the state
board's busing plan. If we want to minimize the disruption in the fall,
I suggest you take the following steps immediately:

"Speak out in clear law and order language on the issue in the State
of the City message — 'The courts have spoken, the law is the law, we
will obey the law, etc.'" This would be the key to White's political
strategy throughout the busing crisis — he would come out for keeping
the peace, and he would try to convince people that it was one thing to
keep the peace and quite something else to integrate the schools. As

one aide explained it, "To the degree that he be identified with the busing issue, it would clearly be under the label of public safety. We would try to maintain a low profile as long as we could, while waiting for Garrity to decide."

Schwartz was among those who counseled waiting for Garrity before doing or saying very much publicly. Some were arguing that the mayor should publicly predict what Garrity would do, and others were urging White to come out early and strong against what Garrity was about to do. Schwartz insisted that the mayor keep his own counsel, because in the winter and spring of 1974, people simply weren't about to believe such a prediction.

When White and members of his administration looked beyond busing, or away from it, they saw more pleasant signs. The great population shift from Boston to suburbia seemed to have ended; the city's population not only had stabilized, but there were signs that young middle-class persons were moving into Boston — not just the single men and women who came to study or work for a while and leave, but young couples and young families. They were often the sons and daughters of those who had fled the city; they had grown up in the suburbs, and they had not liked it very much. They were men tired of commuting to work, and women tired of loneliness and dullness. The suburbs were full of crime and escalating taxes and people who looked and thought alike.

White was gloating. He knew that, sooner or later, the city-suburb trend had to turn, and now it was turning. And he had plans to make Boston more attractive. He talked of $12 to $15 billion worth of public and private investment, of 80,000 new jobs, of 15 million more square feet of office space and another 3 million square feet of retail space. For the old neighborhoods, he talked of fix-up loan insurance, of code enforcement and public improvements and tax incentives.

The statistics could be misleading too. Some of those new residents were mobile in nature. They would come and add something to the city or take something from it and then leave. Others planned to stay, but their arrival in the South and North Ends, for example, helped force out poorer people who could not afford the escalating rents that landlords now knew they could get. There was a virtual class war going on in the South End between rich and poor. And slowly, the Italian North End was changing, almost as if to fulfill that old 1944 Boston study that had suggested that the North and West Ends were really chic places for the rich.

"We're not interested in having people move into the area because it's quaint and safe on the streets. So many outsiders now want to

move in and take advantage of something we built up over the years. Our strength is becoming our destruction. Our roots are here. We want to raise our families here." — A conversation in the North End

The statistics were not much help to Alonzo Johnson, black, age nine, who had died in an elevator shaft at the Mission Hill projects. They did not show how an Irish real estate man, who, with Jewish and black realtors and Yankee bank money, had blockbusted Mattapan, tried to move his operations into Irish Dorchester, and got his windows broken.

The statistics did not include the length, depth, or width of a truckload of garbage and trash dumped by Roxbury blacks on City Hall Plaza to protest a lack of street cleaning. They did not tell how Wellesley College killed a cooperative program with East Boston that it had begun four years before, in the headier days of student activism. They did not reflect the propensity of banks to redline neighborhoods in Jamaica Plain, to tell white families they couldn't move in there.

Given everything that the statistics did not or could not reflect, they were still grounds for optimism. They promised a better day, a city that was stabilizing racially and economically. For the first time since its early days as a small Yankee city with limited and manageable social ills, Boston appeared to have a chance to more than survive. It seemed to hold the promise that once again New England could turn proudly to its capital city and see a leader, that Boston would regain its nineteenth-century prestige as a place to which people turned for knowledge and example. Were it only not for busing, the mayor and his closest aides thought, all this could be.

In Dorchester, a dozen whites with baseball bats, clubs, pipes descended on black kids at the Grover Cleveland Junior High and beat them.

In Dorchester, two Irish teenagers were charged with stabbing to death an eighteen-year-old black.

In Roxbury, Puerto Ricans and Hondurans fought on Dudley Street with fists and rocks.

In Roxbury, gangs of black youths terrorized motorists who were stuck in a traffic jam after a Summerthing concert. They smashed windows. They robbed three persons and beat up a fourth.

As the gala celebration of 1880 had marked an end of an era, as that parade seemed to symbolize the passing of a Yankee Boston and the arrival of an immigrant city, so too the events of 1974 seemed to signal that Boston as the offspring of Yankees and immigrants knew it was passing away. In the early spring, they bade goodbye at Trinity Church to Abigail Adams Homans, age ninety-five. She was the great-great-granddaughter of John Quincy Adams, for whom her father had been named. Her brother was Charles Francis Adams, Secretary of the Navy under Hoover. She was an Adams, married to a Homans, and living on Otis Place. She had been spry and tough. And now it was all gone.

At St. John's Seminary in Brighton, only fifteen men were graduated from the seminary and ordained as Catholic priests. A spokesman for the Church estimated that the Archdiocese would operate with a $3.9 million deficit for the 1974–1975 fiscal year. Church attendance was down, and parochial schools were closing. Humberto Cardinal Medeiros, conservative on abortion, liberal on race, announced that the parochial schools would not take any Boston children trying to escape integrated public schools. From the Catholic wards, bred on the unbending O'Connell and the warm and flexible Cushing, came mutterings and slurs, for the Portuguese-American heir — "Mañana Medeiros" — closed one of their few escape hatches. Now, many would either move, or fake addresses to get their kids into suburban schools, or try to raise enough money for a private school, or just keep their kids home.

The mayor's office, working quietly and behind closed doors to minimize the disaster, was reticent to say much in public about the troubles that were coming. The school committeemen continued to avoid dealing with the issue, even after Judge Garrity issued his June order. The Church could command little or no leadership. The business and labor communities shied away from the issue. Washington, which had told Little Rock once that integration would happen and no nonsense, sir, was now ambivalent. The courts had confirmed that cities would get no help from their suburban neighbors. The city waited it out through the dog days of August.

Radio Station WUNR is playing Irish music. In some songs, the son goes to sea to either Australia or New York or Boston and gets a letter that his mother has died. Her last thoughts are for him. In other songs, men join the IRA to kill the British oppressors. Sometimes the songs are happy, and sometimes they are like travelogues, when the son remembers how blue the water was or how green the grass was. But mostly, they are about dead mothers and British oppressors.

Dorchester Avenue is a major artery that runs through the various wards that make up the neighborhood of that name. Dorchester is a massive, sprawling place and could not itself be called a neighborhood. It is a collection of scores of neighborhoods and parishes — St. Margaret's, Savin Hill, Fields Corner, Mt. Bowdoin, Codman Square, Uphams Corner, Neponset, Meeting House Hill. Parts of Dorchester are dying, the older parts, and it is into the older parts that the blacks and Puerto Ricans and some Gypsies have moved, have replaced the Jews and now, increasingly, the Irish. Pockets of northern Dorchester are integrated. Along with the tension and the hate, there are blacks and white Irish, Poles, and Italians working together to preserve some sense of neighborhood. But the pressures on them are awesome.

Well-kept homes sit next to boarded-up houses and stores, and there are too many vacant lots. There is not enough mortgage money floating around in the precincts, and both the lack of dough and the insecurity of change mean holding off another year on that paint job. The change could flow in from the shore, from the direction of the predominantly black and Puerto Rican Columbia Point Projects, where the state has constructed the large U. Mass–Boston campus, and already, speculators are advertising apartments for transient students, most of whom would give nothing to a neighborhood that cries for stability. The change could come from Uphams Corner, where Puerto Ricans live and shop, or from Ward 14 and Blue Hill Avenue, a long strip of boarded-up kosher butcher stores and specialty shops with an occasional black businessman toughing it out in a failing economy.

Tonight, it is drizzling, but it is still warm enough for kids, blond kids, to play in shorts and undershirts, to play on the sidewalks and in the small alleys and gravel driveways, in the tiny backyards or the abundant vacant lots.

Farther south, on the left, is Mallow's Bar, which advertises itself as "A Good Place to Drink." Subtle, it isn't. Crowded it is, all along the long bar and in the booths lined up a few feet across from the bar. At each end of the bar is a TV, but hardly anybody is watching. Two older guys who have been here a while are singing nicely. They are singing, "It Had to Be You." One of them is standing, singing theatrically, waving his arms about, flashing his eyelashes, miming in front of the bar mirror, while his left hand is draped on the neck of his companion, who sometimes listens and sometimes sings, but always sits. They look lousy, but they sound good.

A woman pushes her way to the bar. She is thin and very white with a cheap coat. The white women are often very heavy or much too thin. They didn't all start out that way. They often started out as just-right thin, with soft long hair and pug noses and some freckles and a sweet smile. They marry young here, just as the blacks marry young. There are large families here, just as in the black neighborhoods to the north and west. The marriage can turn sour early. The strain can make you nervous and thin. The starches, to compensate for the protein, can make you fat. The women often turn hard in the face — the eyes glint, the lips rarely melt in a smile anymore. Some take to the bottle.

"*Is this Maaaaaaalow's Baahr?*" *she asks.*

The bartender, in his fifties, short, freckled Irish, looks suspiciously at her. Scientists embroiled in wars did not invent radar. Bartenders forever hoping to keep the peace invented radar.

"*Is this Maaaaaaalow's Baaaaahr?*" *she repeats in the flattest of a's, the Dorchester a. He says it is.*

"*Is this where Jerry —— hangs out? Jerry? He plays ball, and he has a shirt that says 'Maaaaaaalow's'?*"

The bartender does not change expression, which is somewhere between a smile and a frown; in fact, no expression at all. He gives away nothing. "*I guess so,*" *he says.*

"*Well, I'm his mother,*" *she says. Now, she is talking louder.* "*Yeah, Maaaaaaalow's.*" *She starts to walk away.* "*When you see him, will you tell him I said hello?*" *She pauses.* "*And that I hate him,*" *she yells.*

The bartender shrugs. She stops now, almost to the door, and now berates the bartender. "*That's right. Tell him I hate him.*"

The bartender groans. "*Awwww, whaddya . . .*"

She yells before he can finish, "*It's your fault! You let him drink in here.*"

The bartender says, "*Ahhhh, get outta here.*"

"*It's your fault,*" *she screams. She is yelling over the bar, and then she moves again to the door, and almost as an afterthought, she turns again and yells,* "*He's got long hair now!*"

After she leaves the two guys begin singing again, old songs, mostly from the 1930's and 1940's, and then they sing, "*Heart of my Heart, I love that melody . . . ,*" *which is about the guys who used to hang around. All over the wards, they are wondering what ever happened to the guys who hung around, to the nuns who wore habits, to the Latin mass, to the parochial schools that took your kids, to the Cardinals who didn't talk funny because they talked just like the people here talk, to the political system that promised jobs and power, to the clubhouses and the little stores, to Pesky and Doerr and Williams and York and an all-white Boston Celtics team, to the Old Howard and Hambone Kelly and Rocky Marciano, and the guys with shorter hair. What the hell ever happened around here anyway? And when?*

And what is going to happen now?

On the radio, WUNR has completed its Irish program. Now, later at night, it plays Puerto Rican music.

For all the good and bad that it might do, for all the complex reasons that govern political decisions, the machinery of Kevin White's administration had cranked up to deal with what was going to happen now. By September of 1973, it was clear to some in his administration that time had run out on old Boston. By January, Schwartz delivered his memo. By March, Kiley, Kirk O'Donnell, a bright, pudgy-faced Irishman who had risen fast through the ranks, Quealy, Schwartz, Frank Tivnan, the press secretary, and Rich Kelliher, an aide to Kiley drawn from the Mayor's Office of Criminal Justice, were meeting and trying to put together proposals for the mayor.

Three weeks before Garrity's decision, the Office of Public Service, which runs the Little City Hall program, detached its deputy director, Bill Edgerton, a lanky twenty-nine-year-old former VISTA volunteer with longish brown hair and mod glasses, to organize a dozen neighborhood teams. Each team consisted of Little City Hall officials, the local fire chief, the local police commander, and street workers from the Youth Activities Commission. The team would meet with neighborhood leaders and school officials. From the neighborhoods, it would funnel public safety requirements back to official Boston, and from the latter, it would funnel decisions and plans back to the neighborhoods.

"Chief Greene then spoke of a fire at the D St. Projects, to a non-white apartment. On the mirror in lipstick was written, 'Nigger get out now.' The resident living in project for 7 years and oldest black resident. T.V. was stolen the previous week out of this apartment and she has been beaten. Discussion of removing bad tenants was discussed and all agreed it is difficult to get anyone out, unless harassed by other tenants." — Minutes from South Boston team meeting, July 15

"A few specific questions came out of the discussion: Assurances that the buses will be on time and go from the pickup point to the door of the school. A specific mandate to the police to enforce a no-loitering law within a certain distance of a school building. Also, loitering will be discouraged near liquor establishments in the area of either schools or transit points. This came out of a discussion about the problems with cafes, bars and liquor stores in the Dudley station area being open near school hours, and the concern of a number of people about the potential for violence. . . ." — Minutes from a Roxbury team meeting, August 6

As the summer pressed on, as time became a luxury, the details grew in number.

By August 26, the custodian at the Bradford Annex School had not yet received the wax and other cleaning supplies he needed to get the school ready. Room 6 of the Shaw Annex had a hole in the floor, and the school had no intercom system. The water bubblers were broken at the Thompson School. All over the city, the bus pickup points were as yet undecided. Nobody knew where some of the school personnel were.

That same day, the neighborhood team met again in Southie and was told, "Time is a factor. How many times do we have to say these things? A rumor control center is crucial. The phones have to be manned by creditable people and specialized people who are trained to give correct information and ask the right questions." The popular rumor that week in Southie was that the kids believed the police would not arrest them.

In Roxbury, the community agencies that had been born in the 1960's to integrate schools, to build community control, to help the elderly shop for food, to tell the kids to help the elderly and not mug them, to run security systems in the neighborhoods, were getting together at Freedom House to set up a system, to insure that whatever happened in Southie or Dorchester, or wherever, the white kids coming into Roxbury would be safe. They invited the people from Southie. But the few people from Southie who wanted to go were afraid that their neighbors would think them Quislings.

Both the pro- and antibusing elements in Kevin White's office were worried. There had been confusion in the spring and early summer. Outside "experts," brought in from Maryland and Michigan communities that had integrated, could not believe what they saw in Boston — confusion, created largely by a division of authority between the mayor and the school committee and perpetuated by the school committee's insistence on sabotaging Garrity's order.

By the time the mayor's office was set to move in June, school was out, and the mayor's aides sat by helplessly, while the school department did nothing. William Leary, the Boston-bred and Harvard-educated superintendent, was hamstrung by the politics of the school committee. When he proposed that Bill Reid, the respected, white-haired headmaster of South Boston High School, be named to coordinate Phase One, the school committee voted him down. The school committee lingered as long as possible over the $8 million budget to implement the plan. The budget included summer training programs in human relations for school personnel. Leary had to plan it in the spring; he had to decide who was going to be trained. The budget was dated April 10, 1974. Leary was telling Schwartz he had to see the mayor. Earlier, the mayor had no desire to see Leary — "What the hell am I gonna see him for? I don't even know my own role yet." Finally, the mayor asked Schwartz to set up a meeting between him and Leary and nobody else. On April 15, Leary appeared in White's office. White reportedly told Leary, "You have to make a choice.

You're the superintendent. You tell the politicians to stay the hell out. I don't want to run desegration. If you tell me you're gonna run it, I'll give you whatever support you need. But I don't want to hear it from the committee."

The committee didn't send the special budget over to the mayor's office until early June, and there it stayed for a month, while the mayor's aides tried to get state and federal desegregation funds to ease the impact of the $8 million on the city's taxpayers. Meanwhile, Louise Day Hicks, now a city councilwoman, was vowing there was no way the council would appropriate that money for busing.

As the mayor's office tried to wangle the feds and state to pay half of Leary's budget, White sent the other half to the council July 12. The day before he told the school committee to advance itself the money it needed, and if no federal or state money came in, he'd make up the difference.

The first training workshop was supposed to begin July 15, and Leary was scheduled to go on vacation July 12. Based on the mayor's letter to the school committee, Leary called in an aide and told her to go ahead with the workshops and pay union scale for attendance. The response was overwhelming, because getting union scale to sit in some workshops in the summer was very enticing, and a lot of middle management school officials who didn't need the training ended up in the workshops. The whole idea of carefully selected people went out the window. And when the workshop was four days old, school committeeman John Kerrigan insisted the committee had never given permission for the whole thing and wouldn't approve of anyone getting paid.

As Bill Edgerton got more deeply involved in the neighborhood teams, he became shocked at the response of a school system that long ago had stopped thinking on its own, not because it was composed of dummies, but because the politicians who ran the system created that atmosphere. By late August, Edgerton was angry.

"As of today, there are still no guidelines for principals on safety, no book on how to run an orientation. It's more than just opening day you have to plan for, or just the first few months. As far as we can tell, no master plan has been developed. We've still got some monumental planning to do. In June and July, the school department saw no reason to send out letters to parents. Now, they do. We met with them on the issue of bus monitors, and one said, 'I don't know who's handling that,' and another said, 'I guess I am.' On the subject of training, one of them said, 'They could show up a few days earlier.' There's no plan. It's catch-as-catch-can."

John Coakley, the school administrator who had been punished for not digging into his pocket at testimonial time, was running an educational planning center. He and his aides were competent, but their task was overwhelming.

School department inaction and resistance was only part of the problem facing the city officials trying to preserve both Boston and their boss, the mayor.

The rapid transit system, the Massachusetts Bay Transportation Authority, insisted it needed twelve weeks to get ready to provide buses, and, gee, this was such a bad time, and there are these union policies (the MBTA counts 28 separate unions) in which seniority determines the bus runs, and a lot of notice and training were needed. As it turned out, only 80 runs would be provided by the system, and the city had to contract with private bus companies for more than 400 runs a day. There was a serious question whether these companies could properly train drivers for what might amount to combat runs.

The liquor industry presented another problem. There were 135 liquor licenses operating in Southie alone. Some of them were perennial trouble spots. Some were watering holes for Southie's branch of the syndicate — the Irish hoods who rip off warehouses, hijack trucks, deal in stolen goods, and hold very strong opinions on the issue of race. They got visited by local cops, who know who's who. "Your regular customers aren't gonna be out on the street when school opens," some were told. "You know what we're talking about. We'll close you down. If we can keep you open, we can close you down."

To make sure everybody understood what was going down, Eddie King, who managed the Southie Little City Hall, arranged a meeting at noon one August day at the station house between Kevin White and a pack of influential tavern owners. Most indicated they would cooperate, and one guy looked at the mayor and said he'd bring his kids to whatever school they wanted to go to and he'd get pinched if he had to. "Will you get pinched with me?" he asked Kevin.

The mayor said, "If you tell me who has been pinched, and when it's ever helped, I'll get pinched with you. Have you seen Louise get pinched? Kerrigan? George Wallace?"

A couple of alleged syndicate figures were in the room. They weren't about to get involved, because they couldn't afford to. Social protest isn't good for business; it attracts too much attention. But if any Southie kids were going to get locked up, they might show up with bail money. They were fathers too, and they were antibusing. Nobody realized that day how important that segment of Boston society would become in the busing crisis.

The police and the black community organizations in Roxbury were not the only operatives gathering rumors, tips, information. By the last week in July, the Youth Activities Commission had workers out on the street. Using its own client caseload of 3,000 tough white and black and Puerto Rican kids, YAC found out what schools they were going to and sent letters to the parents ("By working together, we can ensure a safe school year for all our young"). YAC workers followed up the letters by knocking on doors, meeting the parents, and bringing the white and black kids together down to a camp on Cape Cod, where the white and black street kids raised a fair amount of hell — but did so separately. It was not integrated hell. Yet, as school approached, a lot of those kids kept meeting on neutral turf in Boston, talking about bus trips or a dance or an overnight camping trip that they all decided they'd like to do. By late August, the YAC workers were assigned their radio beepers and their schools.

Edgerton and Rich Kelliher were setting up an information center in what used to be the Civil Defense headquarters in the basement of City Hall, the bunker. Here, the school department and the mayor's aides, the police and YAC and fire department would all be assigned phones, would pool information and try to stifle rumors. Coakley, Edgerton, and Kelliher would run the show and answer to Kiley. As they began putting the room together, tacking maps up on the walls, installing switchboards and phones and police radios, Kiley sat six floors up in his office and worried.

"The data base we're working with worries me. I'm not sure the buses will be on time or on the right routes or that the pupil assignments will be done within margins of error. I'm not sure the overcrowding at certain schools is being taken care of. Our role is to badger, kick, scream, shout, gouge, ask people 100 times whether something's been done. I don't doubt Leary, but I worry about the bureaucracy. And I worry about the cops finding themselves at South Boston High School and Jamaica Plain High School and Hyde Park High School and having to move into a crowd with trespass orders, and it's Joe Murphy, their next-door neighbor, and they're struck with questions of conscience — or the cops whose kids are in school or whose brother's kids are in school."

As August closed, the black community pulled together, the white community prepared a gala antibusing march for early September, and the meetings in City Hall, at schools, in the neighborhoods escalated, as the clock ticked away Boston's time.

Schwartz's school reform proposal that would decentralize the bureaucracy, wipe out the school committee, create neighborhood and school district councils, and make the whole system answerable to the mayor was doomed by the busing controversy. The White administration itself was ambivalent over it. Some members worked hard with Schwartz in the unsuccessful effort to win a referendum on it. Others sat back and did nothing. The mayor's election machinery only half-turned in the effort. Opponents linked the plan to busing, and it would go down to defeat.

Meanwhile, out in the precincts and the parishes and the neighborhoods, people rose to their own version of the Boston legacy.

"The Rev. Martin Luther King, Jr., rose to fame fundamentally because he taught his followers to resort to civil disobedience, that is, to refuse to honor or obey laws they considered to be unfair, unreasonable, etc. For this, his birthday has now been made into a State Holiday by our respected leaders. And many of our leading liberals in Washington are working to make it a national holiday. This amounts to giving official and legal sanction to the philosophy of civil disobedience. Very well then. The people of South Boston, Hyde Park and similar communities would be quite justified in resorting to civil disobedience in September of 1974." — "Patricia Henry" — A postcard

ELEVEN

August 27: Kevin Visits
the Trenches

THE MORNING BEGINS cold and cloudy. At night, the moon was full, and the tides were quite high. The waters of Massachusetts Bay were a deep bluish gray, and there were waves breaking over the jetties. On the coast, the last week of August is often a gloomy week, with hints of the clammy winter to come. Later, in September, the muggy days return, but today, the early morning is cool, comfortable, and foreboding. The boulevards along the beaches in and out of the city were crowded all summer with youth. On the last week, only a few sit on the walls and railings or lean against cars, their summer friends and loves and enemies gone, the prospect of dull school or a dull job or no job at all awaiting them. Now, another school year would begin soon, but this would be different, for they are at a loss. As bad as school was, it was a place to go. Now, the only place to go is the corner. Lots of idle young men with just enough dough for cigarettes and booze, hanging on the corner, was a prospect that frightened everyone in charge of making busing work. Already in the morning paper, there are forebodings. The school department said it needs 317 bus monitors and 500 aides. "We are having problems in recruiting them," William Leary said. In the white neighborhoods, the people talked of boycotting the schools. It was clear, said the sources of intelligence on the streets, that many parents would boycott for at least a few days, possibly a couple of weeks, and that at least some kids would never go to Boston schools again.

Kevin White has been drinking coffee with groups of men and women who are as scared as he. He goes to their neighborhood and sits down and tries to convince them that Boston need not fall apart, and he promises to keep the peace.

This morning, he showers and shaves at his Beacon Hill home to get ready for Coffee Hour No. 75. Already, some of his aides are getting to work at City Hall. These are not the issues guys, but the men drawn out of the wards of the city who pledge their fealty to Kevin White the man more than to White's stand on housing, transportation, race relations, or anything else. They are mostly Irish. They drive him places. They make sure the cars and the car radios work. They occasionally drive Henry Hagan's widow or Mother Galvin's daughter Kathryn to and from the Beacon Hill townhouse. Some of them are plainclothesmen, and protect the mayor's body. Some of them sit in the outer office and talk to those people who insist that the mayor of Boston is the only man in the world they will talk to about this broken sewer, or this new invention, or this rumor they just heard. Some of them are with the mayor and his family so much, over at the Beacon Hill house so much, that they are part of the family. The mayor likes them. He can relax with them, knowing they will not bug him, as other aides must, about rent control or revenue sharing.

Michael Feeney is one of seven boys. His father is a police sergeant in Hyde Park. Michael earned a teaching degree from Boston State University and ran for representative in 1972 and lost. He worked his way up in the city by starting in the Parks and Recreation Department and then joined Peter Meade, now an up-and-coming young aide to the mayor, in running the new community schools. Michael Feeney does not have long hair or bushy sideburns. He has a boyish freckled Irish face, and he is always conservatively dressed in a suit. He has a very good sense of humor, but if he is joking around, and the mayor appears, Michael Feeney braces, because he likes Kevin White, and he is loyal to Kevin White, and if all the Michael Feeneys of the world suddenly disappeared, leaving only the issue-oriented professionals, the mobile technocrats, every political administration would die.

Michael Feeney's small office looks out on the Old State House, a colonial red brick building that sits catercorner from the site of the

Boston Massacre. Mike Feeney can look down from his office at the streets where Irish fought with "Prod," where Abolitionists rioted to free black men entrapped by U.S. marshals.

This morning, neither Feeney nor Bernie Callahan, one of the plainclothesmen assigned to the mayor, is thinking about Boston history. They are, instead, making some history of their own, a middle-aged plainclothesman and a fresh-faced young man, taking the city's mayor to his coffee hours so Kevin White can listen to his constituency, get back in touch with the neighborhoods that elected him, pick up some information and thunder at a staff meeting, "Don't tell me! I've been *out* there."

Bernie Callahan has been on the force eighteen years. Until almost three years before, he worked the downtown district. Where were you born, Bernie? "I'm a Brighton boy, your Honor." He lives there still, out in that northwestern tip of Boston that inserts itself into the more affluent suburbs of Newton and Brookline.

Brian Savage has just come in. Savage also always wears a suit. He also can be a wise guy, except when those people call, the people with the rumors, the inventions, and the complaints. Then he is very polite. He is also very loyal, and that gets him a lot of gaff in the neighborhood. "I'm leaving for work this morning," Brian says, "and a neighbor says to me, 'Are you still with the city?' I said, 'Yeah, with the mayor.' He says, 'Oh, with the boss, hah? Yeah, well hit him in the face for me, willya?' Oh they love him in St. Brendan's."

St. Brendan's is a parish in Ward 16. Ward 16 is in Dorchester, and in Ward 16, they are very worried about black folks. "Kerrigan country," says Feeney, who also lives in the ward. It is that ward to which Kevin White travels today to drink coffee and get yelled at.

Feeney, Bernie, and two other plainclothesmen, Tommy Newcomb and Frank Wilson, pile into one of the staff cars parked behind City Hall and take off up a back street that runs between what used to be the West End and what used to be Scollay Square. The car climbs the back of Beacon Hill, swings behind the State House and then onto Mt. Vernon Street, well appointed with trees, townhouses, modern gaslights, and brick sidewalks. As they pull up to 158 Mt. Vernon, almost at the end of the street, Tommy, who warms people with the original Irish grin, looks at the mayor's car and laughs, "The meter maids tagged him again." The mayor's car is the only one parked on the wrong side of the street, as the city street sweeper comes around the corner.

Inside the house is a small foyer and hallway leading to the rear, and a white staircase leading up to the second floor. On the floor of the foyer is a red rug, with an oriental rug on top of it. There is nothing gaudy here, just the tasteful hand of Billy Galvin's well-brought-up daughter. Against one wall is a small table, with fresh-cut flowers in a vase on top of the table and a painting of a ship on the wall overhead. The mayor of the city comes downstairs, with his jacket over his arm and his tie still askew. He had been running again this morning at the Y, and he is tired.

"Gimme that sheet quick," he says to Feeney. "Where we headed?"

"Dorchester," Bernie answers, and Feeney gives the mayor an information sheet prepared by the Dorchester Little City Hall. The mayor reads it, as the car moves south through the city "Background on hostess: Adjie Hurley, sister-in-law of Dave Hurley, and husband Michael is a Boston policeman. Very anti-busing." Dave Hurley works in City Hall, specifically in the Real Property Department. He too will be out in Dorchester to greet the mayor, along with Joe Egan, the Dorchester Little City Hall manager.

The car pulls around a corner and onto a typical Dorchester street of wooden homes, duplexes many of them, built close together, with miniature front lawns and adequate backyards. Adjie Hurley lives in a brown wooden house, on which some renovation is being done. Inside, the rooms are small and clean. It is not a luxurious place to live; it is not a classy place like 158 Mt. Vernon Street, but it is a very nice place to live, and Adjie Hurley wants to make sure she continues to do so. As the mayor is directed to a set of stairs leading down to a small basement playroom, Adjie Hurley comes out of her kitchen, smiles, and says, "Welcome, Mr. Mayor, my house is your house." She is neither nervous nor overwhelmed. She has been in the thick of controversy and neighborhood issues too long to be overwhelmed.

"I hope I get outta here alive," the mayor tells her and proceeds downstairs, and as he goes down, Adjie Hurley says, "You said a mouthful, Mr. Mayor."

Downstairs, seated around a long table that takes up much of the room, are the neighbors, mostly women, but a couple of men, including an Eastern European immigrant who took a day off from work to be here. On another, smaller table is a cake and some doughnuts, which the mayor grabs and starts serving. His jacket is off again; soon he will pull his tie down from his throat. The bulkhead door is closed to keep the kids outside. At first, there is very small talk, some discomfort. Some faces are warm and ready to be friendly. Others are hard, ready to be confronted, ready for argument. "Here, Kevin," says one of the harder faces, "have a napkin." A strange city, this Boston. They regularly ticket the mayor's car, shove him a napkin, call him by his first name, and, as they are about to do, argue like hell with him face-to-face.

"Is everyone here?" Kevin asks, ready to take charge.

"We got six more buses coming," somebody jokes.

The mayor is eating. He says he hasn't eaten at home. A woman named Loretta says, "You deserve a raise if you can't afford breakfast at home." The mayor gets a Marlboro, and a woman lights it for him. He puffs and lets out the smoke and breathes deeply and begins Coffee Hour No. 75.

"I'm willing to talk about anything you want to talk about. I didn't come here to yes you to death, and you didn't come here to smile and let me have coffee and then disappear. If I don't have the answers to your questions, I'll get them, and if I can't, I'll let you know."

One lady produces a prepared list of topics — federal money for neighborhoods, busing, street lights, elderly, and who's on welfare that doesn't deserve it. He takes busing first, and it's busing that monopolizes this coffee hour. They get onto the welfare recipients and crime in the streets and other things, but every time, it comes back to busing.

"There's only two things that can be done. Abide by the order, or don't." He is ready to tell them the city won't persecute them if they don't; he knows they need an escape valve for the anger and frustration, but he never gets to that, because as soon as he has said, "or don't," a woman says, "What if you don't?"

Kevin tells her, "The truant officer won't come and take your child." Then he sighs audibly, "But I don't know. . . . I've been against busing. I don't say it for your benefit, I don't say it just now. I was against it for nine years. . . . You can't shoot the judge or bury your head in the sand. . . . We went to court, and we hired James St. Clair."

Loretta charges that the city was asked to provide lawyers for the court appeal last winter to overturn the Racial Imbalance Law, but that the city reacted too late to help. He jumps at her. "Rumors," he complains. They will destroy the city, rumors will. "Was the lawyer hired before or after the march on the State House?" she asks him. "Before," he snaps and pauses. "Surprised you, didn't it?"

"Yes," says Loretta.

"And $200,000 is a lot of money," he says. He is playing a card now. At the last minute last February, he changed his mind about the appeal. He knew it could come to nothing. People like Schwartz had argued against it, counseling that it was a waste of money, that it would raise false hopes. But Quealy and Barbara Cameron and Frank Tivnan had convinced him otherwise. White folks, some of them anyway, were indicating that Kevin wasn't giving them every legitimate opportunity, and people like Dapper O'Neil and John Kerrigan were out in the neighborhoods, campaigning for office and reinforcing such feelings. So, Kevin White had gambled that politically it made sense to fund the appeal. The *Globe,* which would win a Pulitzer Prize for its coverage of school integration, attacked the mayor for "taking the choke" and wondered how he could have done that, seeing as how people's fears were beginning to subside. Months later, those people, whose fears hadn't quite subsided, would picket the *Globe.* Some would overturn *Globe* trucks. Somebody began shooting rifle bullets through *Globe* windows. But, earlier, the *Globe* carped, and the mayor went on to a summer full of coffee hours.

Now, the mayor is throwing that card on the long table of a playroom in a predominantly white neighborhood, in a precinct and a ward that had favored Louise over him in his 1971 sweep, in an area that Feeney had called "Kerrigan country." And with some, the card looks good, but with others, it means nothing.

"You could've done it, Kevin!" another woman insists. He could have stopped busing, she says. Yes sir, he could've. "We could've won it, if you was with us. If you got on TV and said you were with us, and Sargent backed us, our children would've been in the right schools today."

If she means what she says, then she does not understand. There are so many who do not understand. It is a federal court order, and no mayor, no school committee, no governor, no U.S. Senator, no President is going to stop it now, whether they're on television, on the street, or in a playroom in Ward 16. And nobody could have stopped it a year ago. The whites of Boston had been misled. The old Racial Imbalance Law was academic, pointless. A federal judge was ruling the inevitable.

"Hey," the mayor answers, "if I was going to bag the case, I wouldn't have got James St. Clair as the lawyer. . . . The school committee told you there'd be no busing. What did they do for you? They didn't move three feet, didn't move three feet. . . ."

The mayor talks about the new schools he built, how he's built more schools, fire stations, anything than any previous mayors, including Curley. He lists the schools, but Loretta seems unimpressed. "Those were pacifiers for the blacks," she says. He names the schools in white neighborhoods. "Is the Murphy in a black community? Is the . . ."

"What's the good?" two or three of them ask at once. "Our kids can't go to them now."

The Eastern European man delivers a tirade against black crime.

"You can't walk down Washington Street anymore." They get onto the subject of blacks, and by now, almost everyone wants to talk, to let it out, while the man who symbolizes power is here. They learned a long time ago that a mayor is a boss. They learned that in the lousy textbooks used by public schools and they learned it on the street. So if he's the boss, how come he can't do anything about all these problems?

One lady says she moved into a block, and a black neighbor said he was glad she moved in instead of "some nigger." She says, "*He* said that! I didn't. *He* used that word."

They have a black neighbor up the street. He's okay, they say. But they paint a picture of Roxbury and North Dorchester, a picture of endless violence and depravity. Some are married to cops and firefighters, and the stories brought back home are not the stories of the black guy who is trying to get a mortgage or the black kid who's going to night school.

Over in Roxbury, over in Ward 14 in Dorchester, there are blacks absolutely convinced that white America lives like the Partridge Family, and that people like the ones in this playroom must have it made. The little worlds of Boston orbit by themselves, occasionally brushing with sparks of violence, occasionally exchanging emissaries of goodwill who find common ground, but rarely touching.

"There are two choices," Kevin repeats, for they are back to busing. "You send them to school or you don't. If you don't, there's nothing I can do about it. I've heard guys stand up at meetings and say don't send the kids to school, and that's okay, but what about October, November, December? Maybe you don't go for the first few days, to see if it's safe . . ."

They say it will not be safe. They fear the black neighborhoods. They live in tough neighborhoods, but they fear the blacks.

"Busing, black or white, is personal to the mother," Kevin says. "How would you like to be one of seventy blacks going to Charlestown?"

"Or Southie?" says a woman. They nod and agree. Southie is bad, they seem to feel. Their street doesn't look much different from the streets in the upper end of Southie; the people don't look much different, but there are people in Dorchester who see people in Southie as irrational, violent, less classy. The little worlds orbit.

A woman, smiling sweetly, talking softly, is worried about Judge Garrity's insistence that Boston hire a lot more black teachers. "They're going to the bottom of the barrel to get teachers of insufficient backgrounds." Kevin tells her, "You're assuming they're not qualified. The blacks have fought for black teachers. The Irish did it fifty years ago. There's nothing wrong with that."

The man from Eastern Europe jumps in. "They don't want to work hard." A woman says, "They want it handed to them."

For Kevin White, that's a cue for something he has told other such groups around other tables with other cups of coffee in other neighborhoods. He lights his fourth cigarette and stares off at a wall and rambles about ironies.

"It's funny. It goes from generation to generation. People say why should we do it? For the people who had to fight in the war — that was five years ripped out of them. For me, I was just a kid playing in the streets. I didn't really understand the Depression, but my old man tells me it was the most horrible thing he ever went through. Every generation has a burden to bear. Well, for me, it's a lousy time to be mayor, and it's a lousy time to be a senior in high school or the mother of an elementary school child. I don't know why these things happen. It's just the way it is. For our kids, it'll be a different problem.

"When I had to give my first inaugural speech, I asked my staff to dig up all the inaugural speeches ever given in Boston, because I didn't know what the hell I was supposed to say. There were only forty-five of them, so I read them one night. And I came across a speech by a Mayor Lyman, a mayor of Boston. I don't remember the year. And he started out saying how proud he was to be mayor of such a great city, and how the city had made great progress and all the other baloney mayors say, and then he said, 'There is in our midst an undisciplined people' and how we should send them back to where they came from. He was talking about my grandfather. He was talking about the Irish."

Kevin's eras are fouled up, but he doesn't know it, and they don't know it, and it isn't very important, really, that Lyman was talking about immigrants earlier than Kevin White figured. What is important is the irony, and the people sitting around the table are nodding their heads, half smiling and half curious.

"Now," he says, "there is no reason why the Irish should treat the blacks the way the Yankees treated the Irish, and I even hear blacks say 'spics.'" They nod and mumble with familiarity. Yeah, they know that. They've heard of such things.

"Hey, I'm trying to hold this together. I don't want the whites to leave. If we can get through this, we can hold it together. Taxes didn't go up last year, and they're not going up this year, and they won't go up next year, certainly not more than four dollars, if they do. . . . If you leave, this place will become like Ward 14, blockbusting. You'll go out to the suburbs, and you'll find the taxes are high, and they don't even have sewer lines — they're still working off septic tanks!"

Now, Loretta is saying she expects nothing from any politicians — "Louise, Kerrigan, none of them. They haven't done anything." She talks about visiting the Martin Luther King School in Roxbury, and as she talks, she gets more excited. "They had the poor kids in a gym, with a chain on the door! Firecrackers were going off. We heard stories about teachers being beaten up."

Another woman pleads, "We don't want disruption."

A third offers her own set of ironies. "The black and white kids got along okay at the Grover Cleveland. Now, they're throwing out the black kids who went there, and bringing in black kids who are hostile. I was one of the parents who came to you, asking for that new school addition. My kid had to sit on the floor in the old school. When a kid was absent, that's how he got a seat." And now, their kids will be bused from the schools they fought for.

One of the kids comes down the stairs. He is a little boy, and his name is Douggie, and he says in a loud voice, "Are you having a party?" and everyone laughs, and Kevin White says, "Yeah, they're hanging the mayor."

"Kevin," Adjie says, "I had trouble getting people here. They said, 'I'll get him in the voting booth.' "

"Hey, I grew up in politics. I know the end for all of us is defeat. I can deal with that. I'm forty-four, and I look fifty-eight. . . ."

Adjie says, "I'd work for you, if I felt in my heart that you represented all the people, if you took a stand and said, 'Don't go to the schools.' You're one of us, Kevin."

Kevin White says he is one of everybody's. He says he argues for the whites in the black community and for the blacks in the white community.

"There'll be a black mayor someday, and the city won't fall apart," he tells them.

"It won't be our city anymore," one says.

"That's what the Yankees said about the Irish," he answers.

"It's not the same," they are saying. "It's not the same."

"The Irish," one says, "were not dangerous."

The mayor says he's worried about the city being torn apart. Loretta sighs, "I don't see how we can get out of this."

The mayor looks off to the wall and says, "It'll be a white kid and a black kid fighting over a book neither one wants to read."

"Mr. Mayor, do you know what's causing this?" the Eastern European says. "In the whole country?" The mayor looks at him. "Communists," he tells the mayor.

That one was inevitable. Onward and upward. He turns to them and asks, "Assume busing didn't exist. Would you stay here?"

"Yes," says Adjie. "I was born in Boston. I love it. I don't want suburbia. This is my home. I want the city, the convenience of the city. People in suburbia need buses to transport their kids to school. Here, you pay taxes for those conveniences. You buy a house and you ask about three things — the school, the church, and the shopping. This is an integrated neighborhood. Blacks live right on the corner. . . ." She goes on to crime in Roxbury. Her husband the policeman knows what's going down; the press is hushing up black crime. Loretta jumps in — yes, a lot of incidents are hushed up. They don't trust the press. "I know," she insists, "there are teachers carrying guns. I *know* that."

The mayor of Boston complains, "I still don't have a list of who's to be bused. I still don't know who's being bused where." But he makes his promise. "It's my job as mayor of *all* the people to make sure of safety. . . . If you can get twenty parents together who want to send their kids to school, get them on a bus. Don't walk. Don't ever walk."

They are really asking him what they should do. They're not challenging him any longer. They're pleading. They're scared, and they're asking their mayor, like a kid asks his father, what should they do?

"I guess I'd probably say, hey, don't send them the first week or so. Find out what it's like, who the teacher is, and after two weeks, test it."

He has stayed longer than he was scheduled. He has to do it all over again in another precinct of Dorchester.

Now, he is saying goodbye on the small front porch of Adjie Hurley's house. The women have followed him out the door, including two women from suburban Weymouth, who say they want to know how to handle busing if it comes to them. The Dorchester women look around their neighborhood. "We don't want to lose this, Kevin. You read your liberal papers, Kevin, they don't know what's going on. *We* know, Kevin. We're the *real* people."

In the car, he is sweaty and worn down. This has been a tough coffee hour. "What I'm trying to do is get their confidence. They feel nobody knows what they're saying. You've got to prepare them for changes they don't want, take them over blind terrain. They won't go, unless they've got confidence in the leader."

Later that day, in the early evening, Adjie and Loretta have gone downtown to pick up their husbands, and they are all sitting in one car behind City Hall. They are talking about how a minority controls a majority in the country, about a biased press. Loretta says of the mayor's visit, "He's just campaigning. We're not stupid." And Adjie says, "The voters aren't dumb."

Sixteen days to busing.

Thirteen months to Kevin White's next election.

TWELVE

August 29: Who's In Charge?

IN AN OLD HIGH SCHOOL building that sits on a strip of parkland called the Fens, the Youth Activities Commission gathers around its own long table in a second-floor meeting room. Paul McCaffrey, a tall, muscular man who grew up in Roxbury's Irish Mission Hill neighborhood, wants a neighborhood rundown from his white and black street workers.

"We're supposed to meet with a principal," says a youth worker covering the racially mixed Jamaica Plain, "but we just find out she's returning *tomorrow*."

All over the city, similar reports have come in during the summer, reports of school officials on vacation, away, unreachable, indisposed, as if this were just a normal summer between school years, as if nothing startling or dangerous were about to unfold.

From Hyde Park, the news is not much better. The youth workers have contacted black students scheduled to be bused into Hyde Park, a large, lower-to-middle-income white ward that housed Catholics who had lived in Southie and Dorchester and Roxbury and Jews who had lived in Dorchester and Mattapan.

They were having less success with Hyde Park whites. "We're start-ing to make contact with Hyde Park parents, and they're not," the youth worker pauses, "well, well, very cooperative. But we got a list last week and we've got two workers knocking on doors, about a hun-dred doors or so. The response is noncooperative. They don't wanna talk with anybody. They don't wanna go to any meetings. They don't wanna know about any meetings, and they're not gonna send their kids to school."

"Any positive response?" Paul asks.

"Maybe ten."

"That's a start. You only have a week. Drop everything else and bang," he urges, sinking his right fist into his left palm.

"We're concerned that most kids in our area will be walking," says the Jamaica Plain man. "We're trying to identify spots where kids from different racial backgrounds will be in contact. We're worried about Forest Hills. That's been a trouble spot in the past."

Now, the Hyde Park youth worker is saying, "A lot of kids in Hyde Park are going to parochial schools outside Boston. I know four families — seven children — who were going to public school last year and are now in suburban parochial schools — in Canton, in Milton. I think some Jamaica Plain kids are going to St. Mary's in Brookline. And every night in JP, there's a parade of cars, flying flags and signs, 'Impeach Kennedy' and 'Stop Busing,' and beeping horns, but this is not attracting too many people."

"Every night?" Paul asks.

"Yeah."

"Good."

"Good?"

"Yeah," says Paul, with more hope than realism, "by opening day, they'll be tired."

A black worker reports from Roxbury. "At the King School, we got the names of ten kids to work with, but they're all being transferred *out*."

So much is still unprepared. So many questions hang in the air. Some never get answered. Some get answered two or three different ways. Just yesterday, at the South End team meeting, the fire depart-ment representative asked if a certain decision had been made. "Noth-ing final," said Pedro Mendez, the team leader. "What can I say?" the fire fighter asked rhetorically. "Until they come up with final things, we can't do anything."

And here again today, the confusion is evident. Out there in school bureaucracy land, people of responsibility are either avoiding decisions or passing the buck. The whole political–civil service–union-protected system has operated that way for generations; now that a crisis has been thrust upon it, there is no reason to believe that it will operate any differently.

It is frustrating for McCaffrey and his workers. They do not pretend to be bureaucrats. The workers understand the streets and the kids and the neighborhoods. They are like good soldiers. They're willing to follow humane orders, if the orders make sense. What does seem to make sense to them is what they're doing — or trying to do — now, to keep in touch with those 3,000 street kids and try to work through those kids to their families and to other youths. But it is not easy. There is too much fear out in the land, too much suspicion built into the minds of Bostonians. There have been too many West Ends.

THIRTEEN

September 3: Southie

ON A SHELF in the shining new South Boston branch library are, according to a label, "Spanish Books." There are about 60 of them. On another shelf are "Lithuanian Books," and there are 104 of those. The Lithuanians, like the Poles, have their own church in Southie. The Latins do not. The Latins, and they are few, live in or near the D Street Project. Also living in and near the D Street Project are young whites who like to firebomb the Latins back to the South End or Columbia Point. There may be more books for the Spanish-speaking in the Southie library than there are Spanish for the books in Southie.

Today, there is a team meeting in Southie's new library, in the meeting room. The trouble might not begin in Southie. It could begin at the overcrowded and previously troubled Dorchester High, or at some intersection in Jamaica Plain, where white and black and Latin bump, or in tense, black Roxbury, where trouble in the schools occurs so often that some people think it's a regular course of study. But not one person arriving for this meeting doubts the potential for trouble in Southie.

The team members arrive in groups, and a rear door is opened to the meeting room, a small auditorium that could serve for readings and literary meetings. But the mothers, the local fire chief, the Little City Hall personnel, the local anti-poverty director, the cops, and the eight priests are not here for a poetry reading.

"There's all kinds of rocks, debris, stuff around the high school that could be used in times of trouble to stone the buses," a man tells them, and he asks for their help in cleaning it up. "Maybe if you could chip in a half a day, we could clean it up. It's extremely important. It looks like a dump."

A priest says the clergy have been preaching peace, if not integration, then for Christ's sake, peace. "We're urging a peaceful opening. Yesterday, and the following Sunday, we are preaching on this at the churches. We put out a statement. Beyond that, we'll be there at opening day, at pickup points, to lend our moral support."

There are so many imponderables, so many sensitive points.

One of the alternate routes away from busy, congested Andrew Square involves a bridge, the safety of which is in question. District Six Police Captain Arthur Cadegan, tall, lean, dour, and Irish, says the Metropolitan District Commission cops say it's safe, but "We want it in writing. If not, people in the black community will say we're trying to kill black children, taking them over an unsafe bridge." Yet, if the bars are full, and the day is hot, and the tempers are high among the corner b'hoys, an unsafe bridge might be safer than Andrew Square.

"My son is going to the Gavin," a mother says. The Gavin is a middle school, or junior high, in Southie. "He gets off one block from the Gavin. Will he be protected?"

Cadegan tells her, "Police will be in the area. But it's physically impossible to have police at every bus stop."

Another mother asks about bus breakdowns.

"They'll be going out as an Army convoy," Cadegan says. "If one breaks down, it'll be obvious to the others. They're not going to be floating all over the city. They have regular routes. They should have radios, but I don't know if they have channels authorized by the Federal Communications Commission."

What happens, asks another, when a child takes sick? And everyone who offers an opinion seems to disagree with everyone else as to whose responsibility it is to get the child home. For years, anti-busing leaders have raised the cry of the sick child far from home and have been pooh-poohed by integrationists and liberals. Now, it is September 3, nine days before busing, and there is still fear and confusion over this very same point.

When they exhaust that problem there is yet another. Fire Chief

Bob Greene tells them, "The big problem is false alarms, both within the school and at pickup points. These could raise havoc. If we are tied up at South Boston High School for a false alarm and someone needs oxygen at O and Broadway . . . And we're concerned about small fires at schools. We're not worried about the average person in South Boston, but some awful kooks could take advantage of something like this. So we're asking the Youth Activity workers to watch out and help us."

Ed King, the boyish-looking manager of the Little City Hall, talks about the signs painted on walls and sides of buildings. "Southie Pride. White Power. In Roxbury, it's Black Power. I don't mind, if they just keep on painting. I'll even buy them the paint. . . ." Paul McCaffrey a few days ago hoped the demonstrators would keep demonstrating and maybe they'd be tired. Today, Eddie King hopes they'll paint and do nothing else. They are both joking, because they both know better.

"I've heard they're gonna march up the hill in sheets like Ku Klux," one mother says. "I heard a laundry truck got all its stuff stolen."

Another mother looks at her and smiles, "I hope my kids bring the stuff home," and they all laugh.

Another asks, with a smile, if any Southie citizens have volunteered to be aides or bus monitors. She knows better. But another woman is troubled that there are none. "I think it's wrong. If it happens, there won't be anyone on the bus as concerned as we are." And the first woman explains, "We're afraid." They fear to volunteer. It would seem as if they were supporting busing. The anti-busing organization in Southie is disciplined right down to a precinct level. It is commanding more loyalty than any local politician can now boast. But with the loyalty comes a price.

A woman says her daughters say to her, "How come you're keeping us home? These children are gonna go and gonna wanna go. I'll keep my kids home two weeks. It's hard to keep them at home when they're seventeen. They're big, and I got to sit on them. I say to my boy, it's a good time to set an example, and he says, 'I'll show you a good example.' "

Cadegan preaches, "Anyone throwing a rock or bottle or a can of beer is really a coward, and we should pluck them out and give them swift justice. My concern is not the children, but the adults who show up at school. . . . We can handle the kids, but what about the women? Outside the school?"

A woman says "outsiders" could come in and make things worse, white "outsiders" from other neighborhoods, from suburbs.

Cadegan agrees. He nods his head. He knows that a lot of the people arrested at the St. Patrick's Day parade every year aren't from Southie. "Well, you know what goes on March seventeenth."

What goes on March 17, often, as Marty Gopen can testify, is trouble.

FOURTEEN

September 4: "The Talk Isn't Good"

THIS MORNING in Southie's Little City Hall, Eddie King is worried. His mood changes day by day or hour by hour, depending on events or on what he hears on the street. What he hears this morning is that three black guys showed up last night at Representative Ray Flynn's house, banged on the door and yelled for him. Flynn was out, and his wife yelled as much, but the three kept banging and jiggling the lock. She called the cops, and she called Ray Flynn's brother. Ray Flynn's brother found the other South Boston state rep, Mike Flaherty, and asked for help. Mike Flaherty sent his brother and some other guys down to Flynn's house to wait with Mrs. Flynn until her husband came home from an anti-busing meeting in East Boston. The police also showed up and Eddie King says Mrs. Flynn was hysterical, and Eddie's assistant, Dick Hogan, says Ray Flynn's wife is not the type to make up such a story.

"Rumors are gonna be our biggest problem," Eddie King says. "We'll try to quash them ourselves. When you find a wife who's hysterical and a brother crying for help, you know there's some truth to the rumor. Now I hear the De Mau Maus are coming in. I hope not. If they do, they'll never get out. I heard one black teacher was assaulted at Southie High and another had his window broken. My only bitch, and the parents' too, is I was told the rumor control center would be operating by today. We could've set it up already.

"Up to a couple of days ago, I was getting optimistic. But the things I've been hearing, this thing like Flynn last night, it spread like wildfire last night in town. I'm afraid things are gonna come apart."

Now King is worried that the story of the blacks banging on Flynn's door will really upset people. "They'll start arming, saying, 'We'll get those black bastards.' I'm just worried about the black guy coming home from work."

Hogan says his wife took their daughter to St. Brigid's Parochial School this morning "and all the women are talking about it." King looks at his watch. "It's quarter of eleven now, and I would say by 11:56, it'll be out to Brighton and making its way around West Roxbury. You can bet the Home and School Association is on the phone. Ray's had threats before. But he's scared now."

Yesterday, King and Hogan heard rumors that when the parochial schools opened today, there would be a demonstration at the Gate of Heaven School, because of people's anger at the Church for supporting busing and trying to shut the parochial schools to whites fleeing integration. There was even a rumor of Molotov cocktails. The rumors were unfounded. But each one must be dealt with.

"The leaders of the total boycott are talking nonviolence," King says. "But you hear other people talking violence, talking about stoning buses. The talk isn't good. They just don't wanna go. They're happy with their life-style here. They feel with the blacks coming in, it's a threat to their high school tradition. They prize tradition. 'I'm from Southie,' they say. It's not Irish. It's Southie, and Southie is Irish, Italian, Lithuanian, Pole."

Could black join that tradition?

"It's hard to say," says Eddie King. "The skin is the factor."

The skin and all that it implies. We are not very well off, but *they* are worse off. If they come here, then *we* will be worse off. They must not come here, and we must unite to make sure of that. The whites will chant, "ROAR — *United* . . . Will nevah be defeated!" In unity, there is strength, and in unity, there is the company of misery. In unity, there is pressure to conform, such pressure that Ed King is not so worried about what happens in Roxbury to a white Southie kid who decides to go to school in Roxbury, but what might happen to him when he gets home. "I know a couple of families who were threatened and insulted because they went to a meeting at the McCormack. The resistance is well organized. Don't forget, they've been fighting this thing for nine years, and in the last couple of years, they took a few pages from the mayor's election and set up precinct workers."

Back up town, in the bunker, the rumor control center that Eddie King is waiting for, Rich Kelliher is sucking in air about once every minute and a half, because a tooth is bothering him. He is supposed to see a dentist this afternoon, but he won't. There's just too much to do these last few days. Yesterday, he met with police, fire fighters, the Metropolitan District Commission police, who have some authority inside the city, the Massachusetts Bay Transportation Authority, and the Boston Housing Authority. Today, there will be more meetings, more problems. Rich Kelliher is convinced he will never ever be able to leave his bunker. And he is beginning to wonder about this bunker, these windowless rooms of concrete sunk below some of the oldest ground in America's oldest city, sunk into the hardened waste of the Ice Age. He looks up at the small vents and says, "I don't know how good the air support system is. We might all be dead by 1 A.M. Monday from a lack of oxygen."

Upstairs, in the corner office of the complex of rooms that flank the mayor's quarters, Bob Kiley is holding a 25-page booklet in his hands, the long overdue school department safety guidelines, and he is shaking his head in disbelief. The front page says August, but Kiley says the guidelines have just come out.

"It reads like the Russians after eighteen months in Stalingrad. They have a yellow alert, a white alert, and a red alert. If it weren't just a sticky situation, the *National Lampoon* could do a job on this. I doubt if the principals or anyone with any real life experience was involved in this. We pushed for these guidelines, and now I'm sorry I did. They don't define what an emergency is. They say move the students in the direction of their homes; if the students are waiting for buses, and there are problems, move them into the cafeteria, which means you've moved them out to move them all back in again. Yellow alert means lock all doors, all windows, pull the shades down, close down all scientific experiments, make sure the notes don't fall into the hands of the enemy. The whole mentality is staggering.

"It's unclear who has real authority. One paragraph says it's the principal. In another, it's the superintendent. In another, it seems to be both. When the police get called is obscure. The policy people are not talking to the guys who are doing things. They're already two weeks late. They did it in a vacuum. The next step would be to walk through it with the police. Now, there's no time."

The office next to Kiley's is occupied by Ira Jackson, a young, bright man who, by the age of twenty-three, had already served Ken Gibson, the black mayor of Newark, and for the last two years had been serving Kevin White. Jackson was not the most popular aide among others who served the mayor. He had come far quickly, and his manner rankled them. But one of the things that Jackson did very well was write speeches. The mayor had a tendency to junk speeches and say whatever came into his head, but when he used speeches, Jackson's were there. For the last couple of years, Jackson had been hunting up old FDR quotes to spice up Kevin's appeal to Democratic leaders across the nation. But all the goodwill built up since 1972 and all the political chits that might be owed would come tumbling down if Kevin White were smeared by busing in his own city. He would be smeared, if he suddenly led the anti-busing movement, yet if he took a strong integrationist stand, he could lose the mayor's office. Ira Jackson's job the last few days was to write a speech with which Kevin White could live, a speech the mayor will give Monday night, September 9, on television.

Jackson had asked other aides for ideas. The speech would continue the earlier decision to stick with the law and order issue, to commit the mayor to peace and public safety, rather than forced busing. Stress the safety of the kids, they urged. Stress that the issue is out of Kevin's hands, that the courts have spoken, based on the Constitution.

The mayor's speech is scheduled on the evening following a planned mass anti-busing demonstration downtown. The mayor should compliment the demonstrators on a peaceful march and differentiate between them and the bomb throwers. He should rally the city together against the suburbs, tell the people, "We're expected to fall on our face, but we'll show them!"

Today, Ira Jackson has just finished the speech. It cannot ignore the march, yet it cannot anticipate what will happen during that march and demonstration. As it turns out, no one would anticipate what would happen that day.

"We're trying to convey two things, the call to reason against violence and, without being hokey, to acknowledge the difficult time, the fact that Boston has played a unique role in history, that it's always done things in a different way.

"This gives him legitimacy at the outset. He's been out there five months, meeting mothers and fathers in their own homes. We cite the hardships and inconvenience. We talk about the suburbs escaping responsibility. He's come away from the coffee klatches with a visceral perception of the guy in Dorchester who sees the President and Vice

President resign in shame, who can't sell his house or afford to fix it, who now loses his choice of school, who can't keep hamburger on the table, and it's all coming down around him. In short, that guy's getting fucked. The mayor wants to turn it into a test of courage.

"I've seen every goddamn thing ever filmed or written about busing, but all of that is not appropriate now. This town has too much pride to do violence, because they're watching us? No, not that either. The appeal in the speech is let's do it for one another."

FIFTEEN

September 5, Night:
The Voice of Moderation

SOME HIGH SCHOOL kids in Southie have called a meeting for tonight to allow cops and other such adults to explain what they are trying to do with this busing business. It is a very responsible thing to do, and in South Boston, to do it takes a lot of guts, because, as Eddie King says, the resistance is well organized here and it brooks no deviation. The meeting is to be at the Tynan School, one of those new community schools that the mayor is so proud of.

The Tynan sits in the middle of East Fourth Street, which becomes a dead end at that point. All around it are neat, clean row houses. On one corner is a church and across from the church is a Catholic Youth Organization building where you can register for hockey. The Tynan School basketball courts are busy, but basketball is not what it is in Roxbury. There's Ray Flynn, who starred at Providence, but in Roxbury, the kids take basketball more seriously than almost anywhere, and there are many more Ray Flynns. Now, hockey — well, hockey is another matter. Southie is hockey and football crazy. Its lore centers around its high school athletes, for even with Connolly's Gym on

Broadway, boxing isn't what it used to be in the old days, but hockey and football are better than ever. If all the kids were to follow Judge Garrity's order, with Southie high school kids going to Roxbury, and Roxbury high school kids going to Southie, Roxbury would suddenly have one hell of a hockey team, and Southie would end up with one hell of a basketball team. And, of course, there would be an integrated football team. But nobody will know how such things would work out, because just about everybody from Southie has decided — or their parents have decided — that they are not going to Roxbury.

So, there are not really many kids here, and there are lots of vacant seats in the auditorium, and more than a third of those who do show up are mothers fighting busing and city officials and some men watching from the side and the press. The mothers are passing out pamphlets calling for everyone to participate Monday, September 9, in the big march.

A thin, wiry student, Paul Flynn, calls the meeting to order, says, "This meeting was called by me for information only," and motions to the police and other adult officials as "these guys up here" who are available to answer questions.

Bill Reid moves like a bear. He's growly. His bushy eyebrows hang over eyes that have dispatched messages of stern rebuke and kind retort. His hair and his eyebrows are thick and white. He is Spencer Tracy, the ideal Hollywood headmaster of some private school. Reid is the headmaster of South Boston High School, which bears no resemblance to any private school, except that it is a very proud place.

"We're here only to answer your questions. I will say this — the situation hasn't changed since March. If I were you students, I'd do what your parents tell you. I'm still a believer in the parents telling the kids what to do." The parents applaud. The kids snicker. And Reid goes on, big as a bear, canny as a fox, knowing how to talk to his people. "And, finally, if you do not come to school on opening day, be my guests that day at the beach." He half-smiles and turns away to applause. Bill Reid is telling them to stay away from school, unless they're going to classes.

Now, Charlie Barry is there. He is a police superintendent, and he looks the role, slim, unsmiling, short hair, soft in voice. "If your parents want you on the bus," he says, "they have every right to expect you to arrive safely and return safely, and it's the same with parents from other sections of the city. That's the job of the Boston Police Department. Our goal is to see to it that no student is injured."

Then, it's Arthur Cadegan's turn. "I lived here for over fifty years. And I can appreciate the attitude here, the temperament, the emotions, but one thing I cannot appreciate is someone throwing a rock, a missile. Our job is to keep it cool. I'll be meeting with your folks out on the street. We'll have a very fine time in September."

Michelle Morgan, a striking young woman who looks and acts older than her high school years, reminds the press "this is just an informational meeting." Again, from paranoid Southie, the message goes out — a constructive meeting does not mean support of busing. To the kids and the parents, she says, "If you have any questions, just ask. Don't be afraid of what your neighbor is going to say." There are no questions. The kids giggle or talk. So Michelle gets it going with a question, and then, finally, one of the women yells to Michelle, "Are *you* going on a bus?" Michelle says she's a senior and not assigned to a bus. "If you were a junior, would you?" the woman yells. Not even for the kids will there be any leeway from the hardliners. The pressures in Southie are indeed awesome.

"Ma'am," Michelle tells the lady, "we're here to discuss safety, not my being a junior." That gets applause, and it shows the recalcitrant ones that the shrikes need not dominate all the time. So the questions come, because there are kids who care.

"What if you miss the bus?"

"I suggest," Reid says, "you get home."

"What if you're in Roxbury, and you miss the bus?"

"Go back to the office."

"What happens if you're walking around school, and you have a knife or something on you. What happens to ya?"

"It's against the law. We will handle it with our own staff if possible."

"Will there be monitors to prevent trouble inside the hallways?"

Reid says there are, but "one thing that bothers me, though, is that I can get black mothers to go with their kids to South Boston, but I can't get white mothers to go with their kids to Roxbury. And this bothers me." And a woman yells out, "That's 'cause we're not going, Dr. Reid."

"Yay." Applause.

Reid talks about issues that are rarely discussed by those who view integration in the cosmic sense. "At this time, it doesn't appear we'll have a lot of hockey players from Roxbury." Some guffaws. The last great white hope — hockey. But he stifles the laughs with his next line. "But we'll get some trackmen, which we need because you here aren't producing any." Silence again. "If we get a yearbook staffer from the other school, it's courtesy to have the person on our yearbook. If we get a cheerleader, the same thing goes. It's only fair. . . . You're asking if there'll be courses in black history and culture. We had them last year before busing. We also had them in Irish history and Lithuanian culture, and I'll tell you they don't go over well either."

Charlie Barry excuses himself. He has a meeting down at Columbia Point, where the fear of sending children to white Southie is as strong as the escalating crime rate in that desolate project. "I'll say this," he tells them before exiting. "The same message goes at Columbia Point as goes here. Any action threatening safety means the direct action of the police." There are more questions, more suppositions.

"If you get into a fight with a white person, you'd get suspended, right?" says a kid. "So what if you get into a fight with a nigger?" Some gasps and groans. Some chuckling. Some sarcasm. "Black person," he says. "Neeeeegrow," says another kid.

"You'll get in a fight all right, if you use that language," Reid grumbles. He tells the kids, "If you're in the school building, don't talk to any reporter or the news media without your parents' permission. Let me do the talking." But why do they instill so little confidence in their kids, a reporter mumbles to a youth worker. "Reid is smart," the guy whispers back. "He knows if a kid says something like 'This isn't so bad,' and his parents are against busing, he could get his ass kicked in at home."

When the meeting ends, some of the women remain to vent their anger at the young people who called the meeting. The press will misrepresent this, they yell. It will look as if Southie favors busing.

If it was never clear before, one fact is now clear tonight. Whatever happens will happen not so much because of hotheaded kids, but because of adults, because of people who have grown up with fear and hate and not without reason, but nevertheless with such fear and hate that it becomes a legacy for their children.

As the hall empties, as the women yell at the kids, an Irish police sergeant looks around the hall and says quietly, "Some of the parents rub off on the kids."

SIXTEEN

September 9: And the World
Turned Upside Down

EARLY IN THE MORNING, people wearing armbands were boarding the MBTA's Red Line train at the South Shore suburbs of Weymouth and Quincy, people who had fled the city and will now march with their old neighbors.

By 9 o'clock in the morning, the anti-busing protestors begin gathering on the Boston Common, a few yards from the bas-relief Civil War memorial commemorating the black Fifty-Fourth Regiment and Robert Gould Shaw.

It is not a long march from the Common to Government Center. Boston is a walking city, ready-made for demonstrators. Sam Adams had a marvelous time in Boston. The protestors gather on the red brick plaza of Government Center, where a stage and loudspeaker system have been set up. To their left is one of those nondescript government high-rise office buildings, bearing the name John F. Kennedy.

On the twenty-fourth floor is the office of John Kennedy's surviving brother. His office commands a view of the city, the densely populated suburbs around it, and the magnificence of the bay and the Atlantic beyond. If he wishes or thinks about it, Ted Kennedy can look down at the wards that Honey Fitz and Pat Kennedy controlled, the wards of the North End and East Boston, whose people are now making their way into the office building to demand a meeting with the grandson. One local columnist had pleaded in writing that he come and talk to the protestors, that he and they shared something special and that perhaps he could explain why he could not vote against busing. And perhaps Ted Kennedy believed it, because he was in town, out in Dorchester in fact, visiting an open house at Dorchester High.

In a stairwell leading to the twenty-fourth floor is a Federal Security Service cop with a radio. Inside the Senator's office are some secretaries and an aide, Eddie Martin. "If he's got time," Martin tells a visitor, "he'll be willing to see them. It depends on whether he finishes at the schools. You know, the problem is they supported him on civil rights and desegregation in the South. Now, the problem is here. What do they want? A senator with a double standard? . . ." He asks the visitor, "What do you think? Should he meet with them? He wouldn't mind, but on the other hand, if they're gonna hoot him down . . ."

A delegation of protestors is now in the lobby with uniformed and plainclothes security men. One group walks off to meet two aides to "Brooks." Ed Brooke has been in politics in Massachusetts for almost two decades, but more than half the population calls him Brooks. The other group waits for word from Kennedy. A security man says to one of them, "And do you represent the city of Boston?"

"The whole city of Boston," the man answers.

"And what is the name of your group?"

"ROAR — Restore Our Alienated Rights."

America's security personnel are trained to be so bipartisan, so dispassionate. A man in a maroon jacket stands in front of you and says ROAR to your face, you should at least look a little surprised, if not laugh. How many people yell ROAR into your face? But no, straight-faced, the security man goes back to a phone at the lobby desk and presumably says to his chief, "ROAR," and undoubtedly the chief doesn't laugh either.

A few minutes later, Kennedy's office calls down to the lobby. "Okay," one security man says to another, "send 'em up."

The delegation, most of them women, arrive at the Senator's outer office, and there is that moment of delay, that moment of insecurity on everyone's part. Just for a moment, the hard line of resistance bends among protestors, because they realize they are entering a world about which they have only read or heard. Among those who await them with premonitions of disaster, there is a brief measure of relief to see that those at the door are not green, with fangs. Washington, the state capitals, the centers of political power in America are too distant from those governed. And democracy, still very young and fumbling about, is unsure of itself. Americans insist still that their noisier fellow citizens "show some respect" for the symbols of authority. Two hundred years after King George, there is yet a tendency to be humble before what you perceive as power. So, there is that moment of delay, when Eddie Martin invites them into the Senator's inner office, that moment or two when the protestors, the housewives from Southie and Eastie and the North End, look around at the nice clean office, at the mementos and shift uncomfortably in their chairs. But then, one says, "We'd like him to explain to the people why our children are being kidnapped, why our civil rights are being taken away," and the moment is gone forever.

They want to know if and when Kennedy will be back. Martin urges them to "stay here. He'll be back soon. We can get you some coffee." They say, "No, we'd like the Senator to meet with the group outside."

"Isn't it interesting," says Fran Johnnene from Hyde Park, "for him to pick today to visit the schools?"

Eddie Martin insists his boss "has met with all the leaders."

Martin is told, "He's met with all the leaders, but not with the people."

Martin says his boss has talked to mothers when they were in Washington, and he has talked to them in Dorchester.

A Mrs. Sorrentino from the North End says, "He's never been to my home, and I live just in the North End." She moves her head toward the window in the direction of that neighborhood.

The other women all say they have never met with Ted Kennedy.

Mrs. Sorrentino tells Martin, "He doesn't have the courtesy to respond to our letter."

"The Senator responds to all letters," insists Martin.

"Well, he certainly didn't respond to us, kid," insists Mrs. Sorrentino.

Everybody gets up to leave. "We're getting quite used to meeting with the second in command in Washington, at the state and in every building we visit," Fran says. "We'll be back." They leave the office, and as they go down the hallway, Martin reappears, rushing around the corner, "He's on his way." One mutters, "Convenient he made his way back, hah?" Now, they say, they'll take coffee.

One woman uses the phone to call home. Her oldest of three kids, a twelve-year-old boy, has "a cross between poison ivy and poison oak. He gets it three times a year. He breaks out all over, and it distorts his face. Usually, I'm with him. So, I'm calling every two hours." She has been fighting busing for five years, since she was elected president of her local Home and School Association. "We live it, we sleep it, we eat it, day in and day out."

While waiting, they talk among themselves about this crazy crisis, this thing the school committee said over the years would never happen. "You got a school right across your street," one housewife says. "Why should you move out? It's your turf. Today, they tell you to bus your child. Tomorrow, they'll tell you when to go to the bathroom, when to sleep, when to have an affair with your husband. We are the ones who have the labor pains, and who stay up every night with them when they're sick, not the Senators and the Representatives. It's enough we have to give them to the service. My son was in Vietnam two years. For two years I died. Did the Senator die?"

Mary Binda has four kids, she laughs, four kids and all injury-prone. One day, three of them got hurt at school. "What if they were in different schools all over the place? How would I get to them? I'm not Elastic Woman. The people of the middle class are carrying the whole weight on their shoulders. Carrying the burden."

As they talk, another protestor comes in and says, "Louise says to come down."

"Can't you wait for the Senator?" Eddie Martin asks.

They're getting up. It's clear who has more clout with them. These are not Ted Kennedy's people. Their fathers were not millionaires in the stock market and the liquor business. Most of them didn't go to law school; most don't have summer homes on the Cape. These are Louise's people, and they are not liberals or conservatives or anything else. They are white people with foreign last names who live in a very parochial city that fears change, because so often change has hurt. The world has never been secure, and now it is tumbling down among them, because other insecure people are demanding change, because for *them* change cannot be any worse than what they have got. And in a few moments, all of this will come spilling out into the open, and every newspaper in the country will carry the stories, and the myth of an enlightened Boston will begin to crumble.

"Louise says come down," the man repeats.

"We can't wait any longer," Fran tells Martin.

When they get to the lobby, they learn why Louise may have called for them. "He's here!" a guy says. "He's on the bandstand!"

"I don't believe it," says Fran, and they rush out the revolving door.

"I don't believe it." From the steps on the side of the JFK building, you can see the top half of his head, the wavy hair, the reddish tan, the man who sets them screaming, but instead of screaming with adoration today, they scream with hate and fear. He had gone not to his office, but directly to the rally with a cop and Dapper O'Neil by his side. When he is spotted, he is booed. On the platform, he is jostled, and everyone is yelling. The crowd begins turning its back on him, one after another, and Rita Graul, a Southie ROAR leader and an aide to Louise, says into the mike, "Senator Kennedy, the people have turned their backs on you," and the crowd yells its approval. They keep turning away and they sing, "God Bless America," and a man near the steps shakes his head and says, "He's crazy."

They wave the signs, "Impeach Kennedy . . . Impeach Brooke." Now, the press has become a crowd in itself, a crowd stumbling and tripping over its own wires and equipment, men with 35mm cameras bouncing on their chests and bellies, reporters trying to hold notebooks in one hand and pens in the other, being jostled by the crowd.

"No, no, we won't go!" the crowd chants.

Kennedy turns and leaves. He will not get to speak. Cops escort him off the back of the platform, down its wooden stairs and through the crowd toward the side steps of the JFK high rise. Now, the people are pushing and shoving. Women and men raise their fists, and shake them in his face. They are screaming at him. There is a half-smile on his face, but he is scared. He's not the only one. Some of the anti-busing leaders are scared too. They are learning today that what they began a decade ago is sometimes uncontrollable. Their rhetoric and society's demands have loosed a force that, at times, knows no leaders. Like the anarchists of Spain, it screams Viva Muerte — Long Live Death.

Eggs and tomatoes sail through the air. At least some in that crowd must have done some planning on their own. A tomato hits a reporter and some of the crud splatters Kennedy and another reporter. The crowd gets worse as the Senator nears the revolving door.

"Pig!" they scream at him. "Pig" was what the blacks and the long-haired peace demonstrators yelled at cops. Now, it is their word. "Pig!" They spit it out.

"You're a disgrace to the Irish!" they yell.

He is rushed through the doors and inside the corridor. The feds lock every door they can. The bridge between Washington and the real world is again up; outside, the crowds press against the glass windows, like so many refugees refused passage to a safer world. The glass contorts their faces, and hate contorts their faces too. They pound on the glass, moving lips snarling, hands pointing, pounding, and as the Senator gets down the hall to the elevators, smash, the glass caves in.

Near the rear elevators, with a ring of security men and reporters around him, Kennedy talks to the press. "People have strong emotions, aaaah, and strong feelings about — aaaah — those questions and issues, aaaah, and they've certainly expressed them. They have a — aaaah — right to their position. That's, aaaah, why I came to this meeting today. I hope those voices suggesting violence will be stilled, because I understand what violence can do. Aaaah, the real issue is not busing, but what's at the end of the bus. Parents are concerned about the safety of the children at the end of line. Hopefully, we can direct the emotion and feeling to a quality education. Unfortunately, I was denied the right to speak. I think I had some things to say to them. The idea of pulling the plug out of the microphone . . . that kind of device is deplorable. . . ."

As Kennedy talks, the walkie-talkie held by a nearby cop squawks, "In the lobby, in the lobby . . ."

In the lobby, all the doors to the building but one are chained shut. A custodian smashes out the rest of the jagged glass with a broom handle. Some women shout, "Yay." Brad Knickerbocker, a reporter with the *Christian Science Monitor*, turns to a friend and says, "Welcome to Boston."

On the bandstand, a speaker is saying, "Your newspapers will tell you how good things are in cities that have desegregated. It's not true. The schools in those cities are in chaos."

Dapper O'Neil approaches a reporter and says in his ear, "I hope Kennedy writes me a letter of thanks. I saved him. I was with him until he got to the door."

The big rally is winding down, and the emotions are now keyed up.

In City Hall, on the other side of the plaza, in the corridor outside Kevin White's office, Kiley and Kirk O'Donnell are talking. There is little love lost for Ted Kennedy around here anyway, ever since Miami in 1972, but now there is anger too.

"He gave life to a rally that was dying," Kiley says. "Maybe it was good for him, but it was not good for this city."

O'Donnell wonders, "Can you imagine black people watching this and saying now, 'Wow, if this is what they do to *him* in Government *Center*, imagine what they'll do to *our* kids in *South Boston!*' "

Down in the bunker, the phones are busy where the school personnel are stationed. Around 1 o'clock, there were rumors that some people were stashing weapons near the Fifield School in Dorchester, and a crowd of kids, possibly a spin-off from the rally, were massing at

Roslindale High. By the time police got to Roslindale, there was no crowd. No weapons were found near the Fifield. On a day like today, chalk up two positive signs. In times such as these, negative often means positive.

In the conference room of the bunker, Bill Edgerton, Kelliher, Fred Salvucci, the mayor's transportation aide, and Salvucci's aide, Melanie Ray, and Ed Bailey, a transportation man from the redevelopment authority, are talking about the most basic issue in busing — the buses. The school department's man assigned to bus routes is in the hospital. Nobody can get to him, because he has a heart condition. The city's transportation people are being told less than three days before school opens that the school department has not yet told parents where the bus pickup points are and that some pickup points have not even been established yet.

Salvucci's mouth is hanging open.

"What's the matter, Fred?" Kelliher asks.

"It's unbelievable."

"It's what we've been going through since we started," Edgerton tells them.

Kelliher asks Fred for an overview, for his own gut feelings. Fred promises an overview.

Kelliher turns to Melanie, who has just learned that she must junk everything she's been doing to improve the MBTA and go to work on busing. Busing, the people eater, sucks in everybody. It is all consuming, to the detriment of other issues. "It's gonna really be plugging holes when you see holes," he tells Melanie, "and you'll start seeing them right away."

As they talk, some kids in Southie are stoning an MBTA bus being driven by a black man. All four tires of a black teacher's car have been slashed at the South Boston High annex. A Roxbury woman has registered her kids at that annex, part of a bathhouse that has been converted to classrooms, and calls to complain that local kids threw cans at her and abused her, that one of them yelled, "Southie is lily white and it's gonna stay that way."

At City Hall, the mayor has done what he wanted to do with the speech Ira Jackson had handed him and has recorded it on videotape. Tonight, he will be in every parlor or den that wants to receive him. In the rear of his office, there's a small room with soft furniture and a television and a bathroom, and from this small room, Kevin White will watch himself on television. The room is cluttered, because there are two big cardboard boxes of photographs and old newsclips on the couch. He's going to throw most of it out, he says. He says he's not much for saving junk. He'll throw out what most would think of as sentimental. He'll keep a wedding picture of Patricia Hagan and Joe White and a 1967 full-page ad showing a much younger Kevin campaigning for mayor of Boston. Everything else will go, including a photograph of Kevin White, secretary of state, swearing in one Ted Kennedy as assistant district attorney of Suffolk County.

Now, he and Kiley sit down to watch the speech. He eats crackers and sips a Coke and says, "Today, for the first time, I finally felt I had this thing in my guts." He starts laughing, and his voice gets louder as he jokes around. "I'll walk into the bunker and tell them, 'I'll be taking over the command center at 7 o'clock tomorrow. All right, everyone outta here. I'm running this thing by guts. It's visceral.' "

Kevin White is good on television. The videograph works well. He reads from it effectively. He has what the people in television call good eye contact with the camera. The blue eyes, the thin lips, all serve well.

He reminds those who care to watch and listen that he has been "in over one hundred living rooms in all sections and neighborhoods of this city. I have talked with white and black parents." This speech is supposed to reach out to everyone, to try one more time to show people in Boston that they share, if nothing else, the same misery. A legacy from the dour Puritans.

"I listened to a black mother in Mattapan, a working mother, whose three daughters will be reassigned from the neighborhood school that's now within walking distance of her home, and bused instead to two separate schools. I talked to mothers in West Roxbury whose kindergarten children will have to ride the school bus."

He lashes out against the suburbs. "I don't *want* or *need* the advice of those who live outside our city and who view busing as the solution to racial imbalance so long as it stays within the city limits, who talk of obeying the law, but who remain immune from implementing the law."

No, he implies dramatically, the hell with suburbia. "I trust instead the wisdom and common sense of the mother in Dorchester, the judgment and the instincts of the father in Roxbury." The next few weeks, he promises, will test them dearly. He repeats what he has said at those coffee klatches. "It's a tough time to be a senior in high school. It's a trying time to be the mother of an elementary school child in Boston. And it's not the greatest time to be mayor of this city either. But, it is *our* time, and we must make the best of it."

He reminds the opponents of busing that legal appeals have been exhausted at a cost of $250,000 in city money. Now, Garrity's order stands, he says, and it *will* be carried out.

"We cannot permit our city to be polarized by race or paralyzed by fear." Boston is a city of neighborhoods, he says, and from those neighborhoods come the city's collective strength. The city is one, he says, knowing deeply it is not.

Most who oppose busing, he insists, are not racists or bigots, but responsible people using their right to voice their opinion in a city that has long been a city of free speech.

So, this, then, is his stand, formulated quietly over the year, battered back and forth among his aides, who are capable of every shade of input ranging from the right of Trotsky to the left of Torquemada.

"I am serving notice to those who would resort to violence or use our school children as instruments of political or personal gain in the days ahead — to every mother and every father, I pledge tonight that your mayor and your police department will tolerate no threat to the well-being of your children, that Police Commissioner diGrazia will pursue relentlessly anyone and everyone who endangers our students, black or white, high school or grade school, and that the peril of prosecution faces all who take the law into their own hands in any way. To those who would violate the order and the peace of our city, and to those who would exploit the tensions of next week and the weeks to come, jeopardizing the young and innocent, I promise swift and sure punishment."

The promises are tough. Keeping them will be tougher. Keeping them all will be impossible, and Kevin White will be called to task by black and white for not living up, in their eyes, to the promises of tonight. It will not be for a lack of trying.

He tells them of the twenty-four-hour information center, of cooperation among city and school officials. He does not tell them that as of tonight, not all the pickup points have been established. He does not go into the frustrations that his aides have encountered almost daily since the spring.

"We have not come three hundred years as a city without having faced great change. Boston has never before failed to meet that change with courage, compassion and dignity. And she will not fail now."

A few words more, and it is over. The mayor, concerned with style and his own self-confidence, turns to Kiley and asks, "How was I?"

"It's good," Kiley says. "Very good. It wasn't hokey."

White turns to a visitor and talks quietly. "I'm like a racehorse. I've worked this thing all the way through. The tension mounts up. Finally, there's nothing more I can do in the planning sense. I've dealt with these crises before, though nothing of this length. It's like a political campaign, the day before election, there's nothing more you can do. But on the final day . . . your gut instincts, your emotional stability is what you count on, and the leader has to fill in the holes with those. All the plans may go out the window, all his skills have to be used to plug all the leaks, to know which really are leaks and which are waves. So it isn't planning; it's the years you're in the business. So you just begin to pace and walk and sniff and watch incidents like this afternoon and sniff some more and say, what does that mean, like the candidate watching returns. When there's real trouble, people stop giving orders, they stop and turn to you. I've been on the phone today, doing my own spot checks, calling people like Charlie Barry, probing at people three-fourths of the way down the ladder. I won't have a chance to do that later." He pauses and puffs a Marlboro. He's smoking a lot more now.

"It's funny how your original thoughts hold up — Southie, that Southie will be the problem. Southie is having a nervous breakdown, a collective nervous breakdown. I like Southie, even if it doesn't like me. But they're wrong on this one. The vociferousness doesn't make them wrong, but the violence will. When Charlestown refused urban renewal, it wasn't violent, but loud, the last banshee call of the community before it turned itself around. I think Southie can turn itself around, but not with violence. Not with violence, it won't."

SEVENTEEN

September 10: Kevin's Instincts

NOW, MOST ASSUREDLY, the nation would look east. It had done so once to find the spark for its liberty. It had done so once to seek the persistent source of Abolition so that some could attack it and others could support it, once to find the money for its railroads and its mines and its geographic and industrial expansion, once for cultural and literary impetus. Now, it would look again to Boston, as if what would happen in Boston could indicate what the future held for the republic.

From the border states, from the West Coast, from the Middle West, friends called friends in Boston, Cambridge, and the suburbs and asked, "Why?" The rest of the republic, believing all the cliches it had ever read about the city, was confused or shocked, or, in the case of the South, delighted. In the bunker and five floors above in the mayor's office, nobody is surprised. They simply plod along with their plans.

Kirk O'Donnell is not surprised, but he is still angry one day after Kennedy's appearance and the reaction to it. "He raised the level of tension. He brought the rally back to life. . . . Normally, Kevin's speech would have been the lead story today. . . . Besides, what's he doing stomping all over our turf when we've worked hard to prevent violence?"

Kelliher and Bob Schwartz and Kiley are not surprised. They're still worried that in the details that count, Boston is not ready for busing. They are meeting in Kiley's office, and Kelliher is saying, "Another problem is your normal shakedown. Last year, a black kid would shake down another black. Now, it'll be viewed as interracial. Like the stories coming out of the English High summer session."

Schwartz says, "You mean your normal boys' room extortion. When the kids come home and say, 'I hadda go to the john and couldn't get in without paying them a quarter, and I had to hold it in all day' — that's the kind of things kids don't tell adults in school and wait until they get home."

Kiley says there will be two-and-one-half times the normal number of police outside the schools, and Kelliher talks of YAC workers, but Schwartz worries about the insides of the schools. He ran an interracial high school, and he knows the nitty problems that arise — fights over a place in line, fights over the politics of student assemblies, fights over who should be cheerleaders — and he has no confidence that the Boston school system is prepared for this.

Kevin H. White is certainly not surprised. In the hallway outside his office, he holds an impromptu gathering, and he demonstrates his instincts for the city that has loved and hated him and that now threatens to destroy him politically as it destroys itself. He is not surprised, but he is apprehensive. He is worried about gatherings, the kind that congregate outside school buildings. He had talked to Charlie Barry, who said something about controlling crowds, and Kevin White had slapped himself in the forehead with the palm of his hand and said out loud to himself, "Crowds! What crowds?" Now, in the hallway, with a bunch of aides around him, he recalls his conversation with that policeman whom he trusts so deeply and he delivers a lecture.

"Crowds!" he repeats, "What crowds? What are they *doin'* there? What do you think they're doin' there? If there are four on a corner, shove 'em along." Schwartz, Kiley, Herb Gleason, the city's chief lawyer, and others all stand there, wide-eyed, mouths open, ready to disagree. The mayor seems alone. He is animated, moving his hands around, pacing up and down, charging at an aide here, another there, jabbing his finger.

"'Wait a minute,' they'll yell; 'this is America.' Yeah, this is America — and keep shoving. What is it? A receiving line for booing blacks? We have a loitering law, don't we? Well, let's use it."

Kiley interrupts, "Loitering laws are being struck down all over the country."

"Well not in Boston," Kevin White says, "not yet. There's no need for a crowd to be gathered. No more demonstrations! They had their demonstration yesterday. They had their shot. You're just asking for that kind of thing that happened with Kennedy, when you allow people to congregate. It could happen to a black student as well as Kennedy."

Kiley takes the lead in fighting the boss. Kiley is good at that. Too often, White's aides seem to hold back or to soft-pedal their criticism. Kiley argues now that breaking up crowds sometimes creates larger problems.

"Look," the mayor says, "I've let you guys plan, and I don't wanna interfere, but a crowd has to congregate. It doesn't come up in one big bulk. You let them congregate, you're gonna end up calling me up. No lingering! It'll be a rock from across the street."

Tom McKenna, one of Gleason's lawyers, says, "The strategy is to keep the police presence away from the school." Boston has seen police rush in and police hold back. The administration has had more than six years to look at its police, and there have been times when the police rushing into a crowd have made troublesome situations disastrous. Kevin White knows that, but his instincts are telling him that this time, it has to be the other way. McKenna's reasonable point triggers White's anger, for while he encourages his diverse advisors to debate, he is quick to anger at criticism.

"Listen to me," he says loudly, not quite a yell. "I've got a good mind," and he resumes arguing that no crowd be allowed to congregate. "I don't understand. . . . What the hell are they doing there? Why . . . after that demonstration of crazies yesterday, you're dealing with *insanity*, you're gonna give a permit? Talk about free speech? I'm not issuing any permits. So, the easiest thing is to say to them, 'You're loitering, hey, move along.' "

"Is it mainly Southie you're worried about?" somebody asks.

"Yeah. Chiefly. Their own home turf. Look. I want them broken up at the staging area, before they become a crowd." At one point, Kevin suggests he knows more than Kiley, and Kiley bristles and suggests quietly but angrily that he too has some knowledge in this. Kiley's background includes the CIA and the National Police Foundation, and Kevin's antennae catch the hurt. White retreats $\frac{1}{28}$th of an inch, but not from his argument. White is tenacious.

"If you appear too lenient, you won't get respect for it."

"We're trying to avoid confrontations between police and citizens," Kiley insists.

"I never knew one or two citizens who'll fight with a cop," Kevin counters. "Twenty or thirty, yes. If you let the crowd go! That's what I want to avoid. Right from the beginning. Seven o'clock in the morning. Whammo! Right in the can. Get 'em outta the way early in the morning. Fill up the wagon, throw 'em in. Right in the can! And I believe I know those people. They'll settle down. They respect authority. They blew it yesterday. They *blew* it."

The mayor has other things to do, and the impromptu meeting breaks up. Some aides shake their heads in doubt. Two days later, they will say, "Hey, remember that conversation in the corridor? He was right."

Kiley has received marching orders, and the orders must go down the line. Now, he must meet with Commissioner diGrazia's two top officers — Superintendent Joe Jordan and Deputy Superintendent Paul Russell. Having argued with the mayor, Kiley, as White's administrative assistant, is now the loyal aide, talking softly, tactfully, convincingly, without even a hint of any disagreement he might have had with White.

Kiley reviews the mayor's position on crowds. "It's a fine point, one I hadn't thought about that much. His notion is you stop them from parking near the school at six-thirty or seven in the morning. Any crowds after that, and you move them off."

Russell says the department's approach is supposed to be "low-key."

"The mayor," Kiley says, "thinks one thing they'll understand there is firmness. He feels they won't go to the American Civil Liberties Union in Southie."

Russell laughs at Kiley's joke. "Yeah, not too many in our internal complaint bureau from Southie."

Nobody ever hears of police brutality complaints in Southie, not because police can't be brutal in Southie, but because people in Southie and Charlestown don't react that way. It may not be a deep respect for the law, as some insist. It may simply be a long tradition of keeping your mouth shut and taking one's licks. This too shall change.

Joe Jordan, who has a military manner and wears sunglasses in the style of Patton, predicts kids near the schools who don't belong there, and parents too. He says there has been a debate within the department on how to handle that. "By eight o'clock, it will begin to build up. By eight-thirty, we'll have a pretty formidable group of people, and I'll assume Charlie will have his forces built up accordingly. And the question is — do you want that?"

Kiley says, "The mayor is affected by what he saw yesterday on the plaza. There's a hard-core group of haters who've maybe given up on everything else, and if they see a spot for trouble, they'll do it."

Yet the guidelines handed out in the department as late as last week say arrest only as a last resort.

Jordan laughs. "We keep talking low-key this, low-key that. Meanwhile, we got dogs, we got horses, shields. We got tear gas in the truck. And we're talking low-key it. . . . Whenever police surveillance ends, the hoodlums, the hooligans, whatever you want to call them, will start. . . . If you let things build up, you can be in trouble. If you don't, you can be in trouble. It's delicate."

He worries. "At Southie, you have people opposing it, and politicians supporting them . . . the incident yesterday. Some way, somehow, somebody is gonna want to do something — throw a rock, break a window." And what if the blacks coming into Southie bring friends for protection?

Late in the afternoon, Bill Edgerton sits in the conference room of the bunker and reads the first batch of rumor reports. For beginners, he says, "How would you like a human chain around the Greenwood School?"

NEIGHBORHOOD STATUS REPORTS

Hyde Park   *Elihu Greenwood Elementary School*
Time: 1:45 p.m., Sept. 10th
We have a rumor from several sources that parents intend to form a human chain on opening day at the school. The home and school association members intend to be present to calm the situation.

South Boston   *199 H Street at the Foley Apartments*
Time: 7:30 p.m., Sept. 9th
Three laborers (black) attending a union meeting were shot at by a pellet gun, apparently done by whites living in the area.
D Street Housing Project
Time: ? Sept. 10th
Parents to take occupancy of seats within the school of South Boston High, daring anyone to move them. (well-founded)

Columbia Point   *Columbia Point Housing Project*
Time: 2:30 p.m., Sept. 10th
Rumor that black parents will blockade Mt. Vernon Street, prohibiting buses from entering Columbia Point.

EIGHTEEN

September 11: Generals and Privates

ON THE FINAL DAY of Boston's uneasy peace, on the day before Boston must come to terms with its own history, the diverse personalities who cluster around Kevin Hagan White gather for a morning meeting in the Eagle Room, a carpeted meeting room, furnished with one large desk and some leather chairs and featuring an old wooden sculptured eagle that once adorned the top of the old City Hall.

Paul Parks is here. For a half dozen years, he has presided over the Model Cities program. Parks was very early in the battle to integrate Boston's schools and very early to join Kevin White's administration. Now, he waits to see what years of cajoling, arguing, lobbying for integration will bring. He looks at the morning report from the bunker — a false alarm late yesterday in a Roslindale school, a white deliveryman robbed at knife point by three black youths near the King School in Roxbury.

"Not too bad, huh?" someone says.

"Yeah," Parks answers, "and there's no kids in school yet, either." He shakes his head, folds up the report and sighs, "I don't know. I just don't know."

Kiley, Schwartz, and Tom McKenna from the Law Department are here, ready to fill everyone in on the latest twists in planning, bus routes, meetings, courtroom action; Larry Quealy is here, his antenna sensitive to the white neighborhoods, where he has a wealth of contacts among the anti-busing crowd. And Frank Tivnan is here, worried about what to do with a dozen television crews tomorrow. Already, a room has been outfitted on the eighth floor for the visiting press who have come to cover busing in Boston because that is a national event.

The boss appears in the doorway to the Eagle Room, tired again, slurring his speech, rubbing his right hand across his face, even as he talks. "I wanna get that Southie High School cleared up." Kiley says Russell and Jordan disagree with Kevin's crowd control order.

"Well," says the mayor, "they're wrong, and that's why I'm the commander in chief, and they're not. And I'll tell them, and if they don't do it, I'll fire them. I bow in deference to professional people — nine times out of ten." But, now, he says, he knows he is right. The mayor keeps lines of communication open to just about everyone, including the so-called enemy camps. He values political and combat intelligence more than he does pride. Once, an aide told him that a certain high-level black appointee was really working for one of his rivals, Tom Atkins, and urged the man be canned. "No," White said, "then, we'd have nobody talking to Atkins."

Now, he says, "I have my connections with Kerrigan and Louise, and they have nothing planned. They *want* nothing."

If Southie were the only potential trouble spot, all of this would be so much easier. Just saturate Southie with police and tough it out. But Southie is only one. Roxbury is yet another.

"Most of our security will be handled by community people," Parks says. "We got thirty to forty clergy in addition to the Multi-Service Center anti-crime force, twenty-five to thirty adults. If youths congregate, the twenty-five to thirty adults will move them."

Kiley is troubled. "Paul, I don't think that's a good idea. I have a visceral negative reaction to civilians playing a police role."

"We've done it before," Paul says. Roxbury has a long and controversial history of community security patrols, some of them federally funded and often effective.

"If," Schwartz says, "you were a white kid coming up on a bus, and all you see are these black guys waiting — Paul, if you were a black kid coming into South Boston and saw sixty white guys standing there, wouldn't you be worried?"

"My sense is that I wanna see those preachers there. They *know* people," Paul answers.

Quealy doesn't like it either. "If Southie is an armed camp of police, then the King School has to be, too, or people will get angry."

Paul says he's worried about the King, about blacks being whipped up to blocking the buses. "We've used the civilians for two or three days to let the white parents go into the school. When they first arrived, the people wouldn't let them come in, but for two or three days now, the white parents have been able to come in. . . . The security force is working in teams of five. The thesis is we got to control the community so the police don't have to come in. Cause if they do, some people are gonna be messed up. The King School is shifting from 100 percent black to 60 percent white. That's the problem. That's like taking the George Wallace School in Alabama and turning it black."

The beginnings of the siege mentality are evident. In the weeks to come, these men will come to believe more in themselves and less in others. They feel increasingly that they are the ones carrying the load, making sure Boston doesn't blow itself up. The mayor, especially, will feel that other politicians, the press, the federal government, President Ford, and Judge Garrity are too distant from reality and that his critics don't appreciate what he is doing to preserve sanity. He will have cause to believe that. The people in this room, regardless of their views on busing, are standing between inevitable, ugly incidents and wholesale disaster.

Kevin says he plans to be at City Hall by 7 A.M. tomorrow. "There's no need for me to be seen if everything is going well. If there is trouble," he pauses. "I haven't decided yet. If I'm in Southie at all, I'll be inconspicuous, but readily available to all, very close by in a house. When the audience clears, things quiet down. Nobody wants to get hit for nothing, only for the television tubes." He says he's handled all kinds of demonstrations. You don't handle all of them the same way.

The subject prompts somebody to ask if everyone has seen a *Globe* story on civil disobedience, in which academics, liberals, and other veteran civil rights types were asked their opinions. Some of them suggested that civil disobedience is good only if the cause is righteous. The Puritan lives. The dichotomy is alive and well. "Cambridge liberals," Kiley verbally spits. There is distaste in the room for such opinions and for such persons, just as front-line soldiers carp at those back home who are free with their opinions on a war. Kevin and his loyal aides have no patience anymore with such judgments. The time for talk is almost over. Someone has to drive the tanks. And perhaps take one last smoke.

Kiley looks up and says, "Anything else?" and the meeting winds down, leaving lonely men again, each with his own self-doubts, facing situations that neither their schoolbooks nor their precinct politics had prepared them for.

There are doubts that plague Schwartz now. "I'm worried about working parents dropping their kids on a corner for a bus that hasn't come yet and going off to work. I'm worried about lost kids out there. I'm worried about kids and parents wandering around." At a meeting with school officials yesterday, he was told each principal was responsible for mailing information out to parents in his district. Had someone been assigned to check on the principals, to make sure the mailings went out? No. Had anyone gone out to eyeball the MBTA buses to make sure the words "school bus" were written on each one, so that motorists would stop when the buses stopped? No.

At 2 o'clock in the afternoon, Tivnan and Kiley share their doubts in a special briefing for the out-of-town press.

"There are four high school trouble spots — the South Boston complex, Dorchester, English, and Hyde Park High School and its annex, the Rogers School. The Rogers was a middle school, which is like a junior high, and the people were happy with it. To make the busing plan work, Hyde Park had to give up its junior high school. The students from there are going to two other junior high schools in the black neighborhood."

"Are you expecting trouble from Boston Latin?" one asks. Oh, what a neat story that would be! Ancient, prestigious Boston Latin, from where patriots and statesmen and concertmasters and writers had matriculated for three centuries. A little busing violence there, two minutes of film, with the old school framed neatly behind the correspondent's head — yessir, that would wrap it all up.

"Only," says Tivnan, "if the two student bodies from Latin and English intermingle."

Tivnan stands at the podium usually used by the mayor in a room especially outfitted for television. Kiley stands off in a corner, fighting alone, inside of him, two wars — one that the others fight to maintain their self-confidence in the face of what could be disaster, and another one, a quiet, private one of which he does not speak. Until July 11, Bob Kiley was a married man with two young children. That day, Kiley was to visit his ill father in South Dakota and, while waiting for a changeover at the Minneapolis–St. Paul International Airport, he got a phone call from Kevin White. Kiley's thirty-five-year-old wife, Patricia, and two-year-old daughter, Jessica, had been killed in a four-car collision in New York; his four-year-old son, Christopher, was in critical condition at a Boston hospital. Bob Kiley came back to Boston to arrange funerals for his wife and daughter, and, later, for the boy, who could not survive.

Bob Kiley could easily laugh and could easily be brought to anger, but beyond that, he never displayed much of himself to others. Now, with his family gone, he had made some kind of a steel-framed accommodation with the tragedy eating his insides. He threw himself into Boston's oncoming busing crisis, which, in a perverse way, may have been an antidote. He would eat, sleep, breathe, and think nothing but busing. It would become, for a time, his life. He would complain about the insanity of the plans, the inanities of some of the people involved; he would talk of getting away from it. But just as the crisis needed a Bob Kiley to honcho it, Kiley, subconsciously, may have needed the crisis too. So there he was, two months a widower at the age of thirty-nine, standing in a corner of a room with a bunch of strangers whose job demands that they rush from crisis to crisis, that they be brusque, if necessary, to get the information they need, standing there with his own set of doubts and apprehensions and God knows what else eating up inside of him.

People like Tom Atkins and Ellen Jackson also must be plagued with inner fears. They know enough about racial hatred, for they have spent years doing battle with the school committee. All summer, Ellen Jackson has been putting together the diverse factions that make up the black social service and political community. She has made her headquarters at Freedom House, which for years has served as the focal point for local black movements and inspiration. Atkins, having lost the 1971 race for mayor, was named a member of Frank Sargent's cabinet, and now he is at the helm of the local NAACP, which had fallen in prestige in recent years. Atkins must rebuild the NAACP branch. And as its president, he has immediate access to the press, especially the *Globe,* a newspaper that for years has been very good friends with the NAACP. Jim Curley had his Tammany Club; Martin Lomasney, his beloved Hendricks Club. Atkins has the NAACP.

Tonight, Jackson and Atkins are on a black radio station, WILD, urging parents not to keep their kids home, but to send them to school tomorrow.

"We're training our children for a productive life," Atkins broadcasts, "and not going to school is counterproductive. We need more, not less, school.

"It's against the law not to send them to school. We want to show the rest of the world we're better than them — them, who watched the law being implemented in Selma and Birmingham and who say the Constitution can't be stretched as far as Boston. . . . Our children will be in school, but not alone. I'll be there. Ellen will be there. Other parents will be there. Community people will be there. The police. The federal marshals, if needed. We'll call in the U.S. Sixth Fleet, if that's what it takes. . . . Our children are our most precious property. No one is going to keep them from going to school."

Strong words, words that do not reflect the doubts each of them has, but words geared to combat the doubts they know black parents have.

At 7 P.M., the bunker in City Hall is busy with phones ringing and workers scurrying around and more of the endless meetings. Today's rumor sheets are not conducive to a peaceful night's sleep.

Status Report 9/11/74 12:45
The Martin Luther King School is emerging as a distinct problem on the basis of information thus far received by the center. A group of Savin Hill parents (white) are meeting at this hour in the school auditorium with the principal and the area superintendent. Issues being discussed are not known yet.

Rumors have been received that Roxbury residents plan to block access to the school on opening day. This rumor came from within the school and was transmitted through YAC. Minor incidents which are creating problems at the King include the robbery of a white delivery man in the area yesterday afternoon and reported harassment of white and/or Spanish-speaking parents by black youths. A major emerging problem is the present lack of buses for children from the Uphams Corner area to the King. Public safety is cited as the paramount fear by parents (approximately 70) who have so far expressed their fears to Little City Halls.

In the bunker conference room, the private bus contractors are talking about a 5 percent backup capability — that means one or two buses in reserve for one company; two for another; one to five for a third. Now, people like Melanie Ray join the lengthening list of those with severe doubts and a nagging sense of fear and apprehension. "There's no radio equipment on any of the buses," she tells a friend later. "One company said it has one bus racing around with radio equipment. The MBTA says its policy is to install radios, but they haven't done so. There are a few on some, but the drivers aren't trained to use them. . . . One company is getting buses from all over the place. Drivers are quitting on them already. It's hard to get drivers. They said a lot were frightened off at a safety meeting. There are no maps with routes on them anywhere, and it's hard to tell, but there seems to be no planning for driver training. There's no monitoring system, like a daily reporting procedure. The key thing is that none of these questions were raised earlier. In all of South Boston, none of the pickup points were established until Monday. It's scary that someone as far down as I am is asked to come in and that I should have to come up with these questions that haven't been raised before."

As the bus contractors move out of the conference room, Kiley and his crew move in for one last briefing. Someone picks up from the table a coffee stirrer with an incomplete message, scrawled perhaps at the last meeting — "The shit is on . . ."

Late that night, on the radio news, a familiar voice is heard urging peace and safety for all children. The voice is little-girlish, and it has become familiar to everyone during the last decade, when it was heard so often, urging resistance. It belongs to Louise Day Hicks.

NINETEEN

September 12: Confrontation
with History

NEIGHBORHOOD STATUS REPORTS
September 12, 1974
Time: 10:00 a.m.
South Boston   *Larry Quealy, 7:05 a.m.*
Rumor that 10 to 12 mothers would blockade the
school entrance. That there would be a takeover of
South Boston High next week. That a loudspeaker
was urging students to stay home from school today.

****
Boston Police Department, 7:30 a.m.
Boston Police Department confirms rumor. The BPD
estimates crowd of 200 to 300 parents booing and
jeering as buses from Roxbury roll up to South Bos-
ton High School. The Boston Police Tactical Con-
trol Force forms line between parents and school bus.

****
Incident of photographers of Channel 5 being beaten
up by members of the crowd. One arrest made.

CURRENT STATUS: 10:00 a.m., crowd has dissi-
pated. Further update to follow.

The human chain around the Greenwood School in Hyde Park never materialized, and more than half the student body showed up.

At the King School, the black community's planning paid off. Only eight policemen stood by as buses carrying white kids pulled up. The blacks waiting for them were not the tough kids who had made life miserable or black adults who had threatened to block access to the school. Members of the Roxbury Multi-Service Center stood there and shouted, "Have no fear," as the white kids from Dorchester got off the buses.

At Dorchester High, one of the expected trouble spots, a place with a history of black-white combat, black and white kids registered peacefully and talked to one another.

At the Murphy School in Dorchester, a new school to which the community was looking forward to sending its own kids, the kids who had shown up were inside. Some parents were boycotting, but they were nowhere in sight. "Full house," a YAC worker tells Bob Kiley and Mark Weddleton, who have just pulled up.

In front of the Thompson School in Dorchester, a black guy who works at a nearby community health center tells Kiley the same kind of news. "Good," he says. "Better than an ordinary school day."

For all the premonitions, for all the shouting and the pledged resistance, Boston is peacefully integrating its schools. Attendance is not what it would be normally, but the boycott has not caught on the way everyone figured it would. There is confusion at places like Hyde Park and English High, but no reports of violence from either. The one linchpin that could easily fall out and, thereby, destroy the pattern is Southie, just as Kevin had known all along. Southie.

This morning, the crowds were there. They had pushed and shoved and jeered. They had attacked a couple of left-wing pamphleteers and a TV crew, and the police had shoved them back. To both Southie and Kevin, it was the first indication that the cops were going to put old school and neighborhood ties out of their heads and do what they ordered to do. They might not do it enthusiastically, but they would do it, and in the days to come, some of those same police would come to view Southie the way they viewed Roxbury — with fear and hate.

"Niggah!" the crowd shouted this morning, when the lone black woman was escorted into the school. The can had sailed through the air and landed harmlessly behind her, clanking on the asphalt yard of the school. Even by then, the crowd had begun to thin, and while

Kiley and Weddleton and Eddie King and Joe Jordan and Commissioner diGrazia knew that crowd would build up again, for a few hours, there was actually hope that all the worrying and planning had been for naught, that the resistance had crumbled, that Boston would integrate reluctantly, but peacefully.

Almost every school they visit reinforces that hope for Kiley and Weddleton. As they drive past the Bradford in Mattapan, Kiley looks out his window and exults, "Look at that. Mowed grass. Trimmed hedges."

At Hyde Park High School, confusion abounds. A crowd of black students showed up without identification and were sent back. Now, people are milling around in front of the school. Herbert Jackson, a thickset black community worker, briefs Kiley. "I must've carried fifty kids in my car this morning. . . . I didn't like the idea of three or four dudes walking down the street, because one guy down there" — he points to one of the houses that fringe the high school, houses inhabited by white people — "he had an attack dog on his lawn, and some others were sitting on the sidewalk and started some gibberish, you know, and I said to ours, 'Hey, it takes two to argue.' " Herb Jackson, running around this humid morning, is trying to keep the peace.

After Kiley, Weddleton, and two reporters get back into the official-looking radio car, some white girls saunter over, and one volunteers, without anyone asking her opinion, "You got it all wrong. The kids get along. It's the parents. We *like* school."

Kiley says quietly, "We ought to have a concentration camp for parents."

Roxbury High School, in the heart of the black community, is very quiet. Only a few whites have shown up, but they have not been hassled. A few cops stand around, and one of them is reading a book he must master in order to take the exam for sergeant. On the back of the school building, a kid has scrawled, "Dave J. — he will make your pussy hot." Compared to the messages written in Southie — "Nigger — Boneheads — Ku Klux Klan," — Dave J. and his alleged potential are welcome.

They drive back to South Boston, where they make contact with another radio car, driven by another of Kiley's young aides, Chris Bator, and containing Ira Jackson and Kirk O'Donnell. They trade information — "English High is a ten-strike. . . . They called diGrazia a white nigger. . . ." — and make their way over to South Boston High School again, hoping, if they can just get through this afternoon.

There are knots of kids in yards and in driveways, on the streets that lead as radials into the high school area, on the wooded hill behind the school. "It's like a deathwatch," says Ray Richard, a *Globe* reporter. One kid walks by with a T-shirt that announces, "Black Sucks." Two women walk by the school, past a bus containing the Tactical Patrol Force, past the school that now has black kids in it, and one says, "I'm glad I graduated. I really am."

G Street, in front of the school, is littered with cans and broken bottles and piles of horseshit from the mounted police crews. "If this horseshit doesn't chase them away," Weddleton says quietly, "nothing will."

Nothing will.

Kiley wonders — do you let the knots of people build up into a crowd that you might maneuver, or do you chase down each group like Belfast. Like Belfast, those who stand around do so with arms folded across their chests, with pinched faces of distaste or fear. Sporadically, firecrackers pop off in the woods behind the school or on one of the radial streets.

Kiley calls Rich Kelliher in the bunker again, as he has been doing all morning. "We're just back at Southie. It seems like H hour. There's lots of drinking. There was one incident where mothers and toddlers challenged police."

Superintendent Russell has just talked to Charlie Barry. It seems Barry is establishing a 300-yard range, a demilitarized zone around the school. Outside of that line, he'll permit a little congregating. It isn't exactly what the mayor wants. He wants them broken up. But 300 yards sounds good to those on the scene. "Even the jocks can't throw a bottle that far," Kiley says.

Downtown, a cabbie gets a message on his radio, a message his brother cabbies are getting. "Trouble in South Boston," the dispatcher says. "Stay away from there." The cabbie tells his passengers, "I knew if there was one place in the city it would happen, it'd be Southie. It's a shame. I thought we could get through this all right."

At 2 P.M., the buses roll up to South Boston High School, and the blacks come out. Some people are much closer than 300 yards. A blond woman goes after a black girl.

"Niggah!" the crowd is yelling again. "Boooooo!"

Four white girls come out of school with a teacher, who tries to get them on a bus. "No," says one. "We're not going on there." They'll take their chances walking.

From a stoop, a guy yells at a bus, "Hey, jungle baby, we know what you are."

The cops look tired.

Sam Messina, once a loyal aide to John Collins and now an employee of the school department, tells a friend, "Inside, it was okay." He shakes his head. "Shit. I can't talk to these kids. I can't talk to these kids. It's all emotion. All emotion. They're good kids."

The buses roll out with no more harm than the invective from the stoops and sidewalks. Maybe, just maybe, the city will have made it. If today is cool, then perhaps even more kids will go to school tomorrow and then next week, who knows? But it won't happen that way. It won't because a few streets away, at an annex to Southie High, a bus full of black kids makes a wrong turn and comes back past a built-up crowd of angry whites with hardly any police to confront them. And the rocks fly, and the windows break, and black kids scream and fall, and some touch their cheeks and feel blood. When they get back to their neighborhoods, they will tell the story of what happens at the bogside, and the stories will spread, for the blacks, like the ethnics, have their own grapevines. And as of midafternoon on the first day, while more than 90 percent of Boston's schools integrate peacefully, the story clacks out over the news wires about South Boston, and it is the violence, not the miracle of 90-plus percent acceptance, that will predominate in the news and in the hearts and minds of the key actors.

When Kirk O'Donnell hears the news, he repeats it to a companion. "There were not enough police. The driver took the wrong turn and they got bombarded. We're lucky the buses didn't get out of control. It just didn't have to happen."

Now, from the streets of Southie, from the bunker, from the radio cars, the men answerable to Kevin White trek back to his office late in the afternoon. It is going to be a very long night.

"What's the diagnosis?" Kevin White asks his people.

"Two things," Kiley says. "You have a problem out at Columbia Point with kids and parents, and tonight could be problems. It's a hot night, and people have been drinking all day."

Tivnan, the press secretary, advises them, "You've got to assume there'll be some negative South Boston footage. Our job is to put South Boston in context and give a picture of the rest of the city."

"I want Barry in here and Jordan," Kevin says. "I want their assessment. I want to know what to say for tomorrow. . . . The show of force made a difference at the high school."

Kiley warns, "We may have to keep that up for a very long time."

"No problem," Kevin says. "No problem. . . . There is no responsible element in Southie that has either the capacity or the courage to do something about this. Louise is a bundle of jelly. Larry and I have been buttressing Louise for three weeks in meetings. And even if she tried, she doesn't have the capacity. . . . A good frigging lesson to all the establishment who never understood this town." He lifts his head and exhales audibly. "Well, our job is we do understand this town. I'm worried about the mothers, even the ignorant and ugly among them. I'm worried about the kids. They could do a lot of damage."

Ira Jackson recalls something Eddie King told him earlier in the day. "Eddie's feeling on the crowd was that it was reaching a more feverish pitch, rather than like St. Patrick's Day. He turned to me and said, 'Get outta here. I have to too.' There were black kids giving the finger to white kids throwing rocks."

Kirk O'Donnell smiles. "The black kids were not cowering."

Kevin White mutters softly, "America, America.

"We have three options. You could say it's an isolated, unfortunate incident, but not catastrophic. We were looking for success, not miracles, and even in South Boston, we had success. Or you could isolate it and say Southie has been hurt the most. . . . Then you have to let a night of sobriety curb it. Or say that Southie has thrown its last temper tantrum and put Southie under the closest thing to martial law I can do. I protected 98 percent of the students, but I had promised 100 percent."

Kiley and Jackson immediately opt for the third option.

"I don't like to make threats," Kevin says. "If you say it, you have to deliver on it."

Kiley is now on the phone with Police Superintendent Russell to get more information about what exactly happened this afternoon and how. Tivnan, meanwhile, gets a message from one of his aides who has been up on the special eighth-floor press room, and repeats it. "The press feels we're holding details back."

Eddie King has come in from Southie, and Rich Kelliher from the bunker, and some Law Department guys. Kevin and his aides are still trying to get accurate information on the stoning of the buses, and they're trying to meet a 5 P.M. press deadline. "What are those cops doing, learning how to count?" Kiley says angrily. "Everybody in town knows what's going on except us."

The mayor grabs a Law Department memo on what he can do legally about crowd control, curfews, and other harsh measures. He reads it quickly and says, "Make a short statement based on these points. No more congregating beyond three persons. . . ." As Kevin outlines his strategy, Kiley finishes on the phone — "Five arrests, four injuries and some damaged buses, and now it's quiet."

"Our original premise is valid," Kevin is saying. "That's five guys too many. They should never have allowed anyone to congregate. Never. Never. Never. Never. Never."

Eddie King says, "It never should have gotten to that," and the mayor turns to him with almost a smile, satisfied at least that some-body thinks he was right and says, "Thank you," almost brusquely.

"Arrest them," says Kevin. "Wherever they are. I don't care if they're on the corner of M and D Streets." He pauses and again almost laughs. "Of course, M and D don't meet."

"They did today," says Eddie King. "All the corners in Southie met today."

The mayor opens the door to clear out his living room office. "All right. Back here at 4:15." It is now 4 P.M. "I wanna take a shower." He tells his secretary, "I don't want to be disturbed. I gotta think."

At 4:35, they reconvene in the office. Ira Jackson reports, "The black community is angry. They want to meet with Kevin. They're talking about accompanying their kids tomorrow."

Kirk adds, "The blacks at Columbia Point are meeting now. They're thinking of going to Freedom House and meeting down here tomorrow."

When the mayor reappears, he faces Kiley, Quealy, Parks, Kelliher, Joe Jordan, Russell, Eddie King, Commissioner diGrazia, Tivnan, McKenna from the Law Department, Jackson, O'Donnell, and Steve Dunleavy, a press aide to diGrazia. The mayor sits on an orange chair and lights another cigarette. "All right, who wants to give me a re-view? Who wants to give me a verbal or oral report on what transpired at L Street?"

Bob diGrazia volunteers. He is a tall, husky, handsome man whom the administration has plucked out of St. Louis to revamp the depart-ment, much to the disgust of some officers and the leadership of the patrolmen's union. DiGrazia has countered the union propaganda against him by going out into the neighborhoods and giving a good performance before civic groups. He has captivated the press too, be-cause he is a charming man — a liberal who believes in the law and the police.

"There were some bad agitators," diGrazia says. "The kids got off the buses well in the morning and into school. On leaving today, the buses came up, loaded them all on two buses, again with no incident at the scene. There was one arrest in the morning and five in the afternoon. One policeman got the wind knocked outta him when he was hit by a bottle. One person was arrested on assault and battery on the police, one on assault, three on disorderly conduct. At L Street, a bus driver went down the wrong way, did a U-turn right through the agitators who were coming from the high school."

Eddie King picks up the story. "All of a sudden, 100 to 150 kids came charging down the Strandway. They looked up and saw buses at the Annex. They bolted down the street, throwing bottles and rocks at cars. There were MDC and Boston Police at the Annex. The buses took off, and all of a sudden, the buses came down the Strandway."

Bill Leary, one of his aides, Charles Leftwich, and John Coakley have now arrived, as the mayor asks the police, "Do we have any police following the buses?" Yes, he is told.

"Commissioner, what are our recommendations for tonight and tomorrow?"

"Our officers are gonna be at the schools."

"How many?" the mayor asks.

"Two," says diGrazia.

Kevin worries out loud that two men at Southie High won't be enough tonight. DiGrazia argues it is enough. White reminds them that on the night before school opened, youths painted graffiti on the walls of the school, "which meant they could have burned it down too."

"Tonight," di Grazia says, "two officers will be walking on school grounds. Also, we have cars keeping an eye on the other schools in South Boston."

"And you think that's sufficient?"

"Yes."

"What about tomorrow?"

"Tomorrow, we'll do the same thing we did this afternoon. We will stop them at the checkpoint and escort them. . . ." DiGrazia praises his men, and Kevin White tells everyone — Herb Gleason and Deputy Mayor Sullivan have joined what is now a crowd here — "There's plenty of time for commendations. I'm looking for criticism right now, even of me." DiGrazia says tomorrow, there will be barricades and ropes up around Southie High. Kevin turns to Eddie King for help.

"Seal off Thomas Park," King says. "Keep the kids from going on the grass at the Strandway."

"What's the mood of the community now?" Kevin asks.

"Very bad," says King. "It's gonna boil over. These weren't just eighteen-year-olds." He predicts "a lot more missiles."

"We're gonna have more personnel there," Joe Jordan says. He disagrees with King. "My feeling is tension is going down. If we have enough people visible . . ."

The mayor lays it out. "Let me give you my assessment. I'm not an armchair general, and I don't want to play that role. I'm not trained to. On the other hand, I've had more experience in this thing than most of you. First, if there was any small error in retrospect, I suggest any congregation beyond five is trouble because there are no community leaders who can control them. So, tonight, I'll accept your professional judgment that two officers are sufficient for the high school. I'd suggest at least one officer per school plus cars, and would add the King School to the list. Tomorrow, one day overdue . . . we've had our last public meeting, our last temper tantrum, our last missiles thrown. I wanna know if the police have the capacity to clear the Thomas Park area. Second, I expect any missile thrower apprehended and arrested. Even those with a bum arm. Hitting the target is not a requirement for arrest. They're *cowards*. They're not tough. Do you have the competency to clear Thomas Park?"

Jordan answers in one word, quickly, "Yes."

"You're not planning to put that in a public statement, are you?" diGrazia asks.

"Oh, yes, I am," says Kevin. "I know what I'm doing. This is my town. You can tell me the bus driver took the wrong turn, but that's not the point. There shouldn't have been a crowd in the first place."

DiGrazia worries out loud that the statement could create problems, and others argue the point on both sides, and Kevin stops the arguing. He is in charge. He reads the speech he's put together for the press conference upstairs; he makes corrections out loud; he yells out for the chapter and section on the law that enables him to do the things he's about to do, because there could be civil rights challenges to what he is about to announce.

- The meeting is over. DiGrazia gets up, shaking his head. Kiley and Tivnan join their boss in the back room. There is some yelling, but it is inaudible. It is time to meet the press. The reporters are impatient. They have deadlines to meet and questions to ask.

Upstairs, White lays it out. "The streets will be clear . . . no one will be allowed near school without an ID. . . . No gathering larger than three persons . . . No crowd will be allowed to congregate. . . . All school buses will be escorted by police. . . . I provided 99 percent protection, but I had promised 100 percent. . . ."

Suddenly, a member of the Progressive Labor Party rushes in front of the cameras and begins reading a statement. "Hey, shaddup," reporters yell. "Get him outta there. . . . Hey, get outta there. . . . Awwww, shaddup. . . ." Tommy Newcomb and Bernie Callahan grab him on each arm and rush him out. As they do, another PLP member on the side tries to interrupt with shouts of "martial law" and he too gets the bum's rush.

Walt Sanders, a tall, husky black reporter who patiently covers education in Boston for the local NBC affiliate, asks the Mayor, "Problems were anticipated. Why weren't these measures taken today?"

Kevin doesn't tell them he had preached this kind of crowd control two days ago. He says, "We are a city of great tolerance. We wanted to have as much public assembly as possible. . . ."

DiGrazia follows Kevin to the cameras, and White returns downstairs. It is 5:30 P.M., and Paul Parks is bringing in a group of blacks, including Percy Wilson and Pat Jones, who run social service centers, Bill Owens, a protest leader who has become the first black state senator in Massachusetts, and Herb Jackson, the man who helped keep the peace this morning at Hyde Park High School. There is a mass meeting tonight at Freedom House, and they want the mayor there in person. The community is scared and angry. Kevin reviews for them his arguments against letting people congregate.

"I was operating strictly on my gut. There were tolerant, liberal members of my staff who felt we had handled demonstrations before. I disagreed with my own staff and said if the crowds were far enough away and with good control, I'd give in to their judgment. At least in this case, I was right. They were wrong. We shouldn't let them congregate anywhere. The key to one of your comments, Percy, is hey, we did our part, why didn't the city do its part? You're working in the community that wanted to comply, and the majority extended courtesy to whites. Surprisingly, it worked both ways. Both ways, there were no problems. Just Southie.

"The press and the police couldn't believe how well it was going in Southie. But I also heard reports of 'baboons,' 'niggers,' and other words coming from mothers. I'll tell you, in my guts, I hate that."

The blacks threaten to go into Southie with the kids, and he tells them, "No matter what you do, I'm still gonna implement the three-is-a-crowd order. Black, white, no difference. Any arrest I can make I'll make. I cannot constrain any of you from going in."

One challenges him about his earlier promise. "Mister Mayor, you said the person who throws the first brick, the first tomato or egg will get his head broken."

"That's right. Two of my orders were not met. One, congregating. Two, missiles. I don't give a shit. Any missile. *Arrest* him."

"Why," Wilson asks, "does your staff make so many calculated errors when dealing with the black community? How in hell, knowing South Boston, could they do that unless you don't give a damn about us?"

"Percy, do you think that? I won't give you any shit. Go in yourself. The people in this city worked their ass off. Their error in judgment didn't trigger it."

Another argues, "If the incident had occurred in the black community, I believe there would've been dogs, cats, rats, gas and anything else they could drag in. What we want to see tomorrow, we want to see implementation. If you had seen those girls come off the buses crying and scared . . . We aren't going to that meeting tonight and tell them, 'Kevin *said.*' We want *you* to talk to them."

One argues, "We're in the position we're in now out of consideration to you. We want *you* to speak to the community."

The mayor puts his right index finger to his lips and leans back in the chair and stares up at the ceiling. "I felt I didn't think it advisable — I'm thinking out loud now — I honestly believe 98 percent of the town did better than I thought it would. I don't wanna do what those bastards want us to do — to turn the whole goddamn town upside down. Up till three o'clock, that group thought they were losing the battle. Until that goddamn situation. I don't want to convey that the place is in an uproar. I'd be willing to go to Freedom House — if you can give me a guarantee — no goddamn press. The press is on the verge of going the other way, saying the place is falling apart, and that's just what Kerrigan and Louise want. They'll wake up smiling tomorrow." He raises their devils to convince them.

"My presence begins to start that problem. You get the mayor going from one place to another, you've got a gone situation. Because my police are not coming through, your credibility is out, and they'll say to you, 'You're full of shit.' I've outplayed Kerrigan, and maybe that's not saying much." That gets a few laughs. "In terms of votes, I couldn't give a shit less. You're playing risks, and you're playing them with me. But there's a calculated risk that going there conveys to the media that we got more troubles across the city than we really got."

Wilson tells him, "If we say to those children tonight, back on the bus, kids, the mayor loves you, they're gonna say 'Bullshit to you, bullshit to the mayor. I'll be on that bus, and you'll be waitin' on the corner back on Warren Street.' There should be responsible black folk in that school that they can turn to, even if they're in the basement somewhere."

"So," Kevin says, "you're telling me they're not going to believe me anyway. If I tell them to go, on my credibility and guarantee, and they're willing to go, that's a gamble."

Another says, "We've told these kids, no matter what happens, keep your hands in your pockets and your mouths shut."

The black delegation and the white mayor have been feeling each other out. Now, each side escalates the process.

"I told those kids I'd go on the bus with them," one says. "I didn't go on the bus because of what I had heard about protection. But I'm going to South Boston tomorrow, and the question is how many black males do I have to take with me. And when the arrests come down on us there, all hell breaks loose in Roxbury, because they'll say they're *arresting* blacks in South Boston. You go there tonight and tell us. I'm still going to South Boston, but maybe others won't if they're reassured."

Wilson warns Kevin, "There's a question of retaliation here too."

"I'm not dumb," Kevin says. "I understand that."

"But you don't seem to be dealing with it," Wilson argues.

"Oh, c'mon, Percy, for Chrissakes. I was gonna take police from other areas of the city and double up on Southie. But now you're suggesting to me that I won't get the cooperation in Roxbury that I got today."

"It's a real probability," Wilson says.

They talk of asking for state police, of radio-equipped buses, again of black parents in the schools. The mayor says he wants to review everything with them, now, to make sure he has it straight, so he can clear what must be cleared with Bill Leary.

"How are you gonna deal with prosecution?" one asks him. "You can arrest them, put 'em in the slam and they're out in fifteen minutes."

"I'll do my best," Kevin says, "but I can't control that."

From a corner of the room, Larry Quealy worries out loud about Kevin going to Freedom House. When a black starts to object, Kevin cuts him off. "Hey, this is why I have a staff. We disagree. We discuss."

Kevin says he doesn't want to meet with South Boston parents — Quealy has just learned of a mass meeting in Southie — tonight and tells the blacks, "I wouldn't let Louise Day Hicks through this door today, when she wanted to see us. I don't give a damn what her peace message is." He doesn't tell them that he makes damn sure he stays in contact with her through others.

Wilson has agreed with the mayor about the press, and the blacks also assure White that the questions will be controlled, that the meeting will not be an uproar. The bells from the nearby Custom House tower ring 7 o'clock, and the blacks have to get back.

As they file out, Owens turns and says, "Thank you. Thank you very much."

At 7:45 P.M. Bob Jordan, a *Globe* reporter, and another writer join the mayor and Mike Feeney in one of the cars, equipped with a phone. As they pull out from behind City Hall on their way to Freedom House, Isaac Graves, the black manager of the Roxbury Little City Hall, calls the mayor who listens, grunts, says a few words in anger and hangs up. "Ah, for Chrissakes, Isaac says it's an angry crowd at Freedom House." He is angry too. The delegation had promised him a controlled set of questions — not a censored set, but controlled — no shouting and threats. Now, he will do again what he has done so often since 1968, face a shouting crowd. "I'm friggin' fed up. For five months . . ." He complains of the pressures, the impossibility of running a city. Months later, his friend Dick Dray will say that a long time ago, being mayor stopped being fun for Kevin.

At Freedom House, a car full of Kevin's plainclothesmen and aides appears alongside his, and they and black leaders whisk him inside to the offices of Otto and Muriel Snowden, the veterans of decades of civil rights, social, and educational battles in Boston and the founders of Freedom House. The Snowdens have been at it a long time, and they have outlasted others who appeared briefly in the 1960's and faded away. Some jibe that they are too middle-class, but they are not Toms. They are politic.

Under a picture of Frederick Douglass, who had come here because once blacks were welcome here, Otto Snowden, thin and gray-haired, briefs the mayor on the crowd. "We've cut the mikes," he tells him. "Good idea," Kevin says.

One observer takes a friend aside and says, "The mood here has shifted in an hour and a half. It was bravado. Now, it's fear. The fear is overwhelming. Kevin can't make any promises that will convince them. There's nothing that can be said that will convince them. It's got to be style."

Otto is telling the mayor, ". . . a packed house, and more frightened than angry." The whites, including the aides and the plainclothesmen and the people like Smith, are told — ordered — to stay upstairs. The only white man allowed downstairs at the meeting is Kevin. When Mike Feeney tries to go with him, the normally calm and friendly Ellen Jackson yells him back into the waiting room. Kevin is nervous. From upstairs, one hears first applause, then noise, then shouts and yelling. One black woman, coming up the stairs, says, "The noise you hear are people fussing at people who want to talk and who want Kevin to stop talking so they can talk."

"I believed in you," a woman shouts at the mayor. "I believed in you, and you let me down." The crowd erupts in turmoil. Kevin is worried and sweating. He asks for another shot. He says the city is going to crack down on the troublemakers. He points to the woman who shouted at him and says, "She believed in me, and she sent her kids along, believing they'd be protected. I did let her down."

He promises that Friday will be more peaceful. He promises more crowd control. "It's not the Lord's guarantee, but I'm asking for another chance, and then, if I can't produce, I'll fight alongside you."

There is only scattered applause.

As the mayor prepares to leave, people are milling around outside Freedom House, and there is much confusion. A black woman says to a knot of angry women, "He's trying to get your good graces. He's still white, and what's more, he's Irish."

"They look out for their own kind."

"South Boston should be the same as ours. Why didn't they turn the hoses on them like they did with ours?"

Kevin White, surrounded by white aides and blacks, comes through the crowd scared, sweating profusely, and depressed. His aides push him into the car, and blacks clear a path for them. Nobody is threatening him, nothing visible anyway. The black leaders had no control over the meeting. They control the mayor's exit. As the car speeds off, White, his jacket off, sweating, leans back on the seat, rubs his forehead and his graying hair, his feet up on the dashboard. "I don't want to talk," he says to his companions in the back seat. He sits there, mumbling, swearing. Mike is driving and Bernie sits on Kevin's right and they look at the mayor the way a father looks at a sick kid, the way a coach looks at a favorite player who has played himself out. The car phone rings, and Bernie answers it. Peter Meade is over at the Tynan School in Southie and says there's a mass meeting there at 9 o'clock. He and Billy McDermott are keeping tabs on it, but why isn't the mayor there? McDermott will be angry, until later in the evening, when he will wander into City Hall, take a long look at the mayor, and he will know why Kevin White, better than most humans in a crowd, could not handle any more mass confrontations tonight. Enough was enough.

The mayor is smoking now and calming down, as the car takes him through the quiet streets of Roxbury and Dorchester and back to City Hall. He begins to talk again. "That leadership was no more in control of them . . . If I didn't have my own capacities, I'd have been slaughtered. In my whole political life, this was the most difficult one."

White just goes on, a monologue. "They started to physically fight among themselves. . . . I think I'm tougher than all these bastards, but collectively, they can get to you."

Bernie the father says quietly, "You've been up since five o'clock."

"No," Kevin says, "it's not that."

It is perhaps something larger than even he is thinking about at this moment, hot and unwinding slowly and sweaty in a car on its way back to more reports of more crises. The history of cities, the downward plummet really, had begun long before Grandfather Hagan, even before that awful day in August, 1863. The nation had started out with praise of rural man and his surroundings. It had finally emerged with praise of suburban man and his life-style. The cities were forever left to people others thought less worthy. The attitude was in America's subconscious, but it was there all right, and it was displayed every time the body politic had a chance or a choice. Mayors who ran for governor or President were usually defeated. Generations of suburbanites told their children never, never go into the city, for there is nothing there but death and hate. The federal government seemed to be doing all that it could to keep the cities in their allegedly depraved state. Almost every federal program until the mid-1960's was geared toward the uplift of suburbia and the destruction of urban America. When programs did finally appear, they were almost too late and most certainly underfunded. The idea that America could eradicate urban, suburban, and rural poverty in 50 states for $2 billion a year was a very large laugh. Dribbles and droplets of federal funds, with the hopes they implied, did bring more people into the political process, did provide some employment and some housing, but they also widened the divisions that already existed in the cities — divisions based on heritage, class, race, geography, whatever. Now, a federal court had ruled that the city must bus, but the Supreme Court had so far insured that no cities, not even the predominantly black ones, could cross the artificial lines into suburbia to attain true school integration. By the time Garrity ordered busing, not one single low-income unit of housing had been built under a 4½-year-old state anti–snob zoning law. Meanwhile, slumlords abandoned houses in the city, suburbanites ripped off copper flashing from new and repaired homes in the city, the statistics of crime increased steadily everywhere, and the mayor was told by his frightened, angry black and white and Spanish-speaking and Oriental constituents — protect us. You promised. By any objective standards, Kevin White had bettered the quality of life in the neighborhoods, and he had held the tax rate and he had brought into city government some of the most talented and dedicated people in the country, and right now, it didn't mean shit, because factors now out of everyone's control, factors set in motion more than a century before and assured of continued existence by federal neglect, were now running events in Boston.

At 10:00 P.M., the command staff gathers again in Kevin White's office. Downstairs in the bunker, Kelliher is checking a rumor that Columbia Point blacks are headed for Southie and that Dorchester white kids are smashing traffic lights on Dorchester Avenue to foul up tomorrow's traffic.

The mayor has been talking to Charlie Barry alone in his back room. Now, Barry is back in the living room, sitting with his hands folded in front of him, mulling over how close the city had come to peace today. "Last of the ninth, two out and . . ." The police brass comes in along with Kevin's aides — diGrazia, Russell, Jordan, Kiley, Quealy, Ira Jackson, Kirk O'Donnell, and others.

"Forget today," Kevin begins. "Today is over. All I'm concerned with is tonight and tomorrow. From the reports we have, the white community is all charged up, but the decent element in town is affected by events, and there's great sentiment for not repeating what happened today. The black community can be summed up by saying they are not bullshit, they are not mad, they are not furious, but scared shitless. Scared shitless.

"The orders I want compiled with are that each school has at least two men per school in Southie, so there's no question of entrance tonight on those grounds. The second point is that the area is to be cleared entirely of any congregation of three or more near the high school. Not only out of eyeshot, but out of earshot. I don't want to have those black kids even *hear* them. Anyone who doesn't comply — that includes Louise, Flynn, Dapper, anyone. . . . Arrest anyone who doesn't comply. Any group above ten or engaged in a demonstration, looking for a leader, *anywhere* in town, don't permit it. My instincts tell me the whole town expects it. That includes the press. I cannot think of a reason why that can't be complied with, and tomorrow night I can deliver what I promised I would deliver on Thursday. Start at six in the morning. Full force until the situation de-escalates."

Kevin White would say weeks later that he never expected the city he knows so well to require the full force it did for so long.

"Forgetting today, all right? Can you do that, Charlie?"

Barry nods his head yes. He'll have his men out there.

"Jordan?"

"Positively," Jordan says.

"Commissioner?"

"We'll have to," diGrazia says.

"Paul?" he asks, turning to Russell.

"One condition," Russell says. "It applies to Roxbury too."

"I've been to a tough meeting," Kevin tells him. "The only thing still holding that community together is my credibility. There wasn't one black leader who could control that crowd. I don't think we got any credits there. That black leadership proved to me tonight . . ."

Russell says, "I mention it because everything otherwise went so well today, that English High could erupt tomorrow."

"I understand that," Kevin answers. "If we had gone in there today and done that, we would have eaten up all the credits of patience. . . . I'm hoping if we can control the crowds early enough, then we can spread thin. And the message travels fast in this town, and you don't need phones. We got enough guys?"

"Yes sir," says Jordan.

"That was power today," says diGrazia.

The brass is happy with its men, just as the school department executives are happy with the principals and teachers and aides, who, despite the school committee, made the first day of integration peaceful almost everywhere.

"The policemen there," Jordan says, "had close ties to South Boston. They have relatives there, friends there. Some went to that school." But, Jordan says, they performed.

Barry says, "We had a meeting with the superior officers, and the conclusion we came to is the conclusion you have."

Bill Leary and John Coakley arrive and sit on a couch, as Kevin talks about the vibrations he's getting in the city. "What's going on now is that there's as much control among the black leadership as Louise had over the Kennedy incident." Quealy hands Kevin a note. It says the black leadership is now considering demanding U.S. marshals and a possible school boycott. After White had left the Freedom House meeting, Tom Atkins urged blacks not to send their kids to Southie's schools and said the NAACP would file a motion with Garrity for the marshals. "I don't think the city can do it by itself," he said. "We hoped we could see the city do right by itself, and we have given them a chance, but we cannot sacrifice our children."

About the same time, whites meeting at the Tynan School in Southie were criticizing the large police presence, and as Kevin White meets in his office and gets that note from Quealy about the black community, Ray Flynn walks out of the Tynan School and says, "These people believe the mayor overreacted. Mayor White and the police commissioner used the term 'low profile' in implementing Judge Garrity's order. Then today, the kids in South Boston saw police officers with riot gear, the Tactical Patrol Force and the Anti-Crime Unit and streets blocked off by policemen on horseback. It looked like something out of the Vietnam conflict."

The so-called traditional roles were being reversed. Police overkill, shouted the whites. Not enough police, shouted the blacks.

After getting the note, White reasons that the black leaders must do something to assert their political virility, especially after the raucous meeting. "No different than here," he says.

Now, White tells Leary that black leaders have requested more monitors on the buses. Leary agrees. He had not slept well last night. He rose at 6 A.M. and was in his office before 7 A.M. That morning, as he waited, he said quietly, "It's all on me." Now, as this meeting progresses, Leary is getting angry at Kevin White's administration. He senses that Kevin's people are making decisions about what will go on inside the schools. "I wanna know who's going to be in the schools," he says. "They're *my* schools. I run that show." The mayor is only communicating the request from the black delegation — they want black parents in Southie High.

"I'll have to go to Bill Reid [the Southie headmaster] and tell him," Leary says. "This is pending Reid's okay."

"And if Reid says no?" the mayor asks patiently.

"If Reid says no, we'll negotiate," Leary says and turns to one of the aides who has come in and snaps, "Give him a call at his home."

Kevin also has been on the phone. "I've just talked to the court-appointed monitor," he tells them. "The NAACP is petitioning for U.S. marshals. I talked the court out of it. I asked for an extra day. Is that agreed from everybody?" He knows the answer to that; the question is tactful. There is a general shaking of heads, yes. "We don't need 'em," Russell says.

Leary complains, "The press is pushing me. Sometimes I blow my cool. 'When are you going to name them truants?' they ask me. Sometime this weekend, I've got to come up with a statement to appeal to those parents who are keeping their kids home — to say it worked at the Curley School, it was good at the Cleveland. The problems were opening day problems."

Charles Leftwich, a light-skinned black who's Leary's right-hand man, says, "South Boston is taking a bum rap. It was certain ones. If all of South Boston wanted to stop it, there's no way only buses would have been damaged. It's also dangerous, because blacks will translate South Boston to mean whites."

Kevin, it turns out, will remember this. He will throw it out in front of black leaders in an upcoming meeting.

Leary begins to smile. He pats Kiley, with whom he had clashed, on the back. He says to the mayor, "I wanna tell you your guys are good men. This man," he slaps Kiley's back, "is a darn good man. And Paul Russell. And Kelliher." Kevin tells Leary he too has good people.

"All right," the mayor of Boston says, "let's get the hell out of here and do it tomorrow."

TWENTY

September 13: Containment

AS OF TODAY, the job facing Kevin White is to contain Southie, to make sure the virus, now open and breeding, does not infect the integration in Hyde Park, the racially mixed Dorchester and Jamaica Plain, the angry black Roxbury, the insulated, tough whites of East Boston, Charlestown, and the North End.

On this day, Bob Kiley calls into the bunker. "There are clusters starting to gather. I hear word of a parade through the center of Southie, abetted maybe by a couple of pols. The mayor said yesterday large groups are okay if not steam-gathering. This looks like steam-gathering. They'll need a parade permit. No one should be handing out parade permits like it was St. Patrick's Day 1911."

Then, he calls the mayor. "They give 'em a couple of minutes to make up their minds, and then they move in. It's a different atmosphere than yesterday. Less tense in screaming and shouting. More tense in apprehension."

The afternoon brings trouble — a rumor that a West Roxbury boy was held up at knifepoint by black students, a bomb scare in Eastie.

On Bus #224, a black Roxury kid is cut on the face as a steel bolt smashes through the window. The boy's aunt says she's angry at Kevin White, for Kevin White had promised safe passage. In Southie, the Tactical Patrol Force breaks up the crowds and arrests a dozen men and boys. In Roxbury, a black bus driver tells his white passengers to lie on the floor as he runs his school bus through a gauntlet of stones thrown by black youths.

That night, one of the networks says grimly, in its nightly fashion, "There was a second day of violence in South Boston today. . . ." But that was not the news. Things that are expected are usually not as newsworthy as the unexpected. In Southie and in scattered incidents elsewhere, Boston was acting contrary to the false myth that the press and, therefore, the rest of the nation had of the city. To them, a liberal city was being hypocritical, whereas, in fact, a parochial city with a long history of ethnic and racial distrust and bigotry, was, for the most part, peacefully integrating its schools — and *that* was the news.

But Kevin White and his aides knew that this relative degree of peace would not last long. How long would it be before the youths in Roxbury retaliated? And how long could Kevin White and his administration and the police and community workers contain most of the organized violence to Southie, before it spread? They had to isolate Southie, and as the weekend approaches, this is the task that faces them.

TWENTY-ONE

Indian Summer Day

Part One: The Day

DOVER IS A SUBURB, very plush, where the zoning code insists on one-
and two-acre lots for houses. About five thousand persons take up
fifteen square miles to live in Dover. That would fit about one-third of
Boston's population. There are other differences.

Former U.S. Senator Leverett Saltonstall and family live on a vast
farm with white wooden fences and trimmed hedges, with cows and
horses and chickens, and, unlike some of the families in Boston's South
End, the Saltonstalls are not reputed to keep the chickens in the
kitchen or the bathtub. Today, Sunday, September 15, the Republican
Town Committee of Dover is giving a cocktail party on Saltonstall's
farm. The party is for Salty's neighbor, who lives one mile away. In
Southie and Dorchester, your neighbor lives upstairs. In the old suburbs that ring the city, your neighbor lives next door. In places like
Dover, your neighbor lives a mile away. This neighbor's name is Francis Sargent, and he is the governor, though, as it turns out, not for

long. But even without Saltonstall and Sargent in the neighborhood, it is a pretty good bet that Dover will get its trash collected regularly. The trash in Dover could outfit some apartments in Boston.

About 450 persons will show up for this affair, and two mounted cops from Dover will guide them over the Saltonstall estate, which features an hors d'oeuvres table, a bandstand with a quartet, and several cocktail bars. It is a very nice day, an Indian summer day.

As the caterer in Dover prepares for Yankees and other breeds of Republicans, a priest ascends the pulpit at the Gate of Heaven Church on East Fourth Street in South Boston and pleads, "Our role is to try and keep down any violence that might take place. I know that you will do your part."

In Roxbury, a minister at St. Mark's Congregational Church is urging students to go to school. "God does not fight battles for you, but with you. Bravery is not obtained in isolation of danger. Go forth tomorrow as further demonstration of goodwill."

It is a good day for sermons and outings and press conferences and a ROAR motorcade. But behind the scenes, behind the brick walls of a Beacon Hill townhouse, there is yet another event taking place, and it has not been announced to the press. Kevin White and his advisors are to meet again today to talk about strategy and containment and The Mullens. It will prove to be a long day for Kevin White. In its evening hours, he will talk with white people who share his distaste of forced busing and his fear of Southie, and at night, he will assert his authority over men almost twice his age in the Boston Police Department. Behind it all lurks the enigma of a new and somewhat unexpected factor in the crisis. Gangland.

Larry Quealy is the first to arrive. Larry is concerned about the motorcade today in Southie and rumors of a march tomorrow, when school reopens. A few minutes later, Kirk O'Donnell joins him and talks of blacks scheduled to meet in Roxbury today. His information is that the black leadership is under fire.

In Southie, one source has said, "There'll be an appeal made this morning through the churches, telling them they don't have a permit to march and to stay home. But some of the Irish Mafia are calling parents, telling them to *show up*." When he talks about the Irish Mafia, he does not mean what others have meant. What others have meant were the loyalists around Jack Kennedy, and the term was used humorously. What he means is not humorous. He is talking about Southie toughs, young and middle-aged men, some of whom belong to The Mullens.

Everybody has a different theory about The Mullens. Some say it's nothing more than a social club, a sports club. Others say it's a club all right, and a lot of guys in it do indeed play baseball, and some guys in it are into a different kind of sports, like hijacking trucks, heisting warehouses, loansharking, bookmaking, and other activities on which the law doth frown. It is said further, by some sources, that The Mullens has been in a pragmatic alliance with other elements of Boston's usually freewheeling organized crime set, that one reason the alliance was set up was to cut down on in-house violence. At least one member of The Mullens was given to machine-gunning things and people, and lately, it is said, he was more inclined to just go out and practice firing his machine gun into the harbor. While the Italian and Jewish elements are still deeply involved in gambling, and while the Italian "family," answerable to Raymond Patriarca in Providence, is considered the boss in Boston, there is not the heavy-handed organization here that there is in New York and New Jersey. Former hippies, Chinese from Hong Kong, Puerto Ricans, blacks are all into dope. The blacks run most of the pimping on the street and numbers in their own districts. The Puerto Ricans have their own bookies, and the Chinese, their own gambling clubs. But the man police say is closest to running everything in some organized fashion — allegedly with the blessings of the men in the North End — is a character from nearby Somerville. Theoretically, none of this should have anything to do with busing. But theory is what the academic integrationists and segregationists and, for that matter, federal judges can discuss. The folks gathering here in the morning are not theorists.

It is a strange place to discuss the subject. The Parkman House is almost 150 years old. It sits, all four floors of it, a few yards down Beacon Street from the State House. A plaque on the front informs the visitor, "Here lived and died George Francis Parkman, 1823–1908. Remembered with endearing gratitude by the City of Boston for his bequest of a fund that secures forever the maintenance and improvement of the Common and other public parks." The Common sits across the street. Parkman could look out at it every day. Kathryn Galvin White and some other people raised some money to renovate the old place, now tastefully adorned with donated Yankee furniture and appointments from the best shops. In its rear is the old stable with back doors leading out into an alley. The iron rings to which the horses were tied have been left in the walls. The stable is now a carpeted meeting room with phones in two corners. The phones will be very busy today.

Before they go in, Larry talks about the proposed march tomorrow in Southie, and looks up at the blue sky. "It'll be a nice day tomorrow."

"Shit," says Kirk. "The last thing we need is an Indian summer."

Today, Larry Quealy will hear from people in Southie. Kirk will be talking to his workers in the Little City Halls. Rich Kelliher will be talking to the bunker. Bob Kiley will be talking to everyone from the FBI to the black community.

Inside, Kiley tells everyone he spent Saturday talking with Paul Parks, Percy Wilson, and Police Deputy Superintendent LeRoy Chase, the highest-level black officer in the department, about the King School, "and everyone feels there will be a bigger problem there soon if South Boston continues."

Kirk, a nervous young man given to gnawing on a fingertip or a knuckle, sits slumped in a chair, and predicts the black reprisals will be on "other white kids," not the ones causing trouble in Southie.

"That's the real problem," Kiley agrees. "That's why we've got to stop it here."

"I wonder," Kirk says, "if I could get some hall managers to call the anti-busing leaders in Hyde Park, West Roxbury, Dorchester, and see if they're angry at South Boston. Maybe if their sense of isolation is heightened by all this, Southie will come to grips with this, and maybe the blacks will not retaliate on all whites." This thought becomes the nub of the weekend strategy. The game is to outguess, and to do so, they plumb their intelligence system, which ranges from their Little City Hall people to their political contacts to old friends to worried moderates in the anti-busing camp. Kirk begins calling Little City Hall managers with his divide-and-conquer proposal.

Kelliher hangs up his phone and reports. "The public posture is to fight busing and save the neighborhood," he says of the planned march in Southie, "but the real word we're getting is that it's really to defy the mayor."

Louise Day Hicks has called a contact in the mayor's office. He says she's worried because three mothers have called to tell her their kids were given guns. If the march is to be stopped — the moderates in Southie report — it must be stopped at M Street Park. The gun rumor is the second such heard by White's people.

Shortly after noon, Kevin shows up in brown corduroy slacks, a striped shirt, and a sweater tied by the sleeves around his neck, à la 1950's college campus. Kirk tells him that anti-busing people in other neighborhoods are working the streets against violence. Kelliher, back on the phone, covers the mouthpiece and reports that the police got signals early Saturday and the assumption is the march should be stopped.

Kevin has helped himself to a bunch of blueberries and milk and a cup of coffee and is slurping and talking between and during gulps.

"There's something on my mind. All the prospects of what the English couldn't do in Belfast we gotta do here. I was thinking of something last night. I have a feeling of how the city feels. Like all my feelings, it's a *sense* of something. I have a feeling that the rest of the city is bullshit at Southie, bullshit or sympathetic, and I gotta find out which. But no matter what the sentiment on the other side of the city is, as I see it, there are a number of steps quickly coming upon us. Either the fever is gonna break or it isn't. I think Monday is quite a test for us, a test whether South Boston will come under control, whether it's willing reluctantly to accept slow change. The real test is — can the police contain it? Can we guarantee safety? Can we break up the march without violence? The test Monday is our capacity to break the physical potential for real trouble. I don't have an answer to that. I've heard lots of rumors, bomb threats, even a gun. For the first time in a long time, sitting in bed last night, I was thinking that one of my kids could be in danger. I never thought like that before.

"Are we misreading the sentiment out there? It hasn't gone underground. It has not yet found a leader. We've got a real problem with the psychology of South Boston. So we must not be so stupid as to treat it the same as we would other patients. Our vantage point we have is we can perceive things quicker than anyone else."

He talks about the police ability to contain, the administration's ability to diagnose properly the reaction of blacks, the general public reaction to its decisions. He has been talking with the brass at the *Globe*, people like Editor Tom Winship. "I told Winship yesterday federal marshals are ridiculous, federal troops are not. . . . We've prepared as well as anybody can prepare for this. We've had a sense of patience. We really have to figure out today what happens if all hell breaks loose or if whatever happens, there is not a sufficient guarantee to the black community, and that we won't be able to contain them that night — unless they know what's going on, unless they're part of the process. What are your ideas for tomorrow and tomorrow night? I have some, but I'm not confident they're the right ones."

Kiley argues, "We should make people aware of the parade, that we will not let it get started. We should make it known by midday today. If the blacks could be drawn into the process . . ."

Kevin interrupts, "I agree."

". . . and the whites who may be complying."

"I hadn't thought of that," the boss says.

"Also," Kiley continues, "if there was a way of getting to the people of Southie, people no one's ever heard of before, of appealing to reason, appealing to calm . . . Getting the state police involved won't help. They're not a large enough force, and they're not under our control. The National Guard would be a mistake — like calling in a mob and giving them guns."

"What about Devens?" the mayor asks, referring to an army post in eastern Massachusetts.

"Well, maybe that's it," Kiley says, "a small federal force. If we go that route, we should go about preparing for it, whether we do or not. Any external force, you don't control it. But if the initiative came from you, and it was a small, rather than large, contingent, it would be like exercising some control."

Kevin pulls out some paper. "Let me read a statement I wrote last night. It's not a great statement, but it's a statement. And I agree with you, Bobby. We, in the public eye and in our own, have been in control of the situation, and that's something you don't give up." He stresses that the city's plans should be perceived by the public as part of a process and not just as a reaction to whatever might happen tomorrow.

Just as the mayor starts creating a hypothetical crisis, Joe Jordan walks in. "Don't jump, Joe," he says. "This is Monday night, and the goddamn town is falling apart." He reads, "All across the face of the city for three days . . . white mothers in Hyde Park, black mothers in Roxbury . . . Every section did something to make it proud. Only one section of the city told us they didn't care, that the rest of us have to obey a law that they don't . . . sad . . . a good community with good people. . . . South Boston wishes to be treated differently, so it will be. . . . I will not let any group, black or white, tear this city apart. . . . Because we are still in control, we will take the extra police out and ask Garrity to order federal forces in. . . . That fear will not master us. . . ." It is a good statement.

The mayor says, "We ought to talk to the black leadership here today. We should galvanize the white community. I think that I should talk to [Congressman] Joe Moakley and apprise him and to Garrity to be prepared." Turning to Jordan, he says, "Tomorrow's test is not whether Southie gets over its temper tantrum, but whether we're gonna have a long-term problem like Belfast."

Jordan briefs them on some intelligence from Southie. He says a man who runs a club where all The Mullens hang out and and another guy approached Charlie Barry and told him the men were going to march "come hell or high water. They're supposed to turn around the high school and then onto Broadway. Another source says they'll go directly to City Hall."

"Well, either way," says Kevin, "they're gonna have a march, and we haven't been able to control a march yet."

"We're beefing up with the expectation that the march will form at

Thomas Park," Jordan tells him. Kevin says he wants it stopped before it begins.

"You know who's organizing it?" Jordan asks, ready to tell them if they don't.

"Yeah," somebody says, "I'm told the Irish Mafia."

Jordan says the other day two well-known Southie strong-arm guys were seen with a television reporter who wanted protection while covering the crowd.

Now the question is how to get to The Mullens to convince them to cool it. Jordan says the Somerville hood is supposedly *the* man. A crisis does not come in neat, set pieces, nor does the conversation that men have to deal with it. As some talk of The Mullens, Kirk renews the issue of federal help. "The president himself has to make the decision to send in federal troops. First, you have to go to the state police, then the National Guard. If you want to get federal troops, maybe you could bring in small numbers of state police and National Guard first."

"The state police wouldn't do us any good," Kiley contends, "but no harm either. Federal marshals wouldn't do us any good, but no harm. The National Guard would not only do us no good, but also harm."

They ponder who their links and connections are, to grease the communication lines to Washington. "You've got John and Eddie McCormack," Kirk says.

"We've got Tip," says Kevin, referring to House Majority Leader Tip O'Neill from nearby North Cambridge. But he can't get his mind off the insanity of the hour. Here is a man who has spent most of his adult life in politics, who almost ran for Vice President of his nation and who has been told by admirers to run for President, who has spent some of his most enjoyable nights at the other end of this very same Yankee building discussing cosmic issues with politicians, sociologists, journalists, and economists, and now he is trying to figure out how you contact gang leaders and convince them not to destroy the city. "Until four months ago, I never even knew who that Somerville guy was. But since then, I've learned he's got a lot of clout. . . . Somebody's gonna get hurt. Somebody's gonna take a Saturday night special and fire it into a crowd."

"It's getting to that point," Jordan agrees.

"Where are you gonna let them go?" Kevin worries about the marchers. "They're not gonna sit there like the Bonus Army." He is not crazy about using dogs for control, and fears using them "will lose us good people." He wants to call for help. "Pride is not a point with me. I'm trying to outthink them, though." Suddenly, he looks up and orders, "Larry, get on one of those phones and find out where Tip O'Neill is." He looks at Jordan. "It's like a war, isn't it?"

Jordan rolls his eyes in the direction of the streets. "I'm sure it is over there."

Almost to himself, Kevin says, "I'm not worried about the twelve-year-olds. What really gnaws at me is The Mullens crew. The twelve-year-olds I can contain."

White hands Kelliher a list of blacks to be contacted for a meeting today. Kiley reports on his meeting yesterday and says, "The blacks were urging their kids to go to school, but now they don't know what position to take." Jordan is on the phone with someone from Southie. When he finishes, he reports, "He sounds quite concerned. He says The Mullens are running the affair. He's telling his constituency not to go. He might be a little dippy. I don't really know the guy well." Jordan rings up headquarters and leaves a message for two detectives in the intelligence section to call him.

Kiley and Kirk talk about bringing the FBI in on the hoods, and Kevin says to Jordan, "Joe, I know Clarence Kelley very well. Bob knows him intimately." Kiley adds, "If the Bureau knocks on those doors today, that could stop it dead." Kirk begins pacing the floor. The mayor mumbles acidly, "Great experience."

Kiley is on the phone with Tom Atkins. "Gee, Tom, that's good, but if we could maintain better communications . . . I know the mayor would like to stay in touch. . . ." Kevin whispers, "Where can I get him tonight about six?" Roles are continually reversing and will do so throughout the next few months. First, Atkins urged all blacks to go to school, and White told whites it was up to them, but cautioned that sooner or later they'd probably want to send their kids. Then, Atkins urged a black boycott and said he'd get federal help, while White told his staff the city did not need marshals. Then, Atkins changed his mind about the boycott, and now White wonders if, after all, he'll need federal help to protect black and white kids. Some of it may well be political flanking movement, but a good deal of it is simply responding to changes within the crisis.

Another source is calling in now. He tells Kiley that the Charlestown contingent of The Mullens will help their brethren in Southie. Jordan asks, "What if we start assigning detectives to The Mullens guys and lean on them?" From a front room in the Parkman House, Ira Jackson yells to Kevin that Tip O'Neill is on the other line. White leaves to talk to him, to grease the line to Washington in case troops are needed. Jordan continues, "We'll live right by their club. We'll watch their houses. If only the word can get out to the community that they're the ones in back of it."

"We're worried about panicking the rest of the city." Kiley says.

"We can put a couple of guys on the Somerville guy," said Jordan, "but he's *not* a very agreeable guy. . . . I wonder if we give the men shotguns and we show them we mean business. The Mullens got espirit de corps. South Boston's been threatened, and they're rallying around." Jordan gets up to go. It is 1:55 P.M. and he has a 2 o'clock meeting at police headquarters across town. "Let's keep our fingers crossed."

Kirk half-laughs and shakes his head. He turns to Kiley and says, "Like you said the other night, 'If we were goo-goos, what would we do? Right now.' " The question is poignant — would the theorists, the pro-busing liberals be able to deal with such things as The Mullens? Would they be talking about getting the FBI to knock on doors so that, ultimately, violence might be minimized? Would they know whom to call in the FBI? Kiley, who believes deeply in integrated schools, likes the idea of the FBI knocking on the doors of The Mullens late at night — "Knock, knock, Mr. ——, I'm Agent So-and-So." Tom Mckenna jumps in, "It seems you have this overdue library book?" They roar with laughter.

Samuel Huntington, a Harvard professor and neighbor of Kevin who helped in 1967, calls the Parkman House to offer whatever services he can. "No, thanks, Sam," Kevin says, "not unless there's some textbook I don't know about." But textbooks deal with cosmic issues. They rarely explain political decisions from the point of view of pols. One would not read in a textbook that the key to enforcing *Brown* v. *The Board of Education* in Boston might be, at least today, a Somerville racketeer.

As Kevin begins to unwind, as instructions go out to gather white moderates from the neighborhoods in his office at 7 tonight, staff members talk quietly on both phones, O'Donnell returns from Burger King, Kiley munches french fries as he gets a report on the motorcade — "Sixty from Charlestown, East Boston and the North End? About twenty or thirty behind Broadway waiting to join with signs. Are you on them? Do you have the numbers?" Now, Kiley calls Jordan — "I think it's just a question of having some cars up at the high school to keep them moving."

The boss looks around. "It's amazing how cool everybody's been. I'm really proud of this staff." Again, he talks of how "I'm on the line" and castigates Kennedy, Brooke, Moakley, and Sargent, among others, for not being on the line. In the middle of everything, John Spears, the Jamaica Plain Little City Hall manager, returns Kirk's call. He's calling from Foxboro, where he's watching the New England Patriots. Suddenly, all other conversations stop. Men who moments ago were thinking, talking, and planning containment, riot control, speeches, responses, meetings now yell almost in unison — "What's the score? What's the score?"

The mayor's highly touted Little City Hall intelligence gathering system reports back, "The Pats are beating Miami twenty to ten."

"No shit . . . Jeeeez . . . Heeeeyyy . . . This year, hah? . . . ."

Part Two: Evening

In the Eagle Room, the bridge chairs have been set up in a semi-circle, facing the mayor's desk. The Little City Hall managers, always on call, the new governmental versions of the ancient general practitioner, have brought in white neighborhood leaders, most of whom oppose busing.

In Southie, the motorcade is over. More than 200 cars have taken part, but more important, they included people from outside Southie, people from places like East Boston and Charlestown. The mayor must act quickly to contain the protest, and ROAR leaders know they must act quickly to make sure it's citywide.

Kevin tells the whites here, "If anybody's in the mood and wants to make any suggestions, go ahead. I'm not a fool, and I don't want to make mistakes, but I'm human, and I can make them. I'm not prone to panic, and the situation doesn't call for it." He reviews the events of the last few days, starting with the rally at Government Center.

"There was no political leadership. Nobody, but nobody, could control that crowd. . . . Southie was a bad experience to everyone there. Not much physical damage, but great psychological damage to the kids on the bus. . . . The black community is paralyzed by fear. In the black community, like everywhere else, there's no monolithic leadership. They weren't mad, or angry, just frightened out of their wits, the basic fear of being outnumbered. . . . I'll never say put your child on a bus, only that to those who do, I'll do my best. Well, I obviously didn't do my best for those who were hurt. Friday was considerably better. Late Friday, a group of one hundred teenagers sprung out and cornered a bus; the police went after them, and by and large, it was over.

"In Southie, the great motivation is fear. The boycott there is almost total, and that's their privilege. I don't want Southie cut off. On the other hand, they're equally adamant that no blacks come into town.

I'm really not sure of what that will mean. We'll know tomorrow. There's very little any of you can do. There's not anything that I'm asking you," he tells them, fully intending in this meeting to swing them against Southie, if he senses they're angry enough at what has gone on.

"My job is to insure peace and safety in the city. I suppose your job is to insure peace and safety in your own community. There's no longer anybody in Southie I know of who has the political clout or credibility to make it work. And there are questions and calls coming from other parts of the city. The first is, if you put two thousand police into South Boston, as you have, what about the rest of the city? That's a very real question. How long can I deprive you of that police protection in other areas? I don't know. It depends on Southie.

"The second question is whether the black and white communities will retaliate against each other. Until today, there's been none of that. A few stirrings here or there. Beyond that, I don't know. Look, I'm not shifting responsibility. But I'd like your opinion on, I guess, three areas — will it go as smoothly Monday and Tuesday as it did Thursday and Friday in your communities? What about police protection? What about retaliation?"

An East Boston woman whose children attend public schools contends, "Everything in East Boston is fine. The children aren't being bused. The boycott wasn't being observed. My sentiments are anti-busing, but everybody sent their children to school. I think in East Boston, the sentiments are ninety-eight percent against busing, but we're not being affected this year. With all this trouble, people are outraged. They're very angry that people would threaten the safety of other children with a rock or a pipe. But they're caught in the middle."

One of the original ROAR leaders apologizes for coming in a bit late. "My mother just came back from Italy. I told her to look over the property there, and if it's good, I'll *take* it." She says the anti-busing element in Hyde Park is "completely against violence. We've been in touch with our teenagers. They were gonna wait until you pulled the police out and then erupt. We've been told that Tuesday, the teens will line up River Street."

"Any way of preventing that?" Kevin asks. "Knowing that Roxbury will do the same thing?"

"If there are a lot of police, they won't do it. But there are about ten of them, already out of school, sitting on the steps, already saying to black girls, 'Hey, sister, watch the cunt' and that kind of stuff."

"If it gets like Southie," Kevin says, "it'll be outta control. And we'll have federal troops." He assures everyone that all police protection will remain at their schools.

A Roslindale woman reports, "There's been a transfer of whites from the lower grades to the Mary Curley [Jamaica Plain]. The blacks are kind of — shall we say — taking over there, and the teachers are saying after the second day only, to the white kids, if you don't behave yourself, you'll stay after school and miss the bus, and your father'll have to come get you. So they're fearful. I think the people are appalled at the violence too [in Southie]. Every mother has that in mind. In the grade schools, the black and white mothers are there and want to see it done peaceably."

Bo Holland, managing the Little City Hall in West Roxbury, says that when half the West Roxbury kids got on buses the first day to go to English High, a leader of the anti-busing forces called the Little City Hall and "blamed us for making it work. On Friday, two mothers called me that their kids felt intimidated and harassed and that less kids will go Monday, and my fear is the less that go, the more they'll be subjected to that stuff."

"I don't see how," one man says, "we won't get by the next few days without some retaliation and more bigotry."

The East Boston woman agrees. "I wouldn't use my child as a sacrificial lamb for anybody. If I was a member of the black community, this is how I'd feel. Right now, being a white working woman, we got the short end of the stick. I think white kids in South Boston would give it a shot, but they fear retaliation. Ya know, in a city, with crowded conditions and all, there are gangs, and you got to watch it. You figure you'll get educated some other day. In the Eastie-Southie football game, I go just to make sure my kid gets home." She urges Kevin, "If you could appeal to the anti-busing parents and get them on TV to say 'keep the peace' . . ."

A Charlestown community leader contends, "Fear is picking up in considerable degree. There's talk of increasing the high school and elementary boycott." Her husband says, "There are people going around the community with loudspeakers. We oppose forced busing. We kept our daughter out Thursday and Friday, but we're sending her Monday. She's going into the third grade. She's a sensitive child, and if we don't send her soon, she won't make friends. Some are going further. They're *threatening* people. Somewhere along the line, you're going to have to sit down with the people from South Boston. I'm talking about the responsible people."

Kevin exaggerates, "I've communicated with Louise twenty-five times in the last ten hours. They're stigmatized by talking to me. I talked to Flaherty not an hour ago. I'm not isolating Southie, but I don't want Southie's actions to become contagious and spread across the city."

"No parent will harm a child," the Charlestown man says, "but Charlestown is supportive of South Boston, and if busing ever comes to Charlestown as it did to South Boston, they might react the same way."

The Hyde Park woman explains the splits already showing in ROAR. Because other ROAR members didn't support Southie's actions, she says, Southie figured it was alone. "They felt the rest of the city was going to school," yet Southie, she explains, didn't follow its own boycott rules against violence. A show of support was called for — so, today's motorcade.

A member of the Citywide Educational Coalition reports calls from South Boston parents who are scared and crying. "They have nobody to talk to. They're scared out of their wits. A friend of ours with a kid was threatened," she said, because the family planned to send the kid to school.

"There's an element in Southie now," Kevin says, "that has the whole town paralyzed. I believe Louise has totally lost control of it. We're talking *guns!*" Two women groan.

"There are two armies there," the Hyde Park woman says.

Kevin pushes on, "I'll go a step further. I don't think Ray Flynn has control anymore. So that takes him out of the picture."

After some talk and banter, the mayor asks them, "Do you think I should do everything possible to prevent violence in Southie?" Most of them seem to answer. The answer is "yes." White Irish and Italian men and women, many of whom oppose busing, want the violence in Southie to end. They urge him again to meet with Southie's people. He tells them he had agreed finally Friday to meet with them and was told he wasn't wanted. Perhaps. He certainly was avoiding Flynn Friday. He says now he told people in Southie, "You give me the leadership, and I'll decrease the police." That was the tactic Kevin and Kiley were using that day, and now, the mayor tells these people he'll try again to meet with Southie leaders as a result of this meeting, and he asks one of the white neighborhood leaders to stay and help arrange a meet.

The whites and the blacks are sending messages to City Hall. The messages are basically the same: the people feel lost. And afraid. They fear more violence to their kids. "If we could hear from you," one of them pleads with Kevin. "A lot of people feel their kids were let down because they didn't have protection."

"Would you recommend," he asks them, "I tell the police to arrest anybody and everybody?" He means arrest anyone perceived as causing trouble. The ones who answer seem to agree.

"So," the mayor says, "my failure is not moving hard enough, not providing enough protection." The mayor is building a base of support for a hard line. When he meets later tonight with police commanders, he will refer to this meeting for that very reason.

He has told them he failed to move hard enough, and the delegate from the moderate Citywide Educational Coalition says, "That's what people were saying today." She tells him, "The threats are now going out from Southie to other parts of the community, that if they're not part of the parade, something will happen to them."

A Hyde Park woman worries that blacks will retaliate against the Hyde Park kids.

"That's why I'm trying to contain it," Kevin says. "If the leadership can do it, fine. If not, then more police, more men. But the fear should not spread throughout the city. It's a cancer that'll do us all in."

It is more than fear, the Charlestown woman says. "There's a great state of depression out there, a feeling that their government and the Church have turned their backs on them. They feel they have to *do* something. I tell them to write letters. You know it's Mickey Mouse, and I know it, but at least it's something to *do*."

Kevin asks them to say that they don't condone violence. A lady tells him that politically, things will get bad for him, the longer this goes on. "I've long ago given that up," he says, the self-deprecation of political ambitions getting the usual laugh. But he doesn't swerve from what he wants from them. "I'd like support for nonviolence. I am made of much tougher mettle than my grooming conveys. I told the black community, 'You're gonna be called niggers as long as you're around, but I won't let a child be hurt.'" He stands up. "It's tough. There will be threats. . . ."

The East Boston woman ribs him, "Up to now, your TV speeches have been great. . . ." The Charlestown man interrupts her, "C'mon, he's trying to protect the city." Kevin finishes, "All I'm asking is that you make sure violence doesn't become a catchword in your neighborhood."

The meeting ends, and the white people are not feeling much more secure than they did before it started. Kirk O'Donnell's original idea was to get the whites to embarrass and isolate Southie. What has happened, instead, is the mayor, already having decided to get tough on and contain Southie, has been collecting verbal support for just that, gathering sentiment he will use later. He met earlier with blacks, and he did a similar routine. Now, Kirk says, "Instead of peer pressure, we assume a position of leadership. We're building up support for what we do. In a few hours, we got black and white leadership."

After the meeting, the mayor, sitting in the living room with his aides, suggests, "What we should do is meet with a group from Southie. It can be anybody. Maybe we have them in, meet with them, listen and then say, 'Tomorrow is going to be the same as Friday. If it's disruptive to blacks tomorrow, I'll guarantee federal troops Tuesday, then you won't have to worry about me or Joe Jordan. You're pushing my hand, and nobody across the city has sympathy with you, or to violence or to arms being twisted.' "

"Talk to Garrity," Kiley urges. "You're the only one who can tell him. We should not permit that march. The majority of people thought we weren't firm enough."

"I think it's too late," one contact says. "I really do. Mikey Flaherty and Billy Bulger are hiding as much as they can. Louise has no control. Ray controls a little, and he's been on every corner saying he'll be locked up. The Irish Mafia was in that motorcade today. You could see the license plates. . . . A lotta threats are being made there now. Threats on businessmen not to sell the *Globe*. . . . These aren't high school kids there. They're age eighteen to forty. . . ."

The boss outlines his plan — "One, no parade. Two, the buses will roll. Three, if not, I'll apply for federal troops just for Southie for Tuesday morning."

Maybe he should contact the Somerville gangster, Eddie King urges.

"I'm ahead of you," the mayor says.

Kiley reports, "Clarence's boys [the FBI] are already in the field. They're knocking on doors."

The word back so far from an unscientific survey of gangland is that the older men promise no trouble, but contend they can exercise no control over what some of the younger men do. Eddie King's fears are not calmed by this. He's worried about rumors of guns being passed around social clubs and bars. He's worried about the neighborhood he loves.

Part Three: Night

Tonight, Kevin White must meet with other men, many of them older than he, some of them men who started out when Joe White was a big name in town, and he must assert his governmental virility.

The police sedan pulls up in front of the old Boston Police Headquarters building on Berkeley Street, and the mayor emerges from the back seat. Almost immediately, he points to the office building across the street. "Right there was Johnny Powers' headquarters." That was the night young Kevin White absorbed a few precinct returns, ran out to a phone booth and told his father Johnny Powers was gone. "And John Collins became mayor, and I never dreamt I'd follow him."

But he is mayor, and he cannot escape it, nor, despite his moments of despair, does he seem desirous to doing so, and when he walks into the police conference room, where Robert diGrazia and his officers are sitting around the table, he says, smiling, "Stand up for the mayor," the way they used to say it for Jim Curley. They continue to sit, and a few minutes into the general conversation, Kevin White tells them, "It's a small point, but you should've got off your ass." The next time he meets with them, they will, and it will embarrass him as much as it will please him. A lot of them are older, and some of them are tougher, and the mayor feels he must play this crowd differently from Freedom House or the whites earlier in the evening. Kevin swears a lot more with the police. He feels the need to assert himself more often. Tonight, he will have to do it often, for the police commanders in this room do not agree with Kevin that the march must be stopped before it begins.

A thirty-four-year-old workingman had approached Charlie Barry with the march proposal and promised the march would not get out of hand. "A delegation came to me," Barry says now, "and said the march would be a peaceful demonstration to show the press on the top of the hill that 'We're against violence, against the stoning of buses, that we can have a peaceful demonstration in South Boston.' If they can get press coverage, they'll stay on Broadway. I think we should let them."

Jordan, who had met earlier at the Parkman House with Kevin and who shared fears of organized crime taking over the march, tells the mayor, "All the field officers feel they should be allowed to march, but nowhere near the high school. But we have to make sure we maintain enough equipment and personnel on the line, especially near the school."

Leroy Chase, the black deputy superintendent, cautions, "If we refuse to let them march, we'll be setting a precedent." Of a dozen or so men, with the possible exception of Jordan, it does not appear Kevin White has a kindred soul at this meeting.

"I had my mind made up," he says, "but I think you should know some facts. I'm political. I have some semblance of what's going on. I listen. I have allowed every march on demand, and the only contingent was that its leadership knew what it was doing. But when there *was* leadership," he says, banging the table. "We allow marches, but nothing analogous to what is going on here. You tell me the march is against violence, but the thing I'm dealing with is, by and large, the toughest element in town, The Mullens crowd."

He tells them of his meetings with blacks and anti-busing whites. "It's interesting to hear their views of you and me." He tells them the stories he's heard of threats made by anti-busing radicals on other whites. Well-documented or not, he's using those stories, because he has made a decision, and he believes in what he's doing, and, unless he hears convincing evidence to the contrary, he's using every weapon in his arsenal.

"The crowd that's conducting this parade is a little unique, Leroy," he tells the black officer, "and their methods of recruitment are less than polite. And if they gave you a guarantee of no violence, they probably *could*. Like certain guys can deliver the North End. Bulger is quaking. Louise is shivering. The Mullens know it's a void, and they can step in and control the town socially." He has raised the specter of organized crime running Southie, not just coexisting with the cops, as they often do. Now, he tries to convince them that other whites will not object if the police crack down on troublemakers in Southie, and he raises another specter that scares white cops even more than what's gone on in Southie — retaliation and reaction in Roxbury.

"Southie is in the shithouse. The people I met with tonight agreed I had been too soft. The black leadership realizes that if anyone is hurt tomorrow, their credibility is gone, and they'll have as much power as Louise does now in South Boston — zip. They'd have shot Atkins and taken Owens with him if I wasn't there [Freedom House] the other night. The leadership'll run for cover. . . .

"You always figure you got it until the last moment," he says to those convinced the parade can be controlled. "Like knowing you'll never die. There isn't anybody here who thinks it can't be controlled. But in Southie, it's blown, and I'll know when it's blown in the black community. No one is gonna ask the National Guard to come in, not that ragtag, hayseed outfit. Not the state police. Maybe federal marshals. We're talkin' about federal reserve troops. Now, Charlie's argument is patience, patience, patience. That assumes the other side is playing half-fair. If not, they're about to put you out of business." Now, he has thrown in yet another possibility he knows they detest — the idea of feds running the show, the national implication that the Boston cops couldn't or wouldn't handle it. "It's been a long time since youve been out of business — 1919." The police strike.

"There were people in that room tonight — I couldn't find four of them who had voted for me — not one of them was in favor of that parade at all." Well, technically, that was true enough. Nobody volunteered any support for the parade, and all agreed with the mayor that he should come down hard on troublemakers in Southie.

"We can't control every incident, but we're going to be held accountable for every incident. They're calling your card, because they're telling you they're gonna have a parade whether you like it or not. They respect nothing but authority. That's how they run their own organization — 'Siddown and shaddup!' I'm all for leeway. That's part of my friggin' permissive administration. If they can guarantee a safe parade, those pricks could guarantee you a safe town, cause right now those bastards are *running* Southie. They could guarantee you a safe Tuesday, a safe Wednesday. If we have the parade and violence, we'll all be under indictment — and I mean in the *white* community. The final decision is mine."

Superintendent Russell insists no cops "were faked outta their jock. The alternative is no marching, and we'll have a confrontation earlier." He pictures people from other areas, from West Roxbury, for example showing up for the parade and providing fodder for confrontation.

Kevin says, "I'm a guy from West Roxbury, right? Who's been called and told, 'Show up or else!' Now, I can say, 'Show up? What for? There's no parade.' Give the guy an option so the guy can say, 'Hey, there's no goddamn parade! Show up for what?' "

Russell argues, "They're never gonna get inside that high school. This is their big emotional buildup. After that, it's over." The police see the parade as an escape valve for pent-up emotions that could otherwise lead to violence. But White sees the parade creating an atmosphere where violence will be inevitable, if not condoned.

Kevin says, "If you have any trouble, even without that parade, you'll have trouble across the city. And the blacks will retaliate at the King. The black leaders'll be outta business by tomorrow night. And if you can call one person in Southie and guarantee me leadership, I'll give you anything."

Barry is still arguing that with the parade "you have a shot."

Now, Kevin plays one of his last cards. It's a threat that if things go wrong, the headhunters will be out, and as mayor, he must produce some heads. "I've never interfered with you. I've interfered less with this department than any goddamn mayor. But if there's trouble, the average person will blame you, Charlie, and he'll blame me. But I've got an out. There'll be some goats. There's gotta be. Not to pick on anybody, but you've got to regain the confidence of the community."

DiGrazia tries to back up his men. "The sense of the department is you're gonna have a confrontation all over South Boston instead of a parade, where it's just one spot." He points to a map of Southie. "They're aren't gonna be enough men in South Boston if they start hittin' us in eight or nine places."

"I never fired a gun," Kevin says. "I don't know your business. But I know politics, and I've seen goats hung before."

Eddie King speaks up. He says a sound truck is going around Southie, that it's tearing apart Hicks, Bulger, and Flaherty and announcing a parade for 9 A.M. Kiley turns to Charlie Barry. "Charlie, what do you think is the significance of that? They told you ten o'clock. What do you think that means?"

A police officer answers the question. "It means they'll hold it anyway." Slowly now, the situation is turning around. The specters of black reaction, voter reaction, public image, federal troops, the threat of another department shakeup from the mayor whose administration put many of these same men where they are today, and, now, the possibility that the parade organizers are trying to fake out the cops with contradictory times. The time change could be confusion, of course. But, then again . . .

"I think politically they're out to take over the town," Kevin says. "Even if you never had the damn parade, you're damned if you do and damned if you don't. That's the last day we've got. I got a little credibility in the city, and it'll be gone Monday night if there's trouble. Garrity'll make the moves. What we've got riding is The Mullens crowd, and they'll guarantee safety in the afternoon, okay? But if they're saying there'll be a parade whether you like it or not? It's come to something if we have to depend on The Mullens gang!"

The police are still persistent, though just a touch less than earlier. They argue again that a parade is easier to contain. They talk of "better concentration of our personnel." Kiley and White argue that the marchers can still go in any direction.

"Hey, I've grown up in this town," Kevin says. "You won't have credibility to eat tomorrow. There isn't one pol in town who wants to touch that parade with a ten-foot pole. They're not all dummies. They may be cute, but they didn't survive by being dummies. The worst thing to have in a command decision is the other side moving its troops, and you adjusting to them. . . . One way, they'll blame you. Another way, they'll hang you. . . . You've got no sympathy for Southie right now in this city, and you've got some for yourselves. You give a parade in Southie — next Saturday, you'll have Hyde Park." Kiley injects, "Or what about Roxbury on Tuesday?"

The police commanders are talking now.

"We weren't aware of these facts," one says.

"I live over there, and I haven't met people who've been threatened," another insists.

"I never heard of it," Barry says.

"I always want you to have the balls to stand up to me," Kevin tells them, "but make sure you know the facts."

One staff officer finally says, "What you've told us tonight changes our position."

Kevin assures him, "I think most people in Southie are good people, scared out of their friggin' wits. There aren't many people in or out of Southie who support violence or respect The Mullens crowd."

Another officer says, "We're as aware as you are of the potential for violence. If we have a major incident in South Boston, what we'd have in Roxbury would make what happens in South Boston pale by comparison. If we had had your insight, we might've made a different decision."

Arthur Cadegan, the Southie district commander who had been demoted from deputy superintendent in the White-Kiley-diGrazia shakeup, warns, "If you don't have a parade tomorrow, you'd better close the schools, because you won't be able to control the crowds moving through South Boston."

The mayor gets up to leave them. It is 10:29 P.M. They must arrive at a decision, preferrably in time for the 11 P.M. television news so that they can announce it. It is really the mayor's decision, but the police must be part of it. Two minutes after the mayor leaves, the police command decides Kevin White is right. There will be no parade.

The police sedan moves through the higher-class specialty shop district of the Back Bay, past darkened office buildings and storefronts, from where mannequins watch its progress toward the Public Garden. The sedan bends around the Garden and then moves up past the west side of the Common to Beacon Street and the Parkman House, where Kevin White will spend the night. "I had to put it in perspective, so they could *understand*," he says. "If they decide to go with a parade, heads will roll. I'll shake them up." Pat Brady, a plainclothes police information officer, parks the car in front of the townhouse, where two plainclothesmen are waiting downstairs. Whether he likes it or not, the mayor of Boston will have much protection these days and nights.

Upstairs in the Parkman House, the mayor goes over one issue after another. The meeting he wanted in Southie is off again, but he still wants it. Eddie King urges that the police be ordered to close all bars and social clubs in Southie tomorrow. The mayor opens the refrigerator in a small kitchen off the hallway to get some more blueberries, and he drops some dark bread in the toaster. "I'll tell ya, I'm worried about tomorrow. They could all turn against us. I wouldn't wanna be one of those blacks on a bus tomorrow." The phone rings, and it is Louise Day Hicks, his opponent in two elections. Not only did he beat her twice for mayor, but his organization worked hard to help Joe Moakley beat her in a race for John McCormack's old seat in Congress.

"Hi, Louise. . . . Well, we have a very tense situation, needless to say."

Eddie King says quietly, "She is scared stiff."

Kiley answers, "I can understand that."

On the phone, Kevin is saying. "I know that, dear. I know. . . ."

Eddie King half smiles. "I never thought I'd see the day he'd say 'dear' to Louise."

"I agree, Louise," Kevin is saying. "He's very dangerous."

Louise Day Hicks is the grande dame of anti-busing now. She is cheered and warmly applauded wherever she goes. She was the first to shout resistance, and the people do not forget. But she cannot control the action on the streets, the inevitable result of a decade of pandering to fear and bigotry. Loretta, the woman who chided Kevin at that Dorchester coffee klatch in August, summed up the feelings of many whites in the city — they no longer trusted their political leaders, a position to which many blacks had arrived years ago.

Kevin and Louise finish their call, and Kevin finishes his blueberries and tells Kiley, "You know, I walked out on the Parkman porch today and looked out over the Common. There was music, there were blacks and whites. It was like another world."

Eddie King talks of the world in which they must operate. "The Mullens should have stayed with their first position. They're making money out there. They don't need this. They should've just bailed out kids."

Kiley approaches Kevin and Eddie and the others. He has just been on the phone with Joe Jordan. Barry and Jordan are about to tour the city for three hours with maps. "Now, they're rarin' to go," Jordan reportedly told Kiley on the phone. Kiley cautioned that the police shouldn't overdo it, and quotes Jordan as saying, "Bob, there are only two speeds in the Police Department — on and off — and we're *on*." The police, Kiley is told, feel good about it now. Eddie King, meanwhile, also has been on the phone with a source in Southie who says that the bars should be closed. The rumor persists that "that's where they're stocking up" — on guns, not liquor. The mayor calls Jordan on the phone and tells him to shut the bars down. "I'll take total responsibility," he tells the police officer.

It has been a long and grueling day, from the first meeting at the

Parkman House with his aides to a meeting later with blacks to the gathering in City Hall with whites to the tough session with the police and back here again. But it is not over. There is still Southie, and at 1 o'clock in the morning, Kevin and some plainclothesmen drive out to meet with Mike Flaherty, Senator Bulger, and Louise.

Louise agrees to make calls and talk to her people to get a sense of what's happening, and Kevin goes back to Beacon Hill for a few hours of sleep, interrupted before 4 A.M., when Louise calls him. She feels the rumors of gang influence have been exaggerated and urged that the parade be allowed to go on. White says no, he won't change his mind. Charlie Barry already has called the South Boston man who had originated the parade idea, and told him the parade was off. The angry man said no way, the parade would go on and there would be no violence unless the police instigated it. Now, on the phone, Louise asks that there be no wholesale arrests, and the mayor agrees to no mass arrests of women if it can be avoided, and no dogs.

It is exactly the kind of conversation city officials used to have with black community leaders when the latter were planning protest marches in the 1960's.

At about 6:10 A.M., on the morning of September 16, the disc jockey on a local radio station blathers, "What'd you do this weekend? Did you have an exciting weekend? It's gonna be a nice day. Hey, it may be the last nice day we have in a long time."

TWENTY-TWO
Sons of the Draft Riot

THE SUN at 6:30 A.M. is bright red, rising slowly in a blue sky with just bits and pieces of cloud. In the east, the horizon is red and blue, as it sometimes is early in the summer and spring mornings, and it is clear. There are no ships on the horizon. The French are not on the sea. There is no song for the Shan Van Vocht to sing today. The temperature is expected to be in the 70's. It is a perfect day for a parade.

At City Hall, Rich Kelliher is already in his bunker with the rumor control and information people. Most of them are pale. Some catch a little sun on the weekends, but most are pale. The air circulation in the bunker is not bad early in the morning. By midmorning, it is not good.

Ira Jackson comes into the mayor's office by 7 A.M. He and Mike Feeney are putting on their ties, and Ira is smiling. "Mikey, today's D-Day, Mikey." Feeney, yet another Irish fatalist in a city that specializes in them, does not roar with laughter. Ira has brought two sets of old binoculars, including one of World War II vintage. One is for his crew, and the other is for Kiley's crew, as they travel the highways and byways of shit and strife. "So we can stay outta gunshot distance," Ira says.

This morning's all-time favorite, award-winning rumor is that black guys are renting U-Hauls to load up with Molotov cocktails.

Kiley arrives and reports that law officials were active last night and that the FBI had talked to gang leaders and urged peace. Kiley slides into the car parked behind City Hall. Weddleton is already behind the wheel. Weddleton stops the car on Broadway in Southie, and they pick up Eddie King and drive to Bayside Mall.

Bayside Mall near Columbia Point is the transfer point for buses. Black kids pick up buses here and are taken to Southie. Their number fluctuates each day, depending on the previous day's disturbances. The "mall" is a boarded-up shopping center that died for want of business and no lack of vandalism and shoplifting. Lately, the mall has come to life with motorcycle police, cruisers, foot patrolmen, some TPF, community workers, black kids, some white kids, a lot of buses, and, flying overhead, a state police chopper containing Paul Russell, deputy superintendent.

DiGrazia hears the chopper and looks up and yells, "Hello, Paul. Howareya?" Radios crackle with messages. Kids get shifted around to buses. Some of them decide to split altogether. Others go off to a canteen truck. This is what the struggle has come to, the struggle begun with those black Bostonians of the 1840's who insisted separate schools would only perpetuate the myth of racial inferiority. It has taken 130 years, and it has come to motorcycle cops, scared busdrivers, parents hovering over their kids, a helicopter banking overhead, and men standing on an asphalt pavement that sits between a threatened and threatening black and Puerto Rican community and a threatened and threatening white Catholic community. The Yankees, the ones who brought the slaves and who fought on both sides of the issue of freedom and equality, the ones who enticed the immigrants and then spat on them, are nowhere to be seen this day. They have left the spoils, if indeed there are any, to their inheritors, their tormented, parochial, and frightened inheritors.

"All South Boston High on these buses," a cop yells. "All South Boston High." Most of the black kids seem cool. One girl, being escorted by her mother and another two adults, seems to have been crying. They make sure she gets on the bus. Southie High may not look like much, but there's apparently something there that these blacks see as worthwhile, something they didn't have before. There is a story going around that on the first day of busing, one black looked out the window at the old high school and said, "Sheeeeaaat, take me to Weston," a suburb. But there will also be a story of a black kid showing up at the mall and being told by black adults to go back, that it's too dangerous, and the kid says, "Is there any teachin' going on there today?" and when told there is, he says, "Well, I'm going."

An old car with Ohio license plates pulls up. There will be other nondescript cars with out-of-state plates, and, like this one, they will contain two Irish plainclothesmen, two very Boston-Irish-looking plainclothesmen. What the Boston cops lack in subtlety, they will make up in effort.

Now, the procession of buses, cruisers, cars, and motorcycles begins. They turn out of the mall and take a right onto the boulevard.

The sun has changed from red to blinding yellow. Three MDC horsemen ride on the beach, the men on horseback framed against the bright sun for a moment, so that to stare at them, one sees not distinct men, but forms as on a desert. They ride the sand to the high school annex at L Street, near the scene of the first rock throwing that Thursday afternoon. Across Columbus Park, a motorcycle cop, a yellow bus, and another cycle cop are on their way to the Gavin School. Eddie King takes out one pair of Ira's binoculars and peers at the housing projects to the right of the park, where a group of youths are forming. Projects are perfect places for urban warfare, with their alleys and fire escapes, their broken doors and windows and their look-alike buildings. "Probably about twenty-five of them," King figures.

"They got anything in their hands?" Kiley asks.

"I'm trying to make that out now. The cops are right there."

The helicopter flies over the project, checking rooftops. DiGrazia's car goes by the spot where Weddleton has parked, and one of di-Grazia's aides waves four fingers. "Four buses," Weddleton says. Four buses are supposed to be coming. Heavy morning commuter traffic is moving along the boulevard, as if this were just another workday morning. At 8:21, the buses and their motorcycle escorts are seen. No rocks. Weddleton follows the last one, as they go down the boulevard and turn up the hill to the high school, and Kiley is on the phone, giving a running commentary.

"We've got door-to-door cops on the access route, all holding their helmets." Overhead, the chopper slices the air with its rotary blades. The sound will persist all day, but for a fuel stop. The area near the high school is packed with cops wearing helmets and TPF in blue fatigues. A lot of the TPF are young men, many with long hair and handlebar moustaches. There are a handful of black cops and one woman, and the word on the street is the woman cop knows judo. Four cops sit high in their saddles and face in the direction of Broadway. The buses unload about 200 black kids, and the occupants of Weddleton's car are happy with the numbers. "If we could curb these assholes, maybe we've turned the corner."

Weddleton continues to tour Southie, past the signs that say, "Welcome Niggers" and "Duck, you Suckers" . . . "Klan Country" . . . "This is Southie Country" . . . "Mayor Black" . . . "Mayor White is a Fag" . . . "Boneheads" . . . Eddie King spots a guy on one corner, opening his tavern. The taverns were supposed to be closed. Over and over again last night, Eddie King warned the mayor, close the taverns, and the mayor had told the police to do so. But now, as they tour around, they see one after another opening up for business, and each time, Kiley phones in a report and finally, he hears from the bunker that the bars were ordered closed from 7 A.M. to 9 A.M. only. The bureaucracy doesn't always function the way it should. "What good did it do to close them down from seven to nine?" Kiley asks angrily. When they make their next turn near the high school, Kiley tells Charlie Barry. "Somehow we've fouled up on the joints." Barry takes his command walkie-talkie and orders the police to close them down.

As the car moves up and down Southie's streets, Kiley is on the phone with a running commentary, and Eddie King feeds him details with a street sense that one does not acquire from political science textbooks. "We're getting a lotta dirty looks," Eddie says at one point. "Right now, the lines are drawn, and we're the enemy. . . . Hey, that place opening up at Andrew Square. A bad crowd hangs around there. That should have been one of the first places they closed."

Tough whites are gathering along Broadway, which would be the route of march. "They're gonna march," Eddie says, "I don't care what you say. They're gonna march."

On the phone, Kiley reports, "That's a bad scene. Those bars being open doesn't help anything."

For a couple of minutes, they pull up behind the M Street Park, an open space the size of two large city blocks, which would be the staging area for the parade. The other crew of operatives pulls up too. Ira Jackson comes over with his binoculars and reports, "A lotta people are pulling up in cars, taking a look around and driving off."

But Broadway is active. Men, women, and children are milling about. Some kids are tacking a protest poster on a car. Soon, a disorganized mass, including some young kids and some women wearing hockey helmets and smiling, is moving down Broadway. "Here we go, Southie. Here we go," they chant. Once, it was for high school games, and now it has become the chant of protest, and ROAR chants, "Here we go, Boston. Here we go." But it will forever be Southie's chant, and as they chant it now, these ladies in hockey helmets and kids and some tough guys, the press follows them with their cameras.

The car is driving toward and through the marchers. Weddleton is nervous. He drives slowly, knowing that the slightest accident could cause a riot. The car could be mobbed. King mutters over and over, "Oh, shit. Oh, shit." The crowd is not threatening. They act as if it is just a lark, but some members of that crowd would welcome trouble. Kiley, on the phone to Kelliher, says, "They've dispersed them. A raggly, scraggly group is headed to Dorchester Heights. It's not an unruly crowd yet. More larkish."

From the high school, the cycles speed down G Street, toward Broadway. A little kid stands near the gutter with his own walkie-talkie. "Nothing going on yet," he reports to an unseen friend, presumably carrying his own walkie-talkie. Ahhhh, mechanical America. Kiley shakes his head in disbelief. The police radios crackle, "Information says seventy-five youths are on their way to the high school."

Two buses roll up with TPF troops with helmets and blue fatigues and boots. The motorcycles line up. "Put your helmets on," orders a TPF officer. "Okay, line up right here."

"I think we're gonna have it," Kiley says.

The crowd from Broadway, mostly youths, is moving up G Street toward the school. Some elements are coming up other radial roads leading to the high school. Cops stand in line and block G Street. Cycles and horses break the large groups into smaller ones, as the young demonstrators break through. The cops are getting strung out to a thin line, trying to block all the radial streets at once, but suddenly, from the top of a rise in the woods behind the school, four more TPF cops appear. Two of them, one black and one white, wearing leather jackets, each holds a German shepherd. Each dog barks viciously. The cops stand there, outlined against the sky in their black leather jackets, each holding a leash, against which strains a barking dog, and the crowd across the street disappears. "They're supposed to keep those fucking dogs out of sight," Kiley says, but later he'll happily tell people about the integrated dog patrol and how it made a difference between a noisy demonstration and a full-fledged battle.

The first assault wave has been turned back. It was not a particularly vicious group. The teenagers seemed to enjoy seeing who could slip by the cops. They did not appear to be carrying weapons.

Back in front of the high school, diGrazia looks down the hill. "There's another crowd." The TPF moves down to break it up. Barry approaches Joe Jordan and tells him, "Joe, there are fifty men in two platoons on the other side of the park."

"Now?" Jordan asks.

"Yeah," Barry says, "when you need them."

A platoon of TPF moves down G Street toward Broadway in single file. "Hey, good luck, fellas," a cop yells. Six mounted police also move off at a trot.

Gary Hayes, a civilian aide to diGrazia and a friend of Kiley's, says, "We'll have to keep the horses and cycles after 'em all day till we wear them down."

"Well, why aren't they putting some in the wagon?" Kiley asks. "Right now, it's a lark for them. They're not paying any price. We're just doing the same old thing, and we'll have the same conversation tonight."

Kiley and diGrazia stare down the street. The cops move down, and the crowd moves back. Back and forth, all over Southie, the game will go on all day. Kiley laughs and says, "We could drop leaflets."

"Candy and nylons," suggests diGrazia. "Give up, and we'll escort you out of town."

The messages are spit into the bunker, one after another.

10 a.m. — Arrest at G and 5th St., second arrest today.

10 a.m. — Group breaking up at high school and heading toward H St.

10 a.m. — There is a group of approximately 65 people in front of the South Boston Courthouse.

10 a.m. — Arrest at I and East Broadway . . . booked for disorderly.

10 a.m. — Group heading up Broadway to M St. Park — about 50 youths coming down I St. About 100 people at M St. Park. 100 more heading down E. Broadway toward M St. Park. Rumored regrouping at M St. at 11:00 a.m.

10:10 a.m. — 200 people in M St. Park. "Mullens" people are within this group.

10:15 a.m. — 300 at M St. Park — crowd is being dispersed by police.

10:21 a.m. — Large group of approximately 150–200 people is congregating in front of St. Brigid's Church at Broadway and M St.

Also at 10 A.M., Weddleton is back driving on Broadway, as King and Kiley try to get a feel for what's going on. They have kept their windows closed when the crowds have been close to the car. Now, the windows are open. The day is warm. As they drive slowly down Broadway, Kiley hears one woman yell to another, "It's a waste of time. It's a waste of time up there."

"Right, lady," he mumbles. "Go do your ironing." He gets back on the phone. "We're gonna take the pipe here unless we can get the goddamn places closed. If those places aren't down by two or three this afternoon, it's gonna be bad."

At N Street, Kiley gets out of the car and climbs up the steps of a nearby house. He watches as the TPF move the crowd back toward St. Brigid's Church. "Let's go, Southie! Let's go!" they are yelling. The horses clop-a-clop on the street. The TPF infantry works closely with the cavalry. People are pushed back in one sector, and, almost like a balloon filled with water, the pressure seems to force the crowd back out in another sector.

A Youth Activities Commission worker asks out loud, "How much longer can you push a crowd back before it pushes you back?" Not much longer.

"What happens to equal rights?" yells a woman from her doorstoop. "Don't we have any?" And without waiting for anyone to answer, she vows, "Well, we'll get it."

"Sieg Heil," the whites of Southie shout at the white policemen.

"Heil, Hitler!" they shout.

And now there is violence. Men scuffle on the street. The TPF jumps one man and tries to get him into a paddy wagon. Paddy wagon. To many Irish, it is a racist term. But today, history is replayed. The cops are throwing their own people into the paddy wagon, and as they struggle with one man, another beefy one tries to rescue him — a big guy in a T-shirt. Gary Hayes says, "It's a Mullens." Perhaps. Who knows? Who cares anymore? Mullens or no Mullens, cops and men are fighting in the street. They wrestle the big guy to the ground. Four or five of them are holding him down. Another TPF cop holds by his hair the guy who tries to help the other.

"Leave him alone! Leave him alone!" the people are yelling, from the sidewalks, from the steps, from the windows. Some kid spits on Kiley and a companion who stand on the sidewalk and watch. Back in the car, Weddleton and King are nervous, because demonstrators are all over the car. They yell for Kiley to get back in, and when he's ready, he does. Weddleton drives away, past a young woman who gives the car the finger and quickly shoves her hand back into her pocket. As the car moves slowly back to the high school, past small knots of youths, its occupants hear one little kid say to his friends, "I don't know if they can make the noon news, but it'll be on the six o'clock and the eleven o'clock."

Kiley turns around, his eyes wide with some astonishment. "Do you believe that?" Kevin White may have been right about people performing for the tubes.

In front of the high school, a cruiser pulls up and out jumps Jordan, wearing his sunglasses and a uniform with perfect creases. He's one of those types whose pants never lose the crease. "We'll be playing tag all day long with these kids."

11:34 a.m. Group at Andrew Square heading for MBTA station.

The *Globe* reporters also carry walkie-talkies, and the voice of a police reporter is heard on one. "They're here at Andrew Square. They tore up some phones and did some damage, but the cycles swept them out."

The police radio is also busy. "Motorcycle units to Gavin School. Motorcycle units to Gavin."

11:42 a.m. All available units being sent to Gavin School. Crowd from Andrew Square is heading in that direction.

Three women have approached Kiley as he stands in front of the high school. They strike up a conversation. Their neighborhood radar tells them he's somebody they should talk to. So, they talk. They nag him. "Would you bus your children to Roxbury?" He says, "If I had any, I would." Kiley gets peeved. He doesn't want to be nagged. "My wife and children were killed six weeks ago." They stop. They are uncomfortable and shocked, but they are also relentless, and, so they press on — "We've had Negro kids here, and they were not harmed. . . . Two hundred murders in Roxbury — eighty-seven-year-old woman killed for two dollars . . . and Atkins calls *this* a violent area . . . we don't mind Negro kids here, but we don't want to send our kids out. . . ."

Nearer to the school, a young mother wanders around with her two little kids. The kids hang back, and she tells them, "Go ahead. Look at the school. See what the niggers are doin'. Go ahead. You're not afraid of black people, are you? Shout 'White power.' The two kids shout, 'White power! White power!' " and they collapse into giggles.

The crowd near the high school has slowly but perceptibly increased. Mayor White's insistence that any group larger than three near a school be broken up seems to have again gone by the boards. Someone mentions the crowd to Kiley, who, in turn, asks diGrazia about it, who seems surprised they're there. Cadegan is not crazy about forcibly moving the people away. "Gee," he says, "we stirred up a hornet's nest when we tried to move the women the other day." Jordan walks in and orders his men to clear the area. Most leave quickly. Some who don't want to are cajoled to do so by Cadegan, who gets them laughing and joking and moving.

Early in the afternoon, word comes to the front line that a policeman named Frank Creamer, forty-seven, suffered a heart attack during one of the assaults on Broadway. Three weeks later, he will die.

From the front lines to the bunker, Kiley sends a message too. "Jordan thinks it's gonna be tough getting outta this today. There are kids with pockets stuffed full of rocks." Jordan is right.

The Boston police are pulled thin. There are reports of disturbances elsewhere, and some of the reports are false. Joe Egan, manager of the Dorchester Little City Hall, reports of "rumored diversionary action in other areas of the city to draw police away from South Boston."

12:40 p.m. Rumor circulating at Hyde Park High School that the buses in Bradlee's parking lot at American Legion Highway will be vandalized (rocks, bottles, Molotov cocktails).

1:05 p.m. Approximately 15 non-students gathered outside Roslindale High.

1:35 p.m. Running total of arrests: 17, all in South Boston.

At the high school, as dismissal time approaches, there are two distinct sounds — the chopper up above and the horns of a motorcade in the distance. "Column of threes!" a TPF officer commands, and they go marching down G Street again. Some aides and teachers come out of the high school, but no students yet, because the buses have not shown. They will be late, because crowds have gathered at the Old Colony Housing Project on the boulevard, and police are worried about rocks and missiles. They come late, but they will pick up the students and leave in peace. The action is elsewhere.

"A group up there with bricks on the roof," a radio reports from the housing project.

"Firecrackers going off all over the place here," another says over the airwaves.

A *Globe* reporter talks into his radio, "Every once in a while, a rock is heaved. Some good-sized rocks too."

A community worker gets a message from Freedom House in Roxbury. Some black parents are calling there, worried that their kids aren't home yet from school in Southie.

"A lotta people here," Eddie King says, when the car reaches the boulevard. "Too many people."

Kiley is on the phone. "They haven't done much of a job getting the area cleared out." The other crew pulls up, and Ira Jackson says, "We've been following this gang with the white hats all day. They're bad news guys from Lower Broadway. The detectives just frisked a bunch of them, and they left." The young men wearing white caps, the kind the seafarers sometimes wear, will be seen throughout the afternoon and in days to come. The hat becomes a badge of resistance, like the chant and the ROAR songs, and soon, the different-color berets each neighborhood contingent of ROAR will wear.

As the high school buses leave, 20 minutes late, Weddleton worries, "They let them go too easy. They're planning something." They learn where the catch is. The buses scheduled to pick up the younger black kids at the Gavin Middle School have not yet left Bayside Mall, because of the white crowds massed at the project and near the boulevard and along the route to the Gavin. In the crowd, the white caps reappear. An American flag hangs from the third floor of one project building. A hastily made cardboard sign, held by a protestor, says, "Remember Wegler," a reference to a young white woman torched to death in Roxbury. A family gathered on a grassy strip in front of the project chants, "Yay. Honk if you're with us. Are you with us? Hah? Honk for Southie."

Honk for Southie. Pray for us, Father, for we have sinned. And pray for others of us, for we have not sinned. In the mayor's administration, one of the top-level aides speaks one day over a beer in a place across the street from City Hall. He is given to moments of philosophy and fatalism, though time has not allowed such maudlin luxuries as of late. Boston, he says, is America one century ago. The whites are in the city partly because some wish to be and partly because others must be, and both kinds are in Southie. Now, the national press is gushing over the white ethnics of Southie. How quaint, these Irish folk. "Nobody," he complains, "is really getting into the other part of Southie, what it's like to be in an Irish family where the father is a boozer, where ——'s father [he names another city employee] was killed by a gang of kids because he was shitfaced. The guys drinking at the Rabbit Inn at age twenty-five, but what about the forty-five-year-old drinking there? My own father was an alcoholic. Somebody should really get into that whole thing. What does it mean to work for the city? It means you got a fuckin' red nose at age forty-three and dead at fifty-two of a heart attack before you even got that pension you dreamed about all your life, and you don't even get to see it. The similarities with blacks are amazing — rural migrants, coming from an oppressive political situation which gave them excuses for failure, and both of them have weak family structures — the classic Irish father being drunk, the weak father who becomes an alcoholic and doesn't provide. I can go on forever in terms of my Irish friends in this city and talk about their fathers who had the potential yet never made it."

So, honk for Southie.

Near the Gavin School, there are police all over the lot, and priests who will ride the buses if the buses ever come. On the police radio, a voice from somewhere intrusts, "Ten-three to Operations. Check on

Mercer Street. A group with white caps on." Now, the sounds of the chopper are overhead here.

Everyone waits. The TPF and the regular police and the MDC police all wait for orders. The priests and the kids wait for the buses. The guys in the white caps wait for God knows what. A priest, waiting in front of the school, looks at a young kid smoking and says, forever the priest, "You're too young to smoke." On the sidewalk, older residents joke with uniformed sergeants they know, old neighborhood boys. "Okay, Kojak," one says to a beefy sergeant, and they laugh together.

Finally, an hour and ten minutes after school closed, six buses, escorted by cycles and cruisers, arrive at the Gavin. Kiley has learned that the crisis is not over yet, for these are the same buses used to pick up white children attending the King School in Roxbury. The actions of the crowds in Southie have effectively created trauma for both black parents and white parents, each worried about their kids in strange and sometimes hostile neighborhoods.

Knots of people remain. Someone shouts "Heil Hitler," but the chant against the cops, Garrity, and all the forces that now control Southie is not taken up. "Hey, Michael," a kid yells, "stay here. There might be trouble." Great expectations. There is no trouble now. Cops and priests load the kids onto the buses, and the buses work their way down Broadway back to Bayside Mall, so the kids can transfer to other buses. Broadway looks like a parade scene. Cops line the street. Mounted cops roam the avenue. Traffic cops wave the buses through, and scores of people stand on each block, including, again, the young men in the white caps. They stand and stare. And what is it they have come to look at? A bunch of junior high school kids in yellow school buses.

It is close to 4 P.M. when the buses get back to Bayside Mall, and it seems as if the long day is over. It just seems that way. Jordan has taken his helmet off and wipes his brow with one arm. "If we're gonna do this again tomorrow," he says, "we better go to bed now." But Kiley tells diGrazia their troubles for today may not be over, that white kids still await buses at the King. DiGrazia's expressive face turns from the joy of having brought kids here safely to pain, and Kiley says, "You make an accommodation here, and before you know it, you have a problem somewhere else. Everyone's getting awfully tired."

Weddleton now drives behind the buses on their way to Roxbury. The motorcade moves down Columbia Road in that portion of Dorchester that borders Southie. From the schoolyard of St. Margaret's

Parochial School, some kids throw stones. They miss the buses, but they hit Weddleton's car and one zips through an open window and clips Kiley behind the right ear. On the side of the school is inscribed, "For God and Country."

As the bus bends at Uphams Corner, a focal point for white, black, and Puerto Rican, young white men come out of the bars to stare at the procession and give the finger. A postal worker flicks his hand under his throat, a fine Italian gesture. The motorcade moves up Columbia Road, which changes from white to black, and toward Blue Hill Avenue. It is the evening before Rosh Hashanah, the Jewish New Year. Once, on such a night, there were masses of people here, hundreds of men, women, and youngsters walking to any of a dozen synagogues strung out along the *shtetl* from Roxbury to Mattapan. Now, but for some blacks here and there, the area is deserted. There are no shofars echoing in the late afternoon, no families preparing for the holiest days. But for some pockets here and there, the urban Jew is gone. Slowly, his little stores are boarded up or burned down or converted into something else. His schools become public school annexes or Baptist churches. Only the veterans' memorials on the corners stand out strangely in the black neighborhood, each of them a stiff metal rod Kaddish for the Jews of the city. There is, otherwise, no more trace of them here than there is of the shtetls that once lived in Poland, in Moldavia, in the Pale of Settlement.

Now, in Roxbury, there is the King School, which is not about to win a House Beautiful Award, but it has been cleaned up, and the mood outside is strikingly different from what Kiley has just left in Southie. It is calm. There are no crowds, no black toughs hanging on the corners in the style of Southie, waiting to hurt or to get hurt. Only community workers and YAC workers and a handful of cops are outside. "Hey," one yells to the arrivals in Weddleton's car, "you don't happen to have a bulkie roll on you, do you?" They are tired of waiting, and hungry, but they have waited here, these black adults, to make sure no harm comes to those white kids. The white kids pour out of school the way kids all over America come out, happy to be out. They are more than 90 minutes late. A very tall black eighth-grader with an afro guides them on the buses and lectures them to keep their windows closed. Paul Parks is ecstatic. He talks of how well it has gone, of how earlier in the day, "some dude appears on the hill and lifts a rock and five of the community workers look up at him, and he just puts it down."

The buses pull out with their white charges. Around the corner from the school is the first large group of black teenagers. They are running hard and sweating. They are playing basketball. Most don't bother to look at the buses. Black community workers are stationed at strategic corners. The Multi-Service Center's Sav-More Security Patrol has a car about to follow the buses. Leroy Chase, the department's highest ranking black officer, is out on the street, directing traffic himself, so the buses all get by in one group.

Back in Southie, the police still stand at the curbstones and wear their riot gear. The information center reports 22 were arrested today, all but 3 in Southie, that 9 persons, including 3 police officers, have been injured, all of them in Southie.

At City Hall, the mayor has visited his troops in the bunker and has told them, "I am convinced we made the correct move in banning the march. The police have done an excellent job of combining good judgment with strict enforcement. I think today is a critical day, and so far it has gone well."

At night, he meets again at the Parkman House with black leaders, with the veterans like Ruth Batson, who began making noises about unequal education in Boston in the 1950's, and Ken Guscott of the NAACP, Otto Snowden and Paul Parks, with Pat Jones and Percy Wilson. The blacks are still hoping that something beyond police power can work in Southie, that some social or political pressures by other whites or by some agencies can be brought to bear.

The Parkman House lights burn on long after the end of dusk in nineteenth-century comfort and security. The windows look out on the Common, peaceful in the early fall evening. The Yankee gentlemen of Beacon Hill strolled here at their leisure. Martin Lomasney liked to take a daily walk here. It has been for all sorts of people a place to unwind, to relax. The mayor and Larry Quealy had looked at it, and the mayor said, "You think the president of France is waiting for the last word on busing, and you get out there and hear singing and nobody cares. They're going about their own business." The Common reminds Kevin White that very little of the world shares his worries, his priorities, his problems, his pretensions. The bells of the Park Street Church tone the time, and when the auto traffic is light, it is timeless time. Perhaps the city can endure, as long as young people sing and dance on its Common ground and grown men sit across from the ground and talk late into the night of peace and how to attain it.

Whether peace is attained depends on whether the violence is contained in Southie. It becomes clear in the days and weeks to come that containment has failed. The pus must be let out of the long-festering sore, before anything will mend. The violence, it seems, must run its course.

TWENTY-THREE

Winning the Peace

PEACE DOES NOT suddenly happen. It must be won, and those engaged in winning it must have some measure of control over events. Yet this was the one factor that no party possessed.

The predominantly black, but integrated, Dorchester High football team could come to the rescue of two whites being attacked by blacks, and a skirmish could be transformed into a day or two of peace.

Sargeant Dan Harrington, the cop in charge of a motorcycle squad, could rush his troops into the North End, when Charlestown High students made it across the bridge to demonstrate against busing. He could take a running jump and land on the back of a cycle driven by one of his men, yell "Wooooo Woooooo," and drive the Townies into the city subway system, and thereby gain moments of peace, but it would be short-lived, for the Townie kids would each fork out a quarter, get on the train and get to Southie before the cops did, prompting a TPF officer to comment with some awe, "They beat us back here, the little bastards."

Judge Garrity could deliver stern and rambling lectures from the bench against violence and repeatedly appeal to what he hoped was the goodwill among all parties to work together for a solution, yet he long resisted pressures to take a harder line and crack down with federal authority in the style of Little Rock or, more recently, Denver.

Instead, a national problem being ordered resolved by a federal court on a local city would have to be dealt with by the local powers that be. Those powers included a school committee with no desire to comply, a school bureaucracy with limited abilities, and a mayor.

The mayor complained publicly and privately that while he might be able to keep the peace on the streets, tired as his police were, expensive as it might become, he could not keep the peace within the schools. Trouble within the schools would spill out onto the streets, and even if it didn't, he would be blamed for it. He had no control over what happened inside the schools, yet, that was not something he was sure he wanted. For at least, he figured, he might not be held accountable for the whole business. He would do his part, and let the school committee be damned for not doing its. The trouble with that was that the committee's failure brought about the very thing he hoped to avoid — trouble in the schools meant trouble on the streets. Besides, he complained angrily to his aides, this was a federal court order — let the federal government assume more of the responsibility, cost, and enforcement. And even within his own jurisdiction, ROAR and unaffiliated anti-busing guerrillas were simply too much and too many for a harried police force to contain forever, and the mayor was forever trying to second-guess the next uprising and where it would be. In the weeks to come, he would not only use his built-up intelligence system, but he would also practice his policy of keeping in touch with all parties. Soon, some ROAR members and their relatives were on the city payroll. They didn't sell out, but it didn't hurt to have them around. If patronage could be used to solidify one's political base and keep the peace at the same time, well, why not? Patronage wasn't much, given what the Yankees enjoyed in the previous century and what Hagan's enemies had available to them two generations ago, but it was one of the small luxuries left.

The frustrations of power far outpaced the luxuries.

A few days after the police broke the visible resistance somewhat in Southie, Hyde Park High School exploded and would remain a trouble spot sporadically for much of the school year, as police patrolled its corridors. One day, the mayor's aides told him every high school was a trouble spot, except, perhaps — and most ironically, given the history of racial troubles there — Dorchester High, where black and white faculty and students were making it work as best they could.

"How do we convey to the public outside," he agonized, "that we are *not* responsible for safety *inside* the building? I think we're gonna be blamed for everything by everybody." The more he thought about it, the angrier he became, and he shouted, "Either break through that goddamn school door or convey to the school department that *they* should!" But Kiley, even in tone, said realistically, "There's no way you can break down those doors."

So headmasters, whom he had never appointed, men over whom he had no control, would determine individually whether their schools required police in the halls, and Kevin White, who, unlike head-masters, must run for reelection, concluded that day with a rhetorical question, "Is the headmaster gonna determine for us how *we* are gonna be perceived by the public?" Yes.

And if that were not enough bad news, Kiley, Parks, Peter Meade, and the others told their boss that the police were getting tired, that it might only be a matter of time before some of them overreacted and touched off more troubles on the street. The uneasy peace that seemed to follow the crackdown in Southie had ended with trouble at Hyde Park, they said. As Kiley put it to him, "I think the racial bottle has been uncorked here in the last few days." For the trouble in Hyde Park had touched off black anger at the Lewenberg in Mattapan. Kevin White could come again only to the same conclusion he had reached a few nights before busing began. "They're outfoxing us," Ira Jackson complained. "Monday could be Hyde Park and Roslindale. You just don't know. South Boston kids could end up in Brighton."

"That's right," said Kevin. "You don't know, so what do you do when they get there? You *arrest* them as soon as they show up. For looking the wrong way."

Perhaps it was physically impossible. To make so many arrests would strain Jordan's mobile forces. Perhaps the police would always feel that to make numerous arrests the way Kevin wanted would only provoke more trouble. Besides, once arrested, the culprits would be booked and out of court within a day anyway. Not until federal officials finally made some arrests for alleged civil rights violations did some of the street thugs cool it. For others on the fringe, the mayor's policy of firmness undoubtedly worked in a number of situations. So Kevin White knew by September 20 that the virus was spreading and that one city's police department would be inadequate to contain it. It was a demoralizing time for the mayor — containment had almost worked, almost.

That afternoon, he met with Ellen Jackson, Otto Snowden, Pat

Jones, and other black leaders in the Eagle Room, and he was talking federal troops. Pat Jones had put it succinctly, "Many youngsters are still listening to us, but not in the same numbers."

"I have a clear line to Saxbe [William, then Attorney General]," Kevin said, "and I'm told we need Sargent's okay to get federal troops — that's Tip's understanding — unless the national NAACP knows something I don't know. I need almost immediately some communication with Sargent. I have it personally, but he'll be running around getting opinions from other people too. . . . I'd like to get someone to say to Sargent, if the black community feels it needs protection, that he'll concur with the mayor's request."

Pat Jones warned, "I don't think we should wait until somebody is dead. The TPF is tired, and the cops who aren't tired are uptight and on edge. Those guys had gone for their nightsticks and were ready to move in and crack somebody on the head." Now, as the trouble seeps into the black community, and small outbreaks begin there, black leaders worry again about white cops dealing with black kids, especially white cops who have been shoved, jeered at, and spat upon by their own kind in Southie. "The kinds of things going on inside the schools, I'm not sure the police are the ones who can handle those situations. We've run the course. We're back where we were before. So it seems we should need federal troops at least on standby."

"Well," said Kevin, "why don't we?"

"We saw the battleground shifting from Hyde Park to Mattapan," Jones answered. "We don't want the wrath of federal troops in our own neighborhood."

"What you are saying, Pat," Kevin responded, "is that you want federal troops, but you don't want to *see* them or be *blamed* for them. . . . Pat, nobody is talking about taking your *turf*. I was taking it you want federal troops where the disruptions are, whether they be pink, white, black, purple, or brown."

Kiley warned them, "Once they're here, they have their own command structure and report to Schlesinger [James, the Secretary of Defense]."

Otto Snowden insisted, "We're not afraid of making it public."

Kevin explained tactics. He said there should be a private meeting between Sargent and the black leadership "so he won't think I'm grandstanding," so Sargent's political advisors would not whisper in the governor's ear that the mayor was trying to embarrass him and engineer a victory for Michael Dukakis. "He may well say bring in the National Guard first. He's got to waive the National Guard."

Snowden shook his head. He didn't want the National Guard anymore than Kiley or White did. "There's hardly any blacks in the

Guard. The 82nd Airborne is forty percent black. We don't want another all-white force. Let's put a little color in it."

Kevin pressed for the Sargent meeting. "Sargent has got to understand that this is not something he dwells on." He got up and yelled to a secretary as he walked into his living room, "Get me Sargent's office." While he waited, someone reminded him that every conceivable political and ideological group in Boston — and they are legion — wanted to rally and demonstrate, some at the Common. "Not on the Common," said the mayor of Boston in the middle of a political crisis. "Every damn time I get the Common fixed up, either the pigeons take it or they demonstrate on it."

The call was picked up by one of Sargent's aides, and the mayor put on Ellen Jackson, but the conversation did not go very well. Kevin White got on the phone and talked to one of the governor's closest advisors, Al Kramer. "The black community has not retaliated at all. But their leadership has to have credibility. So they're gonna go back there and say they talked to some aide? I don't want a public statement. I want a political decision that you know in advance . . . . The Guard stinks anyhow. The kids'll play tag with the Guard. My understanding is you have to come in with the National Guard first, and I want to avoid that problem."

Ellen Jackson, holding the other line, yelled, "Hell no, Al. We *need* it because we don't hold that community any longer. Al, you are not *out* there. Respectfully, you are not *out there*. We can hold till two-thirty this afternoon, and we may not be able to hold it after that. We just got a report while we're sitting here that Columbia Point is edgy. We got people in Hyde Park, people in Roslindale . . ."

Isaac Graves, black manager of the Roxbury Little City Hall, got up and shook his head as if to clear it. "This was never in my civics book."

Plans to meet with the governor were not jelling. The governor's office may not have trusted Kevin Hagan White, and Kevin was not crazy about Francis W. Sargent. In the middle of negotiations, he flung a felt-tipped pen across the room.

On Sunday, Kevin White met again at Police Headquarters with the command staff. When he entered, they all stood up.

This time, they talked of how the battles were spreading. Joe Jordan had reports of gunfire at Columbia Point. Ellen Jackson's intelligence was good. The Point was isolated from everyone, including most of the city's black leadership. Now, cops with rifles were at the massive housing project. "Good," says Kevin; "shoot back.

"Firmness," the mayor urged. "Treat each side equally," Southie and Columbia Point.

Some police commanders worried that one incident — of a black kid killed in Southie, or a white girl raped near English High — would bring the citywide riot they all feared. They felt, with or without such incidents, the troubles would be forever with the city, at least through the winter of 1975, like the troubles of Ireland that never disappear, that hang over their fatherland like a perennial shroud.

Kevin got a reading that the cops were ready, willing, and able. Well, maybe it was premature for federal troops. Nobody in the room could assure they'd get feds anyway now, not unless the National Guard was called first, and nobody in the room wanted the National Guard — not after the race riots in Detroit and Newark, not after Kent State. He heard his police worrying the way he does, about a city he and they understand all too well. "I said to my staff — one, this town is more bigoted than anyone wants to admit. Two, this will escalate. Three, the average white believes we are more preferential to the blacks than the whites. Four, the fact is the newspapers are gonna die on us, basically because they don't have the guts and fortitude we have to stick it out. I guess what I'm saying is, never mind how the press or anyone perceives you, if *I* think you've done a good job." Bridling under the siege, he told them, "Ninety percent of the people you deal with will run for the hills. I'll be the exception."

"We'll give it hell again," Joe Jordan promised.

"It's saving the town against itself," Kevin said. "The goddamn town is about to hurt itself. It's *that* important. And nobody will ever know you did it. And I won't get one vote out of it . . . saving the town."

That night, it was exactly one year away from the city primary.

TWENTY-FOUR

The Mayor's Rage

"I'LL OUTLIVE HIM as I have the other fools. The guy in the street knows the judiciary is less than wise. He knows it just as he knows oil prices go up. No one questions them because their third grade civics books say they are wise, humble, and bright. Well, they're lawyers and pols who know a governor or a President. Garrity has made my job more difficult."

The mayor's rage this day knew no bounds. And not one man in the room could control or soothe it. Not Gleason, who had been with him for so long, nor Kiley, whom he trusted implicitly. Nobody.

By the third week of September, Kevin White was convinced that he and his police and the neighborhood leaders could not control or wipe out what had been festering for almost two centuries. He wanted Judge Garrity and the feds to crack down on ROAR and any other agitators. He knew by then that troublemakers picked up for disorderly conduct would be back out on the streets before nightfall. The municipal courts were lenient with most of those arrested, and a hard city guy, be he black or white, is not scared by arrest the way Judge Garrity's Wellesley neighbors might be. White attempted to reach

Garrity privately and was told by a court officer that one cannot talk to a judge about a case unless one is a party to it in court, and then, one speaks in open court.

Well, that was fine textbook material, and White, as a lawyer, knew the rules as well as anyone. But White, the pol, also believed that the judiciary was a bit high-blown at times, that it was out of touch and that, by Jesus, if the court expected him to keep law and order, it ought to damn well give him an ear. He railed against the suburbanite judge in all his courtroom majesty. And he didn't like to be patronized either, he might add.

Late in September, Bob Kiley, speaking for the mayor, urged that blacks and whites in the South Boston–Roxbury high school district be sent to a neutral site, such as Bayside Mall, for their schooling. This, the mayor's people argued, would at least remove the question of turf from the South Boston–Roxbury crisis. Kiley also urged Garrity to begin hearings on Phase Two of the desegregation plan in conjunction with some changes in Phase One, changes such as a neutral site.

In an interview with the *Globe,* White said, "Bob Kiley and I are saying that our job has been done. From now on, it's up to Judge Garrity and the School Department to take over the process of education. And this hasn't been faced up to yet."

Critics felt White was caving into the pressures and the anti-busing crowd. They said he was now separating the issue of safety in the streets from the actual desegregation process. In fact, he had always separated the two. Politically, he did not wish to be perceived as the mayor who brought busing to Boston. But pragmatically, he had very little control over what happened in the classrooms and halls and rest rooms of Boston's school system. No one party or person or agency had total control over the process. Everyone had a piece of the action. Now, that reality was accompanied by a dangerous illusion. Many people in Boston simply did not believe, court order or no court order, that anybody was serious about busing. Opponents seemed to feel that something could be done, somehow, Garrity's instructions to the contrary. If a federal court insisted that Boston bus its children, the federal arm of government should make it clear that it meant business. So, for reasons of pique, politics, and good government, White's administration tried to force the school committee and the court to belly up to the bar and buy a few too.

The school committee's response was to charge the mayor with undermining the desegregation order, and it asked the court to name him a codefendant. That was on September 26. On September 27, Garrity agreed that work should begin on Phase Two. He refused to consider any alterations in Phase One, even though those close to the street felt a neutral site was a good idea. And in a move that shocked the mayor, he named White a party to the suit. The judge said he could see no difference between maintaining safety on the streets and the rest of the desegregation process. Talk of neutral sites could give aid and comfort to truants and their families. Now, as a party to the suit, White would be forced to milk the city treasury for all desegregation costs not covered by the feds. The judge went on to praise the mayor and his efforts at keeping the peace. And the judge admitted publicly that he had not anticipated the "turbulent" reaction to his busing order.

Not having been a party to the suit had been good and bad for Kevin White. It could be good on those occasions when people blamed him for everything, and he could say accurately that he was not a party to the suit, that his hands were somewhat tied, that there was only so much he could do. But it also meant that efforts to reach Garrity, the judge who had not anticipated the "turbulent" reaction caused by busing, to reach that judge with good, solid street intelligence and both social and political readings of what was going on out there, had been stymied. Now, the mayor's office could legally take part in formulating Phase Two, which theoretically made sense. Politically, of course, that was dangerous to White, for it meant a savvy anti-busing candidate could pin the troubles brought by Phase Two onto the mayor.

Garrity's surprise decision came on a Friday, and it drove Kevin White into this rage. He stood in back of his desk in the Eagle Room, while his aides sat uncomfortably around the room, and he raged at the alleged majesty of judges, at the idea of saying anything to the press, at his own aides who tried to argue with him.

"The point is that Garrity is no better than Atkins. He's protecting his flanks. And he's a pompous ass. . . ."

Kevin Moloney, a city lawyer, tried to soothe the mayor. "You've got the best political sense in the room. Why not make the best of a bad deal?"

Larry Quealy asked, why not, as a party to the suit, bring blacks and whites together and come up with a solution. It's better than police action. "Good," Kevin spat out, "and you will satisfy no one, and you'll be in the sewer."

Gleason said the judge had not really prevented Kevin White from dealing with the different parties, with the pols, the neighborhood leaders, the blacks and whites. That was true, but the mayor did not see it, not then. "If you listen to what the order says . . . ," Gleason pleaded.

"I don't wanna listen to the order," the mayor insisted. "He can figure out how to implement this if he wants. *He* can figure out the public safety aspects. *He* can decide who gets public parade permits and who doesn't. It was an affront, and arrogance on his part. Even if he had done it at another time — but in conjunction with the school committee? And it's that kind of goddamn incompetence you've got to fight to do the right thing. Garrity's gonna find us very mute."

Roy Wilkins, chief of the NAACP, had been critical of the White administration, and now Kevin, bristling under that, connected Wilkins's remarks with Garrity's actions. "To think what Wilkins did to us yesterday — after three weeks of a massive dose of an inequitable court plan with no one hurt? How do you justify a Wilkins coming in like that? A Ray Flynn doesn't know better. But Wilkins? Inexcusable. And now Garrity."

Kiley warned, "If we all say nothing, the press will conclude that we're running for cover."

"Blacks and whites are going through major changes in this city," the mayor said, "but apparently the judiciary isn't. . . . What the hell does he think? He's bigger than the mayor of this city? What does he think? We're a bunch of clerks? With all the things we've got to worry about, now we have to worry that we've lost credibility with the *school committee?* Does he think he can make statements without political connotations? . . . Well, I'm gonna give him a goddamn good lesson." To those who argued that being a codefendant could be turned into something useful, into a victory, he insisted, "Better say a mistake than to pretend it's a victory. We will not participate in drawing that plan."

Kevin was lashing out at almost everyone.

To a secretary, who appeared at the door, he snapped, "What do *you* want?"

To Tivnan, who had been urging a statment for the press, "You can no more resist a press release than a drunk can liquor."

To Gleason, who said the mayor cannot say the judge made a mistake, "Herb doesn't want to offend the judge because he's got to practice before him."

"Right," said Gleason, smiling. The token Yankee in White's administration was a true liberal, for he displayed endless patience.

The mayor, talking to Gleason, but really talking to liberals, chided, "Boy, you're quick to say, 'that *Flynn*' or 'that *Flaherty*,' but when it comes to an Atkins or a Garrity or the guys with white hats, we never dare to criticize."

Barry Brooks, Tivnan's aide, tried to sum up what the mayor was saying. "Kevin's point is that he can no longer be neutral."

"But that's self-pity," Schwartz argued.

"What you really don't understand," Kevin lectured, "is you are endeavoring to cover up an indiscretion by the judge. . . ."

"It looked like we were winning the battle. I was reaching out to the Pixie Palladinos and the rest of them. The school committee was thinking it was losing the battle, and a twenty-seven-year-old lawyer [the committee's attorney], without even a vote of the school committee, brings a petition to the judge, and we *lose* it. I was finally getting the Pixie Palladinos *in* without capitulating, without compromising with their attitudes.

"In terms of my making a public comment — it's my dignity and my pride." He left the door open to his staff for independent comments to the press.

Later, with a companion, the mayor, having vented his anger, talked quietly about the court, about busing, about the opposition, about what had happened to him and his dreams and his city.

"I have a one-track mind. Kiley was worried in the spring that I wasn't paying attention to busing, and I told him, 'You don't know me. Once I am in it, that's it — like a viselike grip.' "

Already, less than a month in operation, busing had sapped the strength and energies of white and black neighborhood leaders, of school officials, and of the mayor's staff. Local government generally operates by crisis, anyway. Only in rare moments do those running it have the luxury of planning long-range policies. And now crisis was king, and all other issues and considerations, like faithful subjects, must bend at the knee and wait their turn.

"A number of things have changed. From March to the opening of school, you're playing an adversary role against a defined leadership, like Louise, and the day school opened, the leadership wasn't there. The common denominator now is fear on both sides. I have to develop responsible leadership in the white community." The process, that democratic process so celebrated in print and patriotic blather, requires its successful practitioners to manipulate and cajole, to compromise and demand, to win and lose a dozen battles a day and make end runs that are time-consuming and expensive. The mayor could not join the pro-busing or anti-busing elements, for they are both part of his constituency. He needed elements of both for the city's future. "If this were an autonomous state," he said, "we'd have revolution or repeal." Instead, there are politics and meetings and compromises and offers, and he believed he was the one man in the city who could operate the whole insane scenario.

"Who reaches out now to Tom Johnson [a ROAR leader] to alleviate his fears? Me! Mayor Black. No? Less than true to my ideals? But the ultimate ideal is to hold the community together.

"No one is indispensable," he said, "but this town'll go down as quick as Philadelphia if I go."

But the staff does influence him. If he was angry with them, they will understand, and the anger will pass, and they already know that. "Tomorrow morning," he said, "I'll work my way back in. I'll settle down. Today, it was just a small civic crime." He paused. "Funny, isn't it? To say that of the judiciary."

He talked about mistakes he had made, errors in judgment, he said. "I took my mind off busing for a night. I was up studying inflation, trying to learn economics, preparing for a seminar . . . and that was the day I forgot to check plans for Hyde Park. . . . So there I am learning price indexes. . . . Like Rommel on leave." But this day, he could not help coming back to the judge's decision, for it had stung him personally.

"If Garrity had called and said, 'You're charged not only with public safety but with a real *plan*,' but he didn't do that. He didn't trust my judgment. He just made me a party to the suit. I'll wind up trying to broker something over which I can't have any control. Now *I've* got to work with the school committee on a plan."

To his critics, the mayor was angry because he could not escape responsibility to implement busing. To himself and those around him, Kevin White was angry because he felt the court had restricted his movements as a politician trying to bring about a settlement in the only way he knew how. In fact, the court had not done so, and Gleason was right. Kevin White would continue to work the strings and controls he knew best. But for a short time, he would be seen as a man who lost control or who lost his way, and a malaise would set in among his prized and beloved staff, and it would accurately reflect the mood of the city.

TWENTY-FIVE

Calling For Help

From a reporter's notes . . .
Oct. 3, Thursday.
Mayor tells police, "Don't arrest any public official. They're dying for martyrdom. That's about all they got left; no integrity."
Jordan: "They'll be jumping into the wagon."
Kevin: "Pull 'em out."

Oct. 4, parade in Southie.
Signs at rally: "Whites Have Rights"
              "Tell City Hall You Can't Fight Southie"
Billy Bulger: "Will we surrender?"
The crowd: "Never! No!"
A white-haired guy from Atlanta says, "In 1969 we had the same problems as you. . . . It was in 1773 that you all threw the tea in the harboh, and it was in 1774 that you all got the repressive act. Now, two hundred years later, you still fight repression. . . . I guess it's a lost cause down our way, and we've transferred the battle to you all." He brings them $300, some cornmeal, chewing tobacco, and some snuff.

"Yay."

ROAR pledge of allegiance: "I will not pledge allegiance to the court order of U.S. fed. ct. or to the dictatorship to which it stands, one law, under Garrity . . . with liberty and justice for none."

Virginia Sheehy got dozen roses. "Grateful appreciation from people of SB." She says, "Every time we have something the weather has been good and people saying 'He's with us. It's just the guys in between.' "

Doughnut shop, East Boston, 3 p.m.

Bus driver says busing is crazy. "Every city has its little islands, you know? And they should be allowed to stay that way."

The owner, George. "I'm not busin' my kids. . . . You know, I usta serve colored here. When I was inna army, I usta help them out, you know, if a guy needed a buck. I wouldn't do it today. They put you on your guard. . . . The only reason for this busin' is the city wants the federal money they give you for busin', and I say let 'em keep it."

"And its our money. Whose money do you think it is anyway?"

Late afternoon, City Hall elevator.

Dapper O'Neil, smiling. "It's growing. It's growing, I tell you. People are sick and tired of this shit."

A few hours after Dapper gushed with outward feelings of victory, the traveling ROAR motorcade visited Judge Garrity's house in Wellesley. Some 300 busing protestors sang their songs and chanted their slogans. Some 40 suburban cops wearing helmets, from Wellesley and four other communities, protected the house. For the boys in City Hall, it was comic relief. Wellesley, like Dover, represents wealth and snob zoning and hypocrisy to hard-nosed city dwellers, and the idea that five communities had to turn out cops was somehow a victory, a warped tragicomedy victory. Other than that, there was little to celebrate.

On the night of the motorcade to Wellesley, the myth the people in Southie never cried police brutality was about to come to an inglorious end.

Boston, like Pittsburgh and Baltimore, is a good bar town. The city is sprinkled liberally with saloons, taprooms, bars, social clubs, and veterans' halls. To associate baked beans and brown bread with Boston is to perpetuate a cliche; to talk about booze is to get closer to reality. Some bars are quiet, and some bars are noisy, and some bars can be either, but whatever those choose to be, they are tough, and everybody who knew of the Rabbit Inn on Dorchester Street in Southie agreed that the Rabbit Inn was one tough bar.

That Friday night, October 4, a TPF cruiser passing by the Rabbit Inn caught a brick through one window. Three TPF cops caught the alleged pitcher near the bar. Some 25 to 30 patrons rushed out and gave battle. The next night, Saturday, Boston police swept through the Rabbit Inn — the police later insisting they were responding to anonymous calls about an officer in trouble — and when they came back out, they had left behind them a destroyed, torn-up barroom littered with bruised and bloody patrons. The victims cried police brutality. They said the TPF had come in, clubs swinging. The cops, resented for their very presence in Southie, resented by guys their own age, by people with whom they shared both life-style and antipathy toward busing, had seemingly conducted a revenge raid. It was a raid that matched the overworked Southie counsel — "Don't get mad, get even."

No great wash of liberal sentiment came out of the suburbs, as often happens when police are brutal in minority neighborhoods. Southie, with some ROAR allies, was alone in its Sunday protest to the Police Department. Get the cops out of our neighborhood, they demanded. And on Monday, October 7, they trooped the injured to the City Council chambers to embarrass the Police Department. The trouble was that Southie contained so much hate that while its aggrieved displayed bandages and bruises, the haters were doing a number that would do more to display the virus of bigotry than any other incident.

That afternoon, a mob beat and nearly killed a Haitian immigrant, André Yvon Jean-Louis, who had committed the unpardonable crime of stopping for a red light at Dorchester Street and Old Colony Avenue while en route to pick up his wife, who worked in a Southie laundry. They rocked his car, broke the windows, dragged him into the street, punched him and set upon two motorcycle cops who tried saving him. They chased him, beat him again, and the pictures of a terrified black man, pursued by smiling screaming whites of all ages, flashed across the nation. Liberals may have expressed shock that this was Boston. Boston it was, living up to its dichotomous heritage, Boston, the city with LOVE tattooed on one set of knuckles and HATE on the other. Patrolman Robert Cunningham, nineteen years on the force, fired two shots into the air, and, with Sgt. Charles Deary, got Jean-Louis out of the mob.

It was now clear that increased police forces would be needed in Southie, perhaps forever, and it was equally clear that those forces could not include the TPF, for their very presence might itself instigate incidents among a population that Ray Flynn was insisting was "occupied" as if in war. Trouble erupted in Roslindale. The mayor and black leaders screamed at each other in an angry meeting.

Kevin H. White, as he is mayor of Boston, moves the court to convene an immediate hearing upon such notice to the parties as the court may deem appropriate under the circumstances and thereupon to enter an order requiring the presence and assistance of not less than one hundred twenty-five United States Marshals in the South Boston district of the City of Boston....

It had really been easier in 1863. The mayor and governor simply called for help, and in came armed militia companies, volunteers, and federal troops. Now one made motions, entered briefs. Now the federal government insisted that to put down disturbances, one must first exhaust local police, state police, the National Guard, and then, one may call for federal troops. Of course, a president could decide to order troops in, as Eisenhower had done long ago in Little Rock, but Gerald Ford was not about to do so.

That Monday, October 7, Kevin White sent a letter to Garrity, pleading for federal marshals. "We are utilizing no fewer than 900 police officers every school day — virtually one-half of our active-duty police personnel, to protect children on their way to and from the schools. The cost for police overtime alone is $100,000 a day. The total cost for the first 18 school days exceeds $2 million. The Tactical Patrol Force, comprised of 125 men, has been constantly utilized for school purposes exclusively. And the individual members of the TPF have been averaging no fewer than 55 overtime hours of duty each and every week.

"The police force has strained all its personnel and has exhausted every resource available to it. And the men of the department have acted courageously, with determination, and under frustrating and dangerous circumstances."

The mayor argued in his letter that busing was going well in 90 percent of the city, even though he and the judge knew that trouble had broken out in Hyde Park and other areas. It was Southie, he argued, that had drained the city's resources and patience.

White was asking for a straight-player deal: 125 marshals for 125 TPF cops, whom he would put elsewhere in the city. "Federal presence in South Boston is necessary and needed immediately to guarantee the implementation of the Federal Court order."

Kevin White is relaxed early in the morning of October 8. He does not know what Garrity will do. He does not know now that Garrity will refuse the marshals. It is 9 o'clock in the morning, Beethoven is being played on his stereo, and one of Governor Sargent's aides, Jack Flannery, is on the phone. "Jack," the mayor says, "obviously we don't need those sharpshooters from the National Guard." He reminds Flannery of how the black leaders and he asked for help before. "All the balls are in my court. I'm willing to accept that, but a National Guard? No. I just want him to know — *no*." As the mayor finishes the phone call, Quealy comes in to announce, "One black kid in South Boston High School. *He's* got guts. Talk about a pupil-teacher ratio!"

The blacks have kept most of their kids out of Southie's schools today. The boycott has become integrated, even if Southie's schools haven't. The word from Eddie King in Southie — through Peter Meade — is that "the South Boston people are really scared now. Some are asking if their insurance is canceled."

"They lost it yesterday," Quealy says.

"It's over now," Kevin says, now off the phone. "I won't see them."

In Kevin's mind, three things triggered the events leading to what he has done. One is the character of the city. Another is the belief by many people who feel somehow the law can be changed and busing will disappear. The third is "a familiarity with and at the same time a disrespect for the police. I had two goals — one, for the police to do the job, and two, to protect children. There was a time when we didn't know that the police would *do* the job, and, in my opinion, they've performed admirably. They have been superb."

Because the cops performed and because no one kid had been hospitalized overnight, "everyone has perceived there is turbulence, but no deep problem, because no one was hurt. Past policy was that if no one is hurt, you're in good shape.

"But we're witnessing the end results of ten years of political hate. Candidates have run on it. They beat Pitaro in East Boston on it. It has bred a sense of hate evidenced on the face of those people who beat a black person. After three weeks of the greatest turmoil this city has ever been in, not *one* elected political leader has stood up in this city outside myself. And the court hasn't been much better. It's been distant, not one half as aware of things as the court in Denver. The only communication I get is a hired federal monitor from Washington.

"The blacks wanted to jockey for political position and implementation. The white leadership didn't want implementation and did jockey for political position. So you've got ten years of hate, no respect for the police, the feeling they can change the law, no other political leaders.

"We're not calling the marshals out of panic. I have no intention of being like other cities — bringing in federal support *after* someone is hurt. Second, I believe the federal presence will give the imprimatur that this is a federal act, serious and unalterable. Police presence hasn't done that. This is the only way I know to focus the court's attention on the situation. Also, I have to take out the TPF. Their presence inflames the situation because they've been so forceful.

"It's time for Garrity. Not once did he prevent a parade. But it is a damn sure thing that the public thinks it's the mayor's fault." He says he doesn't like being pushed around by whites, blacks, the court, or anybody. "For once, the judge will get information from people on the scene."

But why not a larger force of marshals? No, he says, it's the federal presence that counts. "Right now, people who are picked up are taken to South Boston District Court, which lets them out. How would they like to go to the U.S. District Court?"

But why not troops? Once, he had talked of troops. Now, he says, "It would be a case of overkill. But it's up to the judge. If the judge wants to call troops, he can. But the judge is so divorced from the situation. The effect of federal marshals is to drive home two points — the law is not to be changed, and it will be enforced.

"Southie will sober up for a moment, or they may well attack the marshals. If they do, the judgment will have to be made by the feds on what to do. Not in our laps. If we don't do it now, we'll run into it in Phase Two, and I can't run a city this way."

Later in the morning, at about 11 A.M., Kevin, now in a suit, sits with Tivnan, their backs to the picture window of the living room, and faces about thirty reporters to explain why he's done what he's done.

One reporter says, "My experience in covering the South was that federal marshals exacerbated the situation."

"Do we have to have a body on the altar to move us to get federal marshals?" Kevin asks. "Three bodies to qualify for the National Guard? And a holocaust means you can get troops? No, that's what other cities do. I've used maximum force to protect children. Obviously, it's a matter of endurance."

Kevin insists he is not following the NAACP demand for marshals. He says the request has come from the Police Department, yet within White's staff, there must have been great disagreement on the usefulness of marshals. Kiley had said publicly the day before, "Federal marshals are not going to be adequate. State Police are not trained for this type of situation. This is not 'Highway Patrol.' The National Guard, in my opinion, has not distinguished itself since the mid-nineteen-sixties. They take seventy-two hours to mobilize and are ninety percent white." Kiley was pushing for federal troops.

When pressed now by Brad Knickerbocker, of the Christian Science

Monitor, on how 125 marshals can control Southie, the mayor answers, "If the U.S. marshals can't help, then the judge is gonna decide how the law is going to be implemented. . . . I don't want under any circumstances the National Guard. I do want the judge, as has been done in Denver, to become actively involved on a day-to-day basis."

Does he expect higher attendance at the schools? "I don't know," he says. "I do know that a situation has deteriorated, and something must change. I have found no one who has given me a better set of alternatives. . . . Now, I'm a practicing Catholic, and I don't think it'll be changed by prayer. And whether it's a black mayor of Detroit or a white mayor of Boston, we *don't* think inner city busing can work. But that is not the issue. The police and I have *tried*."

As the mayor handles questions, a false alarm is pulled at English High, and a few moments later, the police radio reports that black students are running out of English High toward Huntington Avenue. Boston is about to see sporadic incidents of black violence meld into large crowds, assaults, and trashing. It was inevitable, and now it is happening. The TPF, no longer in Southie, now speeds to Huntington Avenue to deal with the blacks. By 11:37 A.M., the police request an ambulance at English High and report that black students are picking up pipes and sticks. At Roxbury Crossing, a neighborhood that was tough when just trees lived there, blacks are reportedly smashing windows. Before the day ends, some 20 persons are injured by rocks, mostly whites, and a fifty-year-old cab driver is beaten by black youths and sent to the hospital, where he requires 20 pints of blood.

It is about this time, as the initial reports come in downstairs, that a reporter asks the mayor, "Did you expect Boston to reach this point?"

"What point?" Kevin asks.

"I ask the question in the light of the reputation of Boston as a liberal city, an enlightened city."

"Are you a local reporter?" Kevin asks, making a face of disbelief, and bringing the crowd to a laugh. Later, apologizing to the man who asked the question, Kevin says, "If you're familiar with the local scene, you'll know a liberal constituency has never been part of the scene. This emotion is not recent, but has been whipped up in five election campaigns. Local pols have been whipping up feelings, and this is the price we are paying. It's marvelous how everyone has disappeared, the ones who were gonna stand in front of the school doors, lie down in front of the buses — as long as the buses are not moving. Someone suggested it would be Armageddon. Well, it's not. It's gone amazingly well. My only regret was when it had half a chance, the locals still had to hold their parades, kid their constituents one more time."

The press briefing ends, and, quietly, a companion presses White again — how can 125 marshals, possibly badly trained, handle Southie if 600 or more cops can't? The mayor says that after yesterday's incidents and last night's meetings with angry blacks, "we came to the conclusion we were being hung." Can the marshals do it? "They *can't*," he spits out. He has had it with W. Arthur Garrity, and he is throwing the ball to him, a ball made up of both petulance and a street sensitivity to reality.

Downstairs in the bunker, the worn and haggard staff is also sensitive to reality. They are getting a good dose of it this afternoon.

"Seventy-five out at Tech," one man yells. "They're breaking windows, stoning cars."

"There's a rally scheduled at two P.M. at Dudley Station," Kelliher says. "We've got the King and the Burke to contend with this afternoon."

"Operations to Two-nine-one," cries a voice on the police radio.

"Two-nine-one."

"Yeah, Ten-thirty-one wants you to start getting your men together."

A man yells to Kelliher, "Richie, they just authorized a one-thirty dismissal at English."

"Roving gangs around the arena and the Carter Elementary School," another woman reports. "They're a teensy, tiny school, and they're very worried."

Rich, on the phone with somebody, says, "These were Spanish kids fighting black kids? Who were they fighting, black kids or white kids?"

"Ten-twelve is sending a busload to District 2 now," the police radio reports.

As the day wears on Kiley wonders out loud, "Why the Christ doesn't it rain?"

Coakley would like to shut the schools down for three days. "There's such a defeatist attitude among all of us. We feel we've lost it. We could use three days to think out a new strategy. There are so many kids out of school anyway. They'll pounce on the ones who are still in."

"Four days, a week ago," Kiley answers, "I would've said, 'Bad idea.' Now, we've got nothing to lose."

Bob Kiley used to talk of political solutions to the crisis of busing. He knew as well as anyone that rushing troops from one battle to another was not the answer. One might extinguish small fires, put down brief rebellions, but soon, one's energy drained, and the cost in money, manpower, goodwill, the very cost to the democratic process, could overwhelm anything good that might come of school integration. Now, while fire alarms ring, and kids trash, and cops rush to different parts of town, he muses over lost opportunities. He feels Garrity has not been as involved as he should be. He knows the real answer lay in a metropolitan solution, not within the confines of the city, but no such solution is anywhere in sight. There is the nagging question too — could the White administration have built a workable coalition of blacks and whites? Maybe. In a few days, the mayor will try to bring blacks and whites together. They will meet together in the Eagle Room, but it won't work, partly because the whites are working stiffs, and the blacks chosen are better educated and more middle-class, and the two groups will be unable to communicate.

But now, it seems all one can do is direct troops and try to avoid bloodshed. A sign on Weddleton's desk in the bunker, a sign put out by the Citywide Educational Coalition before busing, seems strangely out of place now. It says simply, "Take it Easy for the Kids' Sake."

"I've got cycle squads coming in from District 5," the police dispatcher announces on the radio band. "I'm trying to raise them, sir."

Messages come from all directions. The police must be everywhere at once. "Two-nine-one . . . Operations to Two-nine-one. Do you have escort for buses leaving Latin School?"

The mayor is getting his share of troubles too. The NAACP also has submitted a motion in court, arguing that 125 marshals would not be enough. White, it says, should first call on cops in nearby cities and towns and the state police. If they fail, he should then ask the governor for the National Guard, and the NAACP is urging the court to explore the use of federal troops. At 3 P.M., Tom McKenna, of the Law Department, arrives in the mayor's office after having called the Justice Department. "The Justice Department doesn't want to give us any marshals. They suggest the State Police and then the National Guard. If called upon, they'll speak against the utilization of marshals, because other resources are not being used first."

Some of those who hear this news are openmouthed. It is hard enough to train big-city police forces to handle uprisings and street action. Who, in his right mind, would start bringing in small-city, small-town, and suburban police units, most of whom wouldn't know a Puerto Rican from a Cape Verdean from a Sicilian?

Quealy, on the phone to Kelliher, reports out loud, "Dudley Street rally peters out. Mission Hill an unmitigated disaster. Mark Weddleton can't even get near Mission Hill."

"There was a man named Garrity," one aide recites.

"Who refused to give people parity.
"He was a Kennedy man,
"A flash in the pan,
"Created by an act of charity."

Kevin White is railing at the federal government. "We will not move those buses. We will not move those buses. We'll teach the federal government a lesson."

Kiley is arguing they can maintain public safety, but they cannot implement the judge's desegregation order. The judge will see no separation of tasks.

"Maybe we should show up the federal government for what it is," Kevin says. "And that state [desegregation] plan [used by Garrity] that no one agrees with — oh that's good! And those psalm-singing suburbanites."

Kiley pleads, "Aside from all that, isn't there anything we can do to get people talking to one another? Whites to whites, blacks to blacks, whites to blacks."

But Kevin says, "Yeah, but what am I gonna say tomorrow? What are *we* going to do, gentlemen? Do you have any advice before I make my decision?"

Someone mentions Louise, and Kevin urges, "Don't answer them. Don't answer their calls. Let them find themselves. They all call the mayor and say, 'I talked to the mayor, and, oh boy, did I tell him!'"

But tonight, there is a serious question whether white political leaders can find themselves, and by late at night, the question is equally serious for the blacks. For after a day of predominantly black violence — for a change — Bill Owens, having distinguished himself so far in this crisis, reads an inflammatory statement on the 11 P.M. television news — "We are going to walk the streets of South Boston at a time *we* determine. We are going to do it to show that we can go to their schools . . . can go to work there . . . can live there . . . that the people of South Boston *don't own it*."

By the end of the day, 38 persons had been injured, 7 were arrested, and 5 black juveniles had been arraigned for the alleged rape of a white girl earlier in the week. The Cardinal had asked for peace. The mayor had asked for marshals. The NAACP had asked for everything but nuclear submarines. And the *Globe,* the liberal, heretofore cautiously optimistic *Globe,* which, like most newspapers, was no longer in touch with its own city, put to bed an editorial calling for federal troops.

TWENTY-SIX

Confusion in the Ranks

KEVIN WHITE was never ecstatic about Gerald Ford. Kevin White had been known to say that Gerald Ford didn't know anything about the cities, and back when the pressure was on Democratic congressmen to oust Richard Nixon, Kevin White was warning them not to make things too easy for Gerald Ford. If they did, he said, Ford would be a very strong candidate in 1976.

On October 9, the day Kevin White entered W. Arthur Garrity's courtroom, Gerald Ford was having a press conference. In the courtroom, Judge Garrity said no to the request for marshals. He had only 23 of them, he said, and they were assigned to federal courts in Boston — they certainly had no anti-riot training worthy of the name. The feds did have a 1,000-man force that was so trained, but Garrity insisted he had no control over them. Only the Justice Department did, and it ordered them into action only during riotous situations. No, he said, let there be instead a gradual using up of available law enforcement officers — nearby police forces, state police, National Guard, up the bureaucratic line.

So, Tom McKenna had been right. There would be no marshals. White was pissed, but he vowed there would be no suburban police or National Guard either. He went back to his office, called Frank Sargent and asked for 300 state troopers and 100 Metropolitan District Commission (MDC) police. He wanted them at the Bayside Mall by 5 A.M. the next day, October 10. But that was not all on Kevin White's mind that afternoon, for, while still at court, he learned what Jerry Ford had just said in the Rose Garden, when a reporter told Ford of White's request for marshals and the blacks' request for troops and asked what he, the President, intended to do and what comments he might have.

After the standard deploring-of-violence routine, Ford added, "The court decision in that case, in my judgment, was not the best solution to quality education in Boston. I have consistently opposed forced busing to achieve racial balance as a solution to quality education. And therefore, I respectfully disagree with the Judge's order. But having said that, I think it is of maximum importance that the citizens of Boston respect the law. . . ." As far as any marshals were concerned, the President said they were under the court's jurisdiction, not his. About the same time, Garrity was saying that the riot-trained marshals were under the jurisdiction of the Justice Department. Marshals, marshals, who's got the marshals?

Back in Boston, blacks got sick, ROAR took heart, and the mayor realized all his worst fears about President Ford. On the morning of October 10, the state and MDC troopers lined up smartly at Bayside Mall, traveled to Southie and impressed everyone there with military bearing — "They all snapped their helmet visors down together," Paul Parks reported. "They sat up ramrod-straight in the cruisers. Their pride is on the line." Sometime after that, Kevin White and Ira Jackson decided to answer Ford.

At noon, the aides gather in the living room, as Kevin prepares for a press conference. "The President is a hero to that constituency," he says. "But he's undercut our position. We're enforcing their law, and they don't give us the tools to do it."

Jackson comes into the living room with the statement he has prepared for the man whom he would like tò see run for national office.

Kevin reads the three-page statement, and it is strong stuff. "President Ford's statement yesterday acts to impede the enforcement of the Federal court order to desegregate Boston's public schools and thus threatens the safety of our school children. In so doing, he has jeopardized the civil and human rights of the citizens of this city, and his statements challenge the rule of law throughout this land."

The President not only opposes the court's decision, the statement goes on, but is reluctant to provide federal enforcement and, instead, encourages resistance. Eisenhower never criticized the 1954 Supreme Court decision, and Kennedy sent troops to the South when "integration was no more popular in the South than busing is today in the North."

Other cities should beware, for the President and the Attorney General, by denying aid, are telling them — "You're on your own . . . unless you can show me the statistics on the number of children killed, the pictures of the school buses burning, the permanent and devastating damage to your city."

·Well, the mayor goes on, the city will continue to do its best, but . . . Kevin White will not cooperate in developing Phase Two unless Washington is more clear about when federal troops can be dispatched, unless flaws in the integration plan are corrected with the help of city residents and unless the feds come through with more financial aid.

The mayor looks up from the statement and looks at the men he trusts. At Larry Quealy, who every day hears his neighbors complain and worry about forced busing and hears some of them talk of leaving town. At Ed Sullivan, cautious, worried that Kevin could be perceived as supporting busing. At Herb Gleason and Paul Parks, a white Yankee liberal from Beacon Hill and a black integration veteran from Dorchester, who had tried to convince their constituencies that Kevin is still a liberal and has not copped out. At Peter Meade, now running the Office of Public Service, the Little City Halls, a Dorchester Irish boy who has resisted becoming a conservative and who displays equal compassion for whites and blacks caught up in this insanity. At Bob Kiley, who once knew little of Boston and now knows more about it than most of the people who live here, the heaviest crutch on which the mayor has been able to lean during the busing crisis. Of the inner circle, Kirk O'Donnell is not here, because Kirk O'Donnell has been given the job of cranking up the machinery to reelect Kevin White one year from now. That too is something that must be considered with every speech he makes, every press conference he decides to hold. Kevin looks at his people and awaits their reaction.

"We're toying with defiance here," Parks warns.

"The statement is suicidal," Quealy protests. "Ford's an overnight folk hero here."

"The only part that bothers me is where you say you won't cooperate with Phase Two," Meade says. "That sounds like Ford."

"How about 'effectively'?" someone suggests. "You can't 'effectively cooperate'?"

Meade snaps his fingers. "Yeah."

"That's better," Parks says.

"I have no problem with that," Gleason tells them.

Sullivan is worried. He thinks the statement is "politically bad."

Ira is frustrated. "One says don't be against Ford. Another one says be against forced busing." There are opinions all over the lot, he says. "So what the fuck are we having a press conference for?"

"Don't hand out that statement," Kiley warns. "Cancel the press conference. Those of us who like the first part of the statement are not for the second part. Those who like the second part are not for the first part."

Kevin is smiling. He seems most at ease of everyone there. "You see why you're so good? You represent a cross-section. One-half will love it, and one-half will not. I believe in this. Ford is wrong, in my opinion. Second, I am against forced busing, Paul, and always have been. But they *must* know it's possible to be against forced busing and still believe in the *law*." He turns to Quealy, worried about the local votes this could cost the mayor. "Larry, after this statement, I won't run for anything but a gopher hole." He laughs, and Kiley says, "They're all filled up already," and they all laugh.

To no one in particular, the mayor vows, "I'll call on every ounce of federal and state reserves, but I will *not* use the National Guard or suburban police forces." Now, he's trying one-liners that might be used in the upcoming press conference.

"We just had a President who asked us to obey laws which he didn't obey, and now we have a President asking us to enforce a law he won't comply with."

"The public question of busing must be resolved again. It must be either reaffirmed or overturned." On this one, he will prove to be right on the mark, for the events in Boston will come to make Boston a symbol of the difficulties in forced school integration. Combined with increasing black populations and decreasing white populations in some cities, the nation, by the summer of 1975, will be torn over whether and how to proceed with forced desegregation. Academics will snipe at one another. Courts will slow down the integration process in some cities and speed it up in others.

White seems to have a good feel for the trends, for the signs and symbols. He reads the winds and the flights of birds. Yet in the midst of this he must pay attention to his own precincts, where people are worried less about national trends and more about what the next 45 minutes or an hour will bring.

"I believe, talking to Eddie King, there's a hiatus in South Boston, forty-eight hours that we can use." He tells Paul and Larry to get cracking on their contacts in the community. "We can shepherd them together. See if we can have a meeting at six o'clock tonight." He's talking about bringing whites and blacks together. "Nobody will be spotted. Anyone can leave. No one will be embarrassed, held up, quoted, or committed. It's just to explore, to see if they'll be brought together. I'll tell them we have, with luck, forty-eight hours of peace, that we want them to develop their own leadership to tell the mayor, the superintendent of schools, the judge where to go. Co-chair it, one black and one white. I want a commitment from them to stay here for two hours, then leave if it doesn't work out. But stay two hours. Talk about baseball if you want, but stay two hours."

At the press conference, Kevin, just a touch nervous, is reading his own edited version of the Jackson statement that reporters have in front of them. He plays the statement for all it's worth, cool at times, raising his voice when necessary, sighing audibly when he says, "I'll continue to enforce the law," and then hits them with this:

"Therefore, I will not publicly support on my own volition the implementation of the second phase of the plan unless and until . . ." and he lists the guarantees he wants. He has failed to say "effectively cooperate," and maybe it doesn't make a hell of a lot of difference, but to Meade and Parks and Gleason and others, it was more acceptable. It meant the mayor would cooperate, but that his cooperation would be ineffective without federal aid. Now, he is saying he won't voluntarily implement a plan.

Most of the reporters want to know what he means. They keep asking, but the answers are not clear. Kevin does not now appear to be confident or in charge. He is vague. Now he says he'll obey any orders from the judge, but he will not go beyond the judge's orders; he will not be imaginative or use the skills and talents and contacts he has used during Phase One. Perhaps in his own mind, it is clear. He would not bother to go to scores of neighborhoods again or open up a rumor control center. Maybe that's what he means. But it is not clear to anyone listening. He talks about how he tried to make the plan work peacefully without any judge ordering him to do so, and implies he will not be so enthusiastic in Phase Two. He insists again that maintaining public safety and implementing the court order are "separate issues." In the past, the mayor has occasionally — as any leader has — used the tack of frontal assault to force a resolution to an issue, the tactic of a threat. Perhaps he is doing so again, but the result is poor. For those seeking leadership, at this point in time, there are only a blank wall, only dim corridors of confusion — a judge who talks about suburban cops and National Guardsmen, a school committee that resists, a wornout police force, a President who passes the buck, a governor busy running a losing race for reelection and who — unknown to anyone now — will soon play politics with the busing issue, and a mayor who has just confused everybody by seemingly contradictory statements.

At the end of the press conference, the mayor says, prophetically, "True to Boston, she does raise issues, and this is a legitimate issue to be raised — whether the federal government will provide resources to implement the law or whether the President wants to reverse the law. . . ." But the twin thoughts — that once again it is Boston raising the national consciousness on an issue that will tear the nation apart, and that the federal government must decide once and for all whether its full force will be perceived as supporting the decisions of its courts — these thoughts are lost in the confusion.

Back in his office, the boss immediately starts talking to his staff. "Now, let's not panic. All the time we've been together we've allowed an assessment of the mayor. Well, obviously, if it wasn't great, it was the best I.could do. If we get out okay, we were lucky. What we've got to do now is put those groups together [the blacks and whites]."

Late that afternoon and early in the evening, Kevin's people are trying to do just that. It is difficult. Certain whites won't meet with certain blacks and vice versa. Certain whites don't want other whites in the room. Some feel they will lose face. Some feel they will lose votes. The only thing holding is the shape of the table. Kevin is telling somebody that "we liberals innovate, we change things, but we should have the capacity to go back over the road we came and say we made a mistake." Kiley is on the phone, trying to convince the Boston police to patrol Southie between midnight and 6 A.M. because the state is complaining that the troopers and MDC units should not have to patrol around the clock.

Between phone calls, he reviews the mayor's press conference — Kevin didn't mean to say he wouldn't deploy the National Guard, because only a governor can anyway; he meant he wouldn't request the Guard; yes, the mayor is flirting with trouble from the court. In the middle of all his phone calls, Kiley picks up a receiver and tells his secretary, "Get me the Korean truce team." Kiley too must maintain some appearance of sanity and perspective.

Kevin appears in Kiley's office, where he gets a phone call from a *Globe* reporter, who asks again what in hell he meant. "When I said, 'I will not on my own volition support' . . . I put that phrase in. The court has not ordered the performance I put on. It had not ordered me into the coffee klatches. Into staying up eighteen hours a day. I did it on *my own volition*. My own efforts. What I'm saying now is that I will not give those same efforts, unless the federal government gives me some support. The House of Representatives, which cut the money for desegregation costs. The President, who says, 'Busing? Don't worry about that.' With a judge who won't give me federal marshals. I will not go into Phase Two and give all of that of me, when my people pick up the cost. You can't order me to go to coffee klatches. I am no goddamn Governor Wallace. I've put my shoulder to the wheel. If the people at the *Globe* think down there I haven't gone all the way, they can call Garrity in Wellesley and ask him to do it. I'll tell you what you can tell them about the mayor. I am not defiant, but I am determined."

The statement, tough and clear, makes more sense than what he said earlier. Even Kiley had been confused until now, about 6:10 in the evening, as the mayor explains his position to the *Globe*. But not many do understand. Barry Brooks comes in and announces, "Based on the calls we've got so far, west of the Mississippi, they have *no* idea he meant Phase Two." There are people who think the mayor of Boston is now saying he won't enforce the current desegregation plan.

At 6:30 P.M., Meade, Kiley, Jackson, and Quealy make themselves comfortable in the mayor's back room and turn on the television to see what the networks will do with Kevin White's statement and press conference. Meade has been a key figure in putting together the black/white committee, and he has had a day full of problems. Louise Day Hicks objected to two of the white persons Meade wanted, arguing the committee would be stacked against her people, even though one of the two whites she objected to was opposed to busing. A choice had to be made — forget the whole thing, go ahead with some kind of a committee and publicly embarrass those whites who refused to join it, or cave in to ROAR and replace the two white moderates with two militants. They chose to take the last course, convinced Erwin Canham, the editor emeritus of the *Christian Science Monitor*, to chair the group, and hoped for the best. The meeting would be tomorrow.

Meanwhile all three networks are using footage from Kevin's press conference, and two of them lead with it. "Boston's busing crisis," John Chancellor intones, "turned today into a dispute between Boston Mayor Kevin White and President Ford."

"Yahooooo!" yells Ira Jackson. The mayor is looking good. The tough questions asked of him in the press conference have somehow been forgotten. The networks — as television often does — simply record some of the prepared material. None of the confusion has been captured nationally, at least not enough to make the mayor look bad.

While Ira Jackson thinks about blocs of delegates from the Middle West or the Southwest or the West Coast, Larry Quealy worries about the 22 wards in Boston, and he says to Ira, "I know it's good nationally. What I'm worried about is locally."

Later in the evening, Jackson explains what he thinks the mayor's strategy is. "He's a smart enough politician to know he has to distance himself from this thing, or the crisis aspect will never leave him. . . . But that's a secondary concern. The most important point is the only way they'll see implementation is inevitable is through the threat and immediate presence of federal power — through marshals, the FBI, troops. There has to be a federal presence, a Nicholas Katzenbach on the courthouse steps. . . . There's a hell of a difference between a Judge Feeney and a twenty-five-dollar fine and a federal judge imposing a ten-thousand-dollar fine for a violation of civil rights.

"He wants the judge to be firm with them, but to give them at least a rational outlet, a possibility for discussion. The poorest blacks and the poorest whites are going to the poorest schools in the city, aggravating a racial situation that's been developing for over one hundred years. Anyone with half a brain wouldn't have put those two areas [Southie and Roxbury] together. The mayor is saying you have to understand the mores and racial prejudice of the two communities and the historic animosity between those two communities. If those same black and white kids are gonna mix together, at least it should be in an area, a zone, that doesn't threaten either of them. Maybe that's a sad commentary, but that's the way it is, given the suburbs locking in the city with no alternatives."

The diverse personalities of Ira Jackson and Larry Quealy both believe that whites and blacks together in a room can solve some of the problems that have arisen. The mayor is trying to bring them together tomorrow. It will not work. The personalities within the group will not click properly, and there will be moments of anger and antagonism, as well as moments of sympathy and affection. In the months to come, Judge Garrity will create a citywide interracial council, which will not have as many Boston parents as it should, but will be an improvement over what now exists, which is no coalition at all.

Canham, a very soft-spoken journalist, and the group of five blacks and five whites assemble the next day in the Eagle Room, while the mayor's staff gets trays of sandwiches and coffee ready. Kevin goes in, but only for a few minutes. He tells them why he's asked them to come and thanks them for showing up. When he comes out, he shakes his head, rolls his eyes upward, half-smiles and says, "Boy, is that tense!"

He is relaxing. Last night, before he went out to see his oldest son,

Kevin was handed a Little City Hall managers' report on trends, feelings, emotions, problems. "Depressing," he now recalls. "One said, 'You're dead in this community.' I said to my son, well, as I've told you, a mayor knows everything from the heights to the depths. Well, here's the depths. . . ." But this morning, he was in Jamaica Plain for a coffee hour, and as in Roxbury and Allston the other day, hardly anyone, he says, brought up busing. "Busing, anybody? Busing?" he laughs. "No, catchbasins!" He slaps his hands. "Sewers!" Slap. So, eleven months to the primary, and how does one figure it? How does one measure the heights and depths of the city?

After every coffee hour, Mike Feeney hands the taped proceedings to some other staffers, who make sure the complaints are dealt with and type up letters for the mayor telling the neighborhood people how happy he was to meet with them and how happy he was to fix up whatever it was that broke down. It is a masterful election tool, if it weren't for busing. The machinery has a shot at cleaning those catchbasins in Jamaica Plain. But next door, in the Eagle Room, the voices are rising. The issue there is a bit more difficult. It is less tangible than sewers. It is more complex than race. It is class warfare. And political maneuvering too.

Canham is ready with an innocuous statement against violence. Rita Graul, a ROAR leader and an aide to Louise, says there will be no statement without her organization's approval. Peter Meade will say later he felt Graul and the others were under orders not to agree to anything. The *Globe* would report that Graul excused herself to consult with Hicks.

The versions of what was said that day in the Eagle Room vary, but all agree there was little communication. The blacks were told they destroyed neighborhoods and that the Haitian who was beaten probably deserved it. The whites were told they were not only prejudiced but not honest enough to deal with their prejudice. Ellen Jackson walked out crying. Fran Johnnene, staunchly anti-busing, but a responsible ROAR leader, ended up being consoled by the mayor.

Boston had been building toward these days of violence and hate for too many generations for such a meeting to succeed. History had caught up the city. The long-frocked ghosts of intolerance were afoot. The graves of rabble-rousers and patriots, of Abolitionists and slave traders, of Know-Nothings and Irish defenders of the faith had opened. Boston knows little of moderation. It knows much of barricades and flags around which to rally.

TWENTY-SEVEN
Outside the City

*A polite young man waits in a bakery to buy something for a coffee
break, while the town's public works truck sits outside, awaiting his
return. The lady behind the counter and another customer are talking
about METCO.*

*METCO is an eight-year-old program, conceived by Boston blacks,
to bus their kids into suburban school systems. The state pays the tab,
and no whites are bused. By 1974, more than thirty communities participate in METCO, but there are now signs, given the troubles in
Boston, that more communities will turn it down than accept it.*

*The customer talking with the lady is one of a few liberals in the
town of Winthrop, a suburb bordering the East Boston line. The
suburb is typical of those communities hard by the city. It was wealthy
almost a century ago, but now it is poor to middle-class, densely populated, and burdened with its own urban problems. The liberal says
METCO would be good for the black and white kids, that it wouldn't
cost the town any money, and that maybe it would help ward off a
court decision someday that would force suburbs to cross-bus.*

*The young man has been listening, and he says he doesn't want
METCO. Let them work hard for their own schools, he says.*

"I hold three jobs so I can afford to send my kids to school."

*"What are you talkin' about?" the liberal says. "The schools are
public."*

*"Yeah," says the young man, "but I gotta work three jobs to afford
to live here."*

The noose around the city is drawn tighter. With every rock thrown
by a white crowd, with every act of black violence on white students,
the noose tightens.

An angry Kevin White has called the suburbanites "psalm-singing
hypocrites," but he is glossing over the facts. Indeed, there are pious
suburbanites who are quick to preach equal rights for others, as long
as they don't have to jump into the trenches. But there are others in
suburbia who never claimed to be liberals. They hate the city. They
don't like blacks or Puerto Ricans. Some don't like their own kind
who still live in the city. They have come to the suburbs for much the
same reasons as the Yankees came, and one of those reasons is moti-
vated by class — they really think they are better than the folks they
left behind.

In the suburbs south of Boston are people with strong personal
memories of Dorchester and Southie. Some say they wish they still
lived in the city. Others say they're happy to be out. They were quick
to join the public demonstrations against busing. As ROAR successfully fought Kevin's attempt to contain the protests to Southie, the
demonstrations often occurred in the suburbs and were supported by
suburban allies of ROAR.

Four communities, despite the violence in the city, voted to accept
METCO that year, knowing that a one-way voluntary busing program
had little to do with forced busing and the problems often associated
with that. In one of those four, however, opponents continued to fight
the school board's decision to participate in METCO, and at least five
other communities — including that town of Winthrop — refused
METCO. In Middleton, another suburb that refused METCO, opponents went about spreading all kinds of rumors.

They said a stabbing incident in the North Shore community of
Lynnfield involved METCO students. The stabbing was between two
whites. They said another North Shore community, Marblehead, was
having trouble with METCO finances, even though a Marblehead official insisted the state was footing the bill. They said METCO students
in the South Shore city of Quincy had forced Quincy kids to be bused

out of their own neighborhood school districts. Yet, there was no METCO program in Quincy.

As the resistance built in suburbia, the liberals in both Boston and the suburbs became increasingly frustrated. They were divided themselves over the issue. Some felt deeply that the white neighborhoods in the city were being asked to bear too much. Others said that mixing whites and blacks just in the city was harmful to both groups. Some said *they* would not want to bus their children into Roxbury or Southie, so how could they expect it of others. And, of course, there were those civil rights veterans who would not be moved from any plan to integrate any school anywhere, true to the stubbornness of Garrison.

"Americans for Democratic Action invites members and friends to a Brunch featuring Robert Kiley, Deputy Mayor for Planning and Neighborhood Services, to speak on Desegregation of the Boston Schools, Sunday, October 20, 1974, 10:30–12:30 at the home of Helene and Herbert LeVine, Auburndale. Bring your friends. $4.00 per person."

The liberals told Bob Kiley not to come after all. They were worried about a rumored motorcade of 1,000 ROAR cars coming to their Sunday get-together, because the ADA meeting was publicized in a Dorchester newspaper. Kiley was told not to come, and the meeting was shifted, and the motorcade never happened anyway, but it was a pretty good lesson in who was now calling the shots in greater Boston.

The liberals were reduced to vigils outside City Hall. Rarely were the vigils large, usually, a handful of silent adults standing pitifully in the rain or the sun — a far cry from the days of lobbying for the Racial Imbalance Bill or marching south. Rallies that reminded one of the old civil rights days would be held in the future, and they would make people feel better, but the momentum was no longer in the liberal camp.

They took consolation in small events, small displays of righteousness. Betty Parnes, of the ADA, tells those who have come to the first meeting — minus Kiley — "We stood there a long time in the downpour, and let me tell you it was quite an experience. People looked at us and thought we were mad, but I think we made the point." She pleads with the others in the living room in Newton, "At least join us in the vigil."

One man is indignant that the meeting has been altered because of the rumored motorcade. "What's happening here is what's happening in the city. People are being denied their constitutional rights."

Another member, Ellen Feingold, is concerned that the pro-busing groups were not communicating with one another. "The people in the city who support it need our support. I don't know how to get the word out that people in and outside of the city support this thing, that it is not just a court order being followed."

Helplessness. Frustration.

One man is impressed with ROAR's "spy system" and wants to know how it works so "we can use it."

Another man says ADA must be trained for public confrontations with ROAR. "Individually, you would've taken a shellacking," he tells them.

"That's what it's all about," another argues. Ahhhh, to suffer means to win?

"Martyrs don't win," the man insists. "A planned, controlled response is necessary. You would've lost. You can't just go into this with good hearts and strong backs."

"It's a copout," one woman with a deep Yankee accent interjects. "We're asking blacks to go into those schools without any training. If we're that well trained, we could march into South Boston, and maybe we should!"

The intent to do good is there. These are the late twentieth-century goo-goos, detested by almost everyone. The city whites don't like them, because they think they are leftists and rich hypocrites. The poorer blacks have little or no use for them, and too often their only contact with them is via a houseworker. The progressive pols, basically liberal but very hard-nosed, like Kevin, pooh-pooh them as impractical. What their forebearers did to Curley and Lomasney and Honey Fitz is not forgotten in the political subconscious of Boston or the older cities and towns of Massachusetts. Yet, they have often lobbied and proven effective at votes, rallies, legislation, and reform. They are a force that could be used, yet they remain leaderless and virtually useless. They are reduced to sitting around a living room and talking out their role, their guilt feelings, their own perceptions of hypocrisy. "What's gonna happen next?" one man asks. "There has not been the kind of support from suburban groups or liberals on what to do. How do *they* plan to respond to racial integration — not only in schools, but also economic and housing patterns? I'd recommend we spend the rest of our time this delightful fall morning with all this crazy business going all around the city of Boston and figure out what we should be doing."

Another says, "I feel morally vulnerable living in Lexington and coming here to Newton and not having kids in the schools in Boston. A guy in City Hall can say to me, 'All this is very well, for you. You live out *there*.' And I don't know how to respond to that."

Feingold reports that the virus of hate has spread to the suburbs. "METCO buses are coming back in a state of total disrepair. They're being harassed by cars, including one car that went up on a sidewalk and hit a child, and no one even got his license." She has heard a figure of METCO buses being stoned in 22 towns.

"We've been intimidated, and we do have some weight and sense of morality. Protection should be demanded for the METCO buses — if the cops have to meet those buses and escort them, as in Boston, dammit, they should. The second thing is the vigil, which seems to be the only way we can publicly show support. The third thing is the League of Women Voters is trying to get all political leaders to sit together and issue the just statement they're afraid to make individually."

A few smug laughs and grunts are heard here. Just as the pols hold the liberals in disdain, so too do liberals snort at pols for not being more "forthright." But as Bob Schwartz says, Kevin White is not about to ride up at the front of the bus.

"Fourth," she continues, "CPPAX [a coalition of two liberal groups, including anti-war protestors] is gathering names of whites to ride on the buses if and when necessary."

One man interrupts, "How about a Newton person riding on a METCO bus to Newton? If rocks are thrown with a Newton person on the bus, then you'll get protection."

"Fifth," she goes on, "we need volunteer lawyers at the trouble spots to witness the treatment of those arrested. . . . Finally, this is the first major desegregation case where the U.S. has not entered as a third party. During the Kennedy presidency, there was none of this nonsense about existing local jurisdictions. . . . I think the Congress people we've supported — Drinan, Studds, Harrington, Moakley — should be pressing for the U.S. to intervene."

They haggle over when to hold another meeting, this one with Kiley, and indeed, it will be held. Some fifty persons will come and eat bagels and cream cheese and Danish pastry in an airy old Newton house with lots of books in the bookcase and a copy of a Picasso, a house surrounded by hedges and shrubs and trees, a quiet house with the sound of a crow somewhere in the neighborhood. Bob Kiley will predict that ROAR intends to have something to say about the municipal elections coming up in 1975 and about Phase Two. "We see it as a force for the next two years," he'll tell them.

"A lot of things are changing. The courts are tending to look at desegregation as a process to be consolidated. The Supreme Court is not showing evidence of the forward leanings of the Warren Court" on any novel, metropolitan plans.

There is so much, he says, that is yet unclear. There is so little hard information linking desegregation to the quality of education. The "brief peek" he says he took at Boston's public schools "horrified" him. Their improvement in Boston, he says, is "beyond political reform," and in a way, the mayor was relieved when the referendum to abolish the school committee for more community input and mayoral control was beaten at the polls. The problem, he explains, is that those citizens in Boston who worked so hard for school reform now feel beaten and demoralized. "A challenge to us is to uplift some spirits. Few of us would've predicted how volatile the last two months have been." The tension, he tells them, will continue.

Like the last ADA meeting, this one goes on and on with no real resolution. At one point, a woman says of the whites in Boston, "They're very content to live the way their great grandparents lived — they're not in the twentieth century," and there is laughter. It is derisive. If such things were said about blacks, she would have been jumped on as a racist. But it seems okay to say such things about the whites. And therein lay the old class problem again. The Kerner Commission warned in the late 1960's of two societies, one black and one white. But there are more divisions than that. There are urbanites and suburbanites, whites and blacks and Hispanics, division among each of those groups. And one of the biggest divisions is between the whites with formal education and white-collar jobs and those with neither. Many of the whites in the suburbs lived once in Boston and heard "dirty Jew" or "commie" once too often. There is no love lost between the two groups.

The meeting winds down, and, later, Kiley will say to somebody, "I felt like a student from Bangladesh talking about hunger, and they were saying get him a sandwich to take home."

The liberals are still left leaderless, looking for direction. The mayor of Boston has had neither the time nor the interest to come up with a plan for suburbanites.

"We wanted to have an interdenominational meeting. Out of this meeting came another meeting, which led to a breakfast meeting at the Harvard Club, and that led to another meeting of the educational task force of the Mass. Council of Churches, and the task force was divided by politics. We then went to the Cardinal, and when he came in, everyone stood. . . . Somehow, it didn't work. Everyone agreed to go back and exert moral leadership. There was no joint statement."
— An employee of the Unitarian-Universalists describes the flailing about of liberal clergy, October, 1974

"I have a terrible sense of déjà vu, of Theodore Parker and William Ellery Channing talking to their fellow Brahmins. Let's put out an ad

and tell the country there is racism in Boston. If 50,000 could line the streets and watch Anthony Burns being marched back into slavery, then we could turn out 50,000 for this!" — An angry integrationist, speaking at a Unitarian-Universalist meeting in the Arlington Street Church, October 3, 1974

TWENTY-EIGHT

Survival

THE LAUGH was still there. Somehow, it had survived the times. It would begin somewhere in the middle of his chest and force its way up, pushing the shoulders up and down into a jig and prying apart the tight-lipped frown, smashing through the mouth, forcing back all the wrinkles of a fifty-five-year-old man etched deeply into the face of this man of forty-five. Occasionally, he would laugh, and everyone around him felt better for that moment or two, just as when he was a kid, and his mother always knew what room Kevin was in, because that's where the laughter was coming from. But despite Grandfather Tom White's working so hard at being an American, Kevin was an Irishman, given to erratic moments of belly-laughing and deep pits of gloom and doom.

"I never dreamt in my wildest nightmares," he would say, "that I'd be in a wasteland. I never thought it would go on this long."

Events had been conducive enough to despair. In October and again in December, white high school boys were stabbed by blacks. The first incident prompted Governor Sargent to call out the National Guard without first consulting with the mayor, an act that threw White into a public rage. Sargent, behind in his reelection campaign, would suggest he had shown much leadership by stepping in with the Guard units and that their presence had helped cool the city. How citizen soldiers, safely ensconced in two armories far from the street action, could cool anything went unexplained.

The second stabbing brought out the most vicious and hell-bent crowd in Southie since the attack on Jean-Louis. Police had to charge the crowd and use a ruse to get black students out of the school's rear doors. Some police said it was the most frightening experience they had ever encountered.

Schools were closed and opened again, as were taverns. Rumors floated about that certain persons were marked for death, certain bridges marked for destruction. School committeemen were cited for contempt of court and then given another chance by the judge. The mayor's staff was demoralized by the judge's inaction and by the defeat of their school reform plan by anti-busing forces. To them, it seemed their own boss, the mayor, had gone into exile since his confusing press conference.

At one afternoon at the Parkman House, the conversation was laced with invective and self-pity and notably lacking any direction. Judge Garrity was about to hold public hearings on the second phase of busing, which would be almost citywide, and some staff members wanted to put as much distance as possible between that court process and the mayor. Others were worried about that.

"Are we saying we're not interested in the plan that comes out?" Paul Parks asked.

Kirk O'Donnell mumbled to himself, "We're not interested. We're *terrified*."

Phase Two of busing would begin in September, 1975, the month of the city's primary election, two months before the final election. "We have to discuss politically what we're going to do," Kiley said. "We have to protect the mayor's ass because he's gonna have to be involved again.

"The mayor is caught in a hopeless political situation. To make the plan work would require such force, you'd have to wash your hands of any hope for reelection. . . . That whatever government does, it will be perceived as Kevin White doing all this to make the plan work."

They saw nothing but disaster ahead of them. They had to live up to a public responsibility to enforce the law, and some of them believed deeply in the principle of integration behind that law, but they also had a loyalty to the mayor, whom they regarded as a friend, a good politician, and a progressive leader who understood and responded well to the ills of the city. They believed in integration, and they believed in Kevin White and they were afraid the first would destroy the latter.

"This," Kirk whispered to someone, "is becoming a classic case of principle versus politics."

Bob Schwartz warned, "If we're gonna get sucked in anyway, and retreat is not a realistic option, and the mayor will be in the middle of it in an election year no matter what we decide, then, goddammit, we've got to try to *influence* the plan!"

Almost everyone there knew deep inside that Schwartz was right. A few days later, Kiley told a visitor, "We were acting out our weariness. The discussion was necessary, unavoidable, and mildly therapeutic. Since then, we've all come to realize that we can't afford to get caught in the same bind as last fall, having a plan delivered to us over which we have no influence."

They all knew, as well, that any plan that did not include the suburbs was basically unfair. In their strategy sessions, they could make cogent arguments for forcing the suburbs into the solution.

"We're the sixteenth largest city in the United States, but we have the fourth largest amount of public housing," Kirk noted, arguing that Boston was shouldering the burden of caring for the poor, while the suburbs got away with tokenism and lip service. "There have been numerous cases of low-income housing knocked out by the suburbs."

One of the worst places, he said one day, was Wellesley.

"Ironic," said Kevin Moloney, a city attorney, that Garrity's hometown was so white.

"It's true," said O'Donnell. "One of the greatest problems we're dealing with is the hypocrisy."

But they knew the cogent arguments meant nothing. The reality of white suburbs and increasingly black cities meant nothing. The United States Supreme Court had refused Detroit's plea that busing include the suburbs. More proof of intentional discrimination was necessary. Reality, it seemed, was not enough. De facto segregation in the city was wrong. De facto segregation between city and suburb was, in the mind of the Court, excusable. So nobody on the staff was surprised when Judge Garrity ruled a few months later that Phase Two would not include the suburbs.

Again, it would all fall on the city, a city never equipped to deal with the frustrations and poverty of its whites, much less its blacks, a city that never rooted out its own cancers of bigotry, fear, and insularity, a city burned too often by change and pretensions of reform.

Kevin White's administration would have to get involved, like it or not.

By December, 1974, Schwartz was urging White to get actively involved in shaping Phase Two. Had he one single thing he could do over again, Schwartz argued, it would be not to repeat the 1973 tactic of staying away from the Phase One plan. The result was a poor, unworkable plan. "We wound up picking up the pieces and we weren't even able to say, 'We told you so.' " Kevin White agreed with much of what Schwartz was suggesting, but he doubted that he could have any influence over Phase Two. "Atkins," he said, "is in the driver's seat." When Judge Garrity appointed court experts, including one with whom Schwartz was friendly, and four court masters, including Eddie McCormack, whom Kevin trusted, the picture changed. Now, the mayor, Schwartz, and others saw the possibilities for some leverage.

The White administration submitted a critique of the NAACP's Phase Two plan. The masters rejected the NAACP plan for a more moderate approach that preserved some neighborhood identity and decreased busing. The mayor's office was elated. Most had feared a plan twice as bad as what they had suffered with all through the fall of 1974 and into the winter of 1975.

Early in April, 1975, Schwartz sent Kiley a memo. "It now seems apparent that the mayor will lie low on Phase Two until he is publicly pressured to do otherwise, and that as long as Louise and company remain friendly, he will do nothing to antagonize them. My concern here is not with the political wisdom of retaining a low profile, but rather with the need to convince the mayor that planning and organizing for Phase Two must begin as soon as Garrity issues his final order. Our internal activities need not be visible, but the word must go out throughout the administration that the mayor's survival may rest upon a smooth school opening, and that the Phase Two planning effort is therefore of top priority."

Both Schwartz and Kiley were concerned that the mayor's overtures toward Hicks and ROAR, while justifiable in his roles as a peace keeper, power broker, and politician, might compromise him. The efforts of White's staff "liberals" were not made easier by NAACP arguments that the masters' plan left too much segregation, that it was not tough enough, and by the rumors that Garrity would dismantle the very plan his own experts and masters had put together.

The mayor decided the masters' plan was crucial, that it made moral sense for the city and political sense for him to fight for it. He agreed to sign a two-page letter to Garrity, noting that he had objected to some of the masters' plan, but, "it is my considered judgment that as presently drafted the Masters' Plan is preferable to any of the alternatives currently before you. . . .

"Two years ago, the State Board of Education appointed its own master, Professor Jaffe, to conduct hearings on its desegregation plan prior to its adoption. At those hearings, community leaders testified that the proposed South Boston–Roxbury High School district would never work, and they convinced Professor Jaffe of the educational and sociological validity of their arguments. Professor Jaffe, therefore, recommended against the proposed district, but his recommendation was ignored by the State Board."

It was the State Board's plan that Garrity ordered implemented as Phase One, though White's letter tactfully did not remind the judge of that. The mayor concluded, "Please do not repeat the mistake of the State Board of Education by rejecting the advice of your own appointed masters and experts. Last fall's tragic experiences in South Boston must not be replayed next fall in East Boston. . . ."

Kevin Moloney, the city's attorney, moved that Garrity accept the masters' plan, but the mayor's letter was never delivered.

Louise Day Hicks reportedly called Larry Quealy and warned that if Kevin supported even the moderate masters' plan, he'd get no cooperation or votes out of ROAR. ROAR's diehard position was that the only good plan is no plan at all. Schwartz insisted that Kevin would be supporting the court masters, not the NAACP, but the mayor and his staff pictured newspaper headlines, reading, "Mayor Writes Judge, Urging Masters' Plan." They fantasized Garrity saying on the bench, "In deference to Mayor White's request . . ." Phase Two would become Kevin White's plan, they worried. And Schwartz worried right along with them, but he worried more about what would happen to the mayor and the city if Garrity should reject the masters' plan and cave in to the demands of the NAACP.

Instead, Schwartz, Kiley, Kelliher, and others tried brokering a compromise quietly, behind the scenes. They and people from the school system and the Citywide Educational Coalition agreed on a proposal. They didn't want to submit it formally, because it called for more busing, and nobody wanted to commit suicide, but it was better than what the NAACP was pushing. They convinced a court officer to deliver it to Garrity. The judge would not buy the proposed modifications, but he did ease up on his own changes. A month later, he announced plans for Phase Two. Under Phase One 17,000 students were scheduled to be bused; under Phase Two, the number would be closer to 26,000. The cost would rise from $11 million to $22 million, and those figures did not even include police overtime. But East Boston, a potentially volatile district, was exempted; magnet schools were ordered set up to specialize in certain fields of art, science, and education, schools that would draw students from across the city; the universities that had so long been at arm's length from the city's neighborhoods and their schools were drawn into the system. The judge would create a complex system of district and citywide councils to insure parental involvement in the plan. The sweeteners were there, as was the potential for reform in the school system.

In the spring, summer, and fall of 1975, White concentrated on getting reelected and became much less visible on the busing issue than he had been in 1974, and people like Peter Meade, Kelliher, and Schwartz worked quietly with school officials, Garrity's citizen councils, and Justice Department officials to insure a peaceful opening in September, 1975.

Kevin White felt he had been burned too often in 1974. What was supposed to have been a low-profile performance on his part ended up with him on television almost every night. He felt that, politically and morally, he was sharing too much of the busing burden. Now, in 1975, Judge Garrity was assuming more of a role. While he still refrained, right through the opening days of Phase Two, to lean as heavily on the school system as he should have, he did pass an increasing number of orders designed to force the school system to deal with Phase Two. It was not easy. The school committee did what it was ordered to do and nothing more. It changed superintendents, firing Leary and hiring in his place one Marion Fahey, a career employee who did not appear to have Leary's credentials. Throughout the summer of 1975, the school department moved slowly, if at all, and at times, it seemed the Phase Two plan would be sabotaged.

But history had come too far. Now, the Justice Department had assigned about a hundred brawny marshals to the Boston scene, along with special lawyers. Now, the whole law enforcement machinery of state government would be involved, and it did not hurt Kevin White that Charlie Barry was now the state commissioner of public safety, that Paul Parks was the secretary of education, that one of Parks's troubleshooters was Mark Weddleton, and that the new MBTA chairman, Robert Kiley, was chairman of the transportation and public safety subcommittee of Garrity's Citywide Coordinating Council, the CCC.

The CCC would act as a monitor for the court and report directly to Garrity on what was and was not happening out in the trenches. The law enforcement officials were making it clear there would be more cops on the streets and more different varieties too, and that the feds would be more prone to arrest troublemakers for alleged violations of civil rights.

ROAR continued its motorcades and speeches, but the organization seemed to be losing some of its steam. Now, like the liberals in suburbia, ROAR was clearly split, rent with divisions that were based on politics, tactics, and philosophy. Some ROAR members would jostle Ted Kennedy. Others would be ashamed. The fears among White's staff that ROAR could field a strong candidate dissipated in the spring of 1975. Ray Flynn tried and failed to raise money for a campaign. Billy Bulger considered running and apparently decided there was a better future for him in the State Senate and his private law practice. Hicks preferred to maintain her new political alliance of convenience with the mayor. Only Joe Timilty remained to do battle with the mayor.

Joe Timilty's grandfather, Diamond Jim, was more a reflection of his era than Henry Hagan had been. Diamond Jim started working in the city yards when he was a boy and rose through the ranks. Had he not given a job to a relative without benefit of exam, he might have remained there. Instead, he was bounced and went on to become a major political figure. His construction company did very well under Curley.

Diamond Jim had sired six sons, including Joseph, who also fit very well with Curley and became a controversial police commissioner. One of Joseph's brothers, Walter, ran a laundry business, and Walter's competitors complained that Walter's business did very well when Joseph was police commissioner.

Walter named one of his boys after Joe, and the boy, tall and tough and handsome, became a city councilman. He said conservative things and ran unsuccessfully in 1971 against Kevin for mayor. Later, he became a State Senator and voted for liberal things and made friends with some black pols who didn't like Kevin and decided to run again in 1975 for mayor. But he would do so without capitalizing on the busing issue, which meant that ROAR ended up without a candidate for mayor.

Just as Kevin White was emerging early in 1975 from the doldrums into which he and his city had floundered in the dreary winter of 1974, his administration was hit with a series of scandals, some small and petty, some serious. White had always prided himself on a clean administration, and he often worried out loud that somebody, somewhere in his administration, was somehow going to blemish his record.

The Building Department, which inspects new buildings; the Real

Property Department, which gives out contracts for the cleaning, maintenance, and leasing of city property; the Assessing Department; the Boston Redevelopment Authority were all agencies with the potential of providing such blemishes.

Earlier in his administration, the Building Department was the center of scandal as people died in fires and building collapses in structures that supposedly had passed inspection. Now, in the post-Watergate era, as more journalists turned to the almost lost art of investigative reporting, there were more stories that all was not clean in City Hall. That all had never been clean in City Hall, regardless of who the mayor might be, was never really part of the perspective.

Now there were stories of friends getting contracts, of a misuse of patronage, of jobs going to people in return for political support, and of outrageous soliciting of political funds from firefighters by the fire commissioner. With this coming on the tails of those yellow school buses, White and his staff began developing a persecution complex. Answers to tough questions were either vague, inaccurate, or contradictory, and, at times, there were no answers, no comments. Once the darling of the press, the mayor now became its villain, the gray-haired incumbent pol, the big city power broker, now parceling out favors and patronage and running a machine and all that. For his part, the mayor belittled the press for its revolving door employment of reporters, each arriving with little or no knowledge of the city, its ethics, its problems, its life-style, its mayor. He did not like his honesty questioned, or his sense of dignity offended.

In the midst of those crucial days, when his staff was quietly trying to salvage the Phase Two masters' plan, the *Globe* Spotlight Team — its investigative unit — published a story that White's fire commissioner, Jimmy Kelly, and others were pressuring firemen to contribute to the mayor's campaigns. Of all the real and alleged scandals, this could be the most harmful.

"It looks tough for Kevin out there," one city hall employee said in the spring. "I speak to people these guys don't speak to, to people in the North End, people who got relatives in East Boston and Roslindale. They see on TV some guy saying something about a two-hundred-dollar donation and a transfer, and they say, 'Shit, what is this?' People who are lookin' for an excuse not to vote for him won't now, 'cause they've got one. Before, I used to go out and identify a Kevin voter and make sure he votes. Now, I have to spend time convincing him to vote for Kevin. People out there are broke today. They don't like this stuff, the idea of some guy being forced to take money he needs and donate it, especially the fire department. The fire department is sacred. You can screw around with parks contracts, but not with a fire department."

The continual battering in the press wore the mayor down, increased his petulance, and sapped his self-confidence.

"We're in trouble," Kiley told the other staffers one day. "I don't care how big a campaign organization you've got, it won't work. He's down. We're all down."

Tivnan worried, "He wants to go underground."

"And that's what he did last time," Kiley warned, "and it took ten weeks for him to come out of it. This self-immolation bit."

John Marttila, the liberal Democratic consultant who had helped Kevin in his 1971 sweep, was back for the 1975 race. Marttila, traveling about the country, was sensitive to what the post-Watergate electorate wanted. Come clean with everything. Show the public your tax records, your contributions, your expenses, your father's toupee, your mother's false teeth. The era of campaign reform had arrived, but good.

But Kevin, like his city, worried about reformers. He didn't like fads posing as reforms. "You people have a sham set of morals," he yelled one day at some advisors. "You want me to put on a pretense. Why do we have to do this superficial McGovern act?" The mayor argued that he had to be honest to himself, that he would not play the role of a hypocrite. Simple, currently accepted political techniques such as handing out tax returns became major issues.

"Gratuitious political harm," Marttila worried. "Self-inflicted wounds. It's as if he said, 'Let's see, what can we do to hurt ourselves today?' "

For too long, White had run too loose a ship. To many employees, the mayor's attitude — real or inferred — was: go run your operation and don't tell me how you do it. If a department head wanted to hand out a contract to a favored party, the mayor didn't want to know about it. Such practices, after all, were always a part of the reality of government, be it village, town, county, state, or federal. One either accepted that reality and tried to mold it to progressive purposes or one came riding in like a goo-goo. If one did the latter, he usually got shot down in the street and lay politically dead among the corpses of his progrssive programs. The danger with the former option, dealing with reality as it is, was that such reality could ultimately sabotage a political leader's credibility, and this was precisely what was happening in 1975.

Despite the public and private keening of Kevin and his troops, certain parts of the machinery continued to function. Computers and consultants and public relations men had played an increasing role in the mayor's political life since the heady days of 1967. Now, their assignment was clear.

"In 1971," Jackie Walsh said one day, "it was Kevin White is a tough fuckin' guy — Kevin White tears up the airport plans, raises hell when the landlord raises rents. That's because he was perceived as vacillating. This year, we have to say Kevin White has run the city well, that he's been a good mayor and a good guy. So this is a very conservative act, this year. He's way ahead in the polls, so the idea is to keep him strong."

The polls were taken often, and they were highly polished and professional. They showed that for fifteen years or more, race and class were the two most dominant factors in the minds of the voters, that Timilty could not make any headway with people on either side of those issues, that White was running well just about everywhere and certainly in his areas of strength — such as the black and Italian precincts. If he should falter somewhere, there were mailings and phone callers ready — for liberal precincts, for high-numbered, middle-income precincts, for Italians, for people who tie their shoelaces from left to right.

The machinery clanked on under Kirk O'Donnell. Ward coordinators met and were handed thick loose-leaf booklets with thousands of voters' names and addresses. Instructions were given on canvassing. Briefing sessions were held on how to make a phone call, how to record a voter's reaction. On the fourth floor of a shabby Back Bay office building, volunteers gathered at dusk to call the people in the precincts.

The men from Marttila's office cautioned time and again, if Kevin White ever wants to run nationally, he had better learn the New Politics scripts, the techniques of raising money, the "fun" parties that Kevin White insisted he didn't have fun at, the broadened base of financial support, the revelation of all one's pennies and debts. If not, they said, the professional liberals would zap him again, just as they had in Miami.

On his part, White agonized openly for his troops. New friends and aides were temporarily shocked into inaction, paralyzed by confusion and fear of being yelled at. Old-timers, some as young as twenty-five, shook their heads, had another beer, and plodded on the business of running a government and a campaign. "We are Irish Maoists," said a newcomer. "We operate out of loyalty and will."

"My sense of dignity is being taken away," the mayor yelled one day. "The young people who venerate Harry Truman for his candor

— well, don't you *understand?* The only way to do this is by standing up. 'Oh, just sign this income tax declaration, and you're proven clean. Sign this loyalty oath, and you're not a communist.' It's like the McCarthy era. Well, you gotta have confidence in *yourself*."

National ambitions? Busing, he insisted, ruined any chance of that. It was too late, in mid-1975, to make serious moves for 1976, he argued. "I had a good national strategy," he told a visitor. "I saw that candidacy when no one else did, and I was entitled to try for it. You got to be in a position to capture it, to focus on it — man, you've got to be swinging and moving."

For a time, he wondered whether he could or should be mayor for another four years. It would be the longest consecutive period in office for any mayor in the city's history. He spent two hours talking about it with his mother, for Patricia Hagan White had watched three generations of men torture themselves with the insecurity of politics.

"It's not the running," he said, "it's the *winning*. I'm forty-five years old, and when else can I do other things? I'm not Daley, and I don't like the limelight like Lindsay. I *liked* those Parkman House dinners. So what have I got now? Do I grow, or do I go to Dukakis and say, 'Hey, do you need a new justice of the supreme court?' To be a hack, not to grow anymore, to go to eight more custodians' banquets and ten more parades? Those are the things on my mind. I was closer to not running than people thought. But Timilty can't run this city, and I haven't got a substitute."

He was sitting, slouched in a chair, his legs crossed, the fingers of his right hand pulling and tugging at his mouth and lips and nose and chin. He sat there in the early hours of dusk, looking through his favorite window, out past Faneuil Hall, where Mr. Curtis warned so long ago, "Strife, if not bloodshed," would follow the immigration of blacks, out past the North End, where the Irish had screamed, "To Dock Square, boys. We'll give 'em New York!" out to the Fitzgerald Expressway, where the commuters rushed home to white suburbs.

"Before busing, there was a time when I liked walking around this town, when I felt I was in my own living room. But now, it's hate, hate, hate. I've seen too much of it."

TWENTY-NINE

Survival is Not Enough

"HAIL MARY, full of grace, the Lord is with thee. . . ."

The women of Charlestown kneel in a phalanx on the street leading to the Bunker Hill monument and say their rosary. In front of them, the cops tighten up. The lines tighten up. The faces tighten up. The colons tighten up. Nobody wanted this. Who in God's earth wanted this?

"Blessed art thou among women . . ."

Police Commissioner diGrazia walks along the lines of Boston and MDC police, like a World War I officer visiting his men in the trenches. "Don't push back," diGrazia tells them, "but don't let them through." The women of Charlestown want to march. The city of Boston and the federal district court say they cannot gather in such numbers so near the high school. It is the second day of the second year of forced busing in Boston.

"And blessed be the fruit of thy womb, Jesus. . . ."

"Oh, Christ," mutters a cop. They hold their billies horizontally in front of them. The television cameras of all three networks and a few other countries are poised in anticipation. It costs a lot of money to send a TV crew out of New York, and there has not been much action, not as much as a year ago. Around Bunker Hill, the press outnumbers the Townies. The court order prohibiting crowds near schools does not apply to the press. Now, the cops can already see the pictures on the evening news. Boston cops club women?

Slam. In a body, the women of Charlestown, up from bended knee, have hit the MDC police line. A line of Boston cops rushes to back them up. The federal marshals wait in reserve, seven or eight men with the chief of the U.S. Civil Rights Division of the Justice Department, big men in sports jackets and pressed slacks, with radios and helmets that look out of place with their civilian suits, and snug black gloves that fit tightly on the hands and very long riot batons. They are here too, a year late, but here. And up the street, the Tactical Patrol Force is coming, and soon the people of Charlestown will join the people of Southie to demand in the language of black militants that the oppressors have committed police brutality and that they must leave their turf.

The charge is broken. The cops have pushed back, because that was all they could do. Some women screamed, as if they had honestly expected something different, that the cops would part like the Red Sea. The TPF is working the crowd. There is a thud, and a scream, and a young Townie guy is dragged to the wagon.

Mother Galvin stands quietly on a corner and watches. He turns and goes. This is no longer the Charlestown he knew. This is another time. Let the young men around his son-in-law handle this, young Peter Meade, who has succeeded Bob Kiley as the City Hall man to deal with this particular piece of urban irritation, and Rich Kelliher again, and Bob Schwartz again, and diGrazia.

School attendance is not bad, but most of those attending are not white. The white majority has disappeared, dropped out, enrolled in private or parochial schools, moved to or illegally registered in the suburbs. Now, Boston has a school population unbalanced black and brown, and the suburbs continue with an imbalance of white.

Boston would survive, Kevin White said. But for how long, he asked. How long for Boston and America? And would he survive, he wondered in the summer and fall of 1975. Yes, the city had the potential for greatness, but, he argued, "you need someone to marshal it." After him, he suggested, Boston could float leaderless, without direction. "This city could go down the drain."

His hair was almost completely gray. He seemed to be losing more weight. His wrinkles could not be stretched thin or padded with television cosmetics. He had been an elected official for fifteen years, the last eight of them as mayor. He was the incumbent, but he was an incumbent after Watergate, and the press was after imcumbents, and yellow buses were rolling again, and Joe Timilty looked bright and handsome and aggressive. Joe Timilty had with him those John Collins men who had been waiting for a shot at Kevin White or Bob diGrazia, and he had up front for everyone to see, the aggressive, young liberals, the kind of people who had worked for McGovern and could point to Joe Timilty's liberal voting record at the State House. Joe Timilty, who had railed against Kevin White's expenditures that White translated into increased public services, and who once had attacked the Little City Halls in the neighborhoods, was saying that he was a real neighborhood guy whose kids went to an integrated public school, not like the Whites of Beacon Hill. Joe Timilty could not come up with imaginative programs for those neighborhoods, and when he finished eleven points behind Kevin White in the preliminary election, he said the real issue was corruption.

Kevin White had talked of hate in the city. And it was out there to greet the buses, and now it was going to emerge in the election too, as it had in most of the city's elections for much of the city's history. It was not the running that disturbed him, Kevin White said one day, but the winning. Now, it would be the running too. Leaks to the press, presumably from the Timilty camp, became torrents. The charges of scandal returned. Was it true that Kevin White or Ted Anzalone, on White's behalf, solicited cash from big-shot developers in 1970 for the governor's race? Five years later, two weeks before the election, the question became a cause célèbre, and grew worse as the mayor stumbled and contradicted himself in answering it.

"He can't stand assaults on his integrity," Kirk O'Donnell said one day in his cluttered campaign office. "He can take anything else but that."

With a vengeance — "White Lies," proclaimed the headline on one weekly newspaper — the press pursued White. Yet hardly a story on Timilty appeared. Some in the White camp tried to play the leaks game too, but Timilty's people seemed better at it. Behind the stories were the fine hands of the outs trying to get back in. As for the mayor, he again displayed that tendency to walk away, to sulk, to be personally aggrieved. A regular pol acts differently. The regular pol toughs it out, laughs it off. Screw it, says the regular pol. But there was too much complexity to Kevin White's machinery, and the machine wasn't what he ran, it was what was inside of him.

His advertisements had urged the people to reelect "the Mayor," as if he were a Daley, the tough, responsible, experienced mayor. And now, as the charges consumed him, he became not a tough pol, but almost a pitiable figure, a normal person with normal instincts and levels of pain. His instincts told him it was open season on all incumbents, but his emotions asked, why me? One day, he sat alone on a bench on Boston Common with his head in his hands, as if no one else were around to see him. The city was his living room. He could no more hide his emotions from the city than it could from him.

But there was something at work in the precincts of Boston. For all its latent bigotry and fear and suspicion and class hate, and perhaps because of all that, because it is parochial and small and steeped in its own folk history, there were people — beyond those whose jobs depended on Kevin — who remembered. In East Boston, an old lady cried out, "They gonna take our mayor from us." He was their mayor. And when Timilty announced that John Collins would head his transition team into City Hall, those who had forgotten also now remembered. They remembered what the city had been in the postwar years, when the kids moved to the suburbs, when the neighborhoods began falling apart, when journalists came to gaze at downtown and never stopped to talk to anybody in the back wards. They remembered, and they voted. And the Italians of East Boston voted, those who saw a community revived and an airport defeated, and the Italians of the North End, who saw a large number of relatives and friends and neighbors on the public work rolls; the liberals of Beacon Hill and Back Bay and South Cove who heard Barney Frank, now a state rep, urge that they not forget a man who had begun turning Boston around, who had stopped highways and staffed Little City Halls. In the city's growing black precincts, members of the Black Caucus tried to work up some enthusiasm for their friend, Joe Timilty, but other influential blacks heard old Melnea Cass — an institution in their neighborhood — say she heard all right what Joe Timilty *said* he was going to do, but she knew all right what Kevin White had done. The old came out, the ones who remembered Joe White and who liked it when Kathryn Galvin White shook their hands and smiled. And down in the barrio, Puerto Rican voters, beginning to show up in some numbers for the first time, voted for Kevin Hagan White.

He would not win by a great deal. There would be no ground swell for this man. "I'll be fighting perceptions," he complained the day after the primary vote, perceptions of a man suddenly labeled corrupt. His instincts that day told him, "The Collins people are out there. They're gonna swing with corruption. This is the Hyde Square Brick Throwers Association." Too often, he worried out loud, he ignored perceptions until they went out of control. Out of control. Everything had seemed so. Even without the corruption issue, could any incumbent survive busing?

Election day is sunny and pleasant, and the turnout is heavy. Up in the Presidential Suite of the Colonnade Hotel, a few blocks away from the Sheraton Boston, where the mayor's people have rented a ballroom, Larry Quealy paces back and forth, wearing a path in the soft wall-to-wall carpeting. Soft carpets and an artist's view of the city at night. Room service with shrimp and beer and peanuts. Who brings you peanuts the day after you stop being mayor? Politics is to Quealy's boss what the shoe business was to Hagan. Were he to lose it, his place in it, he could die inside. And were the city to return to what it had been before Kevin, for all his failings and impatience and petulance, then Boston too could die from within. And now Larry Quealy worries and paces. Younger men come in and out, professional men who belong to a newer generation of politics and polling. They seem to worry less. "Some people," Larry says, "wonder why I worry about elections, but when you've lost a few you worry." Larry Quealy had been with Johnny Hynes and John Collins and now Kevin White. He had called Kevin White early that morning in September of 1974 to give him the first reports of what busing might be doing to Boston, and now, with others who had long been with Kevin White, he is up here, loyal and worried.

Kevin's brothers come, and Patricia Hagan White comes too. The Beacon Hill neighbors, lawyers and professors, show up, and the old friends in politics, the guys who go way back with Kevin White and who sit with him in a room closeted from the rest, and get reports from the headquarters a few blocks away on Boylston Street. In the main room of the suite is a blackboard with his name and Timilty's and a line next to each, a line awaiting numbers. But no one comes out of the room to chalk the numbers on those lines, and for a while, that motley assortment of pols and professors, neighbors and relatives, do not know whether they are at a celebration or a wake.

At 9 P.M., one hour after the polls have closed, it appears that Kevin Hagan White has won reelection by a very narrow margin. He sits, his shirtsleeves rolled up, his face pale, gaunt, and drawn, on a bed with a phone receiver in his right hand and turns and says softly and not very happily to a visitor, "Well, we did it with a small margin." Kathryn paces the room, while reading precinct returns, which she picks up from the mess strewn across the beds. "He's never been through a campaign like this before. He's exhausted. Can you imagine what his credibility has to be to survive busing, and Watergate and the economy and these last three weeks? Tonight, before he left the house, he was getting the children ready for defeat."

Across the room, the door opens, and Kirk O'Donnell comes in with his wife. Sometime between the routing of a school bus and the mailing of a Kevin White reelection circular, they had a child. In the last few weeks, she would bring the baby up from Dorchester, and they would walk up and down the Commonwealth Avenue mall. Kirk O'Donnell was a young man who had come far quickly, and he almost lost what he had fought for, and now he stares at the mayor for a split second, and the mayor and he hug each other, and Kevin White says, "You've done it. You've done it." Kevin White is smiling, as if he has just won a massive victory, because he senses that Kirk O'Donnell wants him to look like that. Now O'Donnell, who pushed ahead with his campaign like a bull, pushed against contrary opinions and advice from every corner of this most politically attuned city, is crying. "You've done it," his boss says. "It's all *yours*." And he grabs his boy — "These young guys have saved the city," he tells others — grabs his boy by the elbow. "C'mon, let's go for a walk."

Later that night, the mayor sits in a chair in yet another room and writes an acceptance speech. He loosens his tie and yells, "Well, that's my nineteenth fight and my thirty-fifth opponent," and everyone laughs.

Bob Kiley, like Barney Frank and Hale Champion and others who have worked for Kevin White and gone elsewhere, has been back with the mayor, and he is here. "You've got a constituency," he tells him. "Your people came out. They're there. And they came out under the worst possible circumstances."

The constituency is a strange one. It lives all over Boston, but it comes mainly from the northern wards, the older and less suburban parts of the city. Timilty has laid claim to the southern tier of Boston, heavily Irish, heavily civil service, and heavy on voting. They are one part of Boston. That other part, that strange conglomeration of Irish, Italian, WASP, Jew, black, and Puerto Rican, that mix of conservative Democrat and liberal Independent, of loyalists who don't ever forget a favor, and thereoreticians who rail against giving any, that Boston voted with allies to the south for Kevin White, for the goo-goo in him and the pol in him.

Now, with a felt-tipped pen, he writes a few words of thanks to that constituency. He will meet them shortly in a noisy, boisterous throng at the Sheraton Boston, and he will tell them, "Now our battle in this campaign was for the very soul of this city because for the past, particularly for the past two years, this city that we all love has suffered great tensions and great traumas that have brought about in our city great change. Few big cities of America today have faced the pressures we face and tonight this city passed the test."

That same night, Boston returns an all-white school committee to administer a now predominantely nonwhite school system. Pixie Palladino, who had made her vows against Father Pitaro in Eastie, against scattered site housing for the poor and against busing, had come from obscurity to take a seat on the committee. The moderately liberal Kathleen Sullivan has topped the ticket. The committee that emerged from the ballot count promised to be more reasonable about the reality of the twentieth century's demands on Boston.

In the back wards of the city, blacks and Spanish-speaking had flexed muscle. Both candidates had courted them. No candidate could ever again ignore them.

The questions of race and justice and opportunity posed by the Boston Abolitionists remained unanswered, as did the larger and more complex and divisive issue of class, an issue that Boston had made palpable and, so often, bloody and real throughout its history. It was possible, as Kevin White had told his screaming, delirious constituents, that Boston had passed the test, if he was speaking of a test of whether a city could survive class hatred.

But survival is not enough for Boston or America. Each must flourish. As long as the quality of one's public education depends on the property and wealth of one's family and neighborhood, Horace Mann's dream would remain a farce. There was no great equalizer at work in Boston, unless spreading crumbs equally is regarded as a fair and just solution. As long as America had one set of rules for its cities and another for its wealthier suburbs, there could be no reasonable talk of justice.

Very little had been resolved since the clarion calls of Garrison and Phillips. The black had been freed from the plantation to be made slave again to a computerized industrial system that displayed little use for him, a slave to welfare. The white workingman's fear and loathing of the black had endured, for he too had remained a slave to events out of his control. The raucous voices of separatism went unabated in the land, more than a century after men who called themselves patriots made such noises at Faneuil Hall. The stridency of Abolition was evident and unassailable in the hearts and on the tongues of whites who could most afford integration and yet who remained segregated in suburban enclaves. In the midst of busing, men who once were perceived as liberals now warned that busing would further divide the nation, that it would fail, for now the buses had come to their districts, and the voters were making noises. Some urged simply that it end. Others, more responsible, insisted other means were available, that children could be integrated gradually by grade, that teenagers could be brought together voluntarily. Perhaps.

Neither extreme sang any longer Julia Ward Howe's less than subtle predictions of what side God was on and whose grapes of wrath he was trampling. Now, they both sang, "We Shall Overcome." We the people. The Irish and Italians and Poles at the corner of the State House sang that they would overcome. The blacks and white allies countered on the Common that they would overcome. Which people? The only ones who had overcome were those who lived beyond the Pale. The ones who voted quietly behind closed doors to continue fighting the state law that purported to ban discrimination in suburban housing. For such subtle actions, there were no network television crews waiting outside the doors. Only for the rock throwers in Southie. Too often, the powerless make the news more easily than the powerful.

As the nation began its two hundredth year, it was clearly divided still, as so many experts had warned it would be. But the division was not race. It was class; it was money and the privileges and access that money can buy. Because so much of the nation really began in 1775 in Boston, the city began its Bicentennial one year earlier than the nation. There was pomp and sentiment. Old-timers in the neighborhoods talked for posterity to tape recorders. Imaginative historic trails were laid out; inventive games were offered to the tourists. On the banks of the filthy Charles River, the Boston Pops indulged itself in the 1812 Overture, while thousands applauded and cheered and gasped as an army artillery unit and a local fireworks manufacturer outdid themselves.

But few with close ties to the real Boston wished to celebrate. For if the issue was freedom, then the issue had yet to be defined two hundred years after Adams and Hancock and Otis and the others proclaimed it.

From Wilmington, Delaware, with its tired, rickety slums festering in the shadows of an American interstate highway, there was no definition forthcoming. Wilmington had been able to convince the Supreme Court to send buses into the suburbs, but analysts cautioned that other hard-pressed cities should not take heart from this, that what applied to Delaware might not apply to Michigan.

From Louisville, Kentucky, with its old and mellow traditions, its reputation for progressive and quiet movement, there was no definition, only a reminder that Kentucky had been a border state and that within that state, there were men and women who would make common bond with Southie.

From Washington, official Washington, which had so long glared in marble contrast to the filth and hopelessness of black Washington, no one offered any definitions. There was no leadership evident. Not even a Lincoln who could excite emotions and force an issue. There was nothing.

So, in Boston, the answers would have to come. Boston had begun it all, so perhaps, there it must end. The city had no choice. It was imprisoned by its own history, and somewhere in that history was the key.

The violence continued in Boston, as the nation celebrated its two hundredth birthday. On a sunny Friday in April, 1976, Kevin White led tens of thousands down the old streets of the city in a parade against violence. Many of those marching were from outside the city, and some of those marching had been told to do so, but only some. The march was not touted to end Boston's problems, and it did not. It was simply a beginning.

"Liberty was born in Boston," the mayor said two days earlier, "and it will flourish here so long as courageous people of high moral principle are willing to speak what is in their hearts."